# Girl (Hiking) with 4 Dogs:

## An Epic Journey Traversing the Eastern United States on the Appalachian Trail from Georgia to Maine with four Dogs!

# Girl (Hiking) with 4 Dogs:
## An Epic Journey Traversing the Eastern United States on the Appalachian Trail from Georgia to Maine with four Dogs!

**Sandra MacKenzie**

MacKenzie Press
2017

First Printing: 2017

ISBN 978-0-692-88825-4

MacKenzie Publishing
P.O. Box 8266
Columbus, GA 3108

# Dedication

- My Dad, Malcolm George-Holland MacKenzie.

    My biggest helper on the trail

    January 7, 1946 - August 5, 2015

  - Colt MacKenzie, aka Mtn. Goat.

    March 2005- March 26, 2016

The silence you leave behind is filled with poignant memories of the crazy fun and laughter you brought to our lives.

- My loyal friend & companion, Shepp MacKenzie, aka Kujo.

    January 2006- April 21, 2017

    Your loss is almost unbearable.

    Who will chase the bad guys away?

# Contents

# Acknowledgements

Thank you, Father, Son, and Holy Spirit, for making my dream adventure come true.

Thank you, Donna, for reminding me, "You don't try. You do what you say you are going to do."

Thanks to my trail helpers; Dad, Granny Rocket, fellow hikers, Trail Angels, and maintainers.

Thanks to my Mom, brothers, sister, and sister-in-law for at home support.

Thanks to all my friends and family who helped with editing, working so I could have a day off, etc., Teresa, Kelly, Grandma Carmen, Kim H.

Thanks to Jay Cooper who gave me advice on how to improve my writing.

Thanks to Todd for buying me an awesome computer and office equipment for Christmas!

# Prologue

**Prologue**

*Black Despair swirls around me. Laughter terrorizing me, shredding me to pieces. The shards of my life are tossed around inside. Trapped.*

*There is no escape!*

*Panic suffocates me.*

*I can't do this I can't survive!*

*I thrash around and struggle to find hope, anything to pull me from this never ending black pit.*

A soft furry head wedges itself under my hand.

*My breathing calms. I am not alone.*

My eyes snap open. I look into the warm brown eyes of my 16-year-old, four-legged, furry, friend. My trusty terrier mutt, Purple aka, "The Old Man."

*I have to take care of my friend, then I must mark a red "X" on the white calendar.*

How can AJ be cheating? We haven't even been married for four years!

I roll reluctantly off the bed, then drag myself to the kitchen to feed and water my four-legged companion. The bleakness hovers at the edge of my consciousness, waiting to consume and destroy me. Slowly bright memories filter into the darkness. The relentless pain eases to a dull ache.

I almost smile as I remember how long I've wanted to hike the Appalachian Trail (AT), ever since my Big Bro, Steve, started a hike with our church youth group, in Amicalola Falls when I was 8 and he was 16. The church group hiked a section over Thanksgiving vacation. When Mom, Dad, my brother Andy, and I picked Steve up in the Georgia Mountains, I remember seeing guys with long hair and beards carrying backpacks through the woods.

"Why do those hikers look scraggly?" I ask Steve.

"They are thru hikers," he answers excitedly. He tells about the Appalachian Trail that goes from Georgia to Maine and the amazing people who hike the trail.

My mind wanders as Steve continues talking.

I want to thru hike one day…

My thoughts drift back to Steve, he is excitedly telling about the huge mountains he climbed and how he had to hang his food in the trees at night to keep the bear from eating it.

"Why didn't you hike the whole trail?" I ask.

"It's too hard for most people to complete a thru hike," Steve answers.

My eight-year-old mind begins to form a plan, I will hike the whole trail. If I hike one hill at a time I will eventually reach my destination

I am a fighter.

I want to prove that I can hike the entire AT. I don't want to always be the bratty sister who can't keep up.

*How determined and confident I was at eight years old.*

I've never done much planning in my life. I grew up in the country. We didn't take many trips, except to visit grandma in Tennessee. Once she died we didn't go anywhere. We didn't have much money either. In the winter time if it was supposed to freeze we let the water drip in the bathroom and kitchen sink, then we all slept in the living room on pallets by the wood fire, the only heat source we had. When the roof leaked, we had to place pots and pans on the floor to catch the water. It might be months before we had enough money to fix the roof.

Our church has a youth group. We do crafts, go hiking and weekend backpacking on local trails. The year after Steve's trip, we had a church school trip to the mountains in North Georgia.

*I remember thinking, I can hardly wait until I have the time and money to hike the entire AT. It is green, beautiful, and peaceful in the mountains.*

My memories fast forward to 11th grade.

My heart rate increases, my throat tightens. Panic is ready to overtake me.

I squeeze my hands against my head trying to make the memories and the pain stop. The tears continue to build in my eyes.

*Stop! Stop! Stop!*

*I have to run. I don't like to run.*

*I have to get away from my mind!*

I leave the house and run a mile to the park. I keep running, faster and faster, but the memories won't stop.


In 11th grade, I meet AJ at church. He likes computers and avoids spiritual discussions in Sabbath school. He goes to a private church school out of town, but comes home on the weekends. He's 5'9'' with dark brown hair and brown eyes. He wears glasses and is a year older than me. He has an infectious laugh.

After church one week we start talking. We talk throughout fellowship lunch. Almost everyone has gone home and we are still talking.

Mom says, "Why don't ya'll exchange phone numbers and you can finish this conversation later."

"Can I have your phone number?" AJ asks shyly.

"Sure," I say. Our hands briefly touch as I pass AJ the paper.

# Girl (Hiking) with 4 Dogs

I give a small smile as we hug and say goodbye.

Thursday AJ calls, "There is a new 'Star Wars' movie I want to see. Do you want to come with me?"

"Not really, I have school tomorrow, I don't love Star Wars, and I still don't have my license back from my speeding ticket."

"Please come with me," AJ pleads.

"Why don't you take Jewel. Doesn't she like 'Star Wars'?"

"Jewel's busy and not as much fun to talk to as you are. Besides, I can pick you up and take you home afterward."

I finally agree.

We have a great time at the movies. AJ walks me to the house and gives me a warm cozy hug before saying goodbye.

"Call me when you get home, so I know you made it safe," I say.

"I will," AJ says.

After a few weeks of talking, AJ and I are officially "dating." AJ is the first guy I've ever dated. I feel so loved and cherished.

My memories fast forward again.

Panic is closer.

*My brain is screaming the memories are too much!*

*I can't do this! I can't do this!*

I run faster. My legs ache and burn, my throat is raw.

The memories won't stop!

After dating for four years, AJ and I talk about getting married.

"Sandy, I love you. I want to be with you forever. Please marry me. We can hike Appalachian Trail together when we have enough money," AJ pleads.

"AJ, I'm scared to get married. I don't want to go through the pain of a divorce like my parents did."

"I promise to always love and cherish you," AJ says nuzzling my ear.

"Are you willing to be honest with me? Are you willing to communicate with me even when it is difficult?"

"Yes," AJ says kissing my forehead. "My parents have been through a lot and they are still married."

I hug AJ and squeeze my eyes tightly closed as the painful memories of my parents' divorce come back to haunt me.

I was nine.

It's after 9:30 p.m. on a school night and I see my mom getting her purse and car keys.

I ask her, "Where are you going?"

She says, "I'm going to your uncle's house, do you want to come?"

I answer, "No," thinking she won't leave me.

She leaves.

Shortly after she leaves, I cry and scream "I want my Mommy!" until my dad takes me to my uncle's house.

Why doesn't dad stay?

I walk slowly inside.

My mom is drinking wine and cuddling with a man I've never seen.

I plead, "Please mommy, read me a bedtime story?"

She says sternly, "Go lay down, I'll be there in a minute."

I go out of the room and peek through a crack in the door. She's kissing this strange man!

She looks up, sees me, and yells, "Get out!"

My older female cousin finds me sobbing in the floor. She guides me to her room.

My feet and hands are like ice. I am shivering uncontrollably.

*I don't know how to make my mom stop being bad.*

*I'm scared.*

My cousin pats me gently on the back and says, "It will be ok."

I curl in a ball and tears stream down my cheeks.

Mom never reads me a story.

A few months later my mom re-marries. One brother lives with my Aunt, my other brother stays with Dad. I don't know how to live without my mom even if she is busy with her new husband. She no longer has time to tuck me in or read me bedtime stories.

*Why aren't love and commitment enough?*

"AJ, before we get married, I have to tell you about my past."

My heart is racing and I don't know if I can do this. I can't look at AJ. "AJ, when I was six my uncle molested me." I bite my lip, but the tears leak out anyway. I know he's not going to want anything to do with me now, but I have to be honest. I've never had sex, but I'm not a virgin either. I remember my uncle waking me up and wanting me to touch him. I didn't want to. He wouldn't leave me alone.

I used to dream about monsters.

AJ holds me and tells me it is okay. He loves me.

*I hate love! I hate kindness!*

## Girl (Hiking) with 4 Dogs

I run as fast as I can for as long as I can. Tears and sweat run like rivers down my cheeks. My lungs burn. There is a metallic taste in my mouth.

The memories are relentless.

I run home and collapse on the bed sobbing uncontrollably.

The memories destroy me. My wedding day was painfully perfect.


AJ and I married on 07/07 at 0700. I'm in my first year of nursing school.

We have a beautiful sunrise wedding outside at AJ's parents' lake. My Mom and Aunt Bev make my wedding dress. It is has a fitted top and flows out around the waist like a Cinderella ball dress. The dress has a long train with embroidered flowers, and seed pearls. My younger sister, Melissa, is the flower girl. She has hand sewn orange and yellow roses on her white dress. She flings pink flowers petals as she races down the isle. My Dad walks me down the isle. He is handsome in is his dark suit. A church friend plays the keyboard, and my cousins Deana and Teresa sing. Betsy is my matron of honor, Kelly, is my maid of honor, and Elena and Arlene are my two bridesmaids. They have flower print skirts and different color tank tops. The groomsmen, have matching tops, and khaki pants.

A flock of geese fly overhead and land on the lake as we promise to love and honor each other, "until death do us part." The sun is out and a lot of people are present despite it being 7 a.m. We have an outdoor reception. There is fruit, crackers, cheese, and little deserts.

Our wedding cake is white with orange and yellow flowers trailing down the side. My new mother-in-law arranged for two antique Model A Fords to drive us off after the service. AJ and I ride in one, my mom, and mother-in-law ride in the other one. The cars have rumble-seats in the back.

"Where are we going for our honeymoon?"

AJ says, "It's a surprise!"

I keep my wedding dress on. This day is so special, I don't want it to end!

After hours of driving we arrive in the mountains of Tennessee, near Gatlinburg. We have our own cabin in the mountains, it's called "The Squirrels Nest!" It's perfect!

Laughingly I tell AJ, "You don't have to carry me over the threshold."

"Yes, I do."

There is a large window overlooking the mountains. The trees are green and full. There is a balcony, and a Jacuzzi! We unpack then snuggle together...

AJ says, "I wanted to bring you to Gatlinburg so we can hike some on the Appalachian Trail together."

I am overwhelmed with gratitude. All I can do is hold AJ and think about how lucky I am.

The next day we visit the shops in town and buy a wooden plaque with our name on it to hang on the door when we get home. Then we visit the Ripley's "Believe it or Not" museum. The following day we drive to New Found Gap and hike a section of the AT. A taste of the trail; thick green forest, crisp clean air, beautiful, splashing waterfalls, and so much more.

"Once I finish nursing school and work a few years we can save enough money to hike the entire Appalachian Trail. I've read about couples doing thru hikes."

"It sounds fun! We can camp and cook together. We can get away from the stress of the city. Let's do it! It would be too dangerous for you to hike alone, and I wouldn't want anything to happen to you."

*Life is perfect.*

*I want to rip my brain to pieces!*

I'm shaking in the bed. I don't think I'm going to survive the plague of my memories.

Again, a furry head snuggles under my hand. The memories continue.


I graduated college and am working.

"It won't take long to pay of my school debt." I say to AJ.

"We work all the time and never get ahead," AJ says wearily.

"We can pay the bills without you going to work early and staying so late. It is not healthy to work so much. Besides, the new girl you hired, Jezebel, I don't trust her."

"She is a hard worker. She sold more cell phones than I did last month," AJ snaps. "She has to work and take care of her children. Her husband is in the military and is always deployed."

"She says all the military wives are jealous and call her a slut. It's difficult to believe everybody hates her and she is totally innocent," I continue. "I know you would never have an affair, but I don't think Jezebel is a faithful wife."

"She is a top sales rep. so what you think is irrelevant."

"I'm sorry I upset you AJ. I love you and I'm worried. You seem more distant and restless lately. How can I help?"

"I'm worried about paying the bills. I shouldn't have taken the day off. Jezebel needs me at work. I shouldn't have let my mom talk me into going to the Bob Bar Band Concert."

I look worriedly at AJ and finish getting dressed for the concert.

We meet AJ's parents and younger brother at the theater on Broad Street down town. His mom takes pictures, then we put her camera in our car so she doesn't have to walk back to her car. It's the first Saturday in April.

The music is great, but it's difficult for me to relax. My subconscious keeps telling me something isn't right.

After the concert, AJ and I head home to change clothes. He is meeting his brother at Players to play billiards and I am going shopping with his mom at the mall.

"AJ, your mom forgot her camera. Do you want me to text her and let her know we have it?"

"Okay."

"Can I use your phone? I don't want to dig mine out of my purse"

"Sure."

"AJ, there are a lot of messages from Jezebel. Why is she texting you?"

"It's just work stuff."

"Why is she talking about a cow? This doesn't look like work stuff. Are you sleeping with her?"

"No, I'm not that kind of person."

"This doesn't feel right. I can't think. I need to be alone."

AJ yells, "I'm just friends with her!" as I walk off down the street.

I call my foster brother, Joe. His friend works at the mall with AJ.

Joe says, "Chappy saw AJ and Jezebel at the bar in El Carrizo after work a few times. They were laughing and holding hands, and kissing. We didn't know how to tell you."

"You should have said something! How could you let me go on thinking everything is ok! How long has this been going on?"

"More frequently the last couple of weeks. We wanted to tell you, we just couldn't do it."

## MacKenzie

My heart stops. I quietly hang up the phone and turn it ff. I walk through neighborhoods I'm normally scared to drive through. I stay gone all day. AJ never calls.

My husband is having an affair, am I the last in the world to know?! I can't believe this is happening. I gave my heart and soul to this relationship. I gave everything!

"I don't understand!" I cry out in misery.

*On top of cheating, why is he lying? "I'm not that kind of person." What kind of bullshit is that?*

*What is going on? My wonderful, sweet, church going, husband is really an immature, despicable, adulterer. A pitiful body existing on the earth without a soul or a conscience. Like a leaf blown in the wind, without backbone, without substance. A thing to be pitied, like an undisciplined dog that humps any and everything it can. He's sleeping around with that vermin infested slut! Disgusting!*

I want to vomit.

*I can't do this.*

(The following information is added to help anyone going through a painful stressful or otherwise challenging situation that seems insurmountable. If you can't relate, or are a cold hearted, callous bastard, please skip the next couple of paragraphs).

*The pain is intense and unbearable. I want to be dead. My heart is in a million pieces. Sharp edges stabbing me with every breath. I can't take it. Memories poking me throughout the day. Confusion swirling in my head. I thought he loved me. I wish I were dead.*

*I have unshed tears dripping inside. Festering like an infected wound. Pain, and pressure squeeze my throat. I can't breathe!*

*Sentences stopped abruptly, like the life I once had.*

*I focus on nothing. I mark an "X" on the calendar. One more day. And another and another.*

## Girl (Hiking) with 4 Dogs

*I run because I can't walk. I can't sleep. Some friends are there and some are not.*

*I hold on tight to everything, but nothing is there. There is nothing to keep me. Here.*

*Love. Truth. Commitment. The Good Times. Giving My All. It's not good enough. One sided love, it's nothing but a joke. I'm nothing. I'm falling apart.*

*I want to sleep forever. Dreams aren't real when I wake up.*

*I will make my own dreams! I will make my own reality! I am not nothing. He is nothing!*

*I will succeed! I will hike and I will camp! God will take care of me in the city or in the woods!*

*I am Here. I have nothing to lose!*

*He promised to love me. Everything is a lie. He's a walking lie!*

**Lies!**

AJ disgusts me. He is ruled by his F_ _ _ ing penis.

I rip the sofa from the apartment and drag it three houses down, to the street. The neighbors quietly move out of the way.

They fucked on my couch!

My rage builds. It's unstoppable. Consuming.

Hoochie-momma stole my ironing board! What a cunt!

I'm shaking uncontrollably! I can't breathe! I don't want to breath!

I collapse on the floor of our apartment; the bed is a tainted memory. I squeeze my pillow as if my life depends on holding it together.

A piercing scream rips out of my throat. The sound is shrill and pitiful, like a helpless, wounded animal who knows it's going to die.

I shatter.

Finally, there is a moment of silence. Tears pour down my face and saturate my pillow.

*I used to be a fighter.*

*I'm going to hike the Appalachian Trail! I can save the money in couple of years. I don't care if it's safe to hike alone. I don't care about anything. I'll prove I don't need AJ. He can have his fat "apple-shaped" hoochie-momma!*

# Chapter 1: The Dogs

*It's been almost a year since AJ and I split and unfortunately, I'm still alive. I'm not into suicide and God hasn't answered my prayers to let me die in a car accident or other fatal event. I wake each day and put on my armor, a smile and a friendly attitude. No one knows how broken I am inside.*

*I mark another "X" on the calendar.*

*Today is Wednesday, my special day to spend time with my sister.*

"Hey Sookie Woo!" I use my pet name for my sister Melissa, "How was school today?"

"It was okay," she answers putting her books in the car. "Did you see the puppies in the van in front of us? They are so cute. They are free. You should get one."

"I don't want a puppy." *Caring takes too much work.*

"Look!" Melissa says, "There is a puppy coming straight to you. Maybe he is a Valentine's gift from God."

I look closely at the puppy. He is a black and brown fur ball on short stubby legs. His tail is wagging and shaking his whole body. I can't resist his cute cuddliness. I scoop him up and take him back to the people in the van.

"Thank you!" the woman exclaims exacerbated. "We were wondering where he got off to. Do you want a puppy? Our neighbor's German Shepherd broke his chain and jumped the fence into our yard. Now we have all these puppies to give away!"

"How old are they?"

# Girl (Hiking) with 4 Dogs

"He's five weeks old and eating on his own. Occasionally, he suckles on his momma, but only for fun. He is old enough to leave home," the lady answers.

I look again into his sweet innocent brown eyes. He is so cute, and smart. *Maybe he is a Valentine gift from God.*

"Yes, I will take a puppy. I want the one who came to me. Thanks!"

"I'm so glad you got a puppy sissy," my sister says. "He will keep you company."

I give her a hug and we head home.

I name the puppy Shepherd, aka Kujo. He is potty trained from day one, except two accidents. Once, when I set him down in the house after the long drive home, and the second, was when he peed in the floor when I was upset talking on the phone. He's also stubborn and independent! He sleeps all night without making a mess!

The Old Man dies, at 18 years old. He's in heaven.

Kujo needs a new playmate.

Two months later, while shopping at Burlington, I overhear a tall animated woman telling the saleslady, "I rescued a dog from PAWS Humane, Colt. This is the third pair of shoes Colt has chewed! I can't leave him home for a minute without him causing a disaster. One time he broke through the glass on the back door to get in the house and another time he scooted the bottom out of his kennel. He then moved the kennel from the wooden hallway to the edge of the carpeted living room, and chewed the carpet! I hope they will take Colt back. I can't live like this!"

I say, "Wait. I've been looking for a companion for my dog. Let's have them meet and see how it goes. Having another dog around may help with Colt's anxiety."

"We can try. I would hate for Colt to be put to sleep if no one else adopted him."

A week later, after a successful play date at the park, Colt, aka Mtn. Goat joins the MacKenzie family.

Mtn. Goat easily manipulates Kujo, while letting Kujo think he is the boss. Mtn. Goat rarely engages in aggressive behavior. Instead, if Kujo is trying to fight, Mtn. Goat rolls on his back and puts his feet in the air in submission. Kujo sits down in confusion.

Once, while at the dog park, Mtn. Goat frantically scales an eight-foot chain link fence! I close my gaping mouth and inspect Mtn. Goat for injuries. Mtn. Goat is grinning!

Mtn. Goat's favorite activity in the world is escaping, whether he's jumping Fences, squeezing through cat doors or bolting out the front door!

In October, while hiking Kujo and Mtn. Goat in the neighborhood two more dogs join us briefly before returning home. On Saturday morning I see the two dogs being loaded into the dog catcher's vehicle!

I say, "Hey, I know the dogs owner. Can I take the dogs and save you some trouble?"

The dog catcher says, "No. Once they are loaded in the truck I have to take them to the pound. The owner can come by on Monday. The pound is closed on Sunday."

He hurriedly locks the cages and speeds off.

Monday when my neighbor, John, returns home, I explain to him what happened.

# Girl (Hiking) with 4 Dogs

"My sister was supposed to be watching the dogs. The poodle is hers. I had Guard Duty this weekend. I didn't know what happened to the dogs!" John exclaims

"I was considering adopting another dog. If you don't mind, I can adopt your dogs from the pound."

"It might be best for them. I'm going through a divorce. My girlfriend doesn't like dogs and my ex-wife can't have them in her apartment."

"I'll take good care of them," I promise. "I won't be able to adopt them until Saturday."

Bright and early on Saturday I head to the pound. Adoptions are on a first come, first serve basis.

Marley, aka, "Digger," is a Golden Retriever and Smoky, aka, "Instigator" is a small Poodle.

There are so many dogs in the pound. Some are malnourished adults with their ribs showing. Their eyes are pleading for love, and someone to take care of them. Their back hips quiver as they try to stand. Their tails wag just the teeniest bit, not sure if you are there to help them, or hurt them. There is little hope for them. They are old. Past their prime.

There is a German Shepherd adolescent. The pound owners say, "You don't want him." Too much undisciplined energy landed him in the pound. Cast off. Neglected. He looks like he just needs some love and structure in his life. I wish I could save him. My throat tightens.

Seeing the neglected puppies is even worse. They are young, innocent, and full of life. They are playing in their concrete cell, making the best out of a challenging and unpleasant situation. They look at me with curiosity and love. Hoping I will take them to a nice warm home, with love and laughter. They are oblivious to what the future holds for them.

All the dogs live in an open concrete cell. There are three walls and a roof with an open front and a chain link fence for the door. I have to get out of there. Tears threaten to spill down my cheeks. Those wonderful dogs, including the puppies, will be murdered by euthanasia. Their only crime is being born. They are left neglected and alone, to fend for themselves. They end up at the shelter, where their days are numbered. They only have a week to get adopted before they are killed to make room for more cast offs. There are an average of 13 dogs murdered a day at the local shelter. *I'm like those unwanted dogs.*

Irresponsible pet owners should be required to work in a facility and assist with the murder of innocent animals, to see what their irresponsibility leads to. Spay and Neuter!

Be a hero. Save a life! Adopt from the local animal shelter. The dog or cat will be loyal, and will love you forever. Be patient with your new friend. There might be issues of neglect, and abandonment, maybe even abuse to work through. Take classes together, read training books, and make the relationship work.

Whew! My hands are full with 4 dogs!

# Chapter 2: Getting Ready

"Laugh if you want AJ. You will never accomplish anything in life. You are an empty shell. I have a month to prepare for hiking the Appalachian Trail and I will succeed without you. In fact, you're like a ball and chain, holding me back! I'm better off without you! Have your divorce, marry Fertile Myrtle and her well-used vagina! I want nothing from you. You are useless!"

AJ says nothing as I turn my back and walk away.

Then next day, I attend a class at REI in Atlanta, then purchase the recommend warm weather, light weight, moisture wicking, non-cotton clothing, along with a few other items.

The following weekend, I pack my gear and head to the Pine Mountain Trail (PMT) with my 4 dogs. I have a new Jetboil stove, a new standalone REI tent, new REI down sleeping bag, and a new headlamp. I also have enough Mountain House Meals, Roman noodles, Oatmeal, and Grits for a five day four-night backpacking trip, 46 miles.

It's an hour drive to the PMT registration building. I leave the dogs inside my white SC2 Saturn, while I go inside to pay for and pick-up my parking pass. I make a path through the thick fog as I return to the car. I look desperately inside my purse for the car keys, but they are nowhere to be found. I look inside the car and see the keys in the seat. Mtn. Goat has his paw resting on them. It's almost 5:00 p.m. I don't have time to wait on a lock smith. I look at the passenger window, it's down a few inches to give the dogs fresh air. I slide my arm through the largest opening at the top, then I jam my arm down into the narrow opening of the window until my now numb fingers reach the unlock button. I gingerly slide my throbbing arm up and out of the window. There is a maroon and purple bruise forming.

I walk to the driver's side of the car, open the door, shove Kujo, Mtn. Goat, Digger, and Instigator out of my seat, and crawl behind the wheel. Then I call Steve so he can meet me at the trail head. It's a 20-minute drive.

"Be careful," Steve says when I arrive.

"I will," I answer.

"I brought Little Debbie's and jerky for you, in case you need quick energy," Steve says.

"Thanks. I hate starting late, but I am determined to start today. It's only 2.5 miles to the first campsite. I can use my headlamp to see the trail."

"Bye, call if you need anything," Steve says as I start down the trail.

The trail is incredibly difficult to follow. The fog is like a white wall in front of me. The trail is a faint narrow brown line. The thick trees block the sun and obscure the trail even more. I can barely see my hand in front of my face. After 45 minutes of hiking the visibility is zero and the trail is impossible to follow. I trip over a small tree and know I am off the trail again. I shuffle back a few steps and feel the worn trail beneath my feet once more.

I see car lights and hear a car pass a few feet ahead.

I'm not going to make it to the campsite. Maybe I should use my cell phone and call mom to pick me up. I can start fresh in the morning.

No! I am a fighter! I won't quit!

AJ is a fucking looser!

I won't fail!

What would I do if I were on the Appalachian Trail?

I need to stop here. If I keep hiking in the dark and fog I will get lost. Where is a flat spot for the tent?

By now, the horribly thick fog is a cold, misty rain. The dogs are whining and restless. The headlamp is useless in the fog and rain. My glasses are foggy, I can't see anything, I can't find a flat spot. The wind is blowing relentlessly. Finally, I see some very, very small trees about the size of my index finger in diameter. I take off the doggie backpacks, then I tie the dogs to the trees, and begin to set up the tent.

It is a lot more complicated now than it was in the store!

I eventually get the poles together, but every time I try to fasten the poles to the tent, the wind whips the entire tent away from me. I hold on for dear life to one corner of the tent.

Even if I can't get the tent up, I surely don't want to be stuck without it!

The rain is falling harder now in thick intimidating drops. The dogs are whining and fussing. The tent won't stop trying to blow away!  I get out a tent peg and hold the tent with one hand.  I push the tent peg through the loop on the tent and use a rock to hammer it into the soft decomposing leaves on the ground.  As soon as I finish a gust of wind tears the tent out of the ground and attempts to carry it away. I race after the tent and catch it.

Now I can't find the tent peg!

Dear Jesus what am I going to do?

I need to keep the tent in place.  What is heavy enough to hold the tent down while I put the poles and gear inside?

"Umph, umph, umph, umph," the dogs whine behind me.

"Great idea!" I exclaim.  I unfasten the dogs from the trees, then I hold up the tent and find the zipper opening.  I set the bottom down as flat as I can on the hillside and hold open the tent.  "Come on Mtn. Goat," I call encouragingly, knowing that of the four he is the most laid back and will be the least skittish inside a partially collapsed tent.

Mtn. Goat plows in without incident, Instigator rushes in right behind him, poor baby is cold and shivering.  Digger and Kujo don't hesitate.  I grimace as they shake the rain from their fur.

I hadn't intended for all four dogs to go in the tent while I'm still setting it up!

At least they are out of the rain, and the tent isn't flying away. I am able to fasten the poles to the tent, and put the rain fly on. Unfortunately, the tent is contorted, and not on flat ground.  I had to set-up on the middle of the switchback trail.  There is a three-foot-wide flat area and a steep incline above and below the trail.

With four dogs inside the tent I can't move it! I do my best to straighten out the wrinkles, next I tie the rain fly to puny trees, one on each side of the tent.  Finally, I climb inside to get dry.

I use my head lamp to read the instructions for the Jetboil. Hmmm, it says, "Do NOT cook inside enclosed places."

I'll probably burn the tent down if I try.  Thank you, Bro, for the last minute Nutter Butters and dried jerky.

Supper.

I'm glad I fed the dogs before we left home.

Instigator wiggles his wet shivering body under my legs.  I feel like my knees are resting on a wet mop!  The dogs don't have any blankets. I open my sleeping bag so they can get under it to get warm. I have on a warm down jacket, ear warmers and a hat.

I attempt to sleep. I have to keep my knees bent, and sleep at an angle, to keep from falling down the hill. Mtn. Goat is at my head, Digger is on the downhill side by my feet, and Kujo is on the uphill side by my feet.

Finally, after what seems like hours, the wind and rain stops. The dogs begin to settle down and stop shivering. I am warm, dry, and on the verge of drifting to sleep.

Howwwl!

Great! There are wild dogs howling outside the tent. My four dogs jump up from their slumber and begin barking and growling inside the tent.

I put a soothing hand on Kujo's scruff and another on Digger. "Shush. It's okay." I pat the tent beside me. "Lay down and go back to sleep."

Eventually all four dogs calm down. Peace at last. My eyes drift closed.

Suddenly, out of the blue Kujo lunges across my feet, and attacks a calmly resting Digger.

What do I do?

I can either let them fight it out, inside the tent, or risk being bitten, and separate them.

The tent has to survive!

I am wearing a thick jacket. I reach out and grab Kujo, pulling him off Digger, and scream at the top of my lungs, "STOP!"

Kujo meekly backs off. Digger shakes his head to clear his ears, then lays down close to my left side.

I check for tooth marks or blood on both dogs.

After another fifteen minutes, all the dogs are calm again.

"What a first night on the trail!" I exclaim before closing my eyes for the third time.

The next morning is cold and foggy. I notice a gaping hole in the screen mesh on the front door. The result of the dogs gnashing teeth last night.

Next, I quickly feed the dogs, then eat another Nutter Bar while I pack up.

I need to hike 15 miles today to reach my reserved backpacking campsite.

Girl (Hiking) with 4 Dogs

The trail makes a sharp left turn before crossing the road and descending down the mountain. The air is noticeably warmer.

I stop in the afternoon to cook a warm meal, and drink hot chocolate. I use my stove for the first time, and promptly burn a hole in the thumb of my gloves.

Maybe it's not a good idea to wear gloves when playing with fire.

The water is boiling in about five minutes. I drink all the hot chocolate, but save half of my Roman noodles in a Ziploc bag.

I shrug into my backpack and pick-up the dog leashes. My backpack feels heavier. It feels like it takes an hour to walk each mile. My back is aching and my legs hurt.

To distract myself from fatigue and pain, I think about all the neighbors I would normally see on a 1.3-mile hike around the neighborhood. My neighbor Bill walks with me sometimes. He is always talking about his son, Todd, who is an electrician. I can hear the pride in Bill's voice when he says, "I can count on Todd. If he borrows money, he will pay it back."

I wonder what Todd is like?

I encounter other neighbors either working in the garden or taking their dog out to potty. I force myself to recall each house and each neighbor. It helps, and I finally make it to my campsite, appropriately named, "Brown Dog Campsite." I take off the dogs' backpacks and let them run while I set up camp.

I hobble down the hill and to the stream for fresh water. It's relaxing sitting on the rocks while I pump water. I cringe as I stand up. My knees are stiff and painful. I cautiously hike back to camp.

Supper consists of leftovers from lunch, Nutter Butters, and jerky. The wind blows gently and I shiver. I can feel the chilly air sinking into my bones. I quickly feed the dogs, and we crawl in the tent for an early night. Hikers' midnight, is 9 p.m. I am in bed by 8 p.m. The dogs shiver all night. I adjust the mummy bag to cover one dog and then a different one starts shivering. Instigator is sleeping near my feet, and the other three are in separate corners.

The next morning, day 3, there is thick frost on the ground or snow? I let the dogs run around, while I take down camp. The tent poles are frozen. I have to warm them up with my hands in order to pull them apart, now my hands are freezing. I have more Nutter Butters and jerky for breakfast. It's too cold to cook. I also have cold chocolate milk and cold oatmeal.

"Ouch!" I can barely straighten my right knee it hurts so bad. I take a deep breath and slowly let it out as I gingerly straighten my leg.

I don't know if I can hike out.

I turn my phone on. I sigh with relief, I have just enough battery life and cell phone signal, Verizon, to call Steve.

"Hey Steve, have you already left for work?"

"No. Why?"

"I over did it yesterday hiking and I can barely walk today. Can you bring my car to the T.V. tower? Mom has a key. I know I can't hike 30 more miles to finish this trip, but I have all day to make it 7 miles to the T.V. tower parking area."

"Yes, I can bring your car."

"Thanks so much and thanks for the Nutter Butters. I hadn't planned for quick food, but it came in handy. It's colder than I expected."

"Ok, I'll leave your car, then I have to get to work.'

"Ok, bye"

I hang up the phone, then call my four-legged friends.

I whistle and call again. Louder this time.

Still no 4-legged wayward companions.

Finally, after another five minutes of calling three tongue lolling dogs come running back.

"Four dogs whet out to play, over the hills, and far away, but only three little dogs came running back…" Instigator is missing. I call, and call but no Instigator comes running back. I leave my backpack and hobble as I search for him.

I can't find him anywhere! He doesn't like crossing water, and he must have gone with the big dogs, a little way from camp to the stream. He probably crossed the stream when it was narrow, then ran upstream with the other dogs, and couldn't jump across to make it back.

He is wearing a bell, so I can hear him, even when I can't see him, but I can't hear the bell either.

Dear Jesus, what do I do?

Girl (Hiking) with 4 Dogs

I hope someone finds him and takes good care of him. I hope he doesn't get hungry or cold. I can't feel my fingertips anymore. I'll have to leave him behind. It is going to be a long, sad, slow day.

I put on my backpack, and get ready to move on. I take a few steps then stop.

I hear the faint tinkling of a bell. The Instigator finally shows up! I hug him and love on him and promptly put him on his leash.

I limp along, with the dogs slamming repeatedly into the backs of my legs throughout the day, causing my already aching knees to buckle. I want to scream!

There are rock boulders to climb and the trail is rockier on this section of the PMT. I normally love climbing the rocks, but today I wish it was flat and even.

My progress is gruesome and slow.

Halfway to the end, I pass an older couple, the say, "You only have a few miles left."

I say, "Thanks." I already know that, but it is still nice to hear the sound of other people's voices. Except, the dogs are even more hyper and unruly when there are people around. Especially, if those people have a dog!

While crossing one of the streams, Kujo's leash slips out of my hand, and he takes off running in the woods. I call him, but he won't come back! I can't run after him. I can barely walk, and what can I do with the other three dogs?

Kujo finally comes back. He is grinning like a fool.

We continue hiking.

There is frost on the Mountain Laurel leaves.

The trail is only wide enough for one person. Two dogs are constantly trying to walk beside me, and the two in the back, are constantly trying to pass the two in the front. There is no room. The backpack keeps hitting the back of my leg! Kujo in the front, won't stop pulling forward.

Don't they ever get tired? Surely, when we start hiking 8-10 miles every day, then they will get tired. (Yeah right!).

"Digger, PLEASE stop trying to get in the front!" I snap irritably

"Instigator, what are you doing?" I grumble s he digs his feet into the trail.

"Mtn. Goat, I was here first!" I yell as he bumps into my left leg while trying to pass.

We finally make it to the car, and drive home. It is warm, and I can sit down. Moving my legs to use the clutch, gas, and breaks is painful. The dogs promptly calm down and go to sleep. Whew what a trip!

Once at home, I hobble up the 20 steps to the front door, leaning heavily on the rail. The steps must be horrendous for Dad with his bad leg.

Next, I unpack, and analyze how to make the next trip better. First order of business, is to get rid of some weight in the backpack! It's amazing how items that I thought I couldn't live without, suddenly are unimportant.

I call my high school track friend, Kelly, to ask if she can help me make jerky. In high school, everyone thought Kelly and I were twins, or at least sisters. We both have long brown hair and similar physic. I am a little taller than Kelly, and she is thinner than me. Kelly's eye color is brown and mine is hazel. I am three months older.

"Sure, I can help you make jerky. What do you need it for?"

I explain to her I am starting a thru hike on the Appalachian Trail in a couple of weeks.

She says, "Can I hike with you? I want to see how far I can go."

"Sure, but we need to do a pre-hike. I just finished one with the dogs, but I need to do another one before I'm ready for the big 'AT.' I have to fix holes in the tent from when the dogs had a fight. I want to rest my knee a couple of days, get a knee brace, a backpack cover, and a food bag. I also need to figure out a way to keep the dogs warm at night."

"Where are you getting your gear?"

"I usually go to REI, but I don't have time to drive to Atlanta and back. Outdoor World is more expensive, but it's closer. I have my old tent, and an extra sleeping bag if you want to use it?"

"Sure, I have another friend who likes to hike and camp. She might have a backpack I can borrow. I don't want to spend a lot of money on gear."

"I don't blame you."

## Girl (Hiking) with 4 Dogs

I use neon pink duct tape on the tent, it "takes a licken' (or teething) and keeps on ticking," and my mom helps make doggie jackets for the dogs. The jackets have fleece on one side, and blue nylon on the other side for warmth and rain resistance. Mom and I also make fleece inserts, to tie inside the tent, to block the cold air coming from the screen.

The next weekend, Kelly and I plan a 23-mile hike on the PMT.

The weather is clearer, but still cold.

"It's nice to have two cars this time," I say to Kelly as we ride together to the T.V. tower.

"Sorry it took so long to pack," Kelly says.

"I understand. It always takes me longer than I think it will."

After a couple of miles of hiking, Kelly asks, "Why did we start off with the difficult section?"

"Because we will be more tired at the end than we are now," I answer. "I wish we had time for a break."

"I'm already contemplating quitting!" Kelly exclaims.

"We are almost to the campsite. We only have one more mile."

We make it to the campsite, set-up or tents, eat supper, then crawl into the tents for bed.

Howwl!

"Are there wild dogs on the trail?" Kelly asks

"It's probably some dogs that live nearby. Do you want to borrow one of my dogs?"

"Yes, but I don't want Kujo. Can I have Instigator?"

"Yes."

A few minutes later, "Instigator won't stop moving around and whining!" Kelly exclaims.

"Do you want a different dog?"

"No, they are too big. I'm sending Instigator back."

"Okay." I unzip my tent and Instigator runs right inside. "We'll rescue you if any dogs come around."

"Okay. Good night"

"Good night. See you in the morning."

In the morning, I yawn as a roll over and try to go back to sleep. However, no matter which way I turn there is a dog breathing foul doggie breath in my face. With a sigh, I slip on my flip flops, and get up to take them to potty. Once they finish I fasten the leashes to trees while I fix breakfast, and take down the tent.

"I don't want to hike 12 miles today," Kelly says as she crawls out of her tent. "I would rather quit and go back."

"If we don't hike 12 miles today then we will have to hike the extra miles on Sunday or we won't finish."

"Let's go back then."

"How bout we look at the map. Maybe there are shortcuts we can take."

We peruse the map.

Kelly exclaims, "If we had taken the blue blaze trail yesterday then we would have cut our hiking mileage in half!"

"Great! Look, if we take the blue blazes today then we can make it to our campsite in 8 miles."

"I can hike 8 miles." Kelly decides and we continue on the trail.

Hiking is still long and slow. After a few hours, we stop for lunch. Kelly has an alcohol stove she borrowed, and an entire two-liter container of denatured alcohol. We don't know how much she needs and they didn't have smaller containers at Wal-Mart.

The alcohol stove doesn't have a stand for the pot, so in order to keep from putting the flame out, Kelly has to sit the stove between rocks, and sit the pan on the rocks.

After we sit down, she asks, "You already cooked your food in the Jetboil?"

"Yes. It heats water fast. Once I put the noodles in, it stays hot enough to cook them. I can even turn the heat off and the noodles still cook. How is your stove working?"

"It's awful! The water never boiled and now the noodles are cold and soggy. I'm not eating it! I'm throwing it in the woods. Do you think it will attract wild animals?"

"It might. You can give it to the dogs."

The dogs wag their tails excitedly and look expectantly at my friend.

"Okay, but you can put it in their bowls."

Girl (Hiking) with 4 Dogs

"Okay." I make all 4 dogs sit and wait while I hand out their treat. Once they all have their treat in front of them I clap my hands and say, "Ok."

They quickly gobble up the food, then we pack up and continue to our campsite.

Hours later we reach camp. It's a great night for a campfire so we gather pine straw, pine cones, and wood and start a fire.

"Do you hear the cars on the road?" I ask Kelly.

"Yes. We must be close. I see car lights too."

"I think we cross this road tomorrow. I can call Steve. Maybe he can bring marshmallows. Also, we can send extra gear home with him. I'll take Kujo and walk to the road, then I'll see if Steve wants to visit."

"I would love to give Steve this Denatured alcohol! It's heavy and I won't need it tomorrow. I'll see what else I can get rid."

I wait at the road for Steve. It takes a while for him to find us. I frequently look back at our campsite. I know we have a big campfire, but it is easier to see the light shining from six eyes looking in my direction, than it is to see the campfire light.

I start to do the pee pee squirm.

It starts snowing. We only get snow once every 5-10 years in GA!

Steve finally shows up.

"I'm going to pee before I go back to the campsite. I'll meet you there," I say and run with Kujo into a thick patch of woods.

Once we walk through the woods back to the campsite Steve explains why he took so long. "I had to ask a park ranger for directions. The campsite is near a small country road, not the main road we were thinking of. I had to tell the Ranger I was looking for my sister who is hiking on the trail."

"Did the Ranger ask for your sister's name? I didn't register this time, since last time I paid for five nights, and only stayed two."

"I gave Kelly's name. They wanted to know why you were staying at a different campsite than the one on the registration. I explained how you are taking the blue blaze trail because the original site was too far away."

"Thanks! I'm glad you were able to find us. We have heavy surplus gear for you to take back with you," I say.

Kelly says, "I packed way too much stuff. I don't need all this denatured alcohol! I don't need all these toiletries either. I'm keeping the toilet paper though. Everything else can go back, including all this extra food!"

"Good idea," I agree.

"I remember when I hiked years ago, I saved my sour cream and onion chips for the last day. My mouth watered the whole time I was hiking. The other hikers were drooling looking at those chips too! In addition to marshmallows, I brought ya'll some chips, if you want a treat," Steve says.

"Thanks!"

We sit around and eat marshmallows and snacks, while reminiscing about our backing adventures.

"I'm glad we have a fire, but I'm getting cold," I say.

"Me too," Kelly says.

Steve says, "I have to get back now anyway. Good luck on the rest of your trip!"

"Thanks for bringing marshmallows and taking our extra stuff back. Good night!"

"Your welcome. Good night."

Surprise! The next morning everything is covered with snow. At least, a couple of inches of snow! This is the second time this year it snowed!

Kelly says, "I'm freezing, but I'm going to take some pictures of the snow on our tents. We only have five miles to hike today and it's all downhill."

"Me too. Look at the dogs trying to eat it!"

"Ha, ha. Instigator is rolling in it!"

"They are crazy today!"

Not too much later we pack-up and leave.

"Kelly, do you see the turkey and the babies?"

"Yes, but your dogs are scaring them off."

"They were already walking away. They just started walking faster when we got close."

An hour later we make it to the end, about 18 miles total taking blue blazes instead of white! I drive Kelly back to her car near the T.V. tower. Her car is covered in snow! We dig out the handle and knock off the piles, then we follow each other home.

We have a week, for final preparations.

It's surprising and intimidating knowing that after a lifetime of dreaming the time is finally here to make my dreams come true. What if I fail?

Focus. Set the goal, make a plan to reach the goal, alter the plan as necessary to still reach the goal. Prayer. Courage. Persistence. Stubbornness. I'm a fighter!

The next day Kelly and I go to the, The Outdoor World. She buys a Jetboil stove, and a few other items. An employee, Chris, shows us how to pack our backpack better. We put the heavy stuff in the bottom. We also pack the tent and poles on the side of the backpack instead of together, and the food bag goes in the center. Thank you Chris!

Kelly borrows hiking poles from her friends. We also obtain contraband mace from another friend. We cover the label with zebra stripe duct tape.

As I make final preparations Dad says, "I'm coming to help with the dogs."

Dad is 65 years old and retired from full-time machinist and teacher. He still fixes my vehicles when they break and tutors friends and neighbors as needed. He is average height with dark brown/black graying hair and long thick bushy eyebrows. Mostly gray now with spattering of black. He has a full medium length gray beard, prominent MacKenzie nose, sparkling blue eyes, and a friendly engaging smile. I rarely notice his missing teeth. He has upper dentures he doesn't wear and he is missing most of his bottom teeth. He refuses to get the teeth pulled even when they are loose. He is about 75 pounds overweight with average to poor health. He refuses to see a doctor, but I know he has diabetes. He checks his blood sugar every couple of days and when he doesn't feel good. One day he told me, "I don't feel good if my blood sugar is less than 200."

"Dad!" I exclaim. "200 is too high. You are damaging your heart and kidneys you need to see a doctor!"

"I am not going to see a doctor. They don't know what they are talking about."

Dad also has a venous stasis ulcer on his left leg which causes him to limp. He refuses to seek treatment for it and uses a white sock to keep it covered. I educate him over and over again to keep his leg elevated whenever possible and to let me put a light compression dressing on the leg. He refuses. Dad also has borderline high blood pressure. He refuses to take medication.

"Okay Dad, I'm sure I'll appreciate the help. Especially since the dogs aren't allowed in the Smoky Mountains or in Baxter Park in Maine. I should get a camper shell for the truck so we can fit everyone."

Last year, God blessed me with a great deal on a white 1994 GMC Sierra truck. "He knows the plans he has laid..." Jeremiah 29:11.

I'm not great on computers so Kelly helps me search Craigs list for a camper shell. My sister Melissa has a friend with a relative who has a camper shell that fits perfectly, and even matches the color of the truck, but they don't want to sell the camper, they only want to rent it. $100 deposit and $100 for the use of the camper. A new camper shell is $1000+. The camper shell has a few areas where it has been patched on the roof and I'm concerned my dogs will knock out the screen so I keep looking.

I find a camper shell for $60 on Craig's list. Dad looks at it with me. The outside is purple/maroon and it has an Auburn sticker on the back. War Eagle! It is sitting on the ground and there are fire ants on the inside.

It's perfect!

Well, not really. It is two feet too short and a few inches too wide. Dad is able to bolt it to the truck.

"I can fix the back so it will be waterproof," Dad says. "There is no need to spend money on a new camper. This one will work fine."

"Thanks Dad. I'm glad you are handy with fixing things."

February 16, 2011, the day of departure arrives! Meow goes to Mom's house for TLC. He "Yowls" and tries to scratch as he is being loaded into the travel kennel. I reassure him as best as I can. Arrangements are made for friends and family to check on the house, and mail while I am gone. Goodbye house, I'll see you when I get back. I hope the plants don't die. (My baby willow tree died).

Girl (Hiking) with 4 Dogs

I load the dogs into the two kennels in the back for the truck, then Dad and I drive to Kelly's house to pick her up. We have to re-arrange gear in the back for her gear and food to fit. The truck is packed! Two large dog kennels, three medium plastic bins with extra food and clothes. We also have extra sleeping bags, and mats. Two backpacks, two tents, winter clothes, extra shoes and socks, and hiking poles.

We are finally on the road to Amicalola Falls! REI is closed by the time we make it to Atlanta.

Dad says, "We can stay overnight in Atlanta, then go to REI in the morning so you can exchange gear."

"No thanks, I am determined to start hiking on February 17, 2011. I want to be at the park in the morning so no delays ensnare me."

Dad sighs, "Okay."

We arrive at Amicalola Falls Park after midnight. The roads are hard to see at night. We were going to start closer to the trail head, but we can't find the road in the dark. After driving around in circles a few times. I decided, in exasperation, and exhaustion that we should just go to the park visitor center, sleep, and figure out the rest in the morning.

Shortly after parking in the visitor center parking lot, a park ranger checks on us. He taps on the window and asks, "Do you need any help?"

I quickly explain our situation. The park Rangers says, "You can stay parked until morning."

"Thanks," we answer.

After the park ranger leaves I look at Dad and Kelly, "How are we supposed to sleep tonight?"

"That's a good question," Dad says.

Dad walks around to the back of the truck to help get the dogs out to potty. One kennel is pushed all the way to the back and left side of the truck. The door on the long side is facing out. The second kennel is perpendicular to the first, and is all the way to the right of the truck in order to allow both kennel doors to open out. It's a tight squeeze. I have to crawl all the way to the back of the truck to reach both doors. Once the dogs are taken care of we return to the cab. Dad says, "I can sleep in the back and you girls can have the cab."

"Is there room in the back for you Dad?" I ask.

"Yes. I have a spot in mind."

I look at Kelly, "Does that sound okay to you?"

"Sounds good to me. I'm so tired I could sleep on a rock!"

"Good night Dad. I'll see you in the morning."

"Goodnight."

# Chapter 3: Georgia

**Day 1 Thursday February 17, 2011** My eyes open with the first faint rays of dawn. I hop out of the cab and rush to the back of the truck to check on my dogs. I lift the back glass and peer inside. I can hear Dad snoring, but I don't immediately recognize him. He is wedged on top of the dog kennels with a blue ½ inch sleeping foam covering him for a blanket. His feet are hanging over the edge of the kennel. He has about an inch between his back and the top of the camper shell.

He wiggles and the kennels creak underneath his weight.

"Are you comfortable Dad?" I ask in a concerned voice.

"I'm okay," Dad answers in a muffled voice.

"Are you warm enough? There is an extra sleeping bag if you need it."

"I slept good. I don't need the sleeping bag. Give me a few minutes to get out then I will help you with the dogs," Dad answers.

"Okay. I'll see if they have a bathroom at the visitor center, and if anyone can give us directions to the trailhead. Let me know if you change your mind about the sleeping bag." I shiver, "It is colder here than it is back home, but it is warm enough with the sleeping bag inside the cab."

Once I enter the visitor center I notice the ranger right away behind the counter. He seems friendly enough, but I don't immediately ask for directions. I peruse the store hoping to see a map telling us how to get to the trail head.

*How am I going to hike the AT and I can't even find where it starts!*

Dad enters the store and wastes no time in asking for directions. I amble to the counter so I can hear better.

"The reason you couldn't find the road last night is because that road is closed. There has been so much rain it is causing mud slides down the mountain. You can still get to Big Stamp Gap. Here's how…"

I look at his name tag and notice it says, "Ron Brown". I say, "Mr. Brown, thanks so much for giving us directions." By now Kelly has also entered the store. I continue, "My friend and I are starting a thru hike on the AT today! My thru hiker guide has your name in it. Do you want to see?"

Kelly says, "You could sign your name in the book. We can have everyone we meet sign the thru hiker book. Then we'll have a kind of year book."

I look at Mr. Brown, "Do you want to be the first to sign my AT Thru Hiker book?"

"Sure. Good luck to you and your four dogs!"

"Thanks, we'll need it! Dad are you and Kelly ready to go?"

"Let's go!"

We load into the truck. Our path starts on paved road, but before long we have to turn onto a dirt road.

I say, "Dad, I'm glad you're driving. This road is very muddy, and curvy. I am afraid if we have to pass anyone, one of us will slide off the edge of the mountain!"

Kelly says, "Ron said it was a two-way road, but I don't see how!"

We eventually find an area with enough room for about eight cars. We park and get out.

"Dad, we'll take the dogs with us to the top of Springer Mountain. Since we have to come back this way is it okay if we leave the backpacks with you until we are on the way back?"

"Okay"

It's a beautiful, sunny day. It doesn't take us anytime at all to reach Springer Mountain.

# Girl (Hiking) with 4 Dogs

Kelly says, "We made it to Springer Mountain! Look at the plaque."

"Cool."

"There is a book under the rocks. Oh, it looks like a log book. Let's sign it."

The dogs are hyper and smiling. We sign our names, then trek back to the truck.

"Are you tired yet?" Dad asks jokingly.

"Not yet," I answer.

"Let's have lunch here," Kelly suggests.

"That sounds like a great idea!" I say.

After lunch Kelly asks Dad, "Do you want to see the pictures we took?"

"Yes, that would be nice," Dad answers.

Kelly shows Dad pictures, while I divvy dog food into the dog backpacks and get my dogs ready to go. It takes time putting the backpacks on the dogs. Especially since Kujo is trying to squirm out of his backpack.

Eventually we get started on our big hiking trek through the woods. It's uphill and downhill all day. I successfully cross a few streams with four dogs on a leash. Whew, what a relief to still have dry feet! We take frequent breaks to rest, pump water, eat snacks, and air out our feet.

After hiking eight miles, we finally make it to Hawk Mountain Shelter. I kiss the sign, then Kelly and I drag ourselves to the camping area, and collapse in exhaustion.

After a few minutes, I say, "I guess I'm rested enough to set-up the tents."

"Me too," Kelly says. "If you didn't have the dogs we could sleep in the shelter."

"That is true, but if the shelter was full we would still have to put up our tent. After we eat and I feed the dogs we have to figure out how to use the bear cables."

We find a quiet spot a little way behind the shelter. We see a man and his teenage daughter pumping water from the stream. We finish camp set-up and proceed to investigate the bear cables. There are a bunch of cables hooked to the base of a tree. We're not sure what to do with them.

"Hey, do you want some help?"

We turn around and see a handsome, fit man with dark brown hair and friendly eyes. We accept his help and soon have our food bags suspended in air on the bear cables. The guy's trail name is, "Lost Rob."

Lost Rob says, "I started a thru hike a few years ago, but I didn't finish. I spent more and more time in town and spent too much money on alcohol. Do either of you drink?"

We both answer, "No."

"Well, I think you will finish then. I have hot water. Do you want coffee?"

"Sure, thanks."

As we sit talking by the fire, another camper, "Woodrat," joins us. He is on his second thru hike. And lastly, "Niners" and his daughter finish pumping water and hang up their food bag on the bear cables.

At dusk the dogs start barking and whining. "I'm pretty tired. I'll see ya'll in the morning," I say yawning.

"Good night everyone," Kelly calls.

I'm asleep within minutes of laying down.

**Day 2** I yawn and crawl out of the tent. Woodrat is gone already, Lost Rob is leaving down the trail, and Niners is stuffing his tent into his backpack. I look at the bear cables. There are only two food bags hanging up. Kelly's and mine.

I walk the dogs a short distance from camp. When I return, I tie the dogs to trees around the tent, then I remove our food bags, next I quickly dole dog food into the collapsible dog bowls and add water. Kelly and I take a few minutes to heat water for oatmeal and hot chocolate. Finally, we finish eating and packing up. We rush off down the trail.

After an hour of hiking we take a break. Kelly is getting a tender spot on her left great toe. She digs out moleskin from her backpack and protects the red tender skin on her toe. Instigator investigates the inside of a hallow tree while Kujo, Mtn. Goat, and Digger watch enthralled. Once the first aid is complete we resume hiking.

We haven't seen any other hiker. We slowly trudge up Sassafras Mountain.

Kelly says, "Can we take a break? I'm exhausted."

"We've only hiked a mile or two since our last break. Let's hike to the top of the mountain before we take a break."

"You hike to fast and my feet are hot and sore. You have the dogs to pull you along!"

"I'm not taking a break yet." I keep hiking thinking Kelly is right behind me. When I get to the top of Sassafras, I realize I shouldn't have gone ahead. What if something happens to Kelly? I have the dogs for protection, but she doesn't have anyone. I bite my nails as I wait at the top of the mountain.

*I'll give Kelly 10 more minutes, then I'll go back down the mountain to look for her.*

Eight minutes later Kelly storms up the mountain. The first thing she says is, "I'm calling James (her husband) when we finish this section!"

"I apologize for leaving you. I won't do it again. Do you want to hike in the front so you can set the pace?"

"Can we take a break now?" Kelly asks sarcastically.

"Sure."

We eat our lunch sitting on a big bolder at the top of the hill. The dogs sit watching us. They are tied to trees a little way off the trail. We air out our feet, and change our socks. Kelly puts Duct tape over the moleskin on her toe and adds moleskin to a sore area on her heel. Her boots are for snow ski weather. They are heavy and not breathable.

Kelly looks over at me, "Are your boots rubbing blisters?"

"No. I have Gortex hiking boots. They are comfortable so far. They are supposed to be breathable so the sweat can evaporate out."

We pack up and continue our hike. More hills. Everything is brown and looks dead.

On the way up Justus Mountain, we pass Woodrat. He is resting on the side of the trail.

At 3:00 p.m. we cross Justus Creek. We stop to pump and drink water and it is 4:00 p.m. before we leave. We have another mile to Gooch Mountain Shelter. We haven't seen Lost Rob or Niners.

The sun is setting when we arrive at Gooch Mountain Shelter. There is a guy "Ryan," two girls, the "China Girls," and an older man, "Pops."

"Hey, do ya'll know where the privy is?" Kelly asks.

They look at us but don't answer. No big deal. We continue on the trail to the right of the shelter until we find the privy. After we finish at the privy we find the tent area to the left of the shelter. There are a few flat designated areas. We can put up our tents side by side. Kelly feels safer with the dogs nearby.

It's peaceful with the trees overhead.

We sit on a log to eat. I have the dogs tied to trees with string. They get tangled up. (Long drawn out sigh).

Supper is ok. It's dark already, and cold, so we hang our food bags and go to bed.

**Day 3 The** next morning, we overhear the "China Girls" group say, "We are going to have to quit if any more equipment breaks!"

We also meet an older couple, Tom and Brenda from Auburn. They say "We were at this shelter last year at this same time. Once we got to the Smokey Mountains we had take a few weeks off because there was so much snow we couldn't keep hiking. We even had snow shoes! Then we had to quit because my husband got Lyme disease! We were checking for ticks, but we missed one that got between his toes! We are back this year to make it to Katahdin! When you get to Dicks Creek Gap, you have to stay at the Blueberry Patch Hostel. They have the best blueberry pancakes!

"Pancakes sound delicious!" Kelly says.

"They are." Tom says.

"Bye girls, we are headed out!" Brenda calls as she hoists her backpack with blue rain cover on her back.

We finally get packed up. I feed the dogs, then get them packed up. Even the "China Girls" crew is packed and gone by the time we are ready to leave.

"Thanks for waiting on me Kelly. I'm sorry I'm so slow."

"That's okay. I took some cool pictures of the moss and a few mushrooms while I was waiting."

Three miles later, on the way up Ramrock Mountain we pass the Tom and Brenda. They have matching blue rain covers on their backpacks. I call them the "Blue Backpacks."

"Happy Hiking," we call as we pass.

At 2:45 p.m. we see Dad briefly at Woody Gap. I dig in my backpack so I can charge my phone while we eat lunch with Dad.

"I can't find my cell phone!" I am usually good at keeping up with my things.

Dad says, "Did you leave it at the shelter?"

"I didn't see it when we left, and we were the last to leave."

"You can go back and look for it."

"I'm not wasting time backtracking, we still have three miles to hike before dark. Either someone will find it and turn it in, or it's lost forever!" I pray about it, then Kelly and I finish lunch and keep hiking.

I find out later Dad went back to look for the cell phone. He even had a group of boy scouts helping him, but they didn't find it. Dad has a bad leg so I feel horrible that he went to the extra effort of looking for a phone that they couldn't find.

Kelly knocks a pebble down the switchback going down Big Cedar Mountain. Before I know what is happening I am falling toward the edge of the trail. Digger is in hot pursuit of the falling rock. I hit the ground hard. As the wind is knocked out of me, I muster an "Att, att!" which the dogs know means, "whatever you are doing STOP!"

Digger looks back in gleeful confusion as his frolic over the mountain is abruptly ended.

Kelly rushes back, "Are you okay?" she asks while helping me to my feet.

"Never better," I answer brushing the dirt off my pants.

"Your hand is bleeding," Kelly points out.

Girl (Hiking) with 4 Dogs

"It's a little abrasion. It will be fine," I say wiping my hands on my pants.

Kelly continues hiking in front, after another mile of hiking, she yells back, "There is a dog up ahead, coming our direction."

"Thanks," I yell back.

"I don't want your dogs pulling you down when they try to sniff the other dogs butt!"

I take my dogs off the trail to let the other dogs pass. I see one dog on a leash, and when I have my back turned, a second dog, a Dachshund, runs up from behind. Instigator loops behind me, then Digger crosses behind my back from my left side to my right twisting me around. I fall flat on the ground, scrapping my arms and elbow. The four dogs drag me a few feet before I can dig the toes of my shoes into the ground. Kujo nips at the Dachshund. The owner finally snatches his dog up and glares at us.

I lift my head up from the ground. I still have all four leashes in my hands and I say, "Sorry about that. I didn't see your little dog who is *OFF the leash.*"

Once I get back on my feet, Kelly says, "You need to leave the dogs with your dad. You already fell twice when Digger was chasing rocks down the switchback!"

"Okay, if I fall *one* more time today, then I'll leave the dogs with dad for the next section." I look at the dogs, raise my eyebrows, and glare at them. I also slow down and anticipate when Digger is about to lunge!

We have beautiful views of the mountains, they are all shades of blue in the distance. There are low hanging clouds that blend the mountains and cast a scenic haze on the horizon.

## MacKenzie

We make it to Lance Creek, where we are camping. This is our first night camping without a shelter nearby.

I ask, "How are we going to hang our food to keep the bears away? I don't see any cables here."

Kelly says, "We have rope."

"Yes, but I've never used rope to hang a food bag. Have you?"

"No, but I'm sure we can figure it out."

We look around for a tree that looks tall enough to deter the bears and has a limb extending far enough we can throw a rope over it. Each of the dogs has a backpack and they carry their own food.

"We should probably hang the dog food too," I suggest to Kelly.

"I don't think there is a branch strong enough to hold all their food!" Kelly exclaims.

"How 'bout if I put my food in your food bag, then I can put all the dog food in my bag?"

"I guess we will have to make it work," Kelly says. I see a potential limb behind the tents. I'll see if I can get one end of the rope over."

I stuff dog food in my food bag, we tie both food bags to the rope hanging over the tree, then we attempt to pull the food up.

"This is tough!" I exclaim.

The limb cracks.

"Here is a stick. I can push from underneath while you pull."

"Help me get the rope around this little tree," Kelly says. We can use it as leverage. Now hold the rope while I put on my gloves."

"Ouch!" I exclaim as the rope tightens around my hand and digs in. "The rope is painful. I'm glad you have thick gloves."

"You should have bought gloves too, but you were too stubborn to buy any because you couldn't find any that were made in the U.S.A."

# Girl (Hiking) with 4 Dogs

"True. I think we have the bags high enough now. We can tie the string off around the tree."

"Look," Kelly says, "your dogs eyes are glowing in the moonlight."

"It sure is dark for being only 6:30 p.m. I'll put the doggie backpacks on top of this scraggly bush. They smell like dog food, and I don't want a bear hunting me down inside my tent."

"The wind might blow them down."

"I'm too tired and cold to care. It's starting to snow a little."

"I noticed. Let's get in the tents."

"Great idea. One last potty break for me and the dogs, then we are going to bed."

I crawl in the tent with my dogs and drift off toward a dreamless sleep.

Kelly says, "There is something scraping my tent! I'm not going to sleep. I'm going to keep you awake unless you make it stop."

"I can't make it stop. It's probably leaves," I say groggily.

A few minutes later, Kelly says, "I can still hear the scraping."

"Do you want to sleep in my tent with me and the dogs? You will get dog hair on your clothes."

It's quiet a couple minutes then Kelly says, "Okay, I'm coming over."

We manage to fit two people with sleeping mats, sleeping bags, one backpack, and 4 dogs in a 2-person REI tent. There is no chance of getting cold. Kelly is scared of dogs in general, and Kujo a little more than the others. She only allows him near her feet. Instigator is easy to lift up and move. Mtn. Goat is amiable with whatever, and is also easy to move by snapping my fingers and pointing. Digger, on the other hand, is all dead weight. 75 lbs. of unmoving dog.

A few minutes later I tell Kelly, "You are just going to have to use him as a pillow, because even when I pull on his collar I can't move him."

We finally get settled and drift off to sleep. We have our heads at opposite ends of the tent. Later, in the middle of the night, the dogs start barking. Actually, they aren't barking too bad, just a low growl or two and vicious woofs! There are more hikers setting up camp for the night. I want to complain about them arriving so late, but it is only about 9 p.m.

**Day 4** Kujo is breathing in my face. I turn my head to the left and Mtn. Goat is breathing on me. Instigator is standing on my chest. I open my eyes and scoot myself to an upright position.

I smell coffee.

"Good morning Kelly," I say groggily before crawling out of the tent with four dog leashes in my hands. I briefly note two guys in their twenties and a warm fire, then I tightly grasp the dog leashes and take them off into the woods. When we return, I tie the dogs up, then Kelly and I work on getting our food bags down.

As we are packing up, one of the guys says, "We have plenty of hot water and coffee. Do you girls want some?"

I say, "I'd love some. My hands are freezing!" Kelly is also up for coffee and we both get the lid from our Jetboil to use for a cup. We introduce ourselves and learn that Joel, who has black hair and blue eyes, is hiking with his brother Keith, who has dark brown hair and a distinctive military haircut. Both appear muscular and physically in shape.

We say thanks, then I ask, "How were you guys able to hike in the dark?"

Joel answers, "we had our head lamps, and there was a full moon. Also my brother is in the military. We are hiking a section of the trail while he is on leave. We should be able to finish the Georgia section and start the North Carolina section. We hiked almost 16 miles yesterday."

Kelly says, "We are hiking 8 to 10 miles a day and it feels like a lot!"

As they are leaving we yell, "Good luck!"

Kelly and I resume packing. Kelly looks in the side pouch of her backpack for toilet paper (TP).

"Sandy, look what I found!" Kelly yells excitedly.

I look in Kelly's direction and am surprised to see her holding up my red cell phone!

"I wonder how my phone got in your backpack?"

"You must have accidentally put it in my backpack when we were eating supper in the dark at Gooch Mountain Shelter. Since we both have red backpacks you probably put your phone in my backpack thinking it was yours.

I close my eyes for a minute, *Thank you Jesus for helping me find my cell phone. Amen.*

"Are you ready to go?" Kelly asks.

"Yeah," I answer.

Halfway up Blood Mountain we meet "Buzzsaw" and "Frog" going down the mountain. We step to the side so they can pass and I have my four dogs sit so they are more manageable.

Buzzsaw says, "You girls didn't have to move off the trail. We would have moved."

"That's okay. It's nice to have an excuse to take a short break while hiking up the mountain," I answer.

As Frog passes he asks, "Can I pet your dogs?"

"Sure, just be careful with Kujo. He picks and chooses who he likes."

Surprisingly, Kujo walks right to Frog and sticks his head under Frog's hand.

"I guess he likes you," I say. "Are ya'll thru hiking?"

"No." Buzzsaw answers.

"I did a thru hike a few years ago, the best advice I can give is, take nothing for granted and always be prepared. Take frequent short breaks."

"Sounds like good advice," Kelly says.

Buzzsaw looks at his watch, then at Frog. "Are you ready to go?"

"Yes. It was nice meeting you girls. Good luck on your hike!"

"Happy hiking to ya'll as well," I say.

Three miles later we reach Blood Mountain Shelter. It is a rock building with open windows and a tin roof. Blood Mountain Shelter was built in 1934. It is 4461 ft. above sea level. Fires are prohibited at the shelter.

Some hikers have removed their warm outer layers and are wearing only t-shirts and blue jeans. I doubt they are thru hiking as blue jeans are very impractical for long-distance hiking. I have a red fleece headband type ear warmer on, black fleece pants and a black Under Armor shirt. Kelly has a military quality head and neck warmer, a blue fleece jacket, and light blue fleece pajama pants with dark blue and red snowflakes. Fleece is practical for long distance hiking. Kelly found the pants at Goodwill for $5.

Kelly and I take a break to explore and to utilize the privy.

On the way down Blood Mountain, we pass "Dead Man" who thru hiked in 2005. It is steep and rocky going down the mountain. My imagination is going wild! What happens if the dogs pull me over? I'll slide all the way over the mountain. My heart is racing. I take slow deep breaths and focus intently on where my feet are stepping. I angle my body so I descend the mountain at an angle instead of straight down. I am thankful it isn't raining or wet!

I stop to catch my breath. Kelly is right beside me.

"The view is amazing," Kelly says.

"I can see for miles."

There are mountains visible in all directions. The sky is streaked with grayish purple clouds. Occasional sun rays penetrate the clouds. Kelly takes out her camera and to procure a panoramic picture.

I take out the SPOT GPS and send Dad a message letting him know to meet us at Neels Gap in about an hour.

The dogs love to pull! I love it when we are going up hill, but it's not fun going downhill. The down hills hurt my knees like crazy, and I am much slower going down than up. I wear a brace on my right knee. Kelly is just the opposite. She zooms down the hills, then she is really slow up the hills. When it is cold, she wears her black military head and neck warmer over her neck on onto her head. She looks hunch backed when hiking uphill with her backpack. The style makes her resemble a little granny with a scarf on her head.

We meet "Guy" and "Flaxman" from Atlanta, and surrounding areas. It reminds us of home. I mean, we have been away for four entire days, and we have traveled so far, about 30 miles!

We finally make it to Neels Gap. Kelly is ready to quit. We are cold and tired. We call Dad again, so he can meet us, then we take turns going inside Mountain Crossings to use the bathroom, enjoy the warmth, and peruse cool stuff in the store.

We meet Pirate. He helps hikers downsize extra gear. We see hundreds of hikers boots in the tree!

While I'm waiting on Kelly to come out of the store multiple sports cars come zooming up the mountain and around the sharp curves. Wow, a Lamborghini in real life! There are other sports cars too, but the only other car I recognize is a Porsche. The group stops at Mountain Crossings. I am stuck outside holding the dogs. By the time Kelly returns the sports car group is gone.

Dad arrives and we go to town for food supplies. We return to Mountain Crossings for a shower, then we drive back to the Wal-Mart parking lot for the night. Kelly and I share the cab of the truck again and Dad sleeps in the back on top of the kennels again.

**Day 5** I wake up first in the morning, and take pictures of Dad and Kelly sleeping. However, Kelly gets even by taking a picture of me picking up poo after my pets.

*Do I always make a face when I clean up after the dogs?*

Today I am wearing my ear warmers, my second pair of black fleece pants, my teal blue fleece shirt, and my orange and blue down vest. Kelly is wearing her head and neck warmer, light blue fleece pajama pants with white polka dots, and a black down jacket.

The sky is dark blue and grey this morning with bright rays of orange sunlight shining through.

Dad drives us back to the trail head. I notice Mtn. Goat is getting a sore on his leg from where his backpack is rubbing. It slides to the side and rubs his leg. I try, unsuccessfully, to counter balance it. The problem is the backpack is heavy with food and water. Also, when we hike it slams into the back of my calf, which pushes it to the outside, and then rubs Mtn. Goats leg. I wrapped his leg with gauze and tape, but the backpack keeps sliding down his skinny leg. Next, I lighten his load. I remove all the water from the doggie backpacks. They drink from the streams and puddles anyway. I had hoped the extra weight would tire the dogs out, but it's not working so I ditch it. I also put more food in the other two big doggie backpacks, I rotate the backpacks to keep Mtn. Goat's abrasion from getting worse, and to alternate pressure points.

I started with four different backpacks. I have two old style backpacks, a red Kelty K-9 Chuckwagon for Kujo and a blue Granite Gear for Mtn. Goat. I had to buy two new backpacks for the newest family members. After searching everywhere for a backpack, I finally found a blue Ruff Wear for Digger, and a pink camouflage Jeep brand for Instigator. Instigator's backpack is horrible. I had to do alterations to make it fit. Most of the time, I let the big dogs carry his food. He is a master at losing his backpack. Thankfully, Kelly is usually behind us. She lets me know when Instigator ditches his backpack. However, one time I had to backtrack a mile to retrieve his backpack.

In the walking line-up, Instigator kept getting stuck under Digger's belly so I hook him to the loop on Digger's backpack so he can walk tandem to Digger. This gives Instigator and I more room to walk. Kujo walks on the left, constantly pulling ahead. Mtn. Goat walks in the front on the right and Digger is behind him, but continuously tries to pass him.

The best thing about the Kelty backpack is the color. It doesn't have good padding and the chest strap is constantly rubbing under the armpits. Actually, both old backpacks don't have good padding. I sewed fleece on the chest straps, which helps some, except it keeps sliding. The biggest help is to have less weight in the backpacks, which means re-supplying more frequently.

Kujo and Mtn. Goat are also masters at ditching their backpacks. They drop their head and front shoulders, then shake until the backpack falls off. At least when they are on a leash I know when they are trying to lose the backpack.

The dogs love to go fast. I feel like I'm flying! They have so much energy and excitement. They can't wait to get to the top of any hill. It's as if they believe there is a great big steak waiting at the top. They are fun and happy most of the time. They don't know where we're going, but they want to get there fast. We climb a few small boulders as the trail meanders through the woods. We pass a white fungus growing from a dead tree.

At 2:00 p.m. we take a break on a fallen log. We eat trail mix, cheese, and crackers while we let our sweaty socks dry in the wind. Mtn. Goat, Instigator, and Digger rest together. Kujo is a few feet away by himself. All the dogs diligently watch the trail, guarding against intruders.

Once the sun is up the sky is a clear light blue with fluffy white clouds hanging over the mountains. There are a few trees visible. Most are deciduous brown trees, but from time to time evergreens are visible as well.

First, we meet Dad at Tesnatee Gap. When we arrive, Dad says, I can keep the dogs and your backpacks if you want to hike another mile to Hogpen Gap."

I look at Kelly. It is 4:10 p.m. now. It will be dark in less than two hours. "I don't mind walking another mile without the backpacks. I will still bring the dogs though. What do you think Kelly?"

"We can hike another mile."

"Thanks Dad. We'll see you in a little while."

It is a lot easier to hike without our backpacks. We even stop to climb boulders beside the trail. The dogs pose, Kujo looks off into the distance with an arrogant air, Mtn. Goat has a Mohawk and looks with concern at Kelly, Digger looks lovingly at Kelly, and Instigator blends in with the rocks.

## Girl (Hiking) with 4 Dogs

We finish and meet Dad at Hogpen Gap. We use our head lamps to cook supper in the dark in the parking lot. It is dark by 6:25 p.m. We snack on Lance crackers while our rice and cheese cooks in the JetBoil. Dad shares beef hot dogs.

I say, "Dad, thanks for bringing the truck and helping with the dogs."

He says, "No problem."

I ask, "Do you get bored when we aren't with you?"

He laughs and says, "No."

Kelly asks, "What do you do?"

"A little of this and a little of that. I'm working on getting Sandy's mom's taxes done. I look around town, go to the library, or the bookstore."

It is cramped in the cab with Kelly. If I stretch my legs then my back is hunched over, and if my back is straight then my legs are bent. My knees hurt, and cramp when they are bent, and my back aches when it is hunched. Sleep is miserable.

Around midnight, there are crazy people driving their sports cars back and forth on the road! Every time they pull in the parking area and start talking, the dogs bark and get restless. Kelly and I try to eavesdrop on their conversation, but we can't hear. I think they practicing speeding around the curves!

**Day 6** We have an uneventful morning and begin hiking shortly after sunup. The hills are huge, the cooler weather is pleasant. It's not as hot hiking up hill. Kelly claims I have an advantage because the dogs pull me up the hill (she might be right ☺).

We hike Poor Mountain and Sheep Rock Top. Kujo has a talent to stay on the trail. While the other dogs are distracted and trying to pull me in all directions, Kujo always pulls forward. I have to slow down so I don't tromp on Kelly's feet when we are hiking uphill. I challenge myself to see how long I can hike with my eyes closed and the dogs leading. Kelly is ahead of me. I am about to open my eyes to make sure I'm still on the trail.

"What is taking you so long?" Kelly calls back.

"I am seeing how long I can hike with my eyes closed, but I'm about to open them."

"Wait. We are almost to Low Gap Shelter. I will guide you the rest of the way to the shelter."

"Thanks. It is interesting hiking with my eyes closed. One time, I almost fell headfirst over a tree in the trail. I knew it was coming, because I felt Kujo jump, but when he jumped, the other dogs quickly followed, and I smacked into the tree before I could contain the posse. I scraped my leg, but I didn't open my eyes."

"How did you get over the log without falling on your face?" Kelly asks.

"I put all the leashes in one hand, then inched one leg over the log at a time. The log was hip high and as big around as a small person."

"I remember that log," Kelly says. "Did you see the small waterfall crossing the trail?"

"Yes. I heard it and opened my eyes."

"I'm going to use the privy and pump water while we are at the shelter," Kelly says.

"Good idea," I agree.

I rotate the backpack from Kujo to Digger. The dogs are carrying only one pack today, since we plan to meet Dad at the end of the day. Mtn. Goat can recover from his leg abrasion while Kujo and Digger take turns carrying the food. The Ruff Wear backpack is the best one I have, so I use it all the time. Digger loves to wear his backpack. I let him wear it. Instigator is so hyper I have him wear his backpack too.

We resume hiking after our 15-minute break. We hike for another couple of hours before Kelly and I stop for lunch in a sunny spot with a fallen log. It is sheltered from the wind by the ridge on the right. I hook the dogs on various trees so they can lay down.

Kelly asks, "Do you want any more trail mix before I put it up?"

"I'll take one more handful then we can keep hiking. My feet are almost dry."

"Mine are dry. I have my dry socks on and my sweaty socks are hooked to the backpack."

Woof, Woof, Woof, woof!

We both look up and see a hiker stop in his tracks. I assure him the dogs are tied up and they won't bite. We talk long enough to find out his trail name is "Croc" because he always hikes in crocks. He looks warily at Kujo then hikes hurriedly past. We lug our backpacks on, hook up the dogs and resume hiking as well. The mountains are minor today, but we have 13 miles to cover! We see beautiful waterfalls and endless mountain views.

We take a short break at Chattahoochee Gap, the wee beginnings of the Chattahoochee River. Kujo looks around questioningly, Mtn. Goat looks wise, Digger lays down, and Instigator is prepared to attack.

Four miles later, after hiking Blue Mountain, we end our day at Unicoi Gap. Dad is waiting to take us to Helen, GA. Kelly and I split a room at the hiker hotel, Helendorf River Inn. The Blue Backpacks highly recommended it.

The first place we stop to ask is a two-story building. Kelly and I get out of the truck and go inside. Kelly asks the woman at the desk, "Do you know where the Helendorf River Inn is?"

The woman replies, "I have never heard of that place"

"What is the business upstairs? Do you think they would know?" I ask.

"I don't know what is upstairs, but I doubt they will know anything," the woman answers shortly.

"Okay. Thanks." I look at Kelly and raise my eyebrows. "Let's go."

"Let's ask at the restaurant across the street. Maybe they are more intelligent," I suggest.

"You can ask this time," Kelly says.

"Excuse me ma'am, do you know where the Helendorf River Inn is located?" I ask.

"Yes. Keep going down the main street and you can't miss it. Are you thru hiking?"

"Yes. Do you want to sign my thru hiker book?" I ask.

"I would love to. I hope to hike the Appalachian Trail one day."

"Thank you," I look in my book, "Samantha."

"Bless you girls," Samantha says as we head back to the truck.

When we arrive at the Inn I say, "Dad, you can stay in the Inn with us. We are paying for it, you don't have to pay anything."

"No thank you. I'll stay in the truck and listen out for the dogs."

"Okay, but in the morning, you have to make use of the tub so we can get our money's worth out of the room."

Dad says, "We'll see."

The Inn has a lovely metal "Knight in Shining Armor."

# Girl (Hiking) with 4 Dogs

**Day 7** Dad does take a bath. I feed the dogs, then Kelly and I rearrange the plastic bens in the back of the truck in order to make more room. Finally, we eat breakfast! We have cereal and powdered Nido milk.

Kelly and I agreed since we hike 13 miles yesterday, then we are taking the day off today to enjoy Helen, GA. Dad watches the dogs while Kelly and I go sightseeing, and explore the unique shops. Many of the buildings have interesting Muriel's painted on the side. One has hot air balloons, while another building has different pictures of bears, catching a fish in the stream, climbing a tree, and cubs playing.

Dad says, "I can drive you to store. There is no reason why you should have to walk."

"We don't mind walking Dad. It's easy to walk without a 30-pound backpack."

One shop owner makes wooden bowls of all shapes and sizes. They are smooth and beautiful. Another shop has blown glass and other trinkets.

Kelly says, "I bet my sister would love this green glass turtle. I wish I was home with my family."

"If you want to buy them a souvenir we can store it in the truck," I suggest.

"No. I'll have James bring me back one day."

Eventually Kelly and I get hungry and walk to the grocery store. We decide to get ice cream, to split between the three of us. There are all kinds of wonderful limited Blue Bell Ice cream flavors to choose from. We debate between two flavors, Moo-lineum and something else.

Kelly asks one of the employees, "We want the Moo-lineum ice-cream, but it has a messed-up lid. Do you have any more of the same flavor without a messed-up lid?"

"Wait just a minute and I will look."

The employee comes back and says, "I'm sorry, but we don't' have any more Moo-lineum. Do you want something else?"

I look at Kelly. She says, "We don't want Moo-lineum ice-cream if we have to pay full price for a messed-up container."

As we are talking to the employee one of the guys in the store realizes we are thru hikers, and asks the manager to give us the ½ gallon of ice cream for free.

We say, "Thanks for the trail magic!" Then we explain, "Trail magic is a kindness usually involving someone giving thru hikers' food!"

We take the ice cream back to the truck to share with Dad. Dad has the dogs fastened on trees around the parking lot. They each have water and shade.

After ice cream, we load up the dogs and Dad drives us through town, then as the sun sets we return to the parking lot of the Inn to sleep in the truck.

**Day 8** We wake up at 6:30 a.m. I take care of the dogs, then we are ready to leave Unicoi Gap. Dad drives us back to the trailhead. We start climbing Rocky Mountain. We hike from 2971 feet to 4017 ft in under 2 miles. It is freezing cold when we start, but we warm up quickly. Along the way, we pass an interesting tree.

"Kelly, let's take a break. I am curious to see if Mountain Goat can jump up in the tree with the branch sticking out like an arm."

"Okay. I could use a break. Is this mountain ever going to end?"

"It can't be too much farther. Look, Mtn. Goat jumped on the limb. He looks super happy and excited. I think he's laughing because the other dogs can't manage the jump. They are whining, fussing, and looking hopeful, but they just can't make it."

Girl (Hiking) with 4 Dogs

"If you are done playing with your dogs, I'm ready to keep hiking. You wanted to hike 13 miles again today so we don't have time for playing around."

Next, we struggle up Tray Mountain which peaks at 4199 ft. $3/4^{th}$ of the way to the top, we sprawl in the middle of the trail for a snack break. A few minutes later the dogs start barking. I look up to see a hiker quickly approaching. He has black hair, average height and size, and a reasonable size backpack. He stops to talk for a few minutes and introduces himself as Atlanta Dave aka Katmando. He barely seems winded as he struts off down the trail.

We slowly get to our feet and trudge toward Deep Gap Shelter.

Close to 5:00 p.m. we finally make it to Deep Gap Shelter. It's getting dark already. As we get closer to the shelter, Katmando sticks his head out.

"Hey Girl with 4 Dogs, I see you have your tent, but you are more than welcome to sleep in the shelter tonight. I am the only one here and I doubt anyone else will be coming in later. Besides I heard it is supposed to rain after midnight."

"If you are sure you don't mind, then I'll be more than happy to sleep in the shelter."

"This is a large shelter," Kelly adds.

Without further ado, we lay out our sleeping bags, then fix supper. Just before we retire for the night another camper arrives. I don't mention the dogs, and he doesn't complain. His name is Christian.

**Day 9** We only have three miles to meet Dad. We are excited about staying at the Blueberry Patch Hostel. We tell Katmando and Christian about the blueberry pancake breakfast and they seem excited too. We are looking forward to a SHOWER, a BED to sleep in, and possibly real food!

It doesn't take long to meet Dad at Kicks Creek Gap, and he drives us to the Blueberry Patch. It states in the AT Handbook that no pets are allowed at the hostel, but I am thinking it will be ok for the dogs to stay in the parked truck.

As we pull into the driveway of the hostel a man comes out. He says, "Hi, I'm Gary. I own the Blueberry Patch and you can't stay here with the dogs."

My heart stops. "They will stay in the truck," I explain desperately. "We will take them somewhere else when we take them out of the kennels."

"Regardless, you can't stay with the dogs," Gary replies.

I'm getting chocked up. My throat is tight and my eyes are starting to sting. I blink a few times and try to swallow down the lump in my throat. *We just want a shower, somewhere warm to sleep, and real food to eat.*

Gary continues, "I have donkey's in the back and even the smell of dogs upset them." Gary must have noticed my crestfallen face. He continues, "I have a neighbor who owns some land across the street. You might be able to park over there."

I try again to swallow the lump in my throat. I have tears streaming down my cheeks. I take a deep breath and mumble, "No thank you" as best as I can with my throat all constricted.

I can see Katmando in the background near the hiker hostel door.

*Why am I always being rejected?*

I get in the cab of the truck with Dad and Kelly.

Dad says, "It's early, I'll take ya'll back to the trailhead."

Kelly says, "If we don't stay at the hostel, then I'm going home."

I say, "Can ya'll stop the truck? I want to get in the back with the dogs so I can think!

Girl (Hiking) with 4 Dogs

Dad pulls over and I get in the back.

Tears roll down my cheeks.

*It wouldn't be that bad going back to the hostel, the worst part is having to face everyone who saw me crying. I really want a hot shower and Blueberry Pancakes. I also don't want Kelly to quit.*

The next time we stop, I realize Dad brought us back to the trailhead. I am angry. I am tired and I'm not going to let Dad make me hike more than I intend! He isn't exhausted from hiking.

Dad always says, "You can always change your mind," basically encouraging me to quit. It is very irritating. I use his negativity to increase my determination to finish. I want to prove him wrong, he only gave me 60-65% odds of completing the trail.

In this instance, I decide to "change my mind" and stay at the Blueberry Patch.

I get out of the back of the truck and walk back to the cab. "Dad, I've decided to stay at the Blueberry Patch. Gary did say we can park across the street.

"We are at the trailhead now. It will cost more gas to drive back to the Blueberry Patch," Dad replies.

I take a deep breath and try to keep the irritation out of my voice. "That's okay. It won't be the first time we've waisted gas."

"There is another hiker coming down the trail. Do you want to offer a ride since we are going back?" Kelly asks.

"Sounds like a good idea. Maybe we needed to come back just to give this hiker a ride," I suggest.

The hiker, "Magic Bags" agrees to a ride. He is about 5'5," stocky, with reddish brown hair and matching full beard and mustache. He is from Pennsylvania.

We park the truck across the street in the neighbor's pull-out. We keep the dogs in the pull-out area, either on leashes or in the kennels. Dad stays with the dogs most of the time, but he does visit in the hostel briefly. I am back and forth between the truck and the hostel. Kelly stays at the hostel.

While at the Blueberry Patch, we meet Delaware Dave (Delaware). He is middle aged, clean shaven with dark hair. He has a friendly smile and a happy aura. We visit with Katmando again, and we just missed Niners and his daughter.

Delaware Dave says, "I'm glad you decided to stay. I've been reading the trail logs, many of the logs mention "The Girl with 4 Dogs," I was hoping to meet you.

I smile and wish it wasn't so obvious I have been crying. "Thanks."

Later Dad takes a group to the store to re-supply. I buy microwave popcorn to cook at the hostel. There is a path to the showers behind the sleeping quarters. I have toiletries from the truck, but I notice there is extra shampoo and body wash in the shower. They even have razors. I encouraged Kelly to shower first so I don't have to worry about not using up all the hot water.

Finally, I'm ready to retire for the night. I love being clean and sleeping in a bed!

**Day 10** In the morning, true to the trail rumors, we all have a humongous breakfast together. Not only are there pancakes, but also biscuits, bacon, and juice. Breakfast is indescribable! Gary thru-hiked in 1991. The hostel owners are actually very nice and it is worth staying at the Blueberry Patch Hostel. If you don't have trail support to watch your pets,

Girl (Hiking) with 4 Dogs

then you won't be able to stay at the Blueberry Patch because it will disturb the "Assess" living on the farm.

Dad takes us, including Delaware Dave and Magic Bags to the trailhead. We all start hiking together.

As we descend the mountain toward Plumorchard Gap, Magic Bags says, "Wow Kelly, you are slow going up the mountain, but you are like a rocket going down the mountain!"

"How do you like the trail name Granny Rocket?" I ask Kelly.

"It is okay, but I like just Rocket better."

"Okay, your trail name is Rocket, and I am Girl with 4 Dogs."

"It fits us. Although many hikers refer to us as "The Girls with 4 Dogs," Kelly aka Rocket adds.

"That is true," Magic Bags chimes in.

The landscape is brown, but different stumps and trees resemble animals to me. I see a cow, an opossum, and a dragon.

After Rocky Knob, we cross into NC. There is a wooden sign bolted into a tree. The side of the tree has a round metal bar growing into it. It looks like the tree is biting the bar. There is also a tiny American flag wedged between the tree and the sign.

# Chapter 4: North Carolina

**Day 10** Saturday February 26, 2011 Continued "We're never going to reach our campsite," I say. Rocket agrees. Delaware Dave is ahead of us somewhere. Rocket and I are trying to keep up with Magic Bags. He is tireless.

"We're almost to Bly Gap. Less than a quarter of a mile." Magic Bags says without even gasping for air. "Take a break if you need one."

I glance at Rocket and she shakes her head.

"I guess we'll keep going," I say.

Rocket and I keep trudging along. The dogs are pulling me and I struggle not to fall on my face. It feels like an hour before we finally see the camping area. Delaware Dave is setting up his tent. He has on black hiking clothes and a neon orange baseball cap.

Rocket and I collapse on the ground with our packs on for a quick break before setting up camp. The 4 dogs reluctantly sit beside me. After a 10-minute rest, I have enough energy to shrug out of my backpack and assist the dogs out of their backpack. Then I set up my tent and throw all the backpacks inside.

I grab a handful of trail mix and head toward Rocket., "Do you want to explore with me and look for the, 'Old twisted tree often photographed,' referred to in the thru hiker handbook.?"

"Okay."

"I want to see if the dogs can climb the tree."

"I'll take pictures if they are successful," Rocket says grabbing the camera.

We find the tree not far from the campsite. Mtn. Goat makes tree climbing look easy. He jumps up like an Olympic pole-vaulter, then he stops long enough to give me a grin and a hug, before jumping down the other side of the tree. I easily manhandle Instigator into the tree. Digger joyfully follows as I lead him into the tree, however Kujo propels himself off the tree faster than a deer can outrun a forest fire. No amount of coaxing will convince Kujo to climb the tree!

Girl (Hiking) with 4 Dogs

After a few minutes of fruitless coaxing, Rocket and I head back to camp. I tie the dogs to various trees, feed them, then fix supper. I make chili-macaroni with hot water in a zip-lock bag.

Rocket and I head to the campfire Delaware Dave has going. Magic Bags and Delaware Dave are already eating. We sit down to enjoy camaraderie while we eat. I take a huge bite of my macaroni.

I almost gag! The chili macaroni is horrible! The powdered flavor is stuck inside the noodles. The water isn't mixing properly. Every time I take a bite my mouth puckers, my right eye twitches, and my face goes into involuntary contortions. My entire body shudders and convulses. I'm hungry and I didn't bring extra food so I let the saliva collect in my mouth, then I take another bite of food, when no one is looking. It's worse than the first bite. I add extra water to my bag and eventually I consume my food.

The dogs start barking ferociously. When I look up I see Christian approaching the camp.

"It's okay they are tied up," I call.

Christian warily bypasses the dogs and joins us at the campfire.

"What a beautiful evening. The stars are so bright and the sky is crystal clear out here," I say.

"Yes, God is an amazing creator," Delaware Dave adds.

"How do you know there is a God?" Magic Bags asks.

"I read and study his Word," Delaware Dave says. He talks a while longer, then I add, "I know God because when I pray, I can feel his presence. He answers my prayers and provides for my needs sometimes before I even ask."

The dogs start barking again and I go to see if anyone else is coming up the trail. It's dark and I don't see anyone. When I return to the campfire conversation has shifted to what motivates us. We talk about religion, politics, and what motivates us. We talk for hours before finally going to bed.

**Day 11** Rocket the dogs and I are the last to leave camp in the morning. We hike up Couthous Bald at 4669 ft.

"These Mountains are too big!" Rocket exclaims in frustration. "When we meet your Dad today at Deep Gap, I'm quitting! I'm going to call James to come pick me up!"

"Do you want to hike with the dogs? It might help," I offer.

"No! They will pull me over."

I remain silent. We pass Sassafras Gap, Muskrat Creek Shelter, Chunky Gal Trail, and Water Oak Gap. Each sign we pass has 4-5 rocks balanced on top. We only have two more miles until we meet Dad at Deep Gap, forest road USFS 71 to re-supply.

We see Magic Bags and Delaware Dave eating lunch when we arrive at Deep Gap. Delaware looks concerned as we approach.

"Hi! I didn't think we would see ya'll anymore," I say ambling over to look at the message posted on the road sign. I quickly realize the road is closed, and won't open until March 15. It's 20 miles to the next set of parking coordinates. We won't be meeting Dad today.

Rocket and I huddle to the side of the trail. She asks, "What are we going to do?"

We consult the Thru. Hiker handbook. We've already hiked 7 miles today.

I suggest, "We can keep up with Delaware and Magic Bags. They said they are camping at Beech Gap. It is 5 more miles. Then we can hike 15 miles tomorrow and meet Dad at Rock Gap. We usually have way too much food. I think we can make it to Rock Gap and if it is closed, it's only 4 more miles to US 64."

Rocket says, "It sounds like a lot of miles!"

"I'm sorry," I say. "I didn't realize roads would be closed."

"Okay," Rocket sighs.

I call to Delaware and Magic Bags, "Rocket and I are going to hike with ya'll for a couple more days if you don't mind."

"No problem," Delaware says. "I wondered what you would do when I realized the road is closed."

"I'll send my Dad a text message letting him know we are fine and will meet him at Rock Gap in a couple of days. We can ration our food and cut back on how much food the dogs eat at each meal. We'll be fine. Thanks for letting us hike with you."

Delaware says, "I enjoy helping others."

We realize Delaware is stacking the rock piles on the signs. He says it helps reflect his inner balance. Despite our fatigue, every time we see a pile of rocks we think about our friends waiting up ahead. (Rock piles can also indicate a turn in the trail, which comes in handy when I'm looking at my feet instead of the trees.)

## Girl (Hiking) with 4 Dogs

The dogs are having a great time. Their tongues are hanging out, tails are wagging, and it looks like they are grinning.

There is a confusing turn in the trail. Double blazes mean to turn, but the trail obviously goes straight. Kujo keeps us on the right path. A few miles later there is another confusing blaze, it's a single blaze, indicating to go straight, but the trail obviously turns.

I say, "Ok, let's go," and Kujo picks the direction by pulling. I hope the scent he is following is an AT hiker, rather than a random hunter.

When we pass Standing Indian Shelter, we catch up to Delaware. He tells us a story about an Indian and a monster. Later he out hikes us as we continue up Standing Indian Mountain, 5498 ft.

It's been hours since we've seen anyone. Our friends are long gone.

"Rocket, I can't wait any longer, I have to pee really bad. Will you hold the dog leashes for a minute?"

I give Rocket the dog leashes, and run to a large tree. Just as I'm finishing, another hiker rounds the corner. With his Siberian Husky. My face turns red. My dogs start barking. His dog barks.

I give the universal "Hi, how's it going?" nod, then nonchalantly retrieve my dogs from Rocket.

I let out a sigh of relief once he passes. "Other than the wild, crazy jumping and barking from the maniacs and my own racing heart, that went well." I say as Rocket and I resume hiking.

Three miles later, we finally make it to Beech Gap to camp. It is in a little valley with lush green trees and tall bare deciduous trees. Delaware and Magic Bags already set up their tents and have a campfire going. We find a place for our tents then prepare our meager supper.

Delaware says, "I have two extra packs of oatmeal. Do you girls want some? I packed way too much food."

Rocket and I look at each other, "Thanks" we say in unison.

Then Magic Bags gleans we are running low on food and says, "I have extra Roman noodles. I was planning to leave in the hiker box at the last shelter, but I forgot. It would lighten my load if you girls want them."

"Thanks." We answer.

After everyone finishes eating, the guys ask, "Can we give our leftovers to the dogs? We don't want to attract any bears."

"They would love the scraps. Thanks!"

I'm a moron for not planning well.

I learned a couple of lessons: One is that no matter how well I think I've planed, God may have other plans. Another is that when God sends a challenge, he also helps with the solution. And finally, it is ok to accept help from others.

After we finish eating we attempt to hang our food bags. It is difficult to get the rope high enough to get over the taller limbs.

Delaware approaches, "If you tie a rock to one end it is easier to throw the rope. Do you want me to show you?" he asks.

"That would be wonderful!" Rocket says.

While Delaware works on Rocket's rope I tie a rock to my rope. Eventually we get both food bags hanging properly in trees.

Delaware also explains, "When you look for a tree to hang your food bag on you want to make sure it isn't too small or too big. If it is too small the bear will push over the tree and have your food bag and if the tree is too big the bear will climb the tree and have your food. You have to find a tree or branch that is too big to break and too little to climb."

"We didn't know how resourceful bear can be. Thanks for educating us."

We finally have an hour to relax by the fire before going to bed.

**Day 12** Burr! I shiver, it is rainy, misty, windy, and cold this morning!

We hurriedly break camp and scramble to keep up with the guys. They stride quickly off in the distance.

Three miles later we cautiously take a potty break at Carter Gap privy. We are careful not to get turned around when we leave.

After another six miles of hiking, we meet Albert Mountain. Steep, tall, rugged, and beautiful. We are hiking with Delaware and Magic Bags again. I am last in the group. The rock climbs are tedious, thrilling, and tiresome. The boulders are so large, I require distance between me and the next person so the dogs can run and use momentum to jump up.

After so much climbing, I have to stop to catch my breath. When I stop hiking my glasses fog up, then I have to clean the fog off my glasses. My friends look like fuzzy moving trees when I don't have my glasses on. I replace my glasses, and glimpse my friends as they turn the next corner. I race after them. Once I round the corner I come to a complete standstill. My friends are nowhere in sight. Kujo led me to a dead end! There is an eight foot straight up climb. I'm sure Mtn. Goat can climb it, and I can climb it, but not the other three. After frantically searching, I find a narrow steep alternate route just around the corner.

The trail is barely wide enough for my feet with soft loose dirt on the edges. Visibility is limited from the fog in the atmosphere and on my glasses! I feel like I am on the edge of the mountain. Once, after cleansing my lenses, I look down and see a hole in the trail with a never-ending bottom! I force the dogs into a single file line as we chase after everyone else.

I finally catch up to everyone at Albert Mountain Fire Tower. I fasten the dogs to the corners of the fire tower, then Rocket and I climb to the top of the tower. The very top is locked. The higher we go the colder and windier it is. The wind is so strong and cold it literally takes our breath away. We don't stay any longer than it takes for our friends at the bottom to take a picture.

We pass the guy with the dog from the day before. He is eating lunch. His trail name is Fosters and the dog is Kya. He is 5'5" with black wild hair and rich chocolate brown eyes. A mile after Albert Mountain, he passes us when we stop to eat lunch at Big Spring Shelter.

Warmish and cozy inside the shelter, we meet a thru-hiker named, U-Haul. Rumor has it that he started off hiking with a laptop, and an iron skillet! He is learning to get the pack pounds down.

While we are eating, drying our feet, and attempting to dry our socks without freezing, Kujo decides to have his own fun. The dogs are tied to the trees outside the shelter.

Magic Bags looks out and says, "I think one of your dogs is doing something he shouldn't."

I immediately hobble barefoot to the entrance of the shelter to look, and sure enough Kujo is ferociously chewing on his backpack chest strap! By the time I get to him, the damage is done, the backpack is now in three pieces. I rig a temporary fix so I don't have to carry his food and pack. Mine is heavy enough!

Once we start hiking again, Kujo's backpack falls off. I fix it and it falls ff. Every few yards I have to stop and re-attach the backpack on Kujo. He stands grinning the whole time, happy to be giving me trouble. To top it all off, there is vicious sounding thunder rumbling. It is so loud it scares Mtn. Goat and he practically jerks my arm out of socket lunging to get away. I doubt I would have found him if he had run away scared.

At first Rocket is determined to walk slow, despite the impending downpour. However, when the first fat rain drops start falling, we both start running. Unfortunately, Kujo is still losing his backpack. I skid to a stop, run back a few feet, and snatch up the cursed backpack. Since we are getting soaking wet, I relent and carry Kujo's backpack.

It's a torrential downpour, now. If you've ever worn glasses, you know it is impossible to see anything when it is pouring down rain. Rocket and I both wear glasses. We finally see a sign saying, "Rock Gap."

I turn shivering to Rocket, "We either missed the shelter or it is down a side trail. It could be down this trail behind the sign. I think if we keep going straight that will take us further away from the shelter, toward Winding Stair Gap."

"I'm sure the shelter is right on the trail. We must have missed it," Rocket says.

"Okay, we can backtrack. We are soaking wet now so we might as well walk."

We backtrack, then see the trail to the shelter. When we get to the shelter Delaware and Magic Bags admit they saw us run past the shelter.

We say, "Great, why didn't you stop us?"

"We thought you wanted to keep going," Magic Bags says.

"It looks like ya'll made it before it started raining," I observe.

Magic Bags and Delaware at least have the courtesy to look guilty.

I put the dogs' jackets on them, but they won't keep them on. Instigator ends up with all the extra jackets. The jackets get wet from the dogs wet bodies, and muddy from the dirt floor.

I notice a jar of peanut butter on the shelf in the shelter. We don't need it now since we can go to town tomorrow.

Rocket is shivering, and doesn't have nearly as much body fat as I do, "You should change out of your wet clothes then, go lay down in your sleeping bag in the shelter until you get warm," I suggest.

"I can help you s-s-set-up your t-tent and feed the d-d-dogs first." Rocket offers.

"It won't take me long at all. I'll see you in the morning. Get warm, I don't want you to get hypothermic."

Fosters and Kya have already claimed the shelter. I don't trust Kujo to behave when he is in close proximity to another dog. I feed the dogs then shovel food in myself.

Delaware says, "Do you want some hot tea?"

I say, "No thanks. I just want to get the dogs fed and set up my tent. I have a warm sleeping bag!" I clench my teeth to keep them from chattering. The dogs are cold and wet.

Delaware helps me set the tent up under the shelter and then carry it to a campsite. I say thanks. The dogs and I are ecstatic to get in the tent. The dogs don't stir all night, not even when Delaware gets in his tent beside us. Delaware is the nicest guy I've met. Way nicer than AJ. AJ always puts himself first. He wouldn't care if I froze to death! He'd probably celebrate!

**Day 13** There is condensation inside the tent when I wake up. I poke my head out and it is dry today. Yay!

I still have to pack up a wet tent.

"Good morning Rocket. Did Fosters and Kya leave already?"

"Yes. They were awake and packed before the sun came up! He hikes 30 miles a day!"

I turn to Delaware and Magic Bags, "We are meeting my Dad either at Rock Gap or Winding Stair Gap. We can give you a ride to town if you need it."

"That sounds great," Delaware says.

"I would love to find an All You Can Eat (AYCE) restaurant!" Magic Bags exclaims.

"I'm going to look for a doggie backpack!"

"I want sweet tea," Rocket adds.

Without further motivation, we walk the tenth of a mile to Rock Gap.

Wonderful, fantastic, great news, Dad is at Rock Gap! Alleluia!

Rocket, Delaware, Magic Bags, 4 dogs and myself pile into the truck to ride into town. Rocket and I wedge ourselves on top of one plastic bin in the back. Our knees are up to our chin, we are surrounded by backpacks, and we use a foam mat against the back window. Most states it is illegal to ride in the back of a pick-up. The dogs are cozy in the kennels while the guys ride squished together in cab.

Dad finds an AYCE Shoney's, for breakfast. During breakfast Dad says, "I hiked down USFS 71 to the trail to look for you girls. You must have already passed by the time I got there."

"That was a good idea. Was it difficult to walk that far with your bad leg?" I ask

"Not too bad. I just had to go slow."

"Thank you for your help on the trail," Rocket says to Dad.

The other guys also tell Dad thanks for the ride.

After breakfast, we find "Three Eagles Outfitters." Unfortunately, they don't have any doggie backpacks big enough for Kujo. Heather and Sandy assist Rocket and I to find more fuel for the JetBoil, then we head back to the trail.

Once back at Rock Gap Dad suggests, "Why don't ya'll leave the backpacks with me, then you can hike from here to Winding Stair Gap. I will meet you there with your backpacks."

"Thanks Dad," Rocket and I both say. Delaware and Magic Bags, also take Dad up on the offer.

The 3.6-mile hike to Winding Stair Gap is enjoyable without being weighed down by the backpacks. Bread, tea, and strenuous exercise don't mix. Rocket has a quick explosive purge in the bushes and then continues without further incident.

Once at Winding Stair Gap we wait about 30 minutes for Dad to arrive. Delaware and Magic Bags grab their backpacks and head on. It takes longer for me to put the backpacks on all 4 dogs, then Rocket and I follow in their wake. We have less than a mile to the campsite.

Magic Bags wanted to make it to Siler Bald Shelter, six miles away. He is gone by the time Rocket, the dogs, and I make it to the campsite by the stream. However, Delaware is at the campsite when we arrive. He helps us find appropriate limbs for bear bagging.

"Thanks. My food bag weighs at least 25 lbs. since I have my food and the dog food."

Rocket hoists the food bags while I push from underneath.

"I guess if the bear wants our food bad enough he will break the limb, but it is too dark to find another one so this one will have to be good enough. Thanks for your help Rocket."

"Your welcome. Yay, it looks like Delaware has a fire going!"

I say, "Delaware, thanks for letting us use your hiking stick, and I'm sure glad you have a fire going!"

He says, "Anything to help out. What brings you girls out hiking with your 4 dogs?"

I tell him about my dream of hiking and how Rocket and Dad decided to join the adventure. "Dad usually watches my dogs for me when I travel. He decided to come to help with the dogs. What brings you to the trail?"

"When I was a kid, my school in Delaware hiked a section of the trail. Now I'm hiking the whole trail. I have a Girl Scout group who is sort of sponsoring my trip. They send me supplies and girl scout cookies!"

"That's pretty neat. I was working private duty as a nurse. I saved money over the years so I could finance a trip. My patient was sick for a while. He even had hospice. I couldn't leave him as long as he needed me. He was like a grandfather to me. He did so much for everyone in his lifetime. He died in his sleep-in January. I like to picture him dreaming of dancing with his wife. He loved to dance. I knew this was my one chance to hike the trail before I have to get another job. I know he would be cheering for me to succeed. He had many adventures in his younger years."

"It sounds like you miss him," Delaware says.

I bite my lip, then take a deep breath. "Yeah," I say.

I want to prove I'm worth something. I can't make someone love me. I can't bring back someone who is gone... I can control hiking.

Rocket tells about how I asked her to help make jerky, "I want to see how far I can go," she adds

We stare into the fire. After a while I say, "Hey Rocket, do you see the coal in the fire shaped like a horse?"

She looks a minute, then says, "Yeah, do you see the one that looks like an elephant?"

"Yeah." We relax by the fire a little longer then we head to our separate tents.

Delaware puts out the fire.

**Day 14** The sun is out this morning, but the temperature is refreshingly cool. We hike from 3815 ft. to 5012 ft. in a four mile stretch to reach Siler Bald. There are scenic views of the mountains, but everything is still brown. I see a dead limb that looks like a pig snarling, a dragon, and another one that resembles the Atari, "Q*Bert."

Delaware hikes ahead of us most of the day. He creates rock sculptures along the trail by balancing rocks. He says balance is important in life.

Later at Wayah Bald Stone Tower, elevation 5342 ft., Mtn. Goat, Kujo, Digger, Instigator, and I lay on the rock floor surrounding the tower and soak up sun like chameleons. I have two dogs on each side of me. The sky is clear with varying shades of blue. We have a relaxing, sunny lunch break, and dry out our socks without freezing. Rocket and I are tempted to camp at the tower, but we don't want to risk getting in trouble so we hike the final mile to the shelter.

We set up our tents in case any late hikers arrive. It is peaceful and quiet at the shelter. I know the dogs will alert Rocket and I to any visitors, but no one comes. At night, we faintly see the city lights, but we are alone, Delaware is camping somewhere ahead of us.

**Day 15** I reluctantly get out of my tent this morning. It's chilly. I fill up my water bladder from the nearby stream, it's challenging to squeeze in the backpack. I put my food bag in. I see my tent peg bag camouflaged in the leaves, I need to grab it. I stuff the tent and poles in.

Rocket says, "Do you want to hike a few miles then eat breakfast?"

"Sure, that will give me a chance to warm up. It's freezing this morning!"

Girl (Hiking) with 4 Dogs

We finish packing, load the backpacks on the dogs, and shrug into our own backpack, and head out.

The three big dogs are sharing two backpacks. The most hyper in the morning, start off with the backpack.

At Licklog Gap we see evidence of a huge campfire, and two 5-gallon multi-use water containers along with enough unused firewood for a bonfire! Also, there is some green Mountain Laurel, as we trek up yet another mountain.

We pass Cold Spring Shelter. It looks like it was built in the 1930's. A few miles later after Tellico Gap, we catch up to Delaware.

Kelly says, "Delaware, when we get to Wesser Bald will you take a picture of Girl with 4 Dogs and I when we climb to the top of the observation tower?"

He says, "What are you going to do with the dogs?"

I respond, "I can tie them to the trees." After I tie Mtn. Goat up on a tree, he perches himself on top of a nearby rock, Kujo is stationed next to the stairs, and Digger and Instigator are relaxing under the trees.

Delaware says, "Yeah, I'll take your picture. I can barely see you all the way up there."

I say, "We can see your bright orange hat. That's a good idea so you don't get shot by hunters."

Kelly says, "Wow, look at the view from up here. You can see for miles! It is so clear today!"

I respond, "I know. We got lucky to have beautiful weather today!"

We climb down and I retrieve my camera. "Thanks for taking our picture Delaware."

The weather is perfectly warm today as we continue hiking.

My original goal is to climb up each fire tower on the AT. After a while, I give up. Occasionally it's too cold and other times the towers are too far off the trail.

When we arrive at Wesser Bald Shelter we immediately begin to set up camp. I realize I don't have any tent pegs, I forgot to grab them from the leaves this morning! Grrr! I don't have to have tent pegs to set up the tent, but they are useful to keep the rain fly off the tent, and to secure the door so it is easier to open. No wonder my backpack felt lighter!

I rummage around on the ground for a few sturdy sticks.

Kelly asks, "What are you doing?"

I humbly explain, "I forgot to grab my tent peg bag. It was camouflaged in the leaves"

"I have extra pegs you can use."

"I don't want to make your tent unstable."

"It will make my backpack lighter not carrying all these pegs! Please take a few."

Delaware chimes in, "I have a couple extra pegs too."

"Thanks ya'll! Pegs work much better than sticks! Even though the weight of the dogs keeps the tent from blowing away, it is much easier to unzip the rain fly when it is pegged down."

Rocket is the first to use the privy at the shelter. The protocol of privy use is to put in a handful of leaves after you use it. Usually, there is a bucket full of leaves, and if you use the last of the leaves, you refill the bucket. When she returns from the privy she exclaims, "I am not using the privy again at this shelter. I'm going to the woods! The leaf bucket was turned upside down and when I turned it upright to add leaves there were multiple dead, dried, crusted rats in the bucket!"

"That sounds gross," I say.

Delaware is trying not to laugh.

"The privy is disgusting too! It has a metal seat, with tin going down from it, into the bottom of the privy. It echoes!"

I suggest, "Maybe that is to give the rats a way to get out of the privy."

We bust out laughing.

Delaware makes a campfire, but it's still cold. There are logs around the fire for sitting. "Whoa!" I yell as the other end of the log flies up when I sit down.

Rocket and Delaware laugh. They already discovered the seesaw while I was feeding and walking the dogs.

Rocket and I have a variety of flavored marshmallows; Caramel, Chocolate, Gingerbread men, and fruit flavors. I say, "Have some marshmallows Delaware."

He says, "No thanks."

"Come on, I insist. We have plenty. We also have pudding!"

He asks, "How do you have pudding?"

Rocket answers, "We use powdered Nido milk, then we add water, and mix it in a zip lock bag. Voila! Delicious pudding!"

I add, "Nido milk is whole milk powdered, so it has all the calories, fat, and protein we need."

Delaware says, "I'll try some pudding. I carry icing to get my calories."

I cringe and make a face, "That's too sweet for me!"

Rocket looks like she is going to get icing on our next re-supply.

**Day 16** It is pleasantly cool in the morning, however by afternoon we are shedding our outer layer of long sleeves. Rocket, Delaware, the dogs, and I haven't seen anyone else in three days.

We stop at one of the lookout areas and stare in awe. The views are fantastic. The sky is so clear it hurts our eyes.

"Do you see the lake and the Mountain Cabin?" Rockets asks.

"Yes. It would be lovely to have a cabin nestled in the mountains, secluding you from the world. I can barely see any roads. I wonder how they get out if it snows?"

"They probably know how to drive in the snow, or maybe they have a snow mobile."

Delaware doesn't say much although he does gaze longingly across the mountains.

The trail continues through green Rhododendron bushes. There is green moss on the rocks and trees to give variety to the winter brown deciduous trees. It is also rockier with small boulders interspersed. One place has a hole in the rock big enough for a bear and its cubs. We quickly hike past.

Once we arrive in town we realize we weren't really alone. Katmando arrived earlier that day, and there are a few people who arrive after us, Tiger (pronounced Tigger), StormSong, TreeBeard, and Beer Hunter, Dusty, Chris, Dean, Mark, Crow of Insanity, Mike, Eric, Sam, and Covy amongst others. Magic Bags has come and gone already.

Dad meets Rocket and I at the Nantahala Outdoor Center. Dad keeps the dogs for me while I explore town. Rocket and I stay in the bunkhouse one night. They have beds, heated rooms, and showers. What more could we ask for? A towel would have been nice.

Kelly says, "I'm glad we have towels in the truck."

"Me too! Those showers were cold!" I respond.

"Mine wasn't cold, but the floor was nasty! I was jealous you had the large handicap shower, but at least I had hot water."

Later that night, we play games in the community area, and talk to the other thru hikers, many river rafting guides who arrive. Rocket slowly and tediously sews Kujo's backpack with a tiny sewing kit she has.

Stormsong and TreeBeard practiced hiking sections in the Smokey Mountains. They have forded streams. I wasn't anticipating fording streams.

Exhausted we head for bed. Delaware is somewhere outside setting up his tent.

**Day 17** Rest and Relaxation. Dad, Rocket, and I have wonderful meal at the Rivers End Restaurant. We don't have a seat overlooking the river, but it's still relaxing hearing the river rushing by. There is a wooden walking bridge to cross from the restaurant to the bunk house.

Next door to the restaurant, I look for a replacement dog backpack at the NOC Outfitters, but they don't have any. They have silk socks though, and a carabineer. I buy another carabineer. Now I can hook all four dogs o the truck when we aren't hiking.

I weigh my backpack. It is 38 lbs. fully loaded with winter gear, food, and water. While I'm weighing my backpack, Sylvia who works at the NOC Outfitters calls around to find a Ruff Wear backpack for us.

"Girl with 4 Dogs," Sylvia says, "Black Rock has a Ruff Wear Doggie Backpack. They are only a few miles away."

"Thanks Sylvia," I say. "I have been struggling not having enough backpacks."

She gives us directions and we drive to Black Rock. It is a small town with a small movie theater. We find the outdoor store and are relieved to find the exact backpack I need for Kujo.

We spend the second night sleeping in the truck at the bunkhouse.

**Day 18** Cold air blows across the Nantahala River, instantly freezing my fingers. My fingers are numb and, I can't get my flimsy gloves on. After 5 minutes, I give up! Rocket, and surprisingly Delaware, are waiting on me. It takes another 10 minutes to put backpacks on 4 dogs, Kujo resists wearing his backpack. I have to hold Kujo between my knees and bribe him with treats to get his backpack on him. In the meantime, Mtn. Goat is trying to shake off his backpack. Digger wedges his head under Dad's hand to be petted, and Instigator is barking at the water and stomping his tiny feet.

I finally get all the backpacks on, then I have to untangle the leashes. I heft my backpack on with Rockets help. Twenty minutes later we are finally ready to go.

I am more than happy to hike fast because I am freezing. Brrr! We have an eight-mile steady climb to start off with. It's actually not as bad as it seems mentally. It is a fairly gradual climb, 1723 ft. to 5062 ft.

There are beautiful water falls, more Rhododendron, and copious amounts of debris on the trail.

"Okay Rocket, I'll let Mtn. Goat loose first to navigate through all the foliage on the trail. He's probably going to try to escape. Are you ready to catch him?"

"Yep," she responds. "Remember I did the hundred-meter sprint in high school. He won't get past me."

Sure enough, as Mtn. Goat tries to maneuver an escape past Rocket, she quickly tackles him and grabs his leash. Even though Mtn. Goat's fun is cut short, he respects Rocket's superior intellect, speed, and ability to capture him. He looks at her with his tongue hanging out and smiles with admiration.

Digger fumbles his way through the fallen trees. Usually meekly going under the limbs, despite his larger size, and Instigator proudly scrambles over the limbs, despite his smaller size.

I saved the best for last. "Rocket, are you ready for Kujo?"

"I am, but if he growls or barks at me I'm letting him go!"

I laugh and say, "Okay, here he comes!"

He plows through the limbs like a tornado and Rocket snatches his leash. He turns to look at her in surprise, but he doesn't growl or bark.

Rocket says, "Come over here and get your dogs!"

I collect the leashes and we resume hiking.

The higher we go, the colder it gets. We are in an enchanted forest, there is fog in the air, and frost on the trees. The air is crisp and sweet. The ice patterns are exquisite. There is a beautiful frozen spider web. It is so very delicate and serene.

It shatters rather quickly when the dogs accidentally brush against it.

Rocket says, "Why did you let the dogs shatter the spider web?"

I respond, "I'm sorry, we are a wide load. Besides the spider shouldn't build its web near the trail, if he doesn't want it shattered."

We don't take a lunch break. It is too cold, and we are trying to catch up to Delaware and Beer Hunter.

We inadvertently pass them at Sassafras Gap Shelter.

"Hey," I say as Beer Hunter and Delaware pass us.

"We thought ya'll were ahead of us," Rockets says.

"We took a break for lunch at Sassafras Gap Shelter," Delaware says.

"It was too cold for us to stop! We will see you later," I call as Beer Hunter and Delaware leave us in their dust.

Rocket, the dogs and I eventually make it to Locust Cove Gap, and set-up camp. When I hold the leashes in one hand to hook Mtn. Goat up, he escapes confinement, and runs laps around the campsite.

Rocket says, "Your dog is running loose. Can't you catch him?"

I answer, "No, but he'll come back when he's tired."

"Well he's bothering everyone!"

Later, I feed and walk the dogs, then put Mtn. Goat, Digger, and Instigator in the tent so they can stay warm. Kujo has to stay outside with me.

I don't want any more holes in the tent.

Delaware and Beer Hunter have a campfire going, but the wood is damp. It doesn't put out much heat, and it is difficult to keep it burning. Rocket and I find the water source, and fill up our containers, enough for tonight and in the morning and for the dogs. We eat, then Delaware and Beer Hunter help us find a couple of trees to hang our food, and then we go to bed. We're freezing and tired! I see why hikers' midnight is 9 p.m.

**Day 19** I hear Rocket stirring in her tent in the morning. I look up to see a few drops of condensation on the top of my tent.

Girl (Hiking) with 4 Dogs

"Are your tent poles frozen this morning?" Rocket calls.

"I don't think so. I'll check when I get out," I answer.

I slowly wiggle out of my warm cozy sleeping bag. A few minutes later after putting on my warm hiking clothes, I climb out of the tent. I see Rocket Struggling to pull the tent poles apart. I check my poles. "Hmm, my poles aren't frozen. I'll be back in a few. I'm going to take care of the dogs, then I'll pack up."

"Okay," Rocket answers absentmindedly still struggling with her poles.

Delaware brings us our food bags

Fifteen minutes later I return to take down my tent. Rocket is enjoying a bowl of hot oatmeal while talking to Delaware and Beer Hunter. I attempt to pull the poles apart.

They are frozen now.

By the time I finish packing and swallow two packs of oatmeal, Delaware and Beer Hunter are gone.

I know it will be warm later, so I start off with light layers. It also helps me walk faster. My philosophy is, if I'm cold, then I'm not hiking fast enough. I'm used to being last. When, on rare occasions, we start out first, the dogs procrastinate until we get passed. Then, they like to pull my arms out of joint trying to get in front again. They poop about five minutes after we start hiking, and they don't all want to go at the same time. Kujo likes to go at least three times a day. I have to dig a hole and cover it up with leaves, dirt, sticks, moss or whatever is available.

Rocket passes me then says, "Instigator made a mess about 30 yards back."

"Thanks," I respond. "You didn't happen to clean it up?" I ask hopefully.

"Not this time. You were too far ahead of me."

I sigh and backtrack.

Kujo loves Rocket. She likes to make high-pitched noises, just like his favorite squeak toy. He loves it when she is in front of us. He steps on her feet.

Rocket glares back at me and shouts, "If Kujo steps on my feet one more time, then you are walking in the front!"

"I'll hold him back farther. I wasn't paying attention." I don't mind hiking in front, except I hike to fast, and don't realize Rocket isn't behind me

"I feel like he's breathing down my neck!" Rocket exclaims.

Suddenly, two dogs run out of the woods toward us. Rocket stops dead in her tracks, then jumps behind me. Kujo and Mtn. Goat start going nuts, barking, whining, and jumping around. Digger and Instigator are walking in the back. They are looking around trying to see what all the excitement is about. It takes at least five minutes to get Kujo and Mtn. Goat to calm down. What a day!

It is beautiful, but it doesn't warm up, despite hiking fast. The white frost on the tress contrast with the darkness of the trees. We see the mountains in the distance. There is a mystical layer of fog. It is like we are hiking in an ethereal world.

Later we see icicles hanging from huge blue-gray boulders! Along with green ferns and moss dripping icicles the size of daggers!

It finally warms up in the afternoon. This morning, Delaware and Beer Hunter said they were stopping at Cable Gap Shelter. It's 12 miles to the shelter and when we arrive, Delaware and Beer Hunter are nowhere in sight. We set our backpacks down and take out beef sausage, cheese, and crackers for lunch.

I ask Rocket, "Do you want to stay at the shelter, or push on to Fontana Dam where we can meet Dad? It's five more miles."

"It might be nice to stay here," Rocket says.

All of a sudden, there is an incredibly loud BANG! like cannon fire, or a huge tree falling. The dogs are barking like crazy. We look all around, but can't find where the noise came from.

"I changed my mind. I want to keep hiking. Now," Kelly says snatching up her discarded backpack.

"I'm right behind you." I hurriedly put on my backpack and untie the dog's leashes. We leave the shelter sprinting.

Once we are in the safety of the woods a few yards away, I send Dad a text to let him know our plans.

We hike fast, and even run some. It is very rocky.

We pass our "friends" camped by a spring. We smile and wave, but keep going.

At 4:15 p.m. we can see Fontana Dam in the distance. At 5:00 p.m. my watch alarm goes off, screaming it's warning that we are running out of time!  It reminds me to either find somewhere to camp, or make it to the next campsite, shelter, or road before dark.

"Kelly, we have to hurry!"

"I know, but I can't go fast with all these rocks.  You can go on without me."

"I'm not going without you.  I can't run on these rocks either. We can set-up our tent on the trail if we need to.  Do you want to find somewhere to camp or keep going for the dam?  I can see light through the woods."

"I think we can make it to the dam, but we have to stop running because it's getting too rocky!  It is better to make it safe, and alive, than not at all.  Besides, we can keep hiking toward the light. I'm sure your dogs will find the way!"

6:20 p.m. we emerge from the trail in time to watch the final rays of the sun sink behind the water.  We hiked our longest day so far, 16.9 miles.  Rocket and I sit in the parking lot next to the truck, and fix our food.  My knees are sore and throbbing.  After sitting, my legs stiffen, and moving is very difficult.  I have to hobble.

Dad offers, "I'll feed the dogs and take them to potty.  You can rest."

"Thanks Dad.  Thanks for meeting us here too.  It's so much easier sleeping in the truck and it takes a lot less time to get ready to hike in the morning."

"I drove ahead a little way, so I know where the trail enters the woods tomorrow.  It's tricky to find, so I'll drive with you in the morning so you won't get lost."

"Thanks"

The dogs don't act sore.

Rocket and I make use of the bathroom, and take a sink bath. It is warm in the bathroom, but not big enough to sleep in.  We also wash our clothes in the sink.

The truck is parked on the side of the road.  Dad has the supplies arranged in the back so he can sleep on the plastic bins beside the kennels rather than sleeping on top of the kennels.

**Day 20** March 8, 2011 In the morning, after being cramped up in the cap of the truck I am more sore than when I went to bed.

Dad says, "I have an extra map of the Smoky's you can take. It has all the trails in case you get lost."

"Thanks Dad. Where is the map?"

"It's in the cab on the dashboard."

"Okay. I'll get it after we take a shower at the shelter," I answer.

"You don't have to walk the dogs today. I can keep them," Dad offers.

"I know, but since I won't have them for a few days. I want to walk the mile to the Fontana Dam Shelter with them. They will probably miss walking everyday while I'm gone."

Dad smiles and shakes his head as he gets in the truck and Rocket, the 4 dogs, and I start walking.

Yeah, showers! Wonderful hot water. I have always been thankful for hot showers.

We meet Moon Pie, who thru hiked in 2004. She is handing out Moon Pie's, hotdogs, and weather updates. She doesn't offer us any food and I don't ask.

I overhear her telling StormSong and TreeBeard, "You should have good weather hiking through the Smoky's."

Right now, it is sunny and cool.

Rocket has enough phone signal to talk to her husband. She is still talking on the phone when I finish with my shower. She asks me, "When do you think we will be finished with the Smoky Mountains?"

"I'm not sure. In three to five days."

"Well, is it going to be three or four or five?"

"I don't know, it depends on the terrain. I'm hoping three, but it might take longer. It's at least three to Newfound Gap."

Rocket says to her husband, "She doesn't know how long it will take, James, so I guess we can't meet up!"

I know Rocket is upset with me, but I can't guarantee something I don't know. Delaware and Beer Hunter pass us and I am anxious to get started. Russell Field Shelter is 17 miles away. I'm not sure how much longer Rocket is going to hike with me. I have to leave the dogs with Dad, they aren't allowed in the Smoky's.

I look warily at Rocket and ask, "Are you ready to go? We may be able to catch up to Delaware and Beer Hunter."

She glares back, and says "Yes!"

# Chapter 5: Smokey Mountains

**Day 20** March 8, 2011 Continued I've been both looking forward to and dreading the Smoky Mountains. I know there can be snow in the mountains, if we have terrible weather we could be trapped or forced to stop until the trails clear. I'm not worried about issues with snow once we finish the Smokey's.

It's after 11 a.m. when we leave Fontana Dam Shelter. It's sunny and comfortable. We walk across the 48ft. Dam and catch up to Beer Hunter and Delaware when they have to stop to register for hiking in the Smoky's.

After a few minutes of restless waiting I say, "Rocket I'm going to keep hiking. We have 17 miles to cover, and we hike slower than the guys."

Rocket glares at me, but says nothing.

I mentally shrug, then slowly continue along the road toward the base of the first mountain. It is 4 miles from the Dam Visitor Center to Shuckstack mountain fire tower. The elevation increases 2216 ft.

There is 50 feet of steep embankment between the water and the trees bordering the lake. Just before entering the woods from the road, I glance to my right and see a light gray rock shaped like a dragon with folded wings. The tip of the rock barely touches the water and the rock is tilted slightly to the left giving the impression that the dragon is sipping water and listening for danger.

Once I enter the woods the trail elevation begins to increase, even with the numerous switchbacks the trail is steep. I am winded and panting for air within five minutes. I glance back periodically to make sure Rocket is in sight.

Perhaps the dogs do make hiking uphill easier. Either they help by pulling ahead, or I have to concentrate so hard on not getting pulled down that I don't pay much attention to how big or difficult the hills are.

After 45 minutes, Delaware and Beer Hunter pass me as if I'm standing still.

"Do you need a break?" I ask Rocket.

She looks at me, but doesn't say anything.

---

"I guess we'll keep going then."

I pick up my pace. Soon I can no longer see Rocket, but I know she is behind me. I wait at a turn until I can see the top of her head, then I quickly round the corner. If Rocket knows I'm waiting on her she gets irritated and will stop hiking.

The trail twists and turns, left, right, up, down, and sideways like tangled up spaghetti noodles. The trail makes a "U-turn" and I can see Rocket on the other side of a deep ravine. I wave, but either she doesn't see me or she's still ignoring me.

At 1:00 p.m. I give in to my weak shaky legs, and the relentless rumbling of my stomach and stop for a break. The trail is on the edge of the mountain with an endless downward plummet if we fall. The view overlooking the drop off is heart stopping. I can see the endless sky and the tree tops of lesser mountains. Behind me the Mountain is solid rock. It feels as if I am suspended in air.

Delaware is eating a sandwich and gazing reflectively over the horizon.

"It's amazing," I whisper.

Delaware whispers back, "Indeed. God's beauty is indescribable."

When Rocket catches up I ask, "Rocket do you want to stop for lunch with Delaware? It's warm, pretty and we'll have company."

Rocket snaps, "You're the boss, whatever you say goes."

I grit my teeth, look apologetically at Delaware and say, "I'm not going to ruin your view with negative company. Best of luck hiking!" I take off hiking as close to a sprint as I can manage with a fully loaded backpack on my back! I know Rocket can't keep up, and I no longer care. If she wants to be upset with me, then I will give her a reason!

A mile later I see the sign for Shuckstack Mountain fire tower, 0.1 mile off the trail.

I know I won't have time to see the fire tower if I wait on Rocket. If I just go, she will probably realize I took the side trail. Besides she can't get mad at me for leaving her if she is the one ahead!

I take the trail.

Wow! Part of the ladder for the tower is resting in the trees, and there is a hole in the top of the tower roof! I can see mountains for miles in all directions. I can even see the Dam.

Girl (Hiking) with 4 Dogs

     I quickly scramble down the stairs and rush back to the trail. I hike fast for 30 minutes, thinking I will catch up to Rocket any second! She normally takes a lot of breaks.

     I hope she's not behind me.

     I see Delaware camping at Birch Spring Gap. He hasn't seen Rocket since lunch.

     I hike a couple more miles. The elevation is 4520 ft. now and there is snow on the ground!

     How can there be snow? Moon Pie didn't say anything about snow. She said we would have Sunny weather!

     My feet are slipping in the snowy slush. I can't get enough traction to keep up my fast pace. I'm hyperventilating and my heart is palpitating.

     Slow deep breaths. Relax.

     Rocket is ahead of me. I see her boot prints with crosses.

     Dear Jesus, please help me catch up to my friend before Mollies Ridge Shelter. If she doesn't see me at the shelter she will think I went on the Russell Field Shelter and we can't make it that far before dark. Please help. Amen.

     It's only 3:00 p.m., but it is getting dark.

     My calves are cramping! It is excruciating when I walk fast! It is colder and darker! I shiver then cringe at the pain shooting up my leg. I can't keep up this pace, but I have to!

     It's starting to rain. The wind is picking up!

     I keep stumbling along. Another 45 minutes' passes. I round yet another bend in the trail. Finally, I see Rocket. She is sitting on a fallen tree putting on her warmer fleece shirt.

     "Rocket, I'm sorry I didn't have a better answer about how long it would take to get to Newfound Gap. I didn't know what to expect up here. I certainly wasn't expecting snow! I'm also sorry I went ahead without you. I was very angry. Although technically I didn't go off and leave you because I was behind you. Will you forgive me?"

     "Yes, I just wanted a chance to see James. We keep getting farther and farther away and it is harder and harder for him to visit. He says all the guys at work tease him and say, 'Kelly's not really hiking, she's off with some other man. You're a fool!' I want to keep hiking, but I also want to be with James. I miss him."

"I'm sorry. I understand if you want to quit to be with him. It's easier for me to keep hiking because I don't have anyone. I have to keep going so I don't have time to think. If I were married to a good man like James, I wouldn't want to be away from him either."

Rocket sighs, "I'm stuck with you until we get to Newfound Gap. I'll decide then if I want to keep going."

"We'll have to stop at Mollies Ridge Shelter today."

"That's a relief. Why are you limping?"

"I got cramps walking so fast to catch up to you. I couldn't get traction on the snow."

A short while later, Rocket lunges off the trail.

"What are you doing?" I ask in astonishment.

"Look," Rocket says. "I found you a walking stick!"

"You're such a good friend, I don't deserve you. Thanks for the walking stick."

A few minutes later she says, "Here. I found you another one."

"Thanks again."

Having two walking sticks and proceeding at a slightly slower than normal pace, we finally make it to Mollies Ridge Shelter just before dark. Our teeth are chattering and my fingers are numb! There is a tarp covering the front of the shelter and there are two guys inside with a fire going! Rocket and I drop our backpacks, then navigate toward the fire. Once I can feel my fingers again, I dig out supper, then brave the cold to hang our food bag on the bear cables outside the shelter.

We call the guys our Trail Angels, Kelly and Don.

Did Rocket and I get separated so we would keep hiking faster than normal? Had we taken even one break today we wouldn't have made it to the shelter before dark.

We go to bed early so we can continue to warm up in our sleeping bags.

**Day 21** The next morning I retreat under my sleeping bag when cold air touches my face. A minute passes, then I bolt out of my sleeping bag.

If we don't get started we'll never make it out of the mountains!

Girl (Hiking) with 4 Dogs

As I emerge from my sleeping bag Don says, "We took the liberty of bringing in your food bag for you. We had to get ours anyway."

"Thank you. It must be pretty cold outside. There is frost on the top of the bags."

"There is a layer of snow out there," Angel Kelly adds. "How far are you girls hiking today?"

Rocket looks at me and I check the Thru Hiker book. "At least to Spence Field, maybe as far as Derrick Knob Shelter."

The Angels look at each other, then Don says, "We have an extra Smoky Mountain Map if you girls need one."

"Thanks," I answer. "My Dad had one, but I forgot to get it from the truck. Are you sure you won't need it?"

"No." Angel Kelly answers. "We know the mountains like the back of our hand."

"How far are you guys going?" Rocket asks.

"We are waiting until the weather clears up a bit." Don says.

"Do you have enough food?" Rocket asks. "We have extra." I nod in agreement.

Our Trail Angels look worriedly at each other. They start to protest that they don't need any food, but we can tell they are worried they will run out.

"It would help us out if you want some oatmeal, roman noodles and granola bars. We have too much and it makes out backpack heavy," I add.

Our Angels look at each other again and shrug, "If it will help you girls out, we'll take the extra food off your hands and as a thank you we will make you coffee. We have plenty of coffee!" Don says.

After coffee, we bid our Angels farewell, and bravely exit past the tarp on the front of the shelter. The trail is obscured by a light layer of snow.

The morning starts off windy, cold, and rainy, and ends up with all of the previous plus snow. We are hiking in a pristine winter wonderland. There are no footprints, and the trail is only recognizable because it is worn down more than the surrounding terrain.

"Rocket, if you want we can go to Spence Field Shelter for lunch, but it is 0.2 miles off the trail. It is too early to stop for the day, and I'd rather not hike an extra half mile roundtrip."

"What do you suggest?"

"We can eat here at the sign then keep hiking. I'm too cold to stand still for long. My fingers are numb already! If we keep hiking, we can make it to Derrick Knob before dark."

We quickly eat peanut butter crackers and trail mix.

The trail is a combination of snow, and freezing cold stream. On Thunderhead Mountain, elevation 5527 ft. which is over a mile above sea level, the wind pushes me to the edge of the trail.

Rocket stumbles and cries, "Make it stop!"

"The wind is trying to blow me over too! I am having fun trying to be stronger than the wind," I say. "Only God has the power to stop the wind."

Rocket sighs, "You are crazy."

Behind the cover of a few trees we check the map. We still have four and a half miles to Derrick Knob Shelter. We have been hiking all day without breaks except the few minutes we took to eat at lunch time. The sun is sinking behind the mountains. My hair is turning gray from the stress. Derrick Knob is only 11.7 miles from Mollies Ridge.

"Are there any more Mountains before we reach the shelter?" Rocket asks.

"A few small ones, but it is mostly downhill," I answer handing Rocket the map. "When you finish looking at the map do you mind putting it back in the zipper pouch at the top of my backpack?"

"Sure. Let's go," Rocket says.

A couple hours later, I give a cry of delight as I see the gray tarp covering the outside of Derrick Knob. The elevation at Derrick Knob is 4901 ft. Again, we are the last ones to arrive and someone else has a fire going. We immediately gravitate to the fire.

I see the surprised look on the faces of StormSong and TreeBeard. "Where did you girls come from?" TreeBeard asks.

"We started at Mollies Ridge. What about you?" Rocket asks.

"We stayed at Spence Field last night. It was a long, grueling day of hiking today," StormSong answers. "How did you survive the wind on Thunder Head Mountain?"

"It was a fun challenge leaning in to the wind and trying not to let it blow me over," I answer.

"You're are a sadomasochist," TreeBeard says.

"We are glad ya'll have a fire," Rocket says changing the subject.

StormSong grabs TreeBeard's arm and says, "We need to get more wood before it gets too dark to see." They are out of the shelter in a matter of seconds.

Rocket and I settle in, eat supper, and exchange hiking experiences with other shelter residence, White Wolf and Bob.

An hour later StormSong and TreeBeard return with enough fire wood for two more nights. We thank them again before retiring for the night.

**Day 22** I wake up when a blast of cold air enters the shelter. I look up to see White Wolf and Bob leaving. By the time I crawl out of my sleeping bag, StormSong and TreeBeard are also leaving the shelter.

"I'll get the food bags while you finish packing your sleeping bag," I say.

I brush off the snow from our food bags before bringing them inside the shelter.

"Should we bring this black hat with ear warmers, and camouflage glove that was left behind?" Rocket asks holding up the items in question.

"I guess we can. If no one claims the hat, I wouldn't mind keeping it."

There is snow everywhere on the ground. It is freezing cold. My optimism is being frozen! On the other hand, it is kind-a fun hiking in the snow. When I fall, it doesn't hurt.

My bottom freezes when I have to make yellow snow!

The trail is burried under thick snow. It is a depressed, narrow, flat area, surrounded by thick white shrubs and white frosty trees. It is difficult to follow, and at times, it is totally obscured. Rocket and I prefer to be last, because then we can follow someone else's foot prints and hope they are good at following the trail. However, today the snow is falling so heavily, it quickly fills in the footprints.

We come to a "y" in the trail, and don't know which way to go. The sign is pointing somewhere over the edge of the mountain, and the only trail that way is over the cliff, into the sky, then falling in the ravine! There is a trail straight ahead, which seems logical, and there is a trail to the left, barely visible due to low hanging tree branches.

"I'm glad our Angels at Mollies Ridge gave us a map! Can you get it out of the top of my backpack so I don't have to take my backpack off?"

"Yeah," Rocket says. "Here it is."

We consult the map. Rocket and I agree, we need to go to the left.

"It barely looks like a trail. Maybe it's hidden by the tress falling over with all the snow. Thanks for helping with the map. My hands feel numb and I can tell I don't have the same dexterity I usually have," I say.

"I know, my hands are like frozen icicles and I have gloves! Wow, the snow is cold!"

"Brrrr," I say. "The tree just downloaded all the snow it was carrying onto me! The snow is trapped between my backpack and my jacket. I'm glad I have a hood, or it would be down my clothes!"

"Ha, ha," Kelly says. "That's why I'm letting you go first this time."

"Thanks a lot! Yay! I see footprints. At least if we aren't going the right way we aren't the only ones."

"Well they are probably experts at reading maps."

After hiking a few miles in companionable silence, I ask, "Are these fir trees? It's hard to tell with all the snow. Look at the icicles hanging down. They look tasty. I'm going to try one. Do you want one?" I glancing at Rocket.

"No, they might be peed on."

"If you get one from a higher branch it won't be peed on." I bite the tip off my icicle, "Yum, they taste like a Christmas Tree!"

"You can have it!"

"I will. Thanks for the hiking sticks, they are wonderful when my hands aren't full of dog leashes!"

"Your welcome."

We continue to struggle through the thick snow and low overhanging trees. Every time we pass under the snow laden trees more snow falls onto my backpack. The cold seeps through my jacket even though I brush off as much as I can. My feet feel like lead. I keep shivering.

We are hiking in a pristine white world with splashes of grey from the trunks of the trees.

After hours of hiking Rocket exclaims, "Yay! I see the sign for Clingmans Dome tower and parking area. Do you think the bathroom is open? I would love to warm up!"

"It would be nice to get out of the wind and snow, but I'm sure they aren't open. If we hike to the bathroom and it's closed, then we have to backtrack. If we keep going we might make it to Newfound Gap, then we can hitchhike to town and get a room!"

Rocket says, "It's 1 o'clock now. How far is it to Newfound Gap?"

"About eight miles. I'm going for Newfound Gap. I'm shivering just standing here."

The elevation is 6643 ft. I start hiking on the trail. It's like walking through a white tunnel with occasional glimpses of white grey sky.

I let out a sigh of relief when I see Rocket behind me. I don't want us to get hypothermia. We have to make it to a shelter or town tonight. I'm not used to cold weather with snow, but from what I've read it is dangerous. I hike faster, but I'm not getting any warmer.

The fir trees are bowed over, practically in half, from all the snow. They continue to pummel me whenever I hike underneath.

"The water in my CamelBak is frozen!" Rocket says worriedly.

"Mine is too," I respond trying to stay calm. My finger tips are painful and tingly. In addition to my puny gloves I have a pair of neoprene gloves. I put them on, but my fingers are too cold to generate warmth. I pull them off and pull my sleeves down over my hands and fingers. I rub my fingers against my hands to keep them from freezing.

Three miles later, at the sign for Mt. Collins, I say, "Kelly it's 4:15, we have 4.7 miles to Newfound Gap. I don't think we can make it before dark."

Kelly says, "I don't want to get lost hiking at night and freeze to death in the wilderness! We'll have to hike the half mile to Mt. Collins Shelter."

"Sounds like a plan. We've been hiking all day, but we only covered 13.5 miles today."

"I know! I can't hike fast in the snow."

"Me either. I guess the guys form Derrick Knob Shelter made it to town."

"More than likely, they hike so fast."

After a few minutes, I say, "It feels like farther than a half mile to the shelter. Do you thing we missed a turn off?"

Kelly says, "I hope not!"

We round yet another corner and see the tarp covering the front of the shelter. We are practically frozen and we are covered in snow. The snow is frozen onto our rain jackets and our shoes.

I sigh, we are blessed again to have a warm(ish) fire going when we arrive at the shelter. It doesn't resemble, "chestnuts roasting over an open fire," however it keeps us from getting hypothermia, or frostbite. We drop our frozen gear and defrost by the fire before fixing supper.

I look up from laying out my sleeping bag to see my smooth hiking stick with a perfect groove for my hand, glowing uncomfortably on the fire.

"Who put my hiking stick in the fire?" I ask outraged.

"I thought you brought in fire wood when you came. I didn't realize it was your hiking stick," one of the other shelter residents, "Availability," answers.

"Well it wasn't" I say snatching up my other hiking stick and putting it on my sleeping bag. "Please don't burn this one," I say glaring daggers at the culprit.

He holds his hands up and backs away.

We are about to go outside the shelter in order to get water for cooking when the Ridge Runner for the Smoky Mountains, Doug, says, "Do you girls want water? I had to bring some in from the Spring to test it. It's not treated, but it tested clean and if you let the water boil it will destroy any undetected germs."

"Yes!" we both exclaim at once. Yay, we don't have to freeze again to get water.

(Later, we learn that the water source was submerged under ~ three feet of snow.)

"We saw the sign for Clingmans Dome earlier. Are the bathrooms open in the winter time?" I ask Doug.

"No. They are closed," he answers.

I glance at Rocket to see if she is listening. She looks disgruntled so I think she heard. "Still Water" is another shelter resident. He is about 5'9'', has medium brown hair, clear blue eyes, broad shoulders and chest, and an amazing smile. He is from Auburn.

Doug tells us about a group of Spring Break students he had to rescue. They were all wearing blue jeans and T-shirts when there was a sudden storm. They got soaking wet, including their sleeping gear. They were near hypothermic when he arrived. He had to help them get off the mountain and back to town.

Doug laughs, "They looked like drowned rats wearing useless designer clothes."

It's been a few hours and I've finally warmed up, but now I have to hang our food bags and use the privy and I am scared I might get lost or freeze going!

"Rocket, do you want to go with me to hang our food bags and use the privy? We can take turns holding the flashlight."

"Sure." We bundle up then venture outside. The privy is built on a wooden deck. The snow is so high, it is even with the deck. I shuffle my feet so I don't fall off the walkway and into a snow bank.

Rocket volunteers to go first. I'm happy to let her warm up the seat.

We make it back to the shelter and I jump in to my minus five degree sleeping bag, my teeth are chattering and I can't stop shivering. Rocket has disappeared insider her mummy sleeping bag as well.

After a while I'm no longer shivering, but I'm still cold. I'm curled in my mummy bag with a tiny opening for fresh air. I unbraid my hair hoping it will dry and be warmer. It's too cold at the bottom of the sleeping bag to stretch out my legs.

**Day 23** I'm still cool when I wake up in the morning.

I look around for our shelter mates. Availability and Still Water are gone, but Doug is still here. Once he realizes I am awake he says, "I brought your food bags in this morning when I went out to get mine."

"Thanks. Are you staying here today?"

"No. I'm hiking to town to get more supplies. There will probably be a lot of distressed hikers coming in this evening and the next couple of days. It's a five-mile hike. I can give you girls a ride to town from Newfound Gap if you want. US 441 is closed except for four-wheeled drive vehicles until afternoon."

"That sounds wonderful. Thanks."

My hair feels frozen and I can't run my fingers through it.

Rocket pokes her head out of the sleeping bag and looks in my direction, her face contorts into a look of shocked horror.

"What?" I ask in concern.

"Your hair looks like a rats nest!" she exclaims. "You are going to have to shave your head to get out all the tangles. What did you do?"

"I thought if I unbraided my hair it would dry. It still feels wet though."

I worriedly pull my hair back in a ponytail and stuff it under the hood of my jacket, then I reach for my boots. They are extremely stiff this morning.

"My shoes are hard to get on, are yours?" I ask Rocket.

Rocket crawls out of her sleeping bag and reaches for her shoes. "My boots are frozen! I can't get them open wide enough to put them on!"

"Let me see them," Doug offers reaching for the boots. He beats them against the wooden platform of the sleeping area, then he stomps on them, and wiggles them back and forth. In the meantime, I finally force my feet inside my frozen boots.

"My toes feel like they are tiny icicles," I say.

"Don't talk like that," Doug exclaims. "If you talk about your feet freezing they are more likely to do so."

"In that case, my feet feel wonderful. They are so warm and toasty they are on fire," I say jumping up and down to stay warm.

Doug is still working on Rocket's boots. He resembles a bear, strong, but cuddly.

"My feet really do feel a lot warmer when I stomp around. In fact the more I stomp the better I feel. Thanks!"

Girl (Hiking) with 4 Dogs

Rocket is finally able to squeeze her feet into her hiking boots. We exit the semi warmth of the shelter to brave the frigid outdoors.

"No problem. How far are you girls hiking?" Doug asks

"Eventually all the way to Maine."

"I thought you looked like thru hikers. Even though you were caught in bad weather you are prepared. I'm glad I didn't have to rescue you."

"Me too. We almost did get lost yesterday. One of the signs is pointing over the ravine. Two hikers at Mollies Ridge Shelter gave us a map so we were able to figure out the correct direction to go."

We hike in companionable silence.

It is a beautiful winter wonderland. The snow is covering everything! It is perfectly white, and unmarred by footprints or pollution of any kind. There is an average of 1-2 foot of snow with 4 foot drifts in areas. I feel like a snow princess in a lovely winter wonderland.

We make it to Newfound Gap by 10:57 a.m. The roads are somewhat clear, but it looks like there is a thin layer of black ice. The snow drifts beside the road almost reach the bottom of the stop sign. Doug has a black truck, the back of which is about ¾ full of snow.

Rocket says, "Thanks for the ride. Sorry we made you leave the trail."

Doug says, "That's okay. I need to go to town to re-supply anyway. We weren't expecting this kind of weather. People think just because it starts off sunny it's going to stay sunny. The mountains have a weather system entirely their own. At least with thru hikers, you know how to dress warm!"

"It would be easy to get hypothermia," Rocket says.

Doug's radio blares, then a few minutes later he says, "Your hiker friends Availability and Still Water were able to hitchhike into town with a four-wheel drive trucker."

"I'm glad they made it safely," I say.

Doug's truck is delightfully warm inside. The heat is blaring and I can feel my blood return to its normal viscosity. On the way to town, there are 5 ft. long razor sharp, fang-like, icicles hanging from rock cliffs. It looks like teeth ready to tear unwary hikers to pieces. There is also white snow dust drifting over the tops of the trees. The road twists and turns as we descend to Gatlinburg. By 11:36 a.m. there is hardly any snow in sight. The temperature is about 50 to 60 degrees Fahrenheit.

We tell Doug thanks as he drops us off at the Grand Prix Hotel in Gatlinburg. I call Dad to let him know where we are, while Rocket secures us a room with double beds. I look in the mirror and cringe. My hair is indeed a rats nest. Once Dad arrives I dig out the shampoo and conditioner from the truck and proceed to salvage my hair.

"Dad, has the weather been this nice the whole time we have been gone?"

"It was a little cloudy yesterday, but for the most part it has been sunny and cool."

I tell Dad about the freezing temperatures we were hiking through while I unload my 4 legged friends and give them hugs and cuddles.

Rocket calls James. He's coming on Saturday to visit. Rocket hasn't said if she is going to keep hiking with me or not.

We meet more thru hikers at the Grand Prix Hotel, Jelly Pants, then Train Wreck and Two Medicine, I call them, The Brothers. We see Niners, his daughter hurt her leg and is taking time off. Katmando is hiking with Niners.

"I'm surprised to see Fosters here," I say.

Dad remarks, "Is he the one with the grey and white dog with blue eyes?"

"Yes. They were hiking 30 miles a day when they passed us."

"I heard him telling another hiker he is waiting on a doggie backpack. His dog lost hers. The backpack has been on backorder."

"I'm not surprised. It took us a while to find a replacement backpack for Kujo. I'm ready to check out the hiker box and pop some popcorn!" I exclaim.

"Look!" Rocket exclaims holding up a glove. "Do you still have the camouflage glove we found at Derrick Knob Shelter?"

"I do. Now I have gloves to wear!"

I leave a couple of bags of microwave popcorn for the next Popcorn addict. We find a deck of cards in the hiker box and mingle with the other hikers for a while talking and playing cards.

I'm elated to fall asleep in a warm comfortable bed. Dad declined staying in the hotel, saying, "I enjoy sleeping in the cab of the truck and watching the dogs."

Girl (Hiking) with 4 Dogs

**Day 24** I wake up early, but snuggle back under the covers for another hour before getting out of bed. Once I get up, I go outside to the truck to take the dogs out of the kennels for a walk around the neighborhood. Even though it is early, I am comfortable wearing an undershirt and a light fleece jacket. I'm amazed there is no snow or freezing winds. The sun is barely up and Dad and Rocket are sleeping. A few dogs in the neighborhood bark as we pass their house.

I walk a good 30 minutes before returning to the truck. After walking the dogs I hook them to the corners of the truck, feed them, eat breakfast, and then grab a book to read while I wait on Dad and Rocket to get up.

Around 9 a.m. Dad and Rocket are finally awake and finished with breakfast. We discuss our plans for the day.

Dad says, "Gatlinburg has a Trolley nearby. We can pay a few dollars and ride all day."

Rocket asks, "Why do we need to ride the trolley when we can ride in the truck?"

"We don't have a downtown map, there isn't much parking downtown and the traffic is congested," Dad replies.

"I don't mind riding the trolley. It will be fun to see where it goes and to pull the string when we are ready to get off. As long as we don't stay long the dogs should be okay in the kennel," I add.

We walk a few blocks to the bus stop

"Okay Dad. Where to first?"

"We can just ride and see what they have, then before we go back we will stop at the grocery store."

The weather is pleasantly warm. There are a lot of tourist out taking pictures. We ride the bus route and on the return trip, we stop at the grocery store. We see Delaware and Beer Hunter buying food for the next section.

"Hey Delaware," I utter as we bump into each other in the produce isle. The fresh, citrus aroma of oranges surrounds us. "I'm glad to see you survived being in the Smoky's."

"There was a lot of snow that first night, but I'm used to cold weather. I see you and Rocket survived as well. How are your dogs?"

"They missed me and are hyper from not walking every day, but otherwise they are great. Are you staying at the Grand Prix?"

"No. I found a cheaper hotel farther away from town."

I wave to The Brothers as they are picking out trail mix, and introduce them to Delaware.

I hurriedly pay for my purchases. "I'll see ya'll later. I have to catch up to Dad and Rocket. We are riding the bus today."

On the way to find Dad and Rocket I put a few grocery items back. I don't want a bunch of bulky bags to deal with while I get on and off the bus.

We exit the grocery store in time to see the bus driving off. The next one won't be around for another hour. There is a bench for Dad to sit on. Rocket and I take turns sitting beside him. The next bus finally arrives and we head back to the hotel. At the hotel, we wash laundry and talk to the other hikers.

Close to 4:00 p.m. James arrives. He's been driving all day. I give Rocket and James some alone time to re-unite. Dad and I hang out at the truck with the dogs.

By 6:15 p.m. we are famished. I load the dogs back into the kennel, then Dad, James, Rocket, and I ride in James's vehicle into town to check out the local cuisine. We agree to eat at the Alamo restaurant. James has an Alamo New York Strip cooked medium rare, Rocket has San Antonio Chicken, Dad has a loaded baked potato, and I have the SteakBurger cooked well-done. The restaurant is cozy inside with low-lights and soothing background music. The food is mouthwatering delicious. I eat all of mine.

Once outside again, we cross the foot bridge over the creek. Upstream a few yards there is a group of ducks swimming in the water. One duck made it to a small island. The second duck is struggling against the current. She eventually makes it to her partner. I smile.

Back at the hotel I reassure Rocket that I will not be sharing a room with her tonight. I take the dogs for another short walk then get ready for bed.

Dad fixed the kennels so it is easier to get the dogs in and out. He made it so the front kennel opens into the back kennel.

"Dad," I ask. "Can I sleep on the bins in the back rather than in the cab? I hate being cramped in the cab. Don't you sleep in the cab when we aren't with you?"

"I don't mind sleeping in the cab," Dad answers.

"Thanks. Good night," I call as I crawl into the back of the truck and stretch out.

It's cozy back here.

**Day 25** Sunday March 13th I jolt awake when I hear ferrous barking in the morning. I look out of the truck with blurry eyes and see a furry four-legged animal running around. "It's just Kya boys. Go back to sleep," I mumble as I roll over and snuggle inside the sleeping bag.

Mtn. Goat and Kujo keep shifting their weight until I finally give up on going back to sleep and get up to take them all to potty. We walk through the neighborhood again and I hear other dogs barking from within the houses we pass. I quickly return to the truck, then prepare breakfast for myself and the dogs.

I am antsy to hike again, but I'm not sure if Rocket is going to keep hiking with me, or if she is ready to head home. She likes to keep me in suspense. I'm too apprehensive to broach the subject. If I ask the wrong way she is liable to quit hiking for spite.

At 10:43 a.m. I can't contain my restless energy any longer.

I tentatively knock on the hotel door. When Rocket answers I say, "I'm almost finished packing for the next 3-4 days on the trail. Dad is going to take me to the trail head in about an hour. Do you want a ride?"

"Do you have to leave in an hour?"

"I can wait if you want to hike with me, but not long in case the weather is snowy in the mountains again."

"Okay. I'll get my stuff together." Rocket grumbles

At 12:42 p.m., Dad brings us back to Newfound Gap. The roads and trees are clear of snow, however there are 4 ½ ft. piles of snow on the edges of the parking lot.

The dogs whine and paw at the kennel door when Rocket and I put on our Backpacks. Due to park rules, they must stay with Dad.

Rocket and I amble toward the trailhead. We both start out wearing an undershirt and a light weight long sleeve shirt. Rocket has her hiking poles and I have my one hiking stick. On the way to the trailhead a woman in her mid-late adult years is handing out Ziploc bags with a variety of trail magic items, including granola bars, hot chocolate, and macaroni. We also see numerous curious tourists wearing blue jeans, cotton sweat shirts and carrying high- dollar cameras. Rocket tells me later, that one tourists was asking questions, while his partner was video recording.

Yeah, no more snow!

Until we start hiking up the mountain. Then, the clear dry trail turns into mud and slush with areas of ice. The trail is narrow and it seems as if we could fall right down the side of the mountain.

It is only three miles to Icewater Spring Shelter at 6034 ft. It takes us two and a half hours. The next shelter is about eight more miles.

"I think it's best to stay at Icewater Shelter tonight. We won't make the next shelter before dark. The sky is already grey," I say grudgingly.

"I like stopping early," Rocket replies. We can look around, enjoy the fire, and talk to the other hikers more."

"I like to relax, and explore, but I am stressing about the finite amount of time I have to hike the trail. If I don't finish this year, I'll probably never have another chance. We need to hike about 10-15 miles a day. I only paid the bills ahead for 6 months. James takes care of your bills."

"I know, but it is so nice to go slow. To be able to stop and take pictures and long lunch breaks."

I take a deep breath, "I'll try to relax and enjoy the rest of the day."

We meet hikers Harry and Brenda at the shelter, then Rocket and I explore the area surrounding the shelter. The sun shines refreshingly all around. We have plenty of time to cook, eat, converse and play cards before bed.

**Day 26** The following day, we traipse through huge amounts of wet slushy muck. It is long and tiring, although overall, it is warmer, and more pleasant than hiking in freezing snow. We hike through a natural tunnel. The trees form the sides and lean over enclosing the space. There is a five-ft. high snow bank on the left side and in front of us there are fir trees with roots hugging car sized, green moss covered boulders.

We hike 12.6 miles to Tri-Corner Knob shelter. We meet Chappy, Ariel, and Logan, and play a game of spoons using our camp utensils, then we play a couple of hands of spades.

A drop of water lands on my head. "Is the shelter leaking?" I ask the group in general.

Logan looks outside, "It's not raining outside."

"Is anyone else getting rained on?" I ask.

"I see some moisture on my sleeping bag," Rocket says.

"The hot air from our breath is condensing on the roof of the shelter, and dropping down. Let's finish this game, then I'm done for the night," I say yawning.

**Day 27** Our last day of hiking in the Smoky Mountains is almost pleasant. We descend form 5911 ft. to a reasonable 2572 ft. The snow is gone, and the closer we get to the end, the warmer it is. We remain skeptical of the good weather, due to our tortuous previous experience.

In the afternoon, we pass a giant gorilla shaped boulder. We can see for miles over the tops of the mountains. There is no civilization in sight, not even smoke from winter fires. The sky is blue with white fluffy clouds grazing the tops of the mountains. We pass huge boulders with green plant life on all surfaces. It reminds me of trolls. Another boulder has a prominent nose, thin hard lips, and a sharp firm chin. Beside him is a manatee rock couple. They are snuggled side by side embracing with their pectoral flippers. Their body is covered with moss and is stretched out behind them.

As we descend in elevation, we can hear the wind roaring over our heads. It is so nice to be on the other side of the mountain!

After 14.8 miles of hiking we reach Davenport Gap Shelter. It is the last shelter in the Smoky Mountains and it is the only shelter we stayed in that still has the chain link fence on the front for bear protection. Availability and Still Water are at the shelter, along with Paul and a group of standoffish spring breakers.

I notice not everyone has their food hanging up on the bear cables. I ask Availability, "Aren't you concerned the bear will smell your food and try to get in the shelter?"

"I'm not worried about bear," he replies.

I roll my eyes and look at Rocket. "Where are you sleeping? I want to make sure I'm nowhere near you when the bear comes in."

"The bear can't get in when there is a chain-link fence," Availability grunts.

"They can wait on the outside until we all starve," Rocket exclaims.

Finally, Availability stomps off and hangs his food bag on the bear cables. Availability is tall and skinny to the point of anorexia. He has a full medium brown beard and long hair. He doesn't smile.

After eating and cleaning up Rocket pulls out our cards. "Does anyone want to play Rummy or Spades?"

At first only Still Water plays, but after a few minutes Availability is reluctantly drawn over.

"Do you girls like to play spades?" he drawls.

"Sure," we answer.

"How bout we play for money?" Availability suggests.

"We don't bet," Rocket answers.

"We also don't have any money," I add.

"Okay, we can play the sissy way."

We play until we are exhausted and fall asleep at 11:19 p.m.

**Day 28** By the time Rocket and I wake up, Availability and Still Water are gone, however the Spring Breakers are still sleeping.

I find a snazzy Smart Wool long sleeve shirt laying on the ground. I ask one of the Spring Breakers, "Is this ya'lls?"

He gives me a sleepy grumpy look before shaking his head no.

"Thanks!" I reply, shaking the dirt off the shirt and storing it in my backpack, then putting my backpack on so we can start our day.

It's less than a mile to Davenport Gap Road. On the north border to the Smoky's there is as sign telling the story of a bear cup that had to be killed because it attacked a visitor. The bear was habituated to the trail because hikers threw apple cores, candy wrappers, etc. near the trail. The bear cub began to think of the trail and humans as a source of food.

# Chapter 6: North Carolina/Tennessee

**Day 28** March 16, 2011 continued Rocket and I cross a dirt road, then head up a small steep hill with circular wooden logs for steps. Next, we follow a large stream with rushing turbulent water. One section has a small whirl pool and there are multiple water falls cascading over the rocks. Along the banks of the stream trillium is sprouting in abundance.

"I wish the trillium was blooming," Rocket says wistfully.

"I've never seen trillium, I'm glad you pointed it out. It probably will bloom in a couple of days."

"We won't be here in a couple of days. We will be farther north and there won't be any trillium."

"I'm sure we'll see some," I say encouragingly.

It is only a few miles from the shelter to where we are meeting Dad. When the trail exits from the Smoky's we see a woman in her mid-late adult years handing out trail magic.

"Didn't we see you a few days ago, at Newfound Gap?" Rocket asks.

"Yes," the woman replies. "I enjoy providing trail magic to hikers. It helps me feel closer to my husband. He died of a heart attack on the trail last year and I miss him dreadfully."

"I'm sorry for your loss. We appreciate the goodie bag you gave us. My trail name is Girl with 4 Dogs and this is Rocket. We are meeting my Dad today so I can retrieve my dogs."

"My name is Karen, I don't have a trail name."

"Your name could be 'Trail magic' or 'Magic'" Rocket suggests.

"Maybe so. I am looking for a thru hiker I met a few weeks ago. Tall and skinny with black hair, and fresh out of high school. He hurt his leg and stayed with me for a few days. He started hiking again and I want t make sure he is okay. You might know him, his name is, 'Tiger' (pronounced "Tigger").

"I remember Tiger. We met him at the Nantahala Outdoor Center (NOC). He was hiking 20 miles a day. I'm sorry to hear he hurt his leg," Rocket says.

"We didn't seem him on the trail. He could be ahead or behind us though," I say.

"I'll keep looking for him. It's early yet. You girls have a good day."

It's a short distance to Pigeon River Bridge. We see the white truck with the purple camper parked in the shade. We hear the four dogs barking excitedly as we get closer.

I drop my backpack on the tailgate and rush to my four-legged babies. I unhook them from the trees and take them for a short walk to help settle them down. Along the way, I see Dad picking up litter from the ground and bushes.

I yell, "We're back Dad. How was your time with the dogs?"

"It was okay. No fights. I have them outside so they can stretch and have fresh cool air. How was your section?"

"A lot better than the first section. There was still snow in small amounts, but not much. Rocket and I saw a boulder shaped like a gorilla." The dogs are barking again. I idly pet them as I continue talking to Dad. Rocket puts her backpack down and she and Dad sit on the tailgate of the truck.

Rocket adds, "The wind tried to snatch us and take us back into the freezing mountains, but we escaped. We could hear it howling overhead as we descended Mt. Cammerer."

Dad says, "A couple of hours ago, I was sitting here watching a guy who looked suspicious hanging out under the bridge. He had long black hair, and facial hair. He had loose off white cotton pants, matching long baggy shirt with a long shapeless vest overtop. He also had a white turban on his head. He left before I had a chance to talk to him. A few minutes after he left, a policeman drives over to me and asks 'Sir, what are you doing hanging out under the bridge?' I explained about you thru hiking and that I expected you to arrive at any time. He then looked around the area and glanced inside the truck. He looked shocked when he saw the kennels, but then he noticed the dogs. 'You have a lot of dogs with you,' the policeman said. I replied 'Yes. My daughter is hiking with them on the Appalachian Trail, but she isn't allowed to have them in the Smoky Mtns.' The policeman nods, then leaves."

We all have a good laugh.

Girl (Hiking) with 4 Dogs

"Thanks for meeting us Dad, and for taking care of the dogs while we hiked the Smoky's. I guess we better get fresh supplies and keep hiking if we want to make it to Ground Hog Creek Shelter."

"Okay," Dad says. "We meet again in Hot Springs. Send the GPS when you are ready to be picked up."

It's only a quarter mile to the I-40 underpass from Pigeon River Bridge. There is a man and his son, Albert and Jordon, on the road hike giving out cold drinks. The drinks are ice cold and refreshing. We have a 6-mile steady climb ahead of us.

After 15 minutes of hiking Rocket and I are sweating in our layers of clothing.

"I have to stop to take off my rain pants," Rocket says. "I'm used to it being cold in the Smoky's. It is sweltering hot at these lower elevations."

"I'm melting inside my clothes too. This looks like a good place to stop. We can sit on the log if we need to."

Rocket and I stop to peel off layers

I want my rain pants to come off over my boots, but they get tangled up and stuck on my shoes!

Rocket is waiting on me. She says, "There is a large group of people coming this way."

I hobble off the trail with my pants stuck at my ankles half on and half off my shoes! I drag the dogs with me, as far as I can without falling on my face. I hold the leashes to keep the dogs from sniffing everyone going past. Most everyone is pleasantly impressed by my dog handling skills, except the evil dog-hater woman. She has thick, gnarly, wrinkled, leathery smoker skin. Her bones are prominent. Her hair is white, wispy, wild, and brittle. I'm surprised her looks don't scare the dogs into silence. As she approaches she shrieks like a banshee. The dogs jump up and down lunging toward her, trying to get a closer look, to determine what kind of animal she is!

I manage to pull them back off the trail, while she stands four feet away and screams, "I don't like friendly dogs. I had a broken arm from a friendly dog jumping on me!" Each word is louder and more shrill than the last.

I grimace wishing I could cover my ears, and respond, "First of all, Kujo is not friendly, secondly, if you keep hiking they won't be close enough to jump on you, and we would all be happier, and thirdly, my dogs are leashed so remove yourself!"

She continues to stand and shriek.

"My dogs are on a leash!" I reiterate more loudly this time.

Instead of counting her blessings, and being thankful, she squawks, "It should be illegal to have four dogs on one leash!"

I pray for patience and proceed to converse as if talking with someone who is mentally challenged. I calmly respond, "They each have their own leash."

Finally, some others in her group, David and Ryan, manage to drag the hag away.

As the rest of the group passes, they apologize for her ridiculous behavior. Whew! I can finally take my pants off!

At least Rocket and I have something to talk about to keep our minds off the excruciating Snowbird Mountain we are climbing. It is foggy on top of the mountain. We hike from 1375 ft. to 4623 ft., then we hike about 2.5 miles down to Groundhog Creek shelter. We see Tiger, and The Brothers already set-up in the shelter. Rocket stays in the shelter, but I set up the tent for my pups and I.

I walk to the privy after supper. What a nightmare! There is barley sitting room on the toilet, and there must have been a shortage on wood, or they don't want you to be claustrophobic, because there is a two-foot opening at the bottom of the privy, and from the shoulders to the roof is open. I'm glad it isn't raining!

I watch a large group of spring breakers camping a few yards away to the right. I really want to take a dump in peace! I feel like I'm at the fair and any minute someone is going to throw a ball, hit the lever, and dunk me into the privy!

**Day 29** The dogs wake me up when Tiger and The Brothers start moving around in the morning. I quickly put on my hiking clothes and start my morning. It is still 30 minutes later before I am packed and ready to go. As usual Rocket and I are the last thru hikers to leave the shelter.

We hike three miles and are starting up Max Patch when we meet a SOBO (South Bound thru hiker), "Little Engine."

"Wow!" I exclaim. "You are almost finished and we are just starting!"

Girl (Hiking) with 4 Dogs

"It's been a long journey, but worth every step of the way. 4 Dog Girl, I hope you enjoy Maine."

"Thanks!"

"Good Luck finishing," Rocket says.

"Thanks. Tell my Dad I'm still going strong when you see him. He is somewhere behind me," Little Engine says.

"Okay," I reply.

30 minutes later we see Little Engine's Dad. He looks more tired than Little Engine did and he's not carrying a backpack.

It's another four miles to the top of Max Patch. It is a clear, sunny, and warm day, however there are patches of snow. Rocket and I lay down in the sun and eat our lunch. The dogs lay beside me. We want to take a nap, but it is afternoon and we have six more miles to hike today.

It's easier and faster going down from Max Patch. We arrive at Walnut Mountain Shelter at 5:12 p.m. The Brothers are here, but Tiger kept going.

"The water is behind the shelter and down the hill. It looks swampy. I hope you have something to treat your water with," Two Medicine says.

"Thanks. We have a water pump," I answer.

Rocket and I leave our backpacks at the shelter, grab our water containers and the dogs then walk to the water source. It feels like we have to walk a quarter mile before we see any water. It takes a while, but I pump four liters of water so we will have enough for in the morning. The dogs drink straight from the mucky spring. The return trip to the shelter is straight uphill.

I ask The Brothers, "Since the shelter doesn't have a roof, do you guys mind if I let the dogs sleep in the shelter?"

"Why don't you tie them to the entry way?" Train Wreck asks.

"I can try it, but they will probably bark all night. If they are right beside me they are less likely to bark. I can set up my tent if I need to."

"It's okay," Two Medicine says. There is plenty of room."

"Thanks. I will keep them hooked up to my backpack so they won't be able to roam around."

I secure my rain fly over the corner of the shelter where Rocket and I are sleeping. There are four of us in the shelter, not counting the dogs. The Brothers, Rocket and myself. While we are fixing supper, the dogs alert us to the arrival of three more thru hikers, Space Cowboy, Victus, and Youngin'. They look inside the shelter, but decide to set up their tents to the right of the shelter and up the hill.

The dogs are stationed on trees. They bark whenever anyone approaches. Also, they are near the trail to the privy. This privy is much worse than the previous one. This one faces the trail, and doesn't have a door! It is leaning on a tree to keep it from sliding down the hill, and on the uphill side, there is a half-cut log across the front and back bottom support 2X4's. There are 2 rocks the size of my head and neck sitting on the log to hold the privy in place!

As dusk arrives, we get our beds settled in the shelter. The dogs are anxious to go to bed. One minute, I am pulling Digger back from jumping on everyone's stuff, and the next minute, there is a huge dog fight between Digger and Mtn. Goat.

Digger and Mtn. Goat don't usually fight. What is going on?

I finally get them separated, and then Digger and Kujo start fighting. Mtn. Goat joins in, again. I only have two hands and three fighting dogs. Instigator is tied out of harms way, but barking furiously. Finally, I sit on the ground, away from Instigator, who is trying to join the fight, I pull two dogs in opposite directions with my arms, and the third is pushed away with my feet. I lay stretched out on the ground until they finally settle down.

I'm quiet. I make the dogs lay down and look at each other. I feel like I'm a bad parent with mean dogs.

The Brothers look warily in my direction. I pretend not to notice. I crawl in my sleeping bag and commence to arrange the dogs. Mtn. Goat sleeps on the left side by my head, Digger at my feet on the left, Kujo on the right side by my head, and Instigator wherever he wants.

"Good night everyone," I whisper softly.

**Day 30** March 18, 2011 As I feed the dogs in the morning I notice Digger is walking funny. Upon inspection, he has a cut on his foot.

He must have cut his foot on a shelter nail when I pulled him back from jumping in the shelter.

Girl (Hiking) with 4 Dogs

My throat tightens, and a few tears fall. Fortunately, I have first aid stuff in the dogs backpack. I put antibiotic ointment on Digger's foot, and wrap it in gauze. I let him carry an empty backpack, and we head out. Digger is walking okay now.

Not only did Digger get a hole in his foot, but I also got a hole in my rain fly from the wind, and somehow, I got a hole in my sleeping bag. It's a holey shelter, starting with the roof!

We hike 2.5 miles up Bluff Mountain, then take a break. I call Dad to have him meet us at Garenflo Gap, 4 miles away, so Digger doesn't have to walk so far on his hurt foot.

We arrive at Garenflo Gap and sit in the road to rest while we wait on Dad. I hook all the dogs together on my backpack so they aren't coordinated enough to run away. Rocket and I wait forever! We know the road is open, because we see a vehicle drive up, and a trail maintainer gets out. We don't have much cell phone signal, and the battery is low. Rocket is determined to get in touch with Dad. I pray for patience.

"Kelly, I think we should keep hiking and meet at Hot Springs, like we originally planned. If Dad can't find us, then we'll be stuck here. It's six more miles, and if we don't start soon we won't make it before dark. Digger isn't even limping on his foot."

"I wish we had better phone service. We had it in one place, now I can't find enough service to make a call."

"I'll send Dad a Spot GPS saying we will meet at the original place."

A few miles later, it's potty break time. Rocket and I take turns; one holds the dogs and makes sure no one is coming, while the other uses the bathroom. The dogs have no respect for privacy, and stare the entire time. It's like the potty fan club.

We arrive in Hot Springs around seven. It's easy to spot the white truck with the purple camper shell. I contemplate what to do about taking Digger to the vet. The closest town with a vet is 50 miles away. Dad is resistant to going 50 miles, although he isn't paying for the gas, and he wastes plenty of gas on his own time.

"I can keep a bandage on Digger's foot and let him stay in the kennel for a few days. We can take him to the vet when we get to

Erwin TN as long as his foot doesn't look infected before then. Erwin is about 70 miles away," I say.

"Okay," Rocket says. "I called Elmers Sunnybank Inn, but they are inhospitable, and claim there is no room at the Inn. Is there anywhere else you want to stay?"

"I'm not picky. I just want to take a shower, eat and sleep in a bed. How about Alpine Court Motel? They are more expensive, but we don't have that many choices."

"Okay. Let's check them out," Rocket agrees.

The guy running it is hospitable, and possibly senile. He says we can park in the parking lot tomorrow night, even if we aren't renting a room.

The shower at the hotel is terrible. It is like a freaky horror movie. It barely has hot water, then it alternates between freezing and scalding, without any adjustments to the knobs. The pipes are exposed, and the water leaks out of the shower onto the bathroom floor. The bed is comfortable though, and at least we can take a shower, and there is a microwave. Microwave popcorn time! I leave a spare in the hiker box for other souls who are having popcorn withdrawals.

**Day 31** We check out of our hotel room, then I hang out at the truck while Rocket goes to the clinic to have her knees checked out. They buckle randomly when she is hiking, and she isn't sure if she will keep going.

A couple of hours later Rocket returns to report, "The clinicians aren't helpful and didn't even x-ray the knee. How can they tell if anything is wrong with it?"

"You can try wearing a brace," I suggest.

The dogs bark. I look up to see StormSong pass by, then he comes back to check on Digger. He says, "I saw your Dad. He told me about Digger hurting his foot. How is his foot?"

"It doesn't seem to bother him now, but I am keeping him from hiking for a few days."

"Good idea," he says patting Digger on the head.

"We are about to go to the laundry mat. Have you found it yet?" I ask.

"Yes. The Wash Tub at the Edge of Town is cheaper than L & K's. TreeBeard and I did laundry yesterday. We are planning to hit the trail again this afternoon."

"Thanks. We'll see you around."

Dad agrees to dogsit while Rocket and I wash clothes. He doesn't relinquish any of his clothes for us to wash despite my willingness to pay for the machines. While at the laundry mat we see numerous thru-hikers doing laundry. While in town we meet; KOZMIC, elliott, Neil from Colorado, Marnix from the Netherlands, Sensei from Colorado, Nate, Harold, J.T., and Guide Blanco.

Next, we re-supply. And after that we splurge and eat at a delicious restaurant. They have beautiful handmade quilts, and local artistry on the walls. The dogs have a great time greeting new and old friends, with ferocious barking and tail wagging.

The Brothers are our neighbors at the hotel. They tell us they are going to slack-pack.

What?

Slack-packing is when you carry only what you need for the day. You leave your heavy stuff, such as your sleeping bag, tent, and multi-day food supply, with whoever is helping you. Then you hike with a daypack, which has enough food for the day, and water. We always carry rain gear and warm clothes too.

Your helper meets you at a predetermined place. Your thru hike just got a whole lot easier! (And more expensive in gas, but you won't realize that right away).

"Thanks for the information guys. We're going to start slack-packing! We will see you down the trail. Good night," I say as Rocket, Dad, and I head off to sleep in the truck.

Since Dad manipulated the dog kennels so that it is easier to load up the dogs, it is now a prime sleeping place for me. Dad took apart the cages and put them back together in a way that allows the front cage to open up into the back cage. Since I sleep with the dogs in a tent while camping, I decide to sleep in the cages in the back of the truck with them when we aren't camping. Dad sleeps on the plastic bins beside the kennel, and Rocket sleeps in the cab.

**Day 32** In the morning Rocket says, "If we can slack pack then I will keep hiking with you."

"Okay." I consult the map. "It looks like if we hike 15 miles today, then we can meet Dad at the next road crossing. If we pack one bag with our food and water, I don't mind carrying it. Dad can you meet us at Allen Gap?"

"Yes. It looks like NC208/TN70 goes straight to Allen Gap."

"Thanks Dad."

"What should we use to carry our food?" Rocket asks.

"I have this large purse we can try."

"Okay." We stuff the purse full and follow the Appalachian Trail markers through town.

"This purse is bulky to carry," Rocket remarks. "Let's use the laptop backpack? It is larger and we can wear it on our back."

"I didn't want it to get dirty, but you are right, it will be much more comfortable than this purse. I'll call Dad.

Dad meets us at the north end where the trail leaves the road and enters the woods. We trade the purse for the backpack. The backpack is much more comfortable.

Dad says, "The steps are steep to get back on the trail. If you need me to keep the dogs so you don't get hurt going down the steps I can."

"Thanks Dad," I say. "I will let you know if I can't handle it. When we get to the steps, we descend without incident.

If Dad only knew. There are already many places on the trail that were challenging, and more difficult than a few nicely placed steps. It is touching that he is concerned though.

Digger is staying with Dad for a few days.

Rocket and I pass Lovers Leap Rock. It is a tall vertical tower of rock. It is a beautiful day. The sun is shining.

We have great visibility from Rich Mountain Lookout Tower. The sky is blue and white with purplish pink tinged clouds. "The Bruize Brothers" drew self-portraits on the walls of the fire tower. Later we see a tree that has consumed a metal sign! Only the bottom corners remain visible of the sign. It looks like frog lips with the bottom and legs of a bug sticking out.

We have an interesting encounter with a weekend hiker. Earlier, we met a guy and his son hiking, Gator and Flying Fish. Then, we meet a young man, Ben, hiking.

Ben asks, "Have you seen a man and his son hiking. I am supposed to meet them at Rich Mountain Lookout Tower, but I haven't seen them in a while. Some hikers a few miles back said they had seen a man and his son hiking ahead of me."

We tell him about the father and son we met.

It doesn't sound to us like the same father and son he is looking for. Both families have dogs. Ben describes a dog that sounds like it is similar to a French Bulldog, while the father and son describe a dog resembling a Jack Russell Terrier.

"I have a phone with Verizon Service. It normally has signal. You can use it to call home if you want," I offer.

"Okay. I'll call my mom to let her know I will meet my Dad at the fire tower like we decided."

Ben calls his mom and leaves a message. "Thanks," he says. "If you see my dad, please let him know I will wait for him."

Later, we meet his dad and younger brother, Brad and Age. Apparently, Ben had gotten ahead.

"Ben will be waiting at the fire tower for you," Rocket says.

"Thanks," Brad says.

A good rule of the woods is that if you are lost to stay put. You could amend the rule to say, "If you can't find your group, stay where they were expecting you to be until they find you"

We meet Dad at Allen Gap for the night.

"Even though we hiked 15 miles I feel pretty good. How do your knees feel Rocket?"

"They are okay. I think I can keep hiking for a while if we keep slack packing."

"Great!"

Dad warns us, " There is a dead wildcat in the ditch across the street."

"Yuck! It is smelly and gross."

The dogs, of course, are highly attracted to the smell. I make sure they do not get to assuage their curiosity. Thinking about the smell makes me gag!

**Day 33** A half mile after we start hiking we cross paths with a handful of trail maintainers. They are clearing trees, and debris from the trail.

"Thanks, we appreciate your hard work!" Rocket and I say as we pass.

"We are glad to keep the trails clear," one of them responds.

We can hear their chainsaws hours after we pass them.

We have a beautiful, warm, sunny day for hiking. We pass metal property markers and many streams. Kujo loves water. At noon when we cross yet another stream Kujo goes on strike and lays down in the middle of the stream to cool off.

"This looks like a nice place for lunch. Do you want to take a break?" I ask Rocket.

"Sure. I need to air out my feet and change my sweaty socks."

"It's been warm enough, I'm going to soak my feet in the cool stream."

"Good idea," Rocket agrees.

Instigator and Mtn. Goat drink water, but they don't jump in.

A short while after we resume hiking, Rocket says, "Wow! It is so beautiful here!"

"It is! I feel like we are hiking through an ancient Aztec village. The rocks resemble steps, and there are straight up boulders! Maybe any minute we will walk into an ancient temple.

"Yes," Rocket agrees. "It is green from the green Mountain Laurel leaves, moss and ferns. Look, there is a sign for a 'Bad Weather Trail.'"

"That's interesting, but we won't need it today."

A little while later I say, "Grr, maybe we should have taken the 'Bad Weather Trail! This must be a seven-foot drop! Do you want to go first and catch the dogs or do you want to hold the dogs and I'll go first?"

"I'll go first. Your dogs are likely to pull me over if you go first!"

As I jump down I exclaim, "Wow! I'm glad we are hiking north. It's easier going down, than it would be getting the dogs up this drop off!"

A little while later Rocket calls back, "There is a ridge walk. Be careful and don't fall!"

"I have chills. I am glad there are at least puny trees to catch me if I fall with these three hoodlums."

"Don't fall!"

"I'm not planning on it!"

We reach Devil Fork Gap as it's getting dark. We hiked 20 miles!

Girl (Hiking) with 4 Dogs

**Day 34** Early in the day we see a pair of Pileated Woodpeckers. It has bright red head feathers and black and white feathers on its body.

Rocket says, "Wow! I've never seen Pileated Woodpeckers. They are rare. I wish I could get their picture. Did you see where they went?"

"I didn't see them, but the dogs are pulling to the left." The dogs love birds, and the birds love to taunt the dogs. They "tweet" and "twitter," until the dogs go into ecstatic, hyper mode, and stay in an unstable state of mind.

Rocket mimics the birds. Kujo thinks she is the bird, and he is determined to get it. His attitude says, "That bird is just in front of Rocket and I can catch it. I just have to pass her first."

"Rocket," I beg, "Please stop whistling before Kujo pulls my arm off or steps on your heels again."

"If he steps on my heels again, I'm turning around and stepping on him! I hate it when he gets too close. It gives me chills all down my spine."

I laugh, "He's only breathing heavily right behind you."

"Okay, I've stopped whistling so keep Kujo back."

We cross streams on well placed, large rocks, and enjoy seeing a small waterfall, and a black fuzzy caterpillar. After hiking 8.7 miles we make it to Sams Gap, near I-26. When we arrive, Dad is waiting, he says, "I saw one of your hiker friends, Storm something. He came by to check on Digger."

"That's funny," I say. "Digger has his own fan club! He's adopted so maybe that explains his outgoing, loving personality."

Rocket says, "You're not a complete introvert."

"True, but I don't have somebody I just met, coming by to check on me every day either. Hey, do ya'll want to see if the Little Creek Café is open?"

"Sure."

We drive to the Café, but it is closed. Then we check out the nearby Wolf Creek Market. It is expensive, without much to offer for re-supply.

Dad says, "Lets drive into Mars Hill town. It's not far from here. We can fill up the water jugs at the welcome center."

The NC welcome center is, crème-de-la-crème, compared to the privies. There is a lot of history displayed in glass cases inside. They also have plenty of no loitering signs.

"Do you think it is okay for us to fill up the water containers?" I ask.

"Sure," Dad answers. "They put 'no loitering' signs up so they can chase off anyone who is being disorderly."

We have eight, one gallon jugs for water in the back of the truck. They are $0.49/gallon at Wal-Mart. We use the water for the dogs, and for us, when needed. It's easier than having to pump, although Rocket and I still pump while we are hiking, 'cause we sure don't wanna carry 3-5 liters of water a day! It's heavy, and hurts our knees and back!

After finishing filling up the water, we drive into town. Dad is excited to show us around. He drives from one end of the town to the other and back again (more gas money on a fixed budget). He says, "The brick architecture is nice. Do you remember me telling you my dad used to build churches when I was a boy?"

"Yeah, I remember," I answer. "So, part of your adventure, you get to tour all the towns we pass through. You can check-out the architecture and lay-out of the town."

"Yeah," Dad answers. "I also went to the new library and worked on mom's taxes. When I left there, I saw a few options where you can get groceries."

"Thanks Dad."

Rocket points out the blooming Daffodils on the way to the grocery store. We re-supply and splurge on, Lays Tomato Basil Chips which we eat on the way back to Sams Gap. Tasty.

We sleep in the truck in the small parking area at Sams Gap

**Day 35** It's a chilly but beautiful day. The wind whips tendrils of my hair loose from the tight braid I keep it in. Mtn. goat's ears flap when there is an extremely strong gust of wind.

We hike through open meadows, and can see more mountains in all directions!

There is a car size boulder on Big Bald. Rocket says, "Let's stop for lunch on the other side of the boulder. It's not as cold when the wind isn't blowing on us."

Girl (Hiking) with 4 Dogs

"It is warmer without the wind blowing," I agree as we scoot behind the boulder. "Wow! There is a rock fire pit. I wonder if it used to be a chimney to someone's house?"

"It would be interesting to know more of the history.," Rocket says.

We take off our backpacks and dig out our lunch. We made sandwiches before we left the truck this morning. I toss my crust to Kujo, Mtn. Goat, and Instigator. The crust never makes it to the ground.

Rocket and I are enjoying a Snickers before we pack up when I notice Kujo's ears perk up, Mtn. Goat raises his head from his paws, Instigator jumps up and stands tense. I get up and stand near Kujo who is tied to my backpack. A few seconds later a man and his dog barrel around the side of the boulder. My dogs jump up and start barking. It takes a few minutes to calm them.

Once the dogs calm down the man approaches slowly and cautiously. "I'm Kabar and this is Mable," he introduces himself.

Rocket and I introduce ourselves and the dogs.

The dogs remain calm until Instigator starts barking, then Kujo starts growling. "Ugh!" Why can't they all get along? Mtn. Goat is excitedly wagging his tail, so I guess he agrees with me.

"Hush!" I yell glaring at the dogs. They reluctantly resume sitting.

Kujo decides to lie nicely, and beg to be petted, giving the appearance of meekness.

Yeah Right!

Mable is an older dog and looks like she might have arthritis. I look worriedly in Mable's direction then say, "There is an area on the trail about 20 miles South that has a huge jump from the ground to the boulder above. It's at least 7 ft. We were able to jump down. I don't know if Mable will be able to jump up."

"If we can make it through Roan Mountain, then we can do anything!" Kabar exclaims.

"Good luck!" Rockets says.

Does Roan Mountain have more than 7 ft. climbs?

It is getting cold sitting, so we finish lunch and get going.

We continue hiking through the woods, around a gnarly tree with finger like branches extended and a white blaze indicating we are on the right path. We hike through streams and finally after 13 miles of hiking we reach Spivey Gap, Pisgah National Forest.

Dad is nowhere to be found. We wait. And wait. And wait. The longer we wait the colder we get. There's not much of a phone signal. At 5206 ft. on top of Little Bald, we sent out a text, and the Spot GPS signal to let Dad know we were almost at the predetermined destination.

"Do you think your Dad got the messages we sent?" Rocket asks.

"I hope so. It's five miles if we hike to the next shelter."

"I'm getting colder, and it's starting to mist."

"Do you want to wait or hike to the next shelter before we get wet?" I ask.

"We can wait a few more minutes.

Dad finally arrives, I load up the dogs, while Rocket cleans out the cab of the truck.

Once the dogs are taken care of I quickly jump in the truck to get warm and stay dry. As soon as I close the door on the truck the rain comes pouring down.

Dad says, "I was here to pick ya'll up, when a couple and their dog came by. They were tired and sore. It was cold and they needed a ride to town. I left a note on the back of the sign exiting the trail to let you know I would be back."

"Oh," I say. "We didn't see the note." I go back and check the sign. Sure, enough there is a note. "I'll check the sign next time. Did the hikers give you any gas money?"

Dad's a sucker for a hard luck story. He changes the subject and says, "It was difficult to find the trail at first. Once I found the trail I made a small white arrow on the back of the National Forest sign pointing to the direction of the trail, to make it easier for the next person to find where the AT crosses the road."

"That was a good idea," I say.

I doubt the hikers gave him any gas money.

Dad has a habit of piling trash, food, tools, and equipment in the seat while we are hiking. Every day when we finish hiking we have to clean out the seat in the cab in order to sit down. It's become a nuisance. Rocket starts cleaning while I feed the dogs. Recently she has taken to grabbing a plastic bag and throwing stuff inside. Dad won't look for a can opener, flashlight or anything! He smugly says, "I guess it will show up eventually." Rocket and I know where everything is that we move!

It's dusk when the rain stops. We can see a piece of wood outside the window that looks like a mole. At least I think it's a piece of wood.

**Day 36** I yawn, "It's about ten miles to Erwin, TN. Once we get to Erwin I can take Digger to the vet."

"His foot looks fine," Dad says. "Why spend the extra money to take him to the vet?"

"I just want to make sure it is healing fine."

I grab the other three dogs and Rocket and I start hiking. It doesn't take long before we can see Erwin, TN nestled in the mountains, then Nolichucky River is visible meandering between the mountains, with one lone bridge crossing its width. We switchback our way to River Rd. and arrive in time to take Digger to the vet.

Dad drives all of us. It seems like we are driving all around town, but we haven't found the vet yet.

"Dad, stop at the grocery store and I will ask for directions. If we keep driving in circles we will never make it to Unicoi Animal Hospital. Look there is someone at the drink machine outside of the Walgreens."

Dad pulls in the shopping center, drives around the entire edge of the shopping center before finally making it to the drink machine. The man is leaving the machine as we drive up.

I jump out to ask the guy for directions to Main Street.

He says, "Wel', ya' wanna g' a ha bloc then tur le' then g' fo' mi'. U see it."

I say, "Thanks!" I get back in the car and tell Dad and Rocket. "I don't know what he just said. I'm not sure he was speaking English. I think if we turn left at the intersection we will eventually find the Vets office."

At last we find the vets office and I unload Digger. Dad says, "I'll take Rocket and we can shop at the Family Dollar. Call when you finish."

I say, "Okay" and take Digger inside the vet's office.

After a short wait, the vet Karen says "Digger's foot looks fine. There is no indication of infection. It doesn't need stitches. Stitches can only be done within the first few hours of injury otherwise the wound has to be re-opened in order for the wound edges to heal together." She puts a honey dressing on Diggers foot (he loved chewing it off) to help it heal faster and decrease his risk of infection. She says "I didn't know my office was listed in the Appalachian Trail Thru hiker book. My dad is a big fan of the trail and he must have submitted my office information."

"I am glad he did"

"Well, Digger is good to go," the vet says. "He needs to stay off his foot at least a couple more weeks. Good luck and have fun!"

"Thanks," I say. I call Dad on the way out. He says, "I'll be right there."

Dad arrives, but I don't see Rocket. I ask, "Where is Rocket?"

Dad says, "She had a bunch of items to purchase, so I left her at the store. I know how much you hate to wait"

"You didn't have to leave her. I would have waited. I'm not in a hurry today!"

We pick up Rocket and she is livid. She had put everything back in order to not keep Dad waiting, but he had already left!

She says, "I told you I was coming why did you leave without me!"

Dad responds, "I didn't want my daughter to have to wait!"

"I would have been fine waiting. I just wanted ya'll to know I was finished. Do you want to go back to the Family Dollar or do you want to go to Uncle Johnny's Hostel and take a shower?"

Rocket says, "I don't want to go back to the store."

"Okay Dad, can you take us back to Uncle Johnny's?"

We take a shower at Uncle Johnny's Hostel, but decide not to spend the money to stay the night. There are two showers for the ladies, one has better hot water.

"Rocket, since I picked the shower at Nantahala first you can pick which shower you want first."

She says, "I'll take one in the main bathroom."

"Okay," I say. The one in the main bathroom has warmer water, but the one I get is a single shower so there aren't any drafts from people opening the door. The water is lukewarm at best even with conserving the hot water. At least it is warm in the room. Ahhh, I'm clean!

Dad declines taking a shower and instead stays with the dogs at the truck.

Later, we us use the microwave at Uncle Johnny's for popcorn. I use a pack from our plastic storage bin in the truck.

"Hey Sensai, Availability, and Still Water," Rocket says. "Have ya'll been here long?"

"Only a couple of days," Still Water replies.

"Did one of ya'll leave a Smart Wool shirt at Mtn. Collins Shelter? I found one before we left the shelter."

"Is it an XL? I lost mine somewhere," Still Water says.

"Yes. I'll give it back to you, but you have to promise to finish the whole trail. If you don't finish, then you have to hunt me down and give me back the shirt. Deal?" I ask.

"Deal." Still Water says.

Availability asks, "Did you find any Gators at Davenport Gap?"

Rocket says, "I didn't see any."

"Me either. Also, there were still Spring Breakers sleeping when we left Davenport. We wouldn't know your Gator's from someone else's."

We talk a few more minutes before returning to the truck for the night. There is cold air pouring off the nearby Nolichucky River. I snuggle inside my sleeping bag. I am stretched out inside the dog kennels with the dogs. Dad fastens me in before crawling on top of the plastic bins beside the dog kennels.

**Day 37** The pitiful sound of Digger's whining haunts me as Rocket, Mtn. Goat, Kujo, Instigator, and I start down the trail.

"Thanks for taking care of Digger for me. It's okay if you want to give him some extra doggie treats," I call back to Dad.

"Okay. He'll be fine." Dad replies.

We start off at 2022 ft. elevation, dip down to 1712 ft. to cross the Rail Road tracks, then we begin to climb. Mostly a steady climb.

"At least the weather is nice," Rocket comments as we hike through Mountain Laurel, and through fields warmed by the sun. "I still don't understand why we have to hike 20 miles today. I prefer hiking 10 miles a day."

"I won't be able to finish the trail before I have to go back to work if I only hike 10 miles a day," I reply.

"Why can't we stay a couple of days at a hostel that lets us do work for stay? Isn't that part of the hiking experience?"

I sigh, "Maybe some other time. Wow! Look at how the entire tree is uprooted! The roots look like a gigantic porcupine standing on two back legs. All the tiny roots resemble quills protruding from its back and there are two larger roots sticking out like two paws ready to cat fight."

"It is amazing how powerful nature is," Rocket comments as we continue hiking.

A few miles later Rocket glances back then asks, "Why are your dogs so restless today?"

The dogs are pulling more than usual, their scruff is slightly up, their eyes and ears are alert, and they are sniffing intensely at the ground.

"I guess they have too much energy. Do you want to eat lunch here in the shade before we cross TN395?"

"Sure, if your dogs will calm down long enough to let us eat."

"Maybe they smell people from Rock Creek Recreation Area, it's only a few miles away."

"There are some hikers coming from the road. You probably want to wait before you tie up your dogs," Rocket suggests

"Thanks."

As the hikers are passing one of the members warns, "You girls be careful. We stayed at Cherokee Adventures last night. They just dropped us off. The staff warned us there was a momma bear and her cubs spotted in this area a few days ago. You might be okay since you have the dogs. Rangers use dogs to scare bear away, but a momma and her cubs can be unpredictable."

"Thanks for the warning," Rocket says.

We look at each other.

"I don't mind hiking a few more miles to eat lunch. The dogs might be restless because they smell the bear."

"I agree. Let's eat later."

We cross the road and hike a few miles, then we encounter an open field.

"This looks like a good place to eat," Rocket suggests. "Besides I want to get a picture of the tree eating the sign."

"The tree looks like it is smiling!"

After lunch, we begin to climb Unaka Mountain. It peaks at 5180 ft. elevation.

As we approach the top Rocket shivers, "I'm having fl-flashbacks of the Smoky Mountains!"

"It is cold," I shiver and try to keep my teeth from chattering. "L-l-look at all the tiny spruce t-trees."

Rocket says, "The t-trees are the hikers that are d-deluded into believing the cold is over. They s-stop too long, and are t-turned into little trees, frozen f-forever on Unaka Mountain!"

"I can see p-patches of snow through the trees! Let's keep going before we t-turn into another f-frozen spruce tree!"

At bottom of each large spruce tree is a bed of soft green moss.

It warms up as we descend Unaka Mountain. "I wonder why all the spruce trees have broken branches at the bottom," I ask.

"If the snow melts and falls to the ground it might be so heavy it breaks the branches on the way down."

"Could be."

"These trees look like the same brown trees we saw and hour ago!" Rocket exclaims.

"I hope we aren't going in circles! We should reach Iron Mountain Gap any minute, but I don't hear any cars."

"Look up ahead," Rocket exclaims. "It looks like a tire graveyard. There are innumerable tires randomly thrown into the ditch. I guess we aren't hiking in circles."

"I don't see a road. I wonder how the tires got here?"

"I can see the trail twisting down the hill and around the mountain. Maybe a horse brought the tires, or a four-wheeler."

It takes another 45 minutes to finally reach Iron Mtn. Gap.

"Yay! Dad is here," I exclaim as we exit the trail.

"It is close to dark. How long have we been hiking?"

"9 hours and 45 minutes," I answer.

"How was hiking today?" Dad asks.

"Long!" Rocket answers.

"We are low on water," I say to Dad.

"We can drive to town and fill-up the containers."

"Okay. I'll finish feeding the dogs and eat, then we can drive to town.

In town, we buy a carton of ice cream to split, then we return to Iron Mtn. Gap to sleep for the night.

**Day 38** While looking at the map the night before, I realized we will reach Roan Mtn. today. I don't want to tell Rocket because I don't want her to bail on me, but I feel guilty keeping the information to myself.

At the last minute, I blurt, "Rocket, it looks like we will reach Roan Mountain today."

Rocket says, "Did you just now figure that out?"

"Not exactly," I answer. "But I didn't want you to bail on me. Then I decided, even though you hadn't looked at the map and realized we were hiking Roan Mountain, I should still tell you."

"I'm glad you told me, because if you hadn't, then I would definitely quit!" She stomps off to get her backpack and I hitch the dogs to their leashes.

It is cold, again.

We see an entire tree up-rooted and laying on it's side. Later we see white fungus growing from a dead tree, then we see 12 ft. long icicles hanging from a rock ledges.

"I'm tired of the relentless cold!" Rocket exclaims. When we get to the truck, I'm calling James to pick me up!"

"Okay," I respond. "I was looking ahead on the map, there is a hostel in Roan Mountain, TN. It looks like a neat place. They converted the barn into a hiker hostel. We can probably make it there by tomorrow night. Should I make reservations?"

"Sure," Rocket mumbles.

On our lunch break, I call to make a reservation at Mountain Harbour Hostel in Tennessee for tomorrow. Check in time is 5:30 p.m.

We pass little Rock Knob, try not to get turned around at Toll House Gap, wave to the lone Chimney with snow inside, and finally pass Roan Mountain Shelter at 6285 ft., It is reported to be one of the coldest shelters on the trail. Near the shelter, there are craters in the frozen ice of at least 2 ½ feet deep. Kujo, Mtn. Goat, and Instigator are enthralled. They like to sniff it, eat it, and of course turn it yellow! Some of the trail is slushy. The wind doesn't help matters, and the fog makes following the trail challenging.

The snow recedes as we descend the mountain. Just as we exit the trail to Carvers Gap road, I see Dad pass in the white truck with the purple camper shell. I initially think he sees us, but then I consider the thick fog. I say, "Rocket, I'm going to run and catch up to Dad. It's not like him to keep driving once he sees us. Normally, once he sees us, he thinks we can't possibly hike one more step and he stops the truck."

"Good idea," Rocket responds.

I catch up to Dad, and tap the truck window. He brakes suddenly and rolls down the window.

"The fog is so thick, I didn't see you."

"Jesus worked out the timing perfectly. We were just exiting the trail when you drove by. Have you been driving back and forth looking for us?"

"No. I just got here."

"If you want to park the truck in the parking lot, I'll make sure Rocket can find us."

*Thank you Jesus.*

On the way to the parking area, Rocket and I meet a family finishing up a short-day hike with their elderly grandpa.

As we pass, I nonchalantly try to keep the dogs calm. They give the appearance of being well behaved, instead of being the slobbery, barking, jumping, easily excitable monsters they really are.

I'm flattered when people say, "What well behaved dogs you have." I just smile and nod. I wonder if they are blind, or just being nice. Can they not see the tension on the leashes, my biceps bulging from holding back the rowdy dogs, and the mischievous gleam in their eyes? Perhaps, if the dogs hear it enough, they really will be good boys.

We reach the truck. Dad has the heater running. I rush into the cab as soon as I've finished taking care of the dogs.

Rocket says accusingly and venomously, "There is no cell phone service here!"

"Really? We are 5312 ft. above sea level. How can we not have a signal?"

"Somehow you planned this."

I raise an eyebrow questioningly, but I don't dare say a word. It is ironically funny. I dare not laugh, or even grin.

Rocket continues, "You know I was going to call James to pick me up. Now I can't because there is no cell phone service. Even Verizon let me down!"

I do my best to look sympathetic, while on the inside I am singing "Alleluia!" I don't want Rocket to keep hiking if she wants to quit, but at the same time I don't want to hike by myself either. I pray for whatever is best. I am scared to even look at Rocket after we discover there is no phone service. She still accuses me of gloating.

The temperature feels like 30 degrees, or colder, Fahrenheit, but the thermometer says 40.

We cook Roman noodles using our JetBoil stove while sitting in the truck, disregarding the warning not to cook in an enclosed space. The dogs are snuggled together in the kennels in the back of the truck.

**Day 39** The next morning is still cold. While getting ready to leave, eating, feeding the dogs, etc., I see the fuzzy shape of a car pull into the parking lot. Next, through the thick fog, I see the fuzzy shape of a hiker with a backpack on. He walks around the edge of the parking lot, obviously looking for the trail.

"Are you hiking north or south?" I ask the hiker.

"I am meeting some friends. We are hiking south today."

"Go to the end of the parking lot and turn left, follow the edge of the road a few feet and you will see the trail enter the woods." I say.

"I think the trail starts at the other end of the parking lot. I'll look there first," the hiker replies arrogantly.

"Okay," I shrug and raise my left eyebrow. I've hiked 375 miles on this trail, I know what I'm talking about when I tell you where the trail starts, but if you want to waste your time looking, go ahead.

I wave as I see the hiker backtracking.

"You were right," he says humbly as he passes.

"It's all part of the adventure," I answer.

Shortly thereafter, I harness the 4 dogs and Rocket and I continue our NOBO hike. As we near the end of the parking lot through the thick, swirling fog, we see two hikers with backpacks crossing the street and heading north on the AT. The hikers look like twins, and their pace quickens as we start toward them. As we get closer Rocket and I realize The Brothers are ahead of us.

Train Wreck falls behind and we quickly pass him. In passing Rocket jokingly asks, "How many people think you and your brother are twins now?"

Trainwreck mumbles, "I think we are up to 17. You will have to ask my brother."

Trainwreck stumbles and almost falls.

"Are you okay," Rocket asks concerned.

"I'm fine just tired."

"Maybe you should rest for a day or two after you finish this section. We'll let your brother know we saw you when we catch up to him." I say.

"Thanks," Trainwreck says.

The dogs bark and whine excitedly as we pass Trainwreck. I have to jerk back on Mtn. Goat's leash to keep him from accidentally bumping into Trainwreck as we pass.

"Can you keep your annoying noisy dogs quit?" Rocket asks.

"They will settle down in a few minutes."

"They are going to scare away all the wild life. No one else will ever want to hike with us!" Rocket stops ranting and suddenly snatches something from the tree in front of her. I jerk to a stop expecting Rocket to fling a rabid snake on the ground.

"Look trail magic. I wonder why there is only one snickers," she says.

She quickly puts the snickers back in the tree and snatches me forward down the trail.

"What was that all about?" I ask in confusion.

"Two Medicine left the snickers for Trainwreck to keep him motivated." Rocket explains.

"Oh. That was thoughtful of him."

Before much longer we pass Two Medicine, then a half a mile late we see real trail magic hanging in a brown plastic grocery bag in a tree. Rocket and I each take a piece of fruit and candy and leave the rest.

"I bet the family we saw yesterday evening left the trail magic. They seemed pretty excited yesterday."

"Yes. The grandpa looked especially excited yesterday," Rocket agrees. "By the way, your hair looks like a spider web collecting dew drops."

"It must be from all the fog."

A short time later we summit Round Bald and Jane Bald. There isn't much to see other than FOG.

"I'm glad you have the dogs now," Rocket says. "I can't even see the trail; the fog is so thick.

We finally find enough tree coverage, we can take a potty break. Ten seconds after Rocket takes off into the woods, The Brothers and a group of boy scouts round the corner. I am completely blocking the trail with my backpack and the dogs.

"Just a minute and I will get the dogs to the side for you, "I say to the group at large stalling to give Rocket time to finish her business with watering the trees.

"Did anyone stay at the Roan Mountain Shelter? I heard it was really cold," I ask.

"We did, and it is the coldest shelter since the Smoky's," Two Medicine replies.

I hear one of the Boy Scouts mumble, "hurry up," but I continue to dilly dally until I see Rocket on her way back.

"Sorry it took so long to get the dogs untangled," I say as I let the group pass.

We resume hiking, but now we are at the back of the pack.

"Kelly, it's warmed up some. Do you want to take the side trail to look at the Over Mountain Shelter? It is a unique converted barn."

"Not really, but I know how much you like barns, so we can go."

Once we arrive at the barn, Rocket says, "I'm glad we came I like the way the light shines through the cracks in the barn. It looks drafty for sleeping though."

"It would probably be comfortable in the summer time. I'm surprised Instigator's feet don't get stuck in the cracks"

"I guess he watches where he walks." Rocket laughs watching Instigator carefully walk in the barn.

Girl (Hiking) with 4 Dogs

We return to the trail and see The Brothers eating lunch standing where the trail splits to go to the Barn or continues North.

"If you don't want to walk to the Barn we can show you pictures." Rocket suggests. Two medicine says, "Sure, we were thinking about hiking to the barn, but we also want to make it to Apple House Shelter before it is late."

We show them pictures, then decide to eat our lunch while we are stopped.

Rocket says, "We can take your trail trash if you want. We are still slack packing. Also, we are going to the Hiker Hostel tonight and can throw your trash away. Ya'll should come too."

"No thank you. We want to stay in the shelter to save money."

"Okay. Be safe hiking," I say as The Brothers head-out.

Six miles later we cross into Tennessee.

# Chapter 7: Tennessee

**Day 39** March 27, 2011 Continued Another three miles pass, we see The Brothers again at the Apple House Shelter. We try again to convince them to hike to the Mountain Harbour Hostel/ B&B. "No thanks. We are already set-up here," Train Wreck says.

Paul (with) Bunyan's is also staying at the shelter "so my feet can heal," he says.

It sounds like it could take months to years for his feet to heal...

Bunyan has a huge (Bon)fire going, even though it's not currently cold.

I hope he saved firewood for later!

"Do you girls have anything sweet to eat?" Bunyan asks walking toward us. He stops suddenly when Kujo starts growling at him. We check our supplies and spare a few granola bars.

Rocket is elected to deliver the food.

We don't stay long. It's 5:30 p.m.! I have a date with a shower!

The shelters near roads can be trashy, TV's, Refrigerators, and other junk. Also, they are likely to be more crowded since, it is economical and logical to stay close to the road, in order to make it to town early for re-supply, or to stay on your way out of town after re-supply.

It's about half a mile from Apple House Shelter to the Mountain Harbour Hostel. Dad is meeting us at the Hostel. The Hostel is a converted barn built out of weathered wood. The lower level has an opening built into the side to allow the farm animals shelter. There is a brick red painted wooden fence to keep the various farm animals contained. There are sheep, goats, and horses grazing contentedly in the field. There is a creek running between the Hostel and the B&B, with rocks on the sides then beautiful bright green grass. There are also yellow daffodils, and large cedar trees.

Rocket and I leave our backpacks and the dogs with Dad at the truck, then we march up the hill to the main house to pay for our stay. We barely finish knocking when a friendly woman opens the door.

Girl (Hiking) with 4 Dogs

"Hi, I'm Mary and you girls must be the ones who called yesterday. Please come inside. Tell me your trail names."

"Yes," I answer. "I'm Girl with 4 Dogs and this is my friend Rocket.

"We hiked almost 15 miles to get here today," Rocket adds.

"How is the hiking?" Mary asks as she hands us our receipts. "Is there anything unusual on the trail?"

"It's mostly uneventful," Rocket replies. "Although at the last shelter there was a man asking for 'sweet snacks'"

"He said he was staying at the shelter until his feet feel better," I add.

"I wondered if Paul would be here this year," Mary says. "You girls enjoy your stay. We have breakfast in the morning for $9 if you are interested."

"Thanks. We will think about it," I answer as we walk to the hiker hostel.

"Nine dollars is a lot for breakfast," Rocket says.

"I agree."

We get our clothes from the truck and invite Dad to join us for a while inside the shelter. He agrees. Once inside we see fellow hikers, Niners and Katmando. Then Katmando introduces us to Dutch and Colorado.

"You just missed the shuttle to town," Katmando says.

"That's okay. I would rather take a shower!" I reply.

"Me too." Rocket agrees.

While Rocket showers I return to the truck to take care of the dogs and dig out some can food from the truck. The hostel has a sink with running water, a cooking stove, plates and utensils. It also has a wood burning stove for heat and a pile of cut dry wood on the outside porch. Hikers are responsible for replacing the wood we use.

Dutch is from the Netherlands. Dad asks him, "Would you like me to tutor you on English phonics?"

"Yes," Dutch replies.

Dad focuses on the sounds of "o," "a," "e," "r," and "g."

I like the Dutch accent.

After a while Rocket and I crawl into our warm cozy bunks. Dad stays by the fire and no one seems to mind.

The dogs rest in the truck.

**Day 40** March 28, 2011 It is rainy and misty outside. Katmando says, "You girls should stay here another day."

I look at Rocket. She says, "I'm not hiking in this weather."

I sigh. "It is lovely here, I guess we can stay one more day, but rain or shine, I'm hiking tomorrow."

"Bye," Dutch, along with Niners, and Colorado, brave the bad weather to keep hiking. Rocket and I go to the main house to pay for our second night at the Hostel. The owner, Mary, reminds us, "There is breakfast available for $9."

"No thank you," I say. "I'm on a budget. Since I'm paying for two nights of rest, I will eat cereal and milk in the Hostel. It's beautiful here."

Mary says, "When we first bought this property there was a lot of junk we had to take to the dump. We love it here now."

Rocket says, "Thank you for providing affordable housing to hikers."

"We like to meet the different people who hike the trail. They usually have different personalities than those who stay at the B&B."

"Does anyone ever ask Paul (with) Bunyan's to keep hiking?" Rocket asks.

Mary replies, "We see him frequently and try to help him whenever we can. As long as he isn't bothering people he stays at the Shelter, but after a few days the police will go to the shelter and ask him to leave. You can't stay at the shelters for an indefinite amount of time."

"That makes sense," Rocket says.

I take care of the dogs and they are more than happy to return to the kennels out of the rain. Shivering, I return to the hostel to warm up and relax by the fire.

I ask to Katmando, "I thought you were hiking with Niners?"

He says, "I was, but I don't want to get wet today. I'll just hike with someone else."

I ask, "What happened to his daughter?"

"She pulled a tendon in her leg putting on her backpack. She went home to let it heal, then she will resume hiking."

We talk about the different places along the trail.

Rocket says, "Did you see the Overmountain Shelter? When we went, we could see the sun rays shining through the cracks. It was beautiful!"

Katmando says, "I stayed in the Overmountain Shelter. It is really drafty with all those cracks! I froze!"

"It's probably comfortable in the summer." I say.

Toward evening, StormSong, and TreeBeard arrive at the Hostel. They are glad to be out of the rain. A little while later we meet a SOBO from last year, named EWOK. His knees are "shot-out," but he is on track to finish by April.

After a while Katmando says, "We are all going to be here for supper. Why don't we take the 5:00 shuttle in to town and buy food for a home cooked meal?"

"That sounds like a great idea!" Rocket and I answer.

We all discuss what to eat, and settle on salad, garlic bread, and spaghetti with meat sauce. Once we return with the supplies, Rocket starts on the garlic bread, Katmando is working on the spaghetti, and I start the salad. Dad is relaxing on the floor. Again. StormSong and TreeBeard are outside stacking firewood, and EWOK is resting his knees.

Rocket sets the table and we all sit down to eat. Dad lays on the floor to eat.

EWOK says, "I was trying to finish last year, but it started snowing and the trails were too difficult to follow."

I say, "I'm excited to meet you. You are so close to finishing and we are barely started. Good luck finishing."

After the meal, we all clean up together. In this moment, I feel like I belong.

Later, we meet spring breakers, Snickers, Kicks, Rooney and their dog, Roxie.

Snickers says, "We have extra Mountain House Meals, Trail Mix, dried Mango's, and jerky. Does anyone want some?"

"Sure," I say. "Are ya'll finished hiking?"

Kicks says, "We were going to hike more while we are on our spring break, but the weather is so nasty we decided to quit."

Rooney adds, "It's one thing for us to get wet, but we have Roxie!"

"I understand. My 4 dogs are lucky to be able to stay in the kennel with Dad when it rains. Thanks for the trail magic!"

Kicks asks, "What is trail magic?"

Rocket answers, "It's when someone gives you food or supplies when you are thru hiking."

"That's neat. We hope to thru hike one day," Snickers says.

"Anybody want to play a game of Rummy," Kicks asks?

"Yes," Rocket and I answer.

Dad stays sleeping on the floor by the fires.

**Day 41** The next morning, Rocket and I argue about our hiking plans for the day.

"Rocket, if we hike the 24 miles to Dennis Cove, then we can sleep in a bed again!"

"It's 24 MILES in one day!" Rocket exclaims.

"I think we can do it, but I'll carry the backpack with the tent and sleeping bag in case we decide to stop sooner."

"Okay," Rocket finally relents. "Get your dogs and let's go!"

"I can watch the dogs," Dad pipes up.

"Thanks Dad. I'll take Mtn. Goat and Kujo. You can keep Instigator since he didn't eat breakfast, and you can keep Digger. I don't want to risk his foot pad opening up on such a long hike."

I load Kujo with the doggie backpack with dog food. Hopefully after hiking 20 + miles he will finally be tired enough to stop pulling!

Katmando makes sure we are okay and don't need anything, before he starts out with StormSong and TreeBeard.

I watch them hike out of site for a minute until Kujo literally jerks me back to reality.

It starts off cold and overcast. As the sun rises, the sun breaks through the clouds. The sun rays spotlight the numerous purple, blue tinted mountains we will be hiking, reveling more and more beauty as the sun becomes stronger than the clouds. Eventually the sun overcomes the clouds. The mountains are revealed in all their majesty. There is hope.

Day by day the trees lose the brown pallor of winter death and slowly the green buds of life blossom. We cross streams with clear, cold water, and see small waterfalls with happy, gurgling water drops racing down the mountain.

Girl (Hiking) with 4 Dogs

We take a couple of short breaks during the day to snack and to change out of sweaty socks.

It is dusk, but there is just enough light to explore the outside of an old barn near Dennis Cove Road, then we rush toward the road. We round a turn in the trail and glimpse the purple camper on the white truck in a clearing below us. Time to go pee before we get to the road.

When we reach the truck, Dad congratulates us. "I'm impressed. It only took you girls 13 hours to hike 24.4 miles."

"I'm exhausted," Rocket exclaims. "Where is the hostel you were telling me about this morning?"

I sigh, "Let's look at the sign and see what it says."

The dogs have relentless energy as they pull me toward the sign. Mtn. Goat is smiling!

There is a sign indicating two Hostel's. The first one is closed. It's after 8:00 p.m.

I ask Rocket and Dad, "Do you think Kincora is open? What if we are too late and they don't want to let us stay. Maybe we should stay parked here and sleep in the truck."

Rocket says, "I'm tired. It won't hurt to at least check it out."

"You're right," I say. "Let me feed the dogs and get them loaded, then Dad can you drive us to the hostel?"

"Yes," Dad answers.

We reconnaissance Kincora. They are operational!

Dad says, "I'll stay in the truck with the dogs."

I say, "You don't have to stay with the dogs. They will be fine. It's only $4 to stay the night. I can pay for you."

"No," Dad says. "I feel more comfortable staying with the dogs. I'm not really one of the hikers."

"You can still stay," I argue.

Dad responds laughingly, "No, no."

"Okay, suit yourself. I'm going to get a hot shower!"

While walking to the Hostel with Rocket, she asks "Why doesn't your dad ever want to stay in the hostel's or take a shower?"

"I don't know. He doesn't take many baths or showers at home either. I bought him brand new clothes at Christmas one year from TJ Max, and he said he didn't want me to spend money on him.

I insisted he take them, or I would put them in the trash. He says he prefers getting his clothes from Goodwill because it is more economical. He used to take a bath when he would watch the dogs for me when I went out of town. It might be hard for him to get in and out of the tub with his sore leg."

"He smells bad sometimes."

"I know. Maybe we can get him another change of clothes next time we go to town, and we'll tell him we found it in the hiker box. I'll wash his clothes with mine when we do laundry."

We stop talking and enter Kincora. A blissful smile covers my face. It is cozy, comfortable, warm and dry inside Kincora! There are beds, HOT showers, a microwave, a stove, and a refrigerator. Life is great!

"Hey, It's the Brothers!" Rocket exclaims excitedly.

We wave cheerfully and walk toward The Brothers.

They aren't smiling and I wonder if they are still tired from hiking. Two Medicine says, "We got here yesterday and are leaving tomorrow."

"Good luck. We are having a slow day tomorrow," I say.

We visit with Mr. Peoples and the other hikers, Wesley, and William to name a few.

I love it! Mr. Peoples, who oversees the hostel, is an amazing person. He helps with trail maintenance, and is an invaluable source of information. He opens up to us about how he gave up drinking for financial reasons. He says, "I want this hostel to be for long-distance, and thru hikers. I don't want to make the rules. I want those who use it to feel responsible and make the rules. Thru hikers are a different breed of people. They have left the worldly things behind. Weekenders tend to be self-centered and overly concerned about cell phones and business. They don't belong here."

All the hikers in the hostel listen to Mr. Peoples talk as if he is a beloved grandpa. He also opens up about his wife's death. He says, "I was married for 43 years. Being part of trail maintenance helps fill the emptiness left behind when my wife died of pancreatic cancer. I have never hiked the entire trail, but I feel like I have contributed to the trail, by taking care of this section."

My throat is tightening and my eyes sting. I excuse myself to go to the bathroom. I understand emptiness.

Girl (Hiking) with 4 Dogs

**Day 42** In the morning, I notice Kujo is weak and can barely stand up. I palpate his body, check his feet, respirations, and heart rate. Everything is comparable to the other dogs. Other than weakness, I don't discover any acute distress.

I feed the dogs breakfast, then tap the glass on the cab of the truck. When Dad rolls down the window, I ask, "Can you watch Kujo and Mtn. Goat today so they can rest?"

"Sure," Dad answers.

I explain Kujo's weakness this morning and Dad agrees to keep an eye on him. I leave Digger, but I bring Instigator with us.

We are slack packing nine miles. Dad will pick us up at Shook Branch Recreation Area and we will return to Kincora tonight.

There are beautiful water falls, and picturesque wooden bridges. We are at the bottom of a ravine and there is water rushing turbulently past us.

"Watch out," Rocket calls back to me. "There is barely room to hike around this boulder without falling in the water. Make sure Instigator doesn't pull you in!"

I carefully inch my way around the boulder, the tips of my shoes are in the edge of the water. Instigator is on a short leash behind me.

"Thanks for the warning. That was fun," I say catching up to Rocket.

Rocket laughs, "I figured you would say that. I'm glad you only have Instigator today. If you had all four dogs you would have fallen in."

"I would hope not, but you are probably right."

"You would have a difficult time crossing the narrow bridges too."

"True. Wow! Look how the rock wall goes straight up on both sides of the river! If there was a flood rushing toward us there would be now where for us to run."

A few miles later we see Dad at Shook Branch Recreation Area. We eat lunch then I say, "It's early, I want to hike to Watauga Dam. It's only three more miles."

Dad says, "Why not relax for the rest of the day?"

"Because I don't want tomorrow to be too long of a day for hiking."

Reluctantly Dad and Rocket agree to my plans. We let Mtn. Goat hike this shorter section with us. Watauga Dam is interesting. There are rock mountains and we can't find where to meet Dad. Mtn. Goat and Instigator have a blast; however, Rocket and I are frustrated. Dad can't find us despite cell phones, and GPS because Dad doesn't have GPS navigation. He knows where we are, but he doesn't have directions on how to get to us. Also, some of the roads are closed for the season. Dad, has to drive a long way out of the way in order for us to hike three more miles. I should have listened to reason and hiked 9 miles instead of 12.

I sigh, "I'm sorry I wasted our time, but 'It's too late to apologize.'"

"It's okay," Rocket replies, "at least we won't have to hike so many miles tomorrow."

Eventually, we walk out on the road to meet Dad. Along the way, we help a group of hikers. One guy is limping. "I fell and twisted my knee," He explains.

Another guy speaks up, "We are wondering if we hike over this short hill if it will connect with the main road."

"Yes!" Rocket and I answer simultaneously.

"We just came from that direction and the paved road isn't far," Rocket continues.

"Thanks!" the limping hiker exclaims relief evident in his voice. "I don't know how much farther I can hike."

"I'm glad we could help. God is good, all the time!"

We wave and climb into the white truck with the Purple Camper. We have a long scenic return trip to the hostel.

"Dad can we stop at the store to get groceries?" I ask as we enter town.

"Sure," Dad replies.

"I'm making white pasta lasagna," Rocket says.

"Come eat with us Dad. We will have plenty of food," I add.

Dad agrees to joins us. He visits with the other hikers while Rocket and I fix the food. Everyone else has already eaten, but there is a big refrigerator we can keep the leftovers.

Dad gets up after the meal and says, "Food was delicious. I guess I'll go back to take care of the dogs before it gets dark."

I help dad with the dogs, then return to the hostel for another delightfully hot shower. As I am finishing in the shower I can see a light rain falling.

A few hours later many thru-hikers straggle in, tired, exhausted, cold, wet, and hungry. Rocket and I divide the rest of the leftover lasagna and are happy to share in return for a small monetary donation to cover our expenses. It's Wednesday night and the hostel is almost full. Most are thru hikers, but some are hiking a long section of the trail while on leave from the military.

We meet Wolf, Shaiza, and their dog Misha. After talking to them I get the impression Dad has given them a few rides from the trail head into town. We also meet Cypress, and Jelly Pants.

**Day 43** Sigh! we have to leave Kincora.

Dad drives us back to Watauga Dam. The day starts out cool and continually gets colder. It is too chilly for a long lunch. The colder it gets the more Mtn. Goat and Instigator pull.

Around 1:00 p.m., we briefly meet Detour and Packman, a couple from CT, at Vandeventer Shelter. They have been hiking the AT in sections for 19 years and have 500 miles left.

"Wow," Rocket says. "You have perseverance!"

"You better believe it!" Detour says.

Instigator is dancing around like a fighter. The cold is oozing through my jacket to freeze my skin. My bones are starting to ache. I glance at Rocket and see her suppress a violent shiver.

"We're going to keep going before we freeze. We have 11 miles left today. Good luck finishing the trail this year.," I call as we continue north on the AT.

The thick fog turns into mist, then rain, sleet, and finally snow.

"Will this day ever end?" Rocket asks wearily. "How did you convince me to hike 17 miles today?"

"Because we can meet Dad at the next road crossing and avoid carrying our tent and according to the map there aren't any major mountains today."

Rockets sighs, "The constant series of ups and downs is about as bad as one huge Mountain!"

I bust out laughing. Rocket glares back at me. "What is so funny?"

"Look at poor Instigator. He looks like a frozen mop! He's trying to stay warm by running ahead, but he is stopped at the end of his leash. He looks like a maniac. He tucks his tail and his little legs are frantically moving."

"It's getting dark," Rocket comments worriedly.

"We have to be close now. Besides, I'm hoping it is dark because of the snow clouds. My warning alarm on my watch hasn't gone off, so we should have at least another hour."

A short while later we exit the trees and gloriously see the white truck with the Purple camper parked in the parking area at TN 91, Shady Valley.

"I'm glad you're here Dad," I say as Rocket, Mtn. Goat, Instigator, and I all jump in the warm cap. We sit right on top of the piles of junk in the seat.

After warming up about 30 minutes, I brave the cold again to take care of the dogs while Rocket cleans up our seats in the cap, then we cook, and eat in the truck.

It's dark after we finish eating. I tell everyone goodnight and head for the kennels. It is wonderful to stretch in the kennels. I get in first, then Dad lets the dogs in back. I have to claim my spot before Digger and Kujo get in.

I'm warm in the sleeping bag with 4 dogs snuggled around me.

**Day 44** April 1, 2011. It's snowing again! No joke. I've seen more snow on the AT than I have in my entire life thus far!

Usually, I wake up, then wake Dad up, so he can get out, open the tailgate, and get the dogs out.

On April Fools day, I wake up and holler to Dad, "I'm awake can you let me out of the kennel?"

Dad wakes up and attempts to push open the tail gate. He says, "The tail gate is stuck. I can't get it open! I can't climb over the tail gate."

"Okay," I say. As I start moving around in the kennel the dogs get up and start squirming to let me know they want out. I shove the 4 dogs to the far end of the kennel, I stick my fingers through the front of the kennel, and wiggle the latch open. I hold the 4 dogs back with one hand while I squeeze out the six-inch opening of the kennel. The door is restricted from opening because of the tailgate. I manage to twist and turn, until I can wriggle out, while at the same time keeping the dogs in. Then, I have to lift the glass on the camper, hold it up while climbing over the tailgate, and simultaneously trying not to pee my panties, fall, break my neck, or get hit by the glass, which has to be propped up with a plastic gutter piece!

Once I get outside, I have to keep jerking on the frozen tailgate to get it open! There is one to two inches of snow overnight, and it is frigid. We haven't even started hiking!

Finally, I get the tailgate open, then I feed the dogs and wake up Rocket. She isn't keen on hiking today, but we are both fascinated by the snow. I say, "We can have a short day of hiking, just to the next road crossing." Rocket groggily agrees.

The fields and roads are coated in white. The landscape is beautiful, with snow covering the ground. The sky is gray and overcast. Occasionally, we are catapulted by melting ice crystals. We see many animal tracks in the snow. One tree has white froth oozing out and looks like it is peeing! Another area looks like it was catapulted with tiny snow balls.

(The dogs are staying warmish with Dad.)

Rocket and I don't like trail blazing, but we have no choice. One time the trail disappeared, and all we can see is a small lake with streams extending in four directions. Our conclusion is that the stream must be where the trail used to be. I doubt we will have dry feet.

We see a wooden stump at one of the shelters. Someone carved a smiley face in the stump. We also see more animal tracks, and a tree with roots that make it look like it is walking. Occasionally we can see the mountains in the distance. We see fallen trees in the shape of a cross with white ice patterns exploding out with life from the fallen tree. Sharp, beautiful and powerful. We see a tree of pure white reaching into the heavens. Dead brown wild flowers are transformed into white beauty. An abandoned birds nest, now a bowl for snow.

We end our day at Low Gap in Shady Valley, TN after hiking less than seven miles.

**Day 45** We have another snowy day, with us as trail blazers. Again, we let the dogs stay warm in the kennels with Dad. We see a piece of a stone wall, more animal prints, and even bird tracks. We see a shelter full of snow called "The Holiday Inn." There is a spider web inside.

Later Rocket says, "Look at the prints going across the log. I guess the raccoon didn't want to get it's feet wet."

I laugh.

By the end of the day we have descended in elevation, and there is no more snow. The weather is warm and pleasant. The SPOT GPS malfunctioned, and I have to make arrangements for a replacement.

At the sign for VA, we pass a group of hikers. We ask, "Can you take a picture of us at the sign?"

"Yes," one member says and takes a picture. "We are the Kingsport Hiking Crowd and we are glad to meet you. Where are you from?"

We tell them about ourselves and one member says, "I am a nurse too!"

We receive well wishes and wisdom such as, "THE JOURNEY IS THE DESTINATION," from WALL, "Good times at the Line," from the Kingsport Hiking Crowd, and "Much luck!" from Phyllis

Nurses Rock! Thanks for the candy ya'll!

Just before reaching Damascus Rocket and I pass an uprooted tree with a root span taller than our head!

# Chapter 8: Virginia

**Day 45** April 2, 2011 (Continued) Damascus, VA. The sun is shining and the trees are greening. Rocket and I are on our way to "The Place," run by the Methodist Church. We see a sign on the door, saying no pets or parking without permission. Inside, we meet Dust. We discover he owned the gloves we found in the Smoky Mtns., but he doesn't want them back. He is staying at "The Place" while working in town. He takes us to the person in charge of "The Place" so we can ask about parking the truck at the hostel. Dad waits in the truck with the 4 dogs.

Guy says, "Yes, you can park your truck at "The Place," however you cannot let the dogs out on the property."

"Thank you so much for your hospitality Guy. We noticed a park with a walking trail on the way in. We will take the dogs there when we let them out," I say.

We return and let Dad know we have secured housing for tonight. Rocket and I go inside to find a place to sleep. There are many bunks, both upstairs and downstairs. We pick a spot downstairs then lay out our sleeping bags. No one else is downstairs and Dust is upstairs.

I ask Rocket, "Have you noticed it echo's in here?"

"Yeah," she says. I wonder if it echo's when there are more people?"

"That's a good question. I'm guessing probably not."

Later, Rocket and I convince Dad to eat supper with us at Quincey's Pizza. While there we see Katmando, Niners, Stillwater, White Wolf, StormSong, TreeBeard and Sensi, and Face. They invite us to eat with them. Some of them are planning to slack pack back from Elk Gardens to town tomorrow.

After supper, we take the dogs to the park, then return to "The Place." Dad sleeps in the truck and the dogs are in the kennels.

Before going to sleep I ask Rocket, "Do you want to slack pack tomorrow? I'm thinking about showing up and hiking with the guys."

"I'm NOT hiking 23 miles in a day. My knees still bother me. I'm thinking about quitting. I can stay here a couple of days until James can pick me up."

"Do you mind if I hike tomorrow?"

"Go ahead. I'm not going to stop you."

"I'll let you know what I decide in the morning. Good night."

**Day 46** I wake up and look around to let Rocket know I am about to head out.

I don't see her anywhere!

She's not on the bunk across from me. I look in the other rooms, they are empty. I check outside with Dad, and she isn't there either. She wouldn't have left without saying anything, I don't think she's mad at me. What could have happened to her?

Finally, I recheck the downstairs rooms, and find her curled up on a top bunk next to the wall. I shake Rocket awake and ask, "How did you get in here?"

Rocket answers, "You were snoring loud enough to wake the dead!"

"Did you throw something at me or tell me turn on my side?"

"Yes! Then you started snoring louder. I thought you were joking. I finally had to find somewhere else to sleep!"

I laugh and say, "I'm sorry. I came to let you know I'm leaving to go slack-packing with the guys. Do you want to come?"

"No. I'll stay here and keep your Dad and dogs company." Rocket then turns over and pulls the sleeping bag over her head.

I go back outside to let Dad know I found Rocket. He says, "I can take care of the 4 dogs this morning if you want."

"Thanks," I answer and grab my daypack, which has rain gear, emergency blanket, water, and water tablets, and food. The weather is mild.

I heard the guys say they are taking a shuttle to Elk Gardens and slack packing back to Damascus. I walk to where the guys are meeting their ride.

"Good morning," I say. "Is it ok if I take the shuttle with ya'll to Elk Mountain?"

There are five of them, Niners, Stillwater, Katmando, StormSong, and Treebeard. I think of them as, "The 5 guys." They look at each other and shrug. It's not as if they can stop me.

Katmando says, "Yeah, come along with us."

Girl (Hiking) with 4 Dogs

Once at Elk Gardens, there is snow on the ground. Great, I get to hike 23 + miles in the snow, alone. The guys have longer legs and a bigger stride.

We pay our transportation fee, and I start off hiking in the lead.

What if I get lost or hurt in the snow all alone?

It doesn't take long for the guys to catch up, and pass me, one by one, as if I'm a turtle. After everyone passes me, then they stop for various reasons, to take off their jacket, or tie their shoes, etc.

Somehow, I end up in the front again. I push myself until my legs are about to fall off, or I am going to collapse from exhaustion. I don't want to hike alone.

Our hike starts at ~4500 ft., with peaks greater than 5000 ft., and ends at ~2000 ft. It is freezing cold, with snow covering the ground in the morning.

Occasionally, I see deep footprints in the snow.

There are scenic views of the mountains with snow covered peaks, and glimpses of town nestled in the valley below. I turn a corner and stop to assess which way the trail goes. It is challenging to follow the trail. Everything is white, and the blazes are difficult to see. There aren't many trees and the blazes on the rocks are covered with snow. The Five guys catch up behind me and ask, "Why did you stop?"

"I'm looking for a blaze to indicate which way to go over the rocks."

StormSong and TreeBeard take the lead and after climbing through the rocks we eventually see another blaze. Niners and Stillwater pass me, then Katmando. I can keep Katmando in my sight, and it isn't long before everyone stops for water. I drink from my CamelBak and keep going.

Once StormSong and TreeBeard have to stop to determine which way the trail goes. This time I am able to point out a footprint in the distance and we all keep hiking.

As we descend the mountains and the sun rises the day becomes sweltering hot with the sun blazing upon us! The snow is gone. I've managed to stay close to The Five Guys. I keep hiking to the top of the mountain. I have sweat pouring out of me, my face is red, I am consciously taking deep breaths to keep from gasping for air like a fish out of water. My throat is as dry as a desert and my heart is racing and beating so hard it pulsates my entire body. Whew!

We finally take a break. Water. Oxygen. Food. A subtle breeze.

I sit down and lean back against a medium size tree.

I think I will live.

The Five Guys take another break at Saunders shelter. We have nine miles left. I leave first, but have to stop after a couple of miles to purify water with the Aquimira tablets. I feel like I'm about to have a heat stroke. StormSong and TreeBeard stop to make tea. Stillwater and Niners use Aquimira drops then continue to Damascus. Katmando also uses Aquimira drops.

"Well guys, I'll see you back in Damascus," I say as I put my daypack back on. Katmando is also finished getting water and he hikes with me.

Katmando and I hike in companionable silence. After a while I say, "Thanks for not leaving me behind when we started hiking this morning. I was scared I was going to hike by myself."

"We weren't really waiting for you," Katmando replies. "You hike pretty fast and the trail was difficult to follow when we couldn't see any blazes."

We make it to the north end of Damascus and Katmando stops at a store for a drink. I am anxious to check on the dogs and see how Dad and Rocket's day went.

Katmando says, "We are going to eat at Quincy's again later. I hope to see you there."

"Thanks, we'll try to make it."

I hiked 23.5 miles in 8.5 hours, from snow to sunshine, and flowers, well maybe not flowers. Aqua-Mira Water drops are superior to tablets. They work faster. Who wants to wait to drink water, when perishing of thirst, and who wants to carry the water while waiting?

I meet Rocket at "The Place."

She says, "Your Dad left me at the hostel all day without telling me he was leaving, or where he was. I finally got him on the phone this afternoon, and he told me he took the dogs to a wooded area to hang out, so they wouldn't get too hot, or cramped up in the kennels! He could have let me know when he left!"

"I don't know why he didn't call. We gave him your number, didn't we?"

"Yes!"

"Maybe his phone was doing its crazy tricks?"

"Your Dad is very inconsiderate! In the meantime, Dust showed me around town. When we came back to the Hostel at lunch, the Big Boss of "The Place," chews Dust and I out because we parked the truck overnight in the parking lot!"

"I am flabbergasted," I say. "We asked permission from Guy yesterday. He said we could park overnight. Besides this is supposed to be a Christian establishment. Why would the Big Boss be so mean and hateful? No wonder many people are Anti-Christian! I'm leaving a note in the hiker book about how we were treated!"

Why am I discriminated against because I have dogs, and trail support? I am disgusted with "Christian" establishments. First the "Assess," now the "Bosses." I no longer care to stay in "Christian" run facilities. "Do unto others as you would have them do unto you…"

**Day 47** Our new friend, Dust, worked miracles and Rocket is still hiking with me! We volunteer to give the slack-packers a ride back to Elk Gardens. Katmando, StormSong, and TreeBeard already left.

Stillwater says, "I'll take a ride, but I have to finish my laundry."

Niners say, "I'll take a ride also, but I need to wait for the mail. I'm expecting food re-supply from home."

"Okay" Rocket and I agree to wait.

When we finally arrive at Elk Gardens it is hardly recognizable. There is no snow!

I ask, "Dad, can we leave the dogs with you. Rocket and I want to see the ponies of Grayson Highlands without the dogs scaring them away."

"Yes," Dad agrees. "I will keep the dogs. I will see you at Fox Creek, VA."

"Thanks for all your help with the dogs Dad. We'll see you sometime tomorrow."

I have both sleeping bags in my backpack in addition to my regular food and supplies. Rocket is carrying the day pack with her food.

Rocket says, "I have to stop to take my jacket off. I can't believe how hot it is after all the cold we had two days ago!"

"Good idea. I can feel my sweat trickling down my armpits!"

Soon we are hiking in short sleeves.

We see The Brothers. We pass them, and they pass us.

It is warm, with a continual breeze, so it is never too hot, or too cold. We have a leisurely break at Thomas Knob Shelter, conversing and feeding the birds. Next, we hike through and squeeze between huge boulders and enjoy the open fields with the sun gently shining down on us.

We round a corner and all of a sudden we see a pony licking Niners hairy legs, as if he is a salt lick! Of course, we have to have our turn as well.

The ponies tongue feels scratchy and soft when she licks my arm. The ponies aren't scared of us. We pet their thick shaggy fur and look at their tiny feet! We see a mommy and baby pony too!

The Brothers pass us while we are playing with the ponies.

I say, "Rocket, I think we need to stop chasing ponies and get to Wise Shelter before we get soaking wet!"

"You are right. The clouds are getting darker. Just one more picture and then we can go."

Of course, we have to traipse halfway up a small mountain to get a picture of a pregnant brown and white mare grazing in between boulders. Rocket is rewarded for her efforts by being salt-licked! Then we see a dark brown mare with a grey newborn foal. Of course, we have to have a picture of the baby!

We finally arrive at Wise shelter and are able to eat, pump water, and set up inside the shelter before it starts raining, a wise decision. The Brothers are there already and section hikers, "Cool Breeze" with her husband, son, and their Chihuahua.

I ask, "Cool Breeze, is this your first time on the trail?"

She answers, "No. We've been hiking sections during spring break for years. We will eventually finish the whole trail. How 'bout you girls?"

"This is our first time. I am doing a thru hike," I answer.

Rocket adds, "I'm seeing how far I can go."

"Are you just finishing college?"

"No," I answer. "I've been a nurse for years. I was working private duty. I've been saving money so if I ever had the time I would be able to thru hike the AT before I get my next job."

Rocket says, "Girl with 4 Dogs and I have been friends since middle school. We used to run track together in high school. Everyone used to think we were twins. I'm married now. I miss my husband."

I ask Cool Breeze, "Are you a teacher?"

"No. I'm a nurse anesthetist. I just have to put in a request for time off in advance."

"You're such a nice person, I should have known you are a nurse," I say. "We were hiking with some friends; did they already pass by?"

"Yes," Two Medicine speaks up. "StillWater and Niners knew you girls were behind and they wanted to make sure you had room in the shelter."

"That was considerate of them," Rocket says. I agree.

It rains heavily all night long, then early the next morning it starts snowing.

**Day 48** The snow is light and powdery. I can feel the temperature dropping.

What happened to sunny skies and a cool breeze?

We are in a fantastic shelter with a low hanging roof, but the snow is so light weight, and the wind so strong, that it is blowing the snow inside the shelter and onto our gear.

Rocket says, "I don't want to hike in this weather. Let's stay here another night."

I think for a minute then answer, "I'm not hanging out in my sleeping bag all day. Besides, I have a down bag, and if it gets damp from the snow I'm not going to be warm. I am not going to freeze to death in my sleeping bag!"

"Fine," Rocket reluctantly agrees to hike with me. We get up, eat, pack up, and are the first to leave. I have to back track a few steps to retrieve my CamelBak from the top of the picnic table. It is covered in snow, but it's not frozen on the inside.

Our boots didn't freeze either!

Rocket and I are the trail blazers once again. Shortly after starting we see the dark brown pony with the grey baby pony. Even though we are freezing cold, and on the verge of dying from hypothermia, we justify stopping to take pictures of the horses in the snow.

With teeth chattering I say, "We might be famous, the newspaper will print a headline, 'Two Hikers Freeze to Death while Taking Pictures of Ponies in the Snow.'"

Rocket laughs, then we start hiking again.

Everything is covered in snow, including the trees and blazes on the trees. We cross a stream and stand staring, trying to figure out which way the trail goes. There is an upward climb either direction, and no visible blaze. We start up the bank on the right side, but it is the wrong direction, we go straight ahead, then to the left. Thankfully, we finally find a partial blaze. Our hands and faces are numb. Without God guiding us, we would be dead.

The trail is now a creek bed, with large amounts of rushing water and impromptu waterfalls crossing it. We hike on the bank to the side of the trail, squishing plants buried under the snow.

Later, the trail ends at a lake. We are already shivering, and don't want cold water pouring into our boots, freezing our feet, and wetting our clothes even more. We aren't 100% sure the trail is on the other side of the lake, which probably formed due to all the rain the previous night. Given no other options or prospects of where the trail is, we ford the lake.

We plot our path.

I say, "Look, there is a puny tree with a big root sticking up. We can step there first, then there is a little bit of soggy earth, hopefully it won't sink when we step on it. From that stepping place, there is a small island to step on, assuming it isn't floating grass, and from there I see fallen logs and rocks."

"Okay," Rocket says. "Since I have hiking poles, I'll go first. I can check the soggy earth and island to see if it is stable before I put weight on it. Once I get to the other side, I'll throw the hiking poles back to you."

"That's a great idea. Thanks for sharing your poles with me."

"No problem," Rocket answers.

We make it across, and it looks enough like a trail on the other side that we keep going. A short while later, we see an older man hiking South. I ask, "Which trail are you hiking on?"

The man answers, "The Appalachian Trail."

"Thanks," I answer. "We were hoping we hadn't gotten lost. Aren't you scared of getting lost hiking by yourself?"

"No," he answers. "I hike here all the time."

"Be careful," Rocket says.

We continue with more confidence.

After the lake crossing, we have to hike for what seems like hundreds of miles in an open field, with snow blowing, and stinging any exposed skin. It is like fierce needles stabbing into my hands and face. Rocket has thick insulated gloves, I have the sleeves of my shirt, and jacket pulled over my hands. Then, I try to hold the hood of my jacket over my face to block the wind needles.

I'm sure on sunny days the scales and livestock corral are interesting, but for us it is yet another cold exposed area, with a difficult to follow trail upon exiting. So many trails, so few blazes, and not a footstep to follow.

Three miles later, Rocket says, "There is Old Orchard Shelter. Let's stop for a minute."

We check the shelter log and see that our friends were here the night before. They are long gone now. Then we search for the privy. We almost get lost.

I say, "I wonder if StillWater and Niners got wet or if they made it here before it started raining last night?"

"They probably got wet. It took us a long time to get here, and it started raining shortly after we got to the Wise Shelter yesterday. I bet the trail was easier to navigate without so much snow and water burying it."

"True," I answer.

It's only two more miles to Fox Creek, for a total of 7.6 miles hiking.

Rocket and I rejoice as we see the white truck with the purple camper.

"Dad," I say. "I'm so glad to see you!"

"Yes!" Kelly agrees climbing in the truck, shoving trash, food, and tools into a plastic bag so we can sit. We eat a pop tart and an orange while we tell Dad about our adventure.

"It's so nice to be warm," I say. "Thanks for waiting on us. Have you been here long?"

"A little while," Dad answers. "I saw a few other hikers early this morning."

"Probably the 5 Guys," Rocket says.

We are reveling in the warmth of the truck and are starting to defrost, when we see The Brothers, come dragging out of the trail.

"Do ya'll want water, oranges, candy, or trail mix to snack on?" I ask.

They take an orange. Train Wreck looks wrecked and Two Medicine looks like he can use a couple of medicines. I say, "If you need a ride to town or anywhere we can give you a ride. After such a beautiful day yesterday, I wasn't expecting the snow and cold today."

The Brothers consult then agree to a ride to town. We all squeeze into the cab of the truck. Train Wreck says, "I keep falling. I can't seem to recover my strength."

Two Medicine adds, "My wife made me promise I wouldn't hike alone."

"Maybe if you take a few days off then start again you will feel better," I suggest.

Train Wreck says, "I just don't think I can continue."

"There is nothing wrong with quitting," Dad says.

"You'll probably feel better after you rest," I say.

We take them to Marion, VA and they get a room. We go shopping in town and I buy toe socks at the Shoe Show. Life is good.

Before parking for the night, we stop at R&R Station for gas. I use my debit card so we can fill up the truck with gas. It cost 3.79/G and it takes 25.5 G of gas. I'm about to get back in the truck when the inside attendant, Stan, calls on the speaker. He says, "I need you to come inside to pay for the gas."

I go inside and say, "I just paid for the gas on the pump outside."

Stan says, "No, I activated the pump for you, but you have to come inside to pay with a debit card."

I'm still skeptical so I call my bank. It sounds like the attendant is telling the truth. I can't afford to be double charged $89.00!

As I get back in the truck, I explain to Dad and Rocket what took so long. I also ask, "Dad, since you drive a lot in the different towns, is it possible for you to pay to fill up the truck every third time?"

Hopefully if he his helping pay for gas, he won't waste so much driving from one end of town to the other. Also, even though Dad isn't working either, he does get Social Security Retirement checks each month.

Dad says, "Okay." He also suggests, "Why don't ya'll start from Marion in the morning and hike back to Fox Creek?"

I reluctantly agree, however as Dad is driving to find where the trail crosses into Marion, VA, he takes a wrong turn and ends up at Fox Creek.

**Day 49** The next day is sunny again. At noon while eating lunch at Dickey Gap.

Rocket and I see an ambulance parked in the shade. After a few minutes a tall thin man with salt and pepper beard and medium long hair gets out of the ambulance. He has a small brown Chihuahua in his arms.

As the man glances toward us, Rocket asks, "Are you a Medic?"

"No, I just drive an ambulance. My name is Gary and this is my dog Pepper. I take hikers to and from town. For a fee. I can't give you girls a ride with the dogs though."

"That's okay. We don't need a ride. My Dad meets us at the end of every day. How did you end up driving an ambulance?" I ask.

"There was one out of commission, I bought it and fixed it up."

"Interesting," Rocket says.

I ask, "Have you ever done a thru hike?"

"I've hiked the trail before. I can tell you there are sections coming up that will be difficult with your doggies."

"Do you remember any specific places? I can mark them in my thru hiker book."

"I definitely wouldn't take them in the White Mountains in New Hampshire. It is very dangerous even without dogs. Also, the Dragon's tooth just before Newport, VA is challenging."

"Thanks for the information," I say.

Pepper finally sees the other dogs, and then the Chihuahua immediately starts barking. His barking rouses Instigator who jumps up to a fighting stance. Instigator's movement disturbs Kujo who jumps up and lunges toward Pepper, however his foot slips on a banana peel and he is brought back down to his front knees! We bust out laughing, it is just like out of a cartoon. He is pulling along and then, "zoop," down he goes! He has a stunned and confused look on his face!

"It was nice talking to you Gary, but we have six more miles to hike today."

"Good luck!" Gary waves as Rocket and I walk into the woods.

Six miles later I sigh in exasperation, "Great, another fence stile!"

"This one looks pretty easy," Rocket says. "It is wide with wide steps, similar to steps going into a house."

"It has five steps and it isn't too steep. I'll try this one with all 4 dogs, just to see if I can make it on my own."

"Yeah, it's not like the last one where Digger and Instigator went under and Kujo and Mtn. Goat went over. Mtn. Goat is a Booger to catch!"

I carefully inch to the top of the stile while pushing Mtn. Goat behind me. Once I am straddling the top I allow the 4 dogs to join me. Mtn. Goat rushes up and over the stile in two seconds. He jumps to the other side before Instigator is halfway up. Kujo is right behind him. I hook my foot into the steps on the down side to keep from being pulled over. A minute later Instigator and Digger also make it up and over the fence stile.

"Yeah, we made it!" I exclaim, "And my arms are still attached to my body!"

"Good job. Do you see the Daffodils and the purple flowers?" Rocket asks.

"Yes. They are so beautiful. Along with the tree with the red berries. It's such a lovely day I could lay in the grass and take a nap!"

"I wish everyday was this nice," Rocket says. "I see your Dad and the truck on the other side of the river. How much junk do you think we'll have to clean out of the seat today?"

"Probably at least three bags."

We cross the bridge and greet Dad at South Fork Holston River.

**Day 50** April 7, 2011 I consult the thru hiker handbook then excitedly inform Rocket, "We will reach Partnership shelter today. They have showers!"

"Great! How far away?"

"It's eight miles to the shelter and another nine miles to the next major road crossing with GPS coordinates."

"17 miles! Are you serious?"

"It's a beautiful day for hiking."

"Fine," Rocket grumbles as she packs a change of clothes.

A few hours later we arrive at Partnership shelter all hot and sweaty. The shelter looks like a log cabin with a large covered porch. The showers are to the right of the front entrance.

The 4 dogs are sniffing as if there is someone here they know, but the shelter is empty.

"Um, Rocket, I don't think the water is hooked up to the shower. I see a pipe laying here and it looks like it should be hooked to the shower."

"Yeah, nothing is happening when I turn the knob on. Here's a sign, it says 'there is no running water until there is no chance of the pies freezing. That sucks!"

On the top of Glade Mountain, we meet Whole Roll, Bathing Beauty, and Silver Foot.

Bathing Beauty is sitting on a rock in the sun. She says, "I like to check my feet during the day, and let them air out."

"That's a good idea. Are you diabetic?" I ask.

"No, but I am a nurse and I've made it a habit to check my feet, especially when I am hiking."

"Good idea," I answer. "We usually let our feet air out while we eat lunch."

"You girls are an inspiration," Whole Roll says.

"Thanks," I reply.

"It was nice meeting ya'll," Rocket says as we get ready to depart.

"Wish you all the best in your hike," Bathing Beauty says.

A few miles later Rocket points out a jet in the sky, then an hour later we meet up with Dad at the parking area of the Lindamood School.

He says, "Do you want to sleep somewhere else. There is a dead deer carcass a few yards down the road."

"It doesn't smell bad here, but I'll walk the dogs so they can take care of their evening business and let you know what I decide when I get back."

Up closer to the deer, it is gross, nasty, smelly and disgusting. There are flies buzzing around. I quickly haul the dogs back and retreat to fresher smelling air.

"I think this is okay Dad. The deer carcass is far enough away from the truck, I still can't smell it up here."

**Day 51** At the top of the first grassy hill, Rocket and I look back. Rocket points out a police vehicle, "Is that an SUV patrol car?"

"It looks like it. I wonder if they will notice Dad parked at the old school?"

"Probably, unless he moved the truck," Rocket answers, stepping over a fallen limb.

It is sunny with a few rain showers. We cross RR tracks, and swampy areas. We hike thru fields, and over multiple bridges. We see a deer stand in the woods, and green plants resembling Romaine Lettuce. The birds are chirping their motivation for us to keep hiking. There are multiple A-frame fence stiles to cross. The stepping boards are nailed flat to the frame, leaving the two-inch edge to step on, so it is difficult for the dogs to climb over.

"Kelly, thank you for helping with the fence stiles. I don't know how I would manage on my own."

"You would figure something out. For one you can make Mountain Goat crawl under the fence like the other dogs. He thinks he's human climbing over the fence stiles like us."

"I wish Digger wasn't so scared to go over the fence stile. It's annoying having to take his backpack off, then laying on the ground to slide his leash to you, so you can maneuver him through the wooden support boards, and to the other side."

"Maybe this is the last stile for a while," Rocket says.

"I hope so!" I say I putting Digger's backpack back on.

"I can walk Instigator if you want so he doesn't get squished by the big dogs," Rocket volunteers.

"That would be fantastic!"

A short while later, we stop to take pictures of cows. "I'm going to go ahead a way. Kujo, Mtn. Goat, and Digger are pulling, jumping, barking, and trying to get the cows," I say. "I don't want them to get loose and run in the field."

"Okay, I'll be right behind you. I just want to get a little closer to the cows so I can see the calves better," Rocket says as she climbs up a five-foot ramp near the edge of the cow field.

When Instigator sees the other dogs leaving without him, he lunges after us. Rocket isn't expecting his burst of energy, and the wooden ramp she is standing on is slippery and wet from the rain.

"Ouch!" Rocket hollers, "Come get your dumb dog! He just made me fall!"

I rush over and thankfully Rocket isn't hurt. I put Instigator on a short leash.

We hike through more fields, and a deciduous forest. Rocket finds an adorable newt baby to model for some awesome pictures. The newt baby is so cute, he might replace the GEICO gecko one day.

I continue hiking while Rocket is taking pictures.

This is the tallest fence stile I have seen!

It's at least eight feet tall with multiple boards crisscrossed underneath to provide support and stability. Everything is muddy and I really don't want to crawl on the nasty ground today.

I'm still trying to figure out how to cross the stile when Rocket catches up.

"Thanks for waiting," Rocket says. "I can go across first, then send the dogs to me under the stile matrix of boards.

"I was trying to see if I could get across without help, but I wasn't successful," I sigh. "Thanks for helping again."

On the other side of the fence is the Holston River bridge. Also, there is a flood marker, which shows the highest the water levels have reached. Water isn't at the top of the marker, but it is about two inches from flooding the bridge.

1.6 miles before stopping, we have to cross a "stream" that doesn't have a bridge. It is too big to jump across, and there are few stepping stones. The ground leading to the stream is muddy. Rocket manages easily with her hiking poles, whereas I can't use hiking poles because I have 4 dogs on four leashes. I give it my best shot.

"Obviously, if I am using the stepping stones, then you can't" I shout at Mtn. Goat.

He looks at me, looks at the muddy water, then jumps on the rock I'm standing on.

I fall forward stepping in the gooey mud and jerking the leashes forward. Mtn. Goat falls off the rock and not only his feet get muddy, but his nose as well (he hates, muddy wet feet). The other three dogs only have muddy feet.

I look down exasperated, "I have mud on my shoes, and my pants leg. Now my feet are wet!"

Rocket can barely speak for laughing so hard. "Look at Mtn. Goat's face, he looks so disgusted! He keeps shaking his feet as if he can shake the mud off.

Kujo, Digger and Instigator are unfazed by the mud on their feet. Perhaps they are even laughing about the mud on Mtn. Goat's face!

We end the day at the O'Lystery Pavilion. We even have time for a refreshing bath in the stream before supper. The sun is warm and cozy. The pavilion is private and has a sign that says "Do Not use."

I ask, "Dad, did an SUV police vehicle stop and the PoPo get out to talk to you this morning?"

"Yes, they wanted to know what I was doing and if I was okay."

Rocket says, "We saw the vehicle this morning and wondered if they would say anything."

"They seem real friendly," Dad says.

"It's good to know they monitor the trail crossings," Rocket says.

"I agree. This is a nice place to stop," I say. "The stream is nearby and the parking area has gravel. The clouds look like a white splash of water in the clear blue sky."

"I'm going to bring out the bin to sit on when we eat supper." I say sliding the food bin to the ground.

Crack!

"Oops!" Dad says. "I didn't know the bin would break if I sat on it."

"It's probably not as stable because the 40 lb. of dog food I put in is almost empty. I'll have to make sure it is in the back from now on or the rain will drip from the glass onto the container and get the dog food all wet and moldy. I guess we won't be sitting on the bins anymore, and we will have to make sure there is enough stuff inside all the bins to keep them from collapsing when you lay on them Dad," I say.

"I guess so," Dad says.

**Day 52** We see 26, yellow, orange, red and black centipedes, on the way up Bushy Mountain.

We cross streams, which have swelled past the carefully placed stepping stones. Rocket finds a wooden carved hiking stick. I use it to make crossing streams easier. Rocket and I pole vault across one extremely large water crossing.

I am 50% successful. Mtn. Goat lays down in the middle of the stream at the precise moment I'm vaulting across the stream. One foot splashes into water up to my calf. The other makes it to dry land. At the next stream crossing Mtn. Goat stops at the edge at the precise moment I am hopping from rock to rock. The water crsts the top of my hiking boots as I slip off the rock.

I glare.

Mtn. Goat grins.

Rocket says, "Look at the clouds. It is getting darker. There is a fish shaped cloud in the sky, and it is blowing in quickly toward us."

"The wind is blowing in cold air. I can feel the temperature change! It's colder now at 1:45 p.m. than it was this morning at 10:00 a.m.

I shiver. We are in an exposed field. The trees are a long way away, and Chestnut Knob Shelter is at least two miles away, according to the thru hiker book."

Rocket and I both jump as thunder rumbles loudly. Thick black thunder clouds rush in, blocking the sun except for a faint orange-ish pink hue on the horizon. The dogs are anxious and jerk on the leashes as a bolt of lightning strikes the field in front of us. We are close to 4000 feet above sea level, in an open field during a lightning storm! The thunder and lightning is 8 seconds apart!

We run as fast as we can in an attempt to cross the open field. The next bolt of lightning strikes 50 feet away!

We see Chestnut Knob Shelter and sprint toward it.

There is another boom of thunder and almost simultaneous bold of lightning. Seconds later, we make it to the shelter. Immediately the skies open-up. Rain and hail come pouring down. We are under the ledge of the shelter.

Rocket jerks on the door. "I can't get it open," she gasps.

I jerk on the handle too, but it barely moves. Finally, both of us together, pull the door open.

I glance warily upwards as we enter, expecting some kind of booby trap; no buckets of water, or dead rats fall on our head!

Once inside, we notice the door is rigged up with a rope and a rock to keep the door from blowing open in the wind. It is cool and dry inside. I let the dogs come into the shelter. There is no one else around. The dogs are overjoyed to get out of the rain. They behave superbly!

We wait until it looks like the storm has passed, then we start hiking again. After 45 minutes, it starts raining again. The terrain is rocky and rugged. The rain drops collect on Rocket and my glasses.

"I can't see anything in this rain and fog." I grumble.

"Me either," Rocket says. "We are the blind leading the blind."

"At least wc have seeing eye dogs. They are untrained, but better than nothing."

After a while it stops raining again and we are able to clear the rain and fog from our glasses then, we glimpse the town below. We keep thinking, any minute, we will reach the road.

It takes forever! We finally make it to VA 623.

Surprise, surprise, Dad isn't waiting. It's drizzling rain again. Rocket and I have our rain gear on, but the dogs have nothing to keep them dry. We sit huddled together on a cold wet rock near the parking area and try not to freeze. There aren't any grassy areas so the dogs sit in the mud beside the rock.

"Do you think your Dad got the SPOT GPS?" Rocket asks.

"He should have. We sent it two hours ago!"

"What if he doesn't come, or he can't find us?"

"The next shelter is three miles away. We can always hike there for the night."

"What about the dogs?"

"They'll have to stay in the shelter too since I didn't carry the tent with our daypack. I'll try to call Dad again, then if he's not here in an hour we'll hike to the shelter."

"Okay," Rocket replies. "I'm cold, but I want some ice cream."

With my teeth chattering, I call Dad, again. This time he answers, "Hello, are ya'll at the parking area?"

"Y-y-yes. W-we've been here for a few minutes. W-w-where are you?"

"I was there earlier and a couple of hikers came out and needed a ride to town. They were cold and wet so I told them I could take them to town. I'm on the way back now."

"W-w-we're pretty cold too. W-we hurried so we could get out of the rain. I s-s-sent the spot GPS ahead of time. D-d-did you get it?"

"Yes."

"H-h-how much longer until y-you get here?"

"About 25 minutes."

"Is th-there anywhere to get ice cream on the way?"

"If I see anywhere I will get some. See you soon."

"O-o-okay. Love you bye."

Looking at Rocket I explain, "Dad gave s-some hikers a ride to town, but he'll be here s-soon."

Rocket and I sit and shiver until Dad finally arrives.

"Ahh, it feels wonderful in here," I sigh climbing into the cab with Rocket and Dad to get warm.

"I didn't see anywhere for ice cream," Dad says.

"We probably don't need it anyway," Rocket says still shivering despite the warm cab.

"Did the hikers give you any gas money?" I ask.

"No," Dad mumbles, then adds cheerfully, "I bought a rotisserie chicken earlier. Do ya'll want some?"

"Sure," Rocket and I answer.

**Day 53** Upon waking I laugh and quietly sing, "I can see clearly now, the rain is gone, I can see all obstacles in my way..." (Johnny Nash).

I tap on the glass to wake Rocket."

"I'm not hiking in the rain again!" she exclaims.

I laugh harder, "Rocket, the weather is bipolar. There isn't a cloud in the sky today and its already warm enough I don't need my jacket."

"Fine. I'll get up in five more minutes."

I hum to myself as I feed the dogs, "It's hot and then cold..." (a slight variation of Katy Perry's song).

We've barely hiked two miles, when Rocket suddenly stops in front of me. Kujo almost runs her over, then Digger jerks me off the trail toward a gray and brown snake slithering off into the woods.

Rocket scowls at me and says, "You can go first."

I grimace and look questioningly, "I'm sorry if Kujo stepped on you."

"I don't want to step on a snake and I don't want to get run over by your dogs!" Rocket exclaims.

A half a mile later we startle another snake off the trail. Kujo steps on its tail. The first two snakes we have seen on the trail. The snakes didn't look poisonous, but they did blend in with the leaves.

The creeks are swollen and difficult to cross. Laurel Creek campsite is complete with outdoor T.V. recliner, bucket seat from a vehicle, picnic table with 2-liter soda, and a tire swing. A few miles later, we cross the wide, twisting, winding Laurel Creek. The dogs lay down in it.

"I have sweat pouring into my eyes. I'm taking a break and I'm going to rinse my hair it the stream," Rocket says.

"Great idea."

The water is cold enough to steal my breath, but it also feels wonderful on my hot skin. We continue hiking until our snack break at the intersection for Boss Trail.

Rocket comes back from the woods carrying a very nice looking Leki hiking pole.

"Where did that pole come from?" I ask.

I saw it buried under leaves," Rocket answers.

"You sure are good at finding things," I say while longingly looking at the Leki pole.

"It was right in front of you. I don't see how you didn't see it," Rocket says.

"I can't ever find four leaf clovers either, but you seem to find them easily."

"You can use it when you don't have the dogs."

We continue hiking and eventually reach the road walk from US 52 over I-77 to the north end of VA 612. There is a small water fall trickling from the boulder alongside the road and there are tiny yellow flowers blooming.

After the mile and a half hike on hot asphalt we see Dad waiting in the parking area with the white truck with the too short purple camper.

I say, "Yeah, you found us today."

Dad says, "Yes, this place was easy to find."

A few yards away there are more dead animal carcasses.

Dad, Rocket, and I relax and talk sitting on the tailgate of the truck. The dogs are stationed on the four corners of the truck.

Hikers, Elf and Denver pass us, then we meet CloudWalker.

"That's a fine looking Leki pole you have," CloudWalker comments. "I had one, but I lost it a few miles before the road. I laid it down when I took a break, then I couldn't find it again."

Rocket and I look at each other. I raise my eyebrow in question. The pole could be his, or he could be making up a good story.

Rocket says, "I found the pole today, but it sounds like it might be yours."

"Thanks," CloudWalker says.

**Day 54** A few miles after we start there is a ten-foot-high pile of dead animal carcasses. Rocket covers her nose, but I don't have a free hand. I hold my breath and try not to gag when the putrid fumes waft up my nose.

The dogs on the other hand, are barking frantically, and lunging toward the pile of bones. I practically pull my arms out of socket dragging them down the trail. They keep turning around. Their leashes, and feet get tangled! I trip, then cough and gag as a waft of putrid air enters my nose. I frantically pull on the leashes, then break into a run to get away from the smell of decaying animals.

I am determined the dogs will not romp with the dead carcasses. Smelling or touching them after a romp with dead animal juices is ghastly!

It gets hotter and hotter as the sun rises.

After 17.5 miles of hiking, we stop at VA 606 parking area. There are dead fish, and trash littered everywhere.

"Let's drive to Trent's Grocery for snacks, and to get away from the awful smell of dead animals!" I say.

"I second that," Rocket says.

We load up in the truck and drive to the store. We see a sign indicating showers at the campground behind the store.

"I'd love to take a shower!" I exclaim.

"Me too!" Rocket chimes in.

The showers aren't aesthetically pleasing. They are concrete, and there are bugs and spiders. The worst part is the water isn't running properly, and there is NO hot water.

Dad says, "I'll get the hot water running for you girls. I just need to look at the pipes and check the hot water on/off knob."

Dad turns the hot water on. "Thanks Dad, I love you!"

We also do laundry.

"Ouch!" I exclaim jerking my hand back from putting clothes in the dryer.

"What's wrong?" Rocket asks.

"There is an exposed wire on the dryer that shocked me, but I'm okay."

Rocket says, "Is it okay to drink the well water? What if it's contaminated?"

"I'm sure it's fine or they would have to post a sign saying not to drink it," I answer. "You don't have to drink the water, but I am filling the gallon water containers with it."

We spend the night on the toilet violently throwing up, and having diarrhea.

Just kidding. The well water is fine.

However, there is a lot of rain during the night. There is a tornado 30 miles away that causes damage. Back home there are also tornado's that cause damage and destroy many sections of the Pine Mtn. Trail.

Girl (Hiking) with 4 Dogs

**Day 55** April 12, 2011 CloudWalker passes us while we are getting ready to leave the truck. We bring up the topic of the odorous pile of dead bones we smelled yesterday.

CloudWalker says, "Did you know there were dog skulls in that pile?"

"I didn't get close, but that explains why the dogs were so determined to get to the pile of dead bones," I say as chills run down my spine.

"That's disgusting," Rocket says. "How would all those bones get there?"

"I don't know," CloudWalker answers, "but I plan to report it to the authorities."

"Good idea," Rocket and I agree.

I leave the dogs with Dad, so Rocket and I can stay at Woods Hole Hostel. The Hostel is "pet friendly," however, my pets aren't always friendly, (Kujo), or well behaved (Instigator, Digger and Mountain Goat). I want to relax and enjoy the camaraderie at the hostel.

"Is that a squirrels nest?" Rocket asks looking up in the trees.

I look up and see a large nest made from small twigs and leaves hanging in the trees. "I guess so. I don't know what else it could be."

Later I see a mutated tree with an enlarged branch that resembles a porcupine and Rocket points out a black salamander camouflaged in the leaves.

We have a fairly flat day of hiking except one large mountain which increase by 1372 feet over a three-mile distance just north of Wapiti Shelter. Then there are more elevation changes until we Reach Woods Hole Hostel.

Our motivation for the day is supper! For $12, we can have a "family style dinner."

After over 14 miles of hiking, we make it to Woods Hole Hostel in time for supper. We have an entrée, salad with fresh spinach, strawberries, and toasted pecans, garlic bread, and lasagna. Everyone cooks, eats, and cleans up together. A communal living theory. We meet Switch Back and One More, who meet up every year to hike a section of the trail together. We see StillWater, Niners,

Katmando, StormSong, TreeBeard, and a few other thru hikers, however they didn't want to participate in the community meal, they prefer restaurant style service, where they don't have to clean up afterwards.

During supper Switch Back explains, "The reason the trail zig-zags back and forth going up the mountain is to keep the trail from eroding so quickly and to make it easier to hike up the mountain. The more switchbacks there are, the steeper the mountain."

"That makes sense," Rocket says.

We learn, Neville, the current hostel owner is following in her grandmothers footsteps, in opening up the hostel for hiker use. Her husband thru-hiked the trail a few years before, and they both strive to live off the land as much as possible. They have a garden and trade with their neighbors for fresh milk and other items. They also have two cats and a friendly dog, Omakoa, which means spirit leader. The dog receives scraps from hikers, and I wonder if some are sharing their beer as well.

Before we leave the main house to go to the hiker hostel quarters, Switch Back and One More offer to pay for Rocket and my breakfast at the main house in the morning. We say, "Thanks for the Trail Magic!" and then have to explain what that means.

The hiker hostel is in a converted barn, however if you want to pay more money you can get a room in the main house and use the flushing toilet instead of a privy.

Later when we return to the hostel, Rocket says, "Hey, StillWater and Niners, thank you for hiking to the next shelter so Girl w/ 4 Dogs and I could stay at Wise Shelter."

Niners says, "We figured there would be more room at Old Orchard Shelter, but when we arrived the shelter was full. StormSong and TreeBeard had to set up their tent in the rain. We got soaking wet!"

"I'm sorry you got wet," I say.

StillWater chimes in, "The next morning, even though it was chilly, I was hiking in my boxers, I didn't want to wear cold wet clothes, nor did I want them inside my backpack getting all my dry gear and overnight clothes wet. I tied all my wet clothes on the outside of my backpack. I was hiking alone, lost in my thoughts. I rounded a corner and stopped dead still. There was a bear on the trail. Right in front of me! My mouth went dry, I could feel the blood pumping in my brain and muscles. All I could see was the bear in front of me. I stood completely still for a minute, then I raised my hands in surrender and start to back away. The bear looked at me in disgust, huffed at me, then turned and walked back into the woods. I almost pissed all over myself!"

Everyone starts laughing. Someone says, "The bear probably thought you were a bear without fur!" We laugh so hard tears are rolling down our cheeks.

Amenities at the hostel include; an aluminum tub with antique style washing board for free laundry, or $5 for the regular washing machine. Also, there is a kitchen area in the hiker hostel, and most of the thru hikers cook and hang out near the kitchen. The sleeping quarters are bunk style, Mattresses are laid out on the wooden floor. Rocket and each claim a mattress. I curl up in my warm sleeping bag and promptly fall asleep on the soft mattress.

**Day 56** Breakfast is delicious and filling. We have fresh strawberries, pancakes, and milk.

As we finish breakfast and prepare to leave, One More says, "Live every day to the Fullest!"

SwithchBack adds, "May life be a great adventure!"

Again, we thank them for a wonderful breakfast and wish them happy trails as they continue to hike.

Back inside the hiker hostel, I ask, "Rocket, instead of staying another day do you want to hike with our friends as far as Pearisburg, VA today?"

Rocket ponders for a minute then answers, "No offense, but it might be fun to talk to someone besides you for a while. Let's pack up and hike out with the guys. It's only ten miles to town."

It is clear and sunny today. We eat lunch with the guys on top of a small mountain. The view at Angels Rest is beautiful, and we can see a small town in the distance.

After lunch, The Five Guys pick-up their pace and Rocket and I are left behind. We hike thru rock boulders as tall as houses and I am glad Rocket is letting me use her hiking stick today.

As we descend the mountain, into the valley where Pearisburg is, we are passed by the three bears, Teddy, Koala, and Kodiak.

Upon entering Pearisburg, we see a "Hazmat" team at the Ford building. It sparks our curiosity, but we don't get closer since we aren't wearing hazmat gear.

We hike thru town until we see Dad in the white truck with the purple camper. We then ride to the Food Lion and buy a rotisserie chicken to split.

Dad says, "I didn't feed the dogs yet."

"Okay," I say. I unload the dogs, feed them and take them for a walk around town. There is a grassy area on the side of the Food Lion. After hanging out in the main parking lot, we drive to the side of the Food Lion to sleep over night.

**Day 57** Pearisburg VA After breakfast of fresh orange juice and milk, and cereal, we spend the day exploring. We stop at Goodwill, visit the library, then wash laundry at the "washateria," as Dad calls it. We see Jelly pants from Kincora hostel while at the laundry mat. He invites us to visit him at the Rendezvous Hotel later. He has extra change for the washers so we trad dollars for quarters.

"Dad," I say. "We have all these quarters now, please let us wash your clothes, blanket, and comforter. It's wet and it smells stuffy."

"Okay," Dad reluctantly agrees.

Once the clothes are washed, Dad wants to let them air dry. I say, "Dad, we don't have enough room in the truck to lay everything out to air dry. Besides, if it rains again, then it still won't be dry and the money we spent to wash everything will be a waste."

"Okay," Dad again reluctantly agrees. "I guess you can dry it then."

"Thanks," I say and glance at Rocket with a look of exasperation!

While waiting on the clothes to wash and dry, I call home to coordinate with Mom where to send my new SPOT GPS. My last one stopped working and it makes more sense to have the replacement one sent home first and then from there sent to me. The company doesn't know how long it will take to send a replacement.

Rocket's phone with T-mobile doesn't have service, so she takes advantage of the bright sunshiny day. She lays down in the parking lot to take a nap, and soak up the warmth from the sun.

I start chuckling as the police car drives up. I am fairly sure they are coming to make sure we are okay.

The PoPo gets out, looks at Dad and I, then glances to Rocket sleeping on the asphalt, he quickly looks back at us dumbfounded and questioningly, then asks, "Is she okay?"

I know better than to be laughing while the PoPo is so serious so I bite my cheeks to keep from grinning, then as seriously as possible I explain, "Yes she's fine, just tired. She and I are thru hiking. We meet my Dad when we are in town. Today we needed to do laundry. She fell asleep while I was on the phone."

The PoPo says, "She can't sleep in the parking lot."

I gently nudge Rocket and tell her to wake up.

She's wakes up, sees the police officer and says, "What's going on?"

We explain that he was concerned about her. She says, "I'm fine."

After a few more minutes and assurances, the Po Po eventually leaves.

We finish the laundry, then head to The Rendezvous. JellyPants lets us use the shower in his hotel room, and we use his microwave for popcorn. He offers to let us stay with him, but we are okay sleeping in the truck.

We see The Brothers in the parking lot. They are driving a big black, truck.

"Hey guys," Rocket says. "Fancy meeting you here."

Two Medicine says, "We took a few days off and are ready to hike again."

"I'm glad ya'll didn't give up," I say.

"Me too," Train Wreck adds.

It's noisy and crowded at the hotel. The dogs won't settle down, so we drive back to the Food Lion for the night.

**Day 58** Another sunny hot day. We hike up into the mountains, and see mountains and fields throughout the day. Most of the trees are still bare and winter brown. The water supply for the dogs along the trail is sparse today. They happily drink from mud puddles.

Rocket and I stop to investigate a stagnant pond. There are multiple tadpoles and frog-lings in the pond. The dogs lap excitedly as they partake of the water. Then Digger and Kujo jump after the frogs! I lurch toward the edge of the pond, but regain my balance before falling in. They look at me with their tongues hanging out, mouth wide in a grin, tails wagging as if to say, "Thanks for putting these wonderful toys in the water you found for us. It is so much fun to play in our water!"

Rocket excitedly says, "We can't be far from 'The Captains place.' We should see the trail for the zip line any time now."

"I can't do the zip-line with the dogs."

"Fine!" Rocket says, then remains stubbornly silent.

Hours later, we descend into Stony Creek Valley. D'artagnon passes us in the parking area, but we don't see Dad. We don't have phone signal either.

Darkness is quickly approaching.

"Let's hike up the road a little way and see if he is there. He may not be able to find the parking area," I suggest.

"Sure," Rocket agrees. "It beats standing here getting cold."

After hiking two miles on the road we see the white truck with the too short purple camper at the main road, VA 635.

My mouth drops open, Dad has everything jumbled in the back of the truck. It is impossible to get to our food bin or the dog food bin without moving 20 items from the top of the bin.

Rocket is clearing out the cab.

I exclaim, "Dad, what are you doing? There is stuff everywhere. How are we supposed to get to our food or anything else in the truck! There's no room for the dogs to get in the truck!"

Dad is normally "calm, cool, and collected," but he yells, "If you don't like how I arrange the truck then I can take a bus and go home!"

I respond, "If you want to quit that is fine, but at least take the truck and the dogs with you! I don't want to manage the trail, and the dogs by myself and I can't leave the truck or the dogs behind!"

Rocket chimes in as the mediator, "Why don't we eat and feed the dogs, then ya'll can talk about this later.

"Okay," Dad and I both agree.

I grumble to myself as I move stuff around to get to the food. "I've hiked 21 miles today. I'm tired and hungry. It is getting dark and cold, and it looks like rain is coming. Now I have to move all this stuff before I can even relax!"

Maybe Dad's blood sugar is low.

Girl (Hiking) with 4 Dogs

Today is the deadline for filing taxes. I filed mine before I left and it will be direct deposited into my checking account. Maybe Dad had to find his tax papers.

**Day 59** I shiver as I leash up the dogs. The cold damp air oozes through my layers of warm clothing. I glance at Rocket and nod to let her know I am ready. We briskly head off on the trail.

We reach Bailey Gap Shelter, a thousand feet above the valley we started from, in no time.

"I'm hiking back to the truck to stay with your Dad today. It's too cold to hike!" Rocket exclaims rubbing her arms briskly.

Both of us have chattering teeth.

"It's possible he is no longer at the parking area. Do you want to call?"

Rocket gets out her phone, but there is no signal. I pull out my phone. I don't have signal either.

I stifle a smirk.

While we stand arguing about whether or not Dad will still be at the parking area, the Three Bears pass us. They are wearing T-shirts and shorts. Rocket and I have our long pants, undershirt, fleece over shirt, hoodie/ ear warmers, and jacket on.

"We can run to warm up," I suggest.

"I'm not running while carrying my backpack!" Rocket exclaims testily.

Shortly thereafter she agrees to continue north. We each grab a handful of trail mix, then we vigorously keep hiking.

It warms up enough after noon, that Rocket and I finally stop shivering and are warm enough to take off our jackets. We breeze past War Spur Shelter. The Three Bears are eating hungrily at the shelter picnic table. They have a fourth hiker with them. He is thin, pale, and wispy. His unruly black hair stands out in stark contrast to his pale skin. His trail name is Ghost.

As we pass I glance back to see why Digger and Instigator are lagging behind. Instigator kicks dirt backward with his hind feet and Digger is wagging his tail so happily it hits one hip then the other.

"Come on boys," I say tugging on the leashes.

As we disappear down the trail I hear one Bear say, "Maybe we should hike to the next shelter. We can't let those girls with the dogs pass us!"

Their voices fade and Rocket and I bust into hysterical laughter.

Kujo looks at us as if we've lost our minds.

"Did you see the Bears with their mouths hanging open?" Rocket asks.

"They were shocked to see two girls and 4 dogs lumbering by." I double over again in laughter.

The Bears pass us six miles later, just before Laurel Creek Shelter. They are moving furiously up the trail, almost at a run. Kodiak has a look of fierce concentration on his face, Teddy is grim faced, and Koala is resolute. Ghost trails silently behind them. His face is devoid of emotion.

Rocket and I look at each other and grin. We both start laughing so hard again that we have to stop to catch our breath.

We cross yet another stream before reaching Laurel Creek Shelter.

We pass the Three Bears and Ghost again at Laurel Creek shelter.

Rocket says, "It's good to see ya'll again."

"Sure," they mumble, not looking pleased to see us.

"I'm glad it warmed up today. It was freezing this morning. How were ya'll able to hike in shorts?" I ask.

"We were moving too fast to be cold," Kodiak answers.

"How far are you girls hiking today?" Teddy asks in mild amazement.

"Only two and a half more miles. Almost 19 total for the day. My Dad is meeting us at the next road crossing."

"How do you hike with all those dogs?" Koala asks.

"Very carefully," I answer. "We aren't fast, but we have endurance, and hike a consistent pace. Also, it saves time sleeping in the truck. I still have dogs to tend to, but not dogs and tent."

Ghost watches silently from the shadows.

"Good luck Girl with 4 Dogs and Rocket," Teddy says.

"You hike faster than we thought you would," chimes in Koala.

Girl (Hiking) with 4 Dogs

We say goodbye and keep hiking to Sinking Creek VA 42 to meet Dad. The last rays of daylight fade as we pass a barn with hay inside near the road. There is faint pink and dark blue tints in the sky. We cross multiple fence stiles in the fading light before finally reaching Dad.

**Day 60** April 17, 2011 The morning greets me with a beautiful view of multicolored trees in the distance on the mountains. There are dark and light greens with shades of orange and red mixed in. The color scheme is so perfect it resembles a painting. The trees are snuggled together like a big cozy bed. I close my eyes for a minute and imagine myself floating in the midst of such perfection. I no longer have worries or cares.

Did AJ ever love me?

A still small voice whispers inside my head. My love for you is sufficient. See what all I have made for you?

I open my eyes. At this moment, I feel such love and contentment. God has given me the world with such unimaginable beauty. He loves me so much he gave His wonderful son, Jesus, to die for my sins so that one day I can be in heaven with him. The beauty in heaven is even more amazing than the scene before me. The beauty surrounds me and holds me close. It comforts me. I know I am loved.

I am safe.

I am never alone.

Even though I am not perfect and I'm not good enough in so many ways. God still loves me and he always will.

"Jesus loves me, this I know," I smile as healing tears trickle down my cheeks.

In an instant, Rocket brings me back to the present. "Instigator just pooped on the trail," she informs me.

"Thanks," I mutter backtracking to clean up after Instigator.

A short while later, we cross the road and approach Kieffer Oak, which is the largest tree on the AT in the Southern section. It is 18 feet around and over 300 years old.

"Do you want to hug a tree today?" I jokingly ask.

"Sure," Rocket answers. "You get on one side and I'll get on the other. Let's see if we can reach around the tree."

Rocket and I give the tree a big hug, one on each side. Rocket extends her hiking poles around, but the tree is so big, I can't reach the poles.

The dogs just pee on the tree and look at us expectantly saying, "We claimed the tree for ya'll. Can we go already?"

We hike thru a field with cows. There is cow prints, grass, and mud, but not blazes. I look at Kujo suspiciously. Is he following the AT or a cow?

Finally, we see a sign indicating the Eastern Continental Divide, which can be colder and have more snow in the winter due to "orographic enhancement and cooler temperatures with elevation" (Wikipedia.org). It is an imaginary line on the mountains indicating which way the water will fall when it rains (blueridge.now.com). Our sign indicates on the right/east side, the water will travel 405 miles before eventually making it to the Atlantic Ocean and on the left/west side it will travel 1920 miles before reaching the Gulf of Mexico.

On the descent from Sinking Creek Mountain we meet, Red Beard and Curly who are section hikers from Maryland. Next at Niday Shelter we meet Pa Bert, OtterBill, and K8, they are out for the weekend to fish at trout creek.

We meet up with Dad at VA 621, Craig Creek Road, and meet Blanche and Mervin, two trail maintainers. Dad is rummaging in the truck for a can opener.

Blanche signs my thru-hiker hand book, then says conspiratorially, "We were wondering why there was a strange truck parked here with cages in the back. My husband and I are relieved to see you girls here with the dogs, although how you manage to hike with 4 dogs I'll never understand." She looks at Rocket and I and whispers, "No offense but, your Dad is rough around the edges. He has all that facial hair, his hair is long and unkempt, and he looks like he's been wearing the same clothes for days. We wanted to make sure he wasn't up to mischief. We take pride in maintaining our section of the trail and we don't want anything to happen to our hikers."

I sigh, "I understand how you could be concerned. As you now know we have the kennels in the back for the dogs when we sleep in the truck or drive into town."

Rocket adds, "If I came upon a truck with a short camper shell and cages in the back my imagination would go wild too. We appreciate you looking out for campers hiking."

"Your Dad is very nice," Mervin says. "I can see he has difficulty walking, yet he still wants to help you take care of the dogs. He was watching the trail anxiously until you arrived. You are very lucky to have him with you."

"I know. I probably couldn't manage the trail and the dogs without his help," I respond.

**Day 61** We hike up Brush Mountain. It's chilly. At the top, we meet two elderly day hikers, Lois and Ed, with the AVA.org group. Ed looks at Instigator, smiles, and says, "You have your hands full."

"That's true," I say, "I have three more dogs, but I didn't bring them today." I'm winded from hiking up the Mountain and this elderly couple doesn't even look out of breath. I ask, "Have you been up here long? You don't look a bit tired."

Ed laughingly says, "We came up a different trail to see Audie Murphy's Monument. We parked a half mile from here and it was an easy hike."

The monument is honoring the WWII American soldier who died in a plane crash on Brush Mountain. There are butterflies flying around the monument, like a busy family taking care and honoring our fallen soldier. They provide comfort and joy for eternity with their presence. There is even a butterfly chrysalis.

Rocket says, "The rock piles around the monument are neat. We added our own rocks."

Lois asks, "What do you girls do?"

I answer and tell her about working as a nurse and saving money to hike the trail. Before Rocket can say anything, Lois asks, "Is this your daughter?"

What!?

I'm only three months older than Rocket! Do I look like I'm in my 50's?

I'm stunned speechless so Rocket answers, "No, we are just friends." I can tell she's about to have an apocalyptic fit of laughter!

I glare at her.

As we are leaving, Ed says, "You don't look old enough to be your friend's mom. You just sound very mature for your age."

I give him a "yeah right" look and say, "Thanks, now I don't feel so old."

He laughs.

Just before Trout Creek we meet another couple, Sandy and Dale. She is a vet Tech from Naples, FL. He has a homemade walking stick with a snake hook on the end. They don't think I'm an old woman, at least they don't say so.

After Pickle Branch Shelter while clamoring over rocks and boulders, we meet Suicidal. He says menacingly, "I hate it when people hike on the trail with dogs. They don't know how to keep the dogs from running over people." His face is tight and sneered into an ugly scowl as he looks at Instigator. I can see his nostrils flaring and his teeth grinding. He takes an intimidating step forward.

I look him right in the eyes standing my ground and say, "Too bad they don't keep their dogs on a leash like I have mine on a leash. I usually have three more dogs, but a fellow hiker said Dragon's tooth is difficult with dogs so I left the other three with my Dad."

Rocket interjects, "We are meeting Dad at the end of the day today. Are you thru hiking?"

"Yes. I've hiked the trail before, but I didn't finish certain sections fast enough so I have to hike them again." He looks momentarily confused and lost in his own thoughts of hiking the trail faster. He steps back fractionally.

"Okay," I say and look questioningly at Rocket.

She looks back and shrugs her shoulders.

Rocket swiftly passes Suicidal. Instigator and I are right on her heels.

"Good luck," Rocket says and we expeditiously keep hiking.

Once out of ear shot, I say, "I'll be happy to finish the trail in any amount of time."

"Me too," Rocket agrees.

At Cove Mountain, we have a scenic view of the mountains and see tiny chickpea plants, then we meet Stroke and Safari.

Stroke says, "Did you girls pass an older guy with greasy black hair?"

"Suicidal?" Rocket asks.

"Yes. He was yelling and cussing at us. He threatened to push us off the rocks if we didn't move out of his way!" Safari exclaims.

"He told us dogs shouldn't be allowed on the trail," I add.

"He gave us the creeps," Stroke says.

"I think he has mental health issues. He probably stopped taking his medicine," I say.

"Good luck hiking. Be careful," Safari says.

"Thanks. Ya'll too," Rocket says.

In no time, we reach Dragon's tooth. For a short distance the trail consist of hiking on the edge of jagged rocks and boulders. It wouldn't have been a challenge for the other three dogs.

Instigator manages easily. I don't even have to pick him up once!

At the bottom of the boulder, I find the sole of someone's shoe. I pick it up and carry it so I can say I have someone's sole. Within minutes it starts to drizzle. I put down the sole to put on rain gear. Once I have my rain gear on, Rocket and I traipse again on the AT.

The sole is lost again.

We are hiking an average of 15.3 miles a day.

We meet Dad at Newport Rd., then hike to the store for snacks.

On the way back I mention, "Rocket if we hike 25 miles tomorrow then we can still slack pack, otherwise we have to carry our tent and sleeping bags and stay on the trail."

Rocket says, "Do whatever you want. I don't know if I'm hiking tomorrow anyway."

"Why not?" I ask.

"Because I'm tired, my knees keep buckling, I don't want to carry a full backpack, and I don't want to hike 25 miles in a day. That is too far."

"Well if you aren't hiking with me anyway, then I'm going to hike the 25 miles. I'll take my tent and sleeping bag in case I can't make the whole trip."

"Fine," Rocket says.

**Day 62** It's dark when the 4 dogs and I get up, eat and begin our long day. Rocket and Dad are still sleeping.

It's barely 7:00 a.m. when we cross the first fence stile. Then 30 minutes later, we cross another fence stile. By the third stile, I'm ready to pay Rocket to hike with me again. I hook the dogs to the backpack and push it under the fence, then I climb over the fence.

A short while later, another fence stile looms ahead.

I have a fence stile to cross that is surrounded by what resembles an electric fence. There are cows, and calves in the field. I look for a warning sign on the fence to indicate if it is electric. I don't see a sign, I even tap the fence, to make sure I don't feel electricity.

I gently lift the fence, so Kujo can crawl under, he has the dog food in his backpack. However, as I lift the fence and push Kujo under, there is a shock through my right arm and out my left hand. Kujo, who I'm holding in my left hand, yelps and jumps back!

There is electricity after all. Okay, no going under the fence. There is no one to catch the dogs on the other side if I let them loose to go over the stile, and I'm 100% sure they will chase the cows if they are let loose.

There is a piece of wood in the way for going under the stile.

About this time, I look up and see a bull staring at us.

Help! We are all going to be stampeded by a bull!

He is black with white horns. His stance is wide and intimidating. His black eyes look rather perturbed. With my heart racing, and adrenaline pumping, I decide the dogs can go under the stile after all. I push Instigator through the wooden maze under the stile, and hook his leash on the wooden step. I make the other three "sit" and "stay" while I take off the backpack and throw it on the other side. Then, I convince Mtn. Goat to crawl under the stile, I clamp his carabineer onto Instigator's leash. Digger goes under next without too much difficulty. I climb over the stile and hook all three leashes onto the backpack on the other side. The cows on the north side are not as fierce looking and they don't have horns. I glare at the dogs, and in my sternest voice, tell them to be quiet.

Kujo is understandably hesitant to go anywhere near the fence. My hands are shaking and my legs feel weak.

In the meantime, the bull is inching closer and is staring at Kujo and I with hatred in his glowing red eyes. He stomps his foot at us. His head is lowered and his huge, sharp, white, pointy horns are looking viscous. I pick up a rotten piece of wood just in case the bull charges.  I take Kujo's backpack off and with shaking hands, shove him under the fence stile.

We finally all make it safely to the other side.  I gulp in lungs full of air and sit for a minute on the bottom of the fence stile until I stop shaking.

Miracle of all miracles the dogs remain blessedly silent.

Ironically, once on the other side of the fence, there is a sign for SOBO's to see, stating the fence is electric.

Unfortunately, there are two more fence stiles in short succession.  We crawl under the first and over the second. Fortunately, none are as hard to cross as the one with the bull.

I see Dad and Rocket parked at VA 311 parking area in Catawba, VA.

I tell them about my near brush with death and I ask Rocket, "Do you want to hike the rest of the way with me?  I could sure use you help with dogs and the fence stiles."

"No, it's too cold and too far"

"It's warming up and there is only 20 miles left."

"Take your dogs and keep going.  I'm not coming with you."

"Okay, suit yourself," I say.

Dad offers some Little Debbie's, and says, "I'll see you in Daleville."

Next, I hike McAfee Knob.  It is breathtaking.  I know Rocket would love to see the view over the mountains.  She would love to see the eagles flying overhead, the huge rock crevices, and hundred-foot drop offs over the edge of the cliff.  I wouldn't recommend hiking the area with poor visibility.

I see deer a few times and the dogs try to pull my arms off going after them.  Also, there are a million and one up hills and down hills.

I'm never going to finish!

There is a stream crossing near Lambert's Meadow Campsite that has a brown, semi-formed substance that resembled stool.  Gag!

At Lamberts Meadow Shelter, Clod Hopper, a 48 + year old guy is brewing a concoction, and talking about how he enjoys scalding people with hot coffee.

Hmm, I'm not as tired as I thought.

I smile and say, "Good luck hiking." I quickly retreat.

Later, I meet a trail maintainer named, Homer. Homer says, "You only have a few more miles to until you reach town. The hiking is easier from here."

"Thanks for the information and for all your work to keep the trails lovely," I say as we pass.

A few miles before reaching town I notice graffiti on the rocks and litter on the ground.

I finally make it to Daleville, where I meet Dad and Rocket, just as the sun is going down. Luckily, the last stretch of trail before reaching town is flat and easy. I sit for a while in the parking lot of the dry cleaners, too tired to move.

Dad and Rocket take care of the dogs.

While eating we see D'artagnon, Ghost, and the Three Bears walking back from the store.

"Wow," one of the bears says, "You girls aren't far behind."

"Did ya'll get in today?" I ask

"We got in early this morning and are heading out tomorrow morning," Teddy says.

D'artagnon asks, "How are the dogs holding up?"

"They are good. We just hike 25.7 miles and they don't even act tired!"

"Well, Girl with 4 Dogs and Rocket, we are leaving laundry detergent at the hotel. Be sure to use some. It was cheaper to buy a large container since we all had to do laundry," D'artagnon says.

"Ya'll are so kind. Thanks," I say.

Since it is late I can't justify spending money for a hotel tonight. We agree to sleep in the truck in the parking lot of the dry cleaners.

**Day 63** We've had rain over the last week and water has dripped from the too short camper shell into the squished food bin. It's sunny today and we have a few hours to kill before we can check into the hotel room. I feed the dogs then hook them to the outside of the truck.

"Rocket, do you want to help me sort thru the food bin? We can dry everything salvageable and throw away anything that is ruined," I say.

"Sure," she replies.

Dad is in the cab of the truck picking at the sore on his leg.

Girl (Hiking) with 4 Dogs

The sun has been up for about an hour. I few cars drive through the dry cleaner parking lot. One car circles all the way around before disappearing on the opposite side of the building. I begin to wonder whether it is a good idea to hang out in the same parking lot we spent the night in, but I ignore my subconscious.

Around 10 a.m. Rocket and I have the truck fully unloaded. Food, multiple gallons of water, thrift store purchases, wet dog backpacks and jackets, wet clothes and sleeping gear, a shovel for outdoor bathroom use, along with bags filled with trail litter, are strewn everywhere.

We are drying out the last salvageable food items when I look up and see a cop car pulling into the parking lot. I look at Rocket and we both shrug.

"What can be happening this early on a Wednesday morning, to attract the attention of the police?" I ask.

"I don't know. We were here all night and I didn't see or hear anything unusual. The dogs are relatively calm and quiet. For once." Rocket answers.

"I wonder if the dry cleaners are laundering dirty money," I jokingly ask Rocket.

"If so I don't want to be here," Rocket replies.

We finish sorting and drying items, then we put our extra clothes, store purchase, and gear in the broken bin and stuff it farther into the truck.

Shortly after the first police car arrives, a second car drives up. One officer goes inside the dry cleaners, and the other one stays outside in his vehicle.

"What is going on?" I ask again.

We don't have to wait long to find out.

The first officer, who is slightly heavy set with dark prematurely balding hair, returns from the dry cleaners, then both officers cautiously approach us. When they are a good 20 feet away "Baldey" stays back while "Slim," the taller skinny, dark haired officer ventures closer.

"What are you girls doing here?" Slim asks pleasantly.

"We are just drying out some of our wet hiking gear," I answer cheerfully.

"What are you doing with all these dogs?" Baldey demands insolently.

Rocket can see my defenses go up. She quickly explains, "We are thru hiking and we hike with the dogs for protection. Our Dad meets us when we reach town to help us re-supply. We saw ya'll drive up. Is there some kind of problem at the dry cleaners? We have been here for a while and we haven't seen anything unusual."

Baldey scowls, and Slim laughs before saying, "The owner of the dry cleaner is wondering what you are doing here!"

"You girls will have to leave immediately!" Baldey demands.

"If the owners didn't want us here all they had to do was ask us to leave. Instead, they created unnecessary drama," I respond irritably.

Rocket looks at me and shakes her head to shut me up. "We'll leave as soon as we finish packing. We are planning to stay in a hotel room tonight. Thanks for letting us know the owner was concerned." She smiles and waves until both officers are in their vehicle.

Rocket says laughingly, "They look like the good cop vs. bad cop roles from the movies. Baldey is mean, and trying to intimidate us, while Slim nicely asks us what we are doing."

Hurriedly, we finish packing. The salvageable food is now in a new bin with an intact lid and no cracks in the container. We can now leave it on the outside edge of the truck so it is easier to get our food in and out and water can't get in the container when it drips down.

We load up the dogs and exit the parking lot, all under the watchful eyes of thc PoPo!

From the dry cleaners, we go to the Howard Johnson hotel, and are able to check into our room early. Then, we go to Blue Collar Joe's for a free donut. Dad and Rocket had picked up the SPOT for me from the post office the day before and found an AYCE restaurant for us.

We explore town, then pick up a new creamy, fruity flavor ice cream to split three ways. In town, we meet May, Karen, Kristen, BJ, Deborah, and John

While at the hotel, we meet three kids who immediately fall in love with the dogs. A teenage girl, with red stylishly short hair, and her two younger brothers, William and Shawn. One with short brown spiky hair and the other with longer brown hair. Instigator is the immediate favorite, followed by Digger and Mtn. Goat.

The kids are enthralled with Kujo. He tolerates a little attention before growling.

Why do kids continue to want to befriend Kujo when he makes it clear he doesn't want to be bothered?

Kujo growls again. "Leave the black one alone before he bites you!" I snap at the youngest boy.

The kids are so in love with Instigator, I am concerned they might try to puppy-nab him. Fortunately, the sleeping arrangement for the dogs are as follows: First Mtn. Goat goes in the back kennel. He is always enthusiastic about getting in. Digger rushes in next. Mentally, Digger has to have a running start, or he doesn't think he can jump into the back of the truck. I have to trick him into jumping. Then Instigator, his Highness, is elevated into the truck, he also goes in the back kennel. We close them up in the back and Kujo gets the front kennel by himself to prevent fighting. There aren't many people who are brave enough to get past Kujo to try to take any of the other dogs.

In the hotel room, Rocket and I load pictures from the camera onto the computer while eating pizza and popcorn. Dad visits with us until it gets dark then he meanders to the cab of the truck to sleep for the night. Rocket and I finish washing and drying all the laundry, then we crash for the night.

**Day 64** "Bye Dad, see you at Taylors Mountain Overlook on the Blue Ridge Parkway (BRP) 97.0 this evening. We'll send a Spot GPS signal two hours before we will be there."

Daleville quickly disappears behind Rocket, the four dogs and I. We hike under I-81 on VA 779, then we pass Us 11. About two miles into our hike Rocket slows substantially and eases herself nonchalantly behind Kujo. She whispers, "There is a burly, unkempt man up ahead carrying a crowbar."

As the harsh, beady eyed, stringy, greasy, black haired man approaches I hear Kujo growling softly and menacingly. When I look down Kujo's is snarling and his scruff is up. I ease to the far-right side of the trail keeping Rocket protected behind us and Kujo between the man and us.

"Hey, how are you?" I ask in a friendly voice as we pass.

The man remains silent and looks even angrier. His hand clenches tighter on the crow bar.

As soon as Rocket and I round a turn in the trail we break into a sprint. We run a good ten minutes before settling in to a fast-paced hike.

I shiver despite the warm day.

"I'm glad you have the dogs with you," Rocket says.

"Me too!" I've never seen anyone hiking with a crowbar before."

We hike another eight miles in relative silence, occasionally commenting on the terrain or the scenery, until we reach Wilson Creek Shelter. At Wilson Creek Shelter we meet "General Sherman" from Atlanta and "Art Rainbow" from New York. We take time for a snack and trail conversation before hiking another three miles to meet Dad at BRP 95.9, Montvale Overlook.

There are a few picnic tables overlooking the mountains. We see StormSong sitting alone at one of the tables.

Rocket asks, "Where is TreeBeard?"

"He had to hike back to Wilson Creek Shelter because he forgot his rain gear. He thought it would be faster and easier to hike on the road until he had to enter the trail again," StormSong answers.

"I understand," I say. "Are ya'll still enjoying hiking?"

"We are. Tree Beard is having pain in his calf. I am watching his gear. Once he gets back we still have to hike to Bobblets Gap Shelter."

I look at Dad then ask, "Do you want to pick up TreeBeard where the trail exits onto the road a few miles back? He will know it's you because of the white truck and the too short purple camper shell. It would save him time, and strain on his leg."

"Yes," Dad says. "I would hate for him to have to hike any more than absolutely necessary."

Rocket and I grab out food and our Jetboil to cook with from the truck, along with the dog food and water for us and the dogs. Digger is thrilled to be re-united with StormSong, his fan club member. The AT parallels and crisscrosses the BRP many times. We are parked in one of many pull-out areas.

We have a cold, but uneventful night.

Girl (Hiking) with 4 Dogs

**Day 65** Rocket and I sit in the cab to eat cereal and powdered Nido milk. We have a pop tart, and split an orange. Dad is at the back of the truck, sawing a piece of wood for the gap between the camper shell and the back of the truck.

"Dad," I say. "Do you want to sit in the cab with us where it is warm. I don't want you to be cold outside. We have plenty of cereal and milk to share. We would love to have you join us."

"No thank you," Dad answers. "I'm not cold. You know I don't have to wear a lot of clothes to be warm. I'm still working on fixing the back so it won't leak inside when it rains."

"Are you sure you don't want to join us?" Rocket asks.

"I'm sure," Dad replies and continues sawing on the wood.

I look at Rocket, raise my eyebrows, and shrug.

A little while later we see a ranger checking the trash cans, and decide to get moving so Dad can move the truck.

It's about three miles to Bobblets Gap Shelter. After hooking up the dogs we quickly hike to the privy. It is the best privy on the trail! It is luxurious, has handicap bars, and plexi-glass skylights!

We have a beautiful clear day for hiking with few major elevation changes. We see majestic mountains, fragile, fire red flowers, soft moss, yellow and green spider like flowers, upright charred remains of tress and barren landscape from a past forest fire. Tiny new trees are budding from the earth. One area has moss that looks like tiny flames of life. It is green on the base with reddish orange stems reaching toward the sun and ash white blossoms soft enough to fall asleep on. Other ground foliage is also present, three to four varieties forming a community for survival in the barren landscape.

Did the fire destroy or cleanse?

We see another bud, it is circular with geometric blossoms enclosing the bud, and 10 sprouts extending from the edges, resembling an asterisk. We also see a lady slipper on the verge of blossoming

The 4 dogs are exuberant. The sun is shining. Spring is in the air!

We hike 12.6 miles before reaching Jennings Creek.

"I don't see the truck or your Dad," Rocket says.

"I'll give him a call. He probably thinks we are still hiking."

I walk up the road a few feet in order to get a phone signal. Dad answers just before the voicemail picks up.

"I am on VA 619," Dad says, "but I don't see where the trail crosses."

"We are at the road now. There is a creek and s small parking area. We will stay near the road so you can see us."

I hang up with Dad then explain to Rocket about the difficult time Dad is having finding where the AT crosses the road.

"I wonder if the trail is obscure near the road crossings to make it safer for hikers?" Rocket asks.

"I've heard VA is the worst state for crime against hikers. Is it because so much of the trail is in VA, or because it is close to civilization? So far, the cops in VA are very diligent, perhaps even overly cautious."

A few minutes later the dogs jump up from laying on the ground. I listen closely and eventually hear the truck approaching. I wave my hands near the edge of the road as Dad finally approaches the trail crossing at Jennings Creek. "Yeah, you found us," I say.

"Yes. It was a long ride from the BRP to this spot on VA 614 road. I can see on the map where it is a straight line for you girls to hike from point 'A,' to 'B,' but I had to drive a 180 degree out of the way twisting convoluted road to arrive at this spot."

"I'm glad you figured it out. It sounds like a fun adventure," I say.

Dad looks at me as if to say, "yeah right." Then he says, "I don't think we should stay parked here. We should go somewhere else, off the AT."

"Not when you just explained how out of the way this place is. I don't want to drive a few hours away, wasting gas, to find somewhere to park, then have to drive back in the morning," I say.

"Before you girls start unpacking and cooking supper, I need to explain what happened after you left this morning. As you know I was working on cutting the wood to fit below the class on the camper shell to keep the rain out, well not long after ya'll left a police officer stopped by. He asked what I was doing and if I had parked at the overlook all night. I explained about fixing the camper shell and he said, 'It is illegal to sleep overnight anywhere on the Blue Ridge

Parkway pullouts.' Then he gave me a warning ticket and said I could be fined or thrown in jail if it happens again!"

"Well, this place has parking coordinates and a tent symbol in the Thru Hiker Guide book. We should be okay, as long as we stay in the parking area and are incognito. I say we stay. We can point out to a PoPo that we didn't know where else to park, we thought we could park at the parking coordinates, and this area isn't on the BRP. What is your vote Rocket?"

"It's your truck. I'm staying out of it."

"Okay then. I say we stay and if we get in trouble, then it can be all my fault. I don't think anyone will even come this far out in the boon docks."

Dad grudgingly agrees.

As we are eating supper I ask, "What did you do after the officer told you to leave from the overlook?"

"I went down a few miles to another overlook and continued sawing the wood and working on fixing the camper shell so it won't leak. I had planned to have it finished before we started on this trip. I never imagined it would take so long."

Rocket says, "At least now we have it set up so the water doesn't get into the food bin, and as long as you park the truck with the back tailgate going slightly down hill, the water doesn't get inside the back of the truck either."

We are close to a beautiful creek that I'm sure is lots of fun to swim and wade in, if it isn't so COLD. There are trout in the water. Two fishermen bring back a trout each and they assure us that anyone can catch trout just about every time you put your line in the water. There is a limit of three fish per person per day. The dogs alert us every time someone comes to the water hole to catch a fish.

Rocket says, "I wish I had my fishing poles. I talked to James earlier. He's been fishing with his buddies every weekend. He even fixed the fishing boat and takes it out."

"We can buy fishing poles next time we go to town," I say.

"It's not the same. Besides I would have to buy a fishing license before I could fish."

We fill up the dog water containers and gallon jugs from the ice-cold creek water. The dogs have the recycled sweet tea jugs, so as not to get confused with our water only gallon jugs.

Dad meanders around the parking area picking up trash.

"Dad, when are you going to drop the trash bags into a garbage dump?" I ask as Dad puts another full garbage bag in the back of the truck.

"Next time we go to town, I guess," Dad answers.

After taking care of the dogs, I jump into the warm cab of the truck to eat supper.

"It got cold fast once the sun went down," Rocket says.

I'm beginning to have sleep anxiety. I pray that I can sleep through the night, and Dad can leave in the morning without being questioned by the PoPo's.

**Day 66** I wake up to the dogs barking. I wiggle my way out of the kennels and pray there isn't a PoPo.

Whew! it's only two men fishing. One of them says, "Good luck on your journey and stop for berries."

Dad takes two dogs to the woods with him. He calls, "Come look at this flower hiding in the woods." I come over to investigate. It is yellow and has large green leaves.

Dad says, "I think it is a Lady Slipper. I haven't seen one of these since I was a boy."

"It is a beautiful flower. I'm glad to see something besides brown barren trees."

Once Rocket wakes up, I show her the flowers before we leave.

A few miles down the trail we take a break at Bryant Ridge Shelter. Kujo stands guard while the other three dogs sprawl out on the porch and look like they've lived at the shelter for years. The shelter has a large roof overhanging an outdoor porch area. The porch overlooks a deciduous forest. Inside there are bunks on both the downstairs and upstairs sleeping areas.

"Hey Rocket," I say, "Let's move in here."

"I wouldn't mind staying here a few days," Rocket answers making herself comfortable on one of the downstairs bunks.

We eat snacks then drag ourselves away from the AT home in the woods and trek on in search of the Guillotine, whatever that is.

Girl (Hiking) with 4 Dogs

Along the way, we see purple lady slippers, trillium, sassafras, white flowers with green leaves, and yellowish brown, sponge-like Sorel mushrooms, and mushrooms that are light brown and look like a tube sock. We see a circular rock wedged between two boulders.

Rocket says, "This must be the Guillotine. I'm not sure I want to hike under that rock. What if today is the day it decides to fall?"

"I agree. I'll go through first. I'm not going to linger!"

After the Guillotine, we pass hikers, Dutton Duo and OttoNoBedder at the Thunder Hill Shelter.

At the end of the day we meet at Thunder Ridge Overlook.

I say, "I wish we could stay here instead of driving out of the park."

"I know," Rocket agrees, "but I'm not going to chance going to jail because we parked in the wrong place!"

Just as we are getting in the truck, a hiker and his family approaches.

"Hi," he says "I overheard you are thru hiking and need somewhere to park tonight. I am from the area and can help. My trail name is Sundance and I did a thru hike on the AT a few years ago. I know around here they treat the BRP like the White House Lawn. There is always somebody monitoring it, however I can tell you how to get to Jefferson National Forest, it is like the red-headed-stepchild, it is barely supervised, and has fewer rules and regulations. The area we camp at is called Hunting Creek."

"Thanks," we say.

Sundance shows the way since he and his family are going the same way.

There are lots of other drive-in campers in the Forest. Some have dogs. We drive around for 20 minutes and come back to the first place we saw. Once we stop and start to get out we hear dogs barking a few campsites away.

Dad says, "We should go find somewhere else to park. You know how your dogs don't get along with other dogs."

"There's probably dogs everywhere," I say, "and besides we didn't see anywhere else. It's Saturday night!"

"I'm getting hungry. Let's see what happens if we stay here," Rocket adds.

"Okay," Dad says.

We let the dogs out on leashes, after 15.4 miles of hiking, they are too tired to cause trouble.

The forest is calm and peaceful.

**Day 67** When we finally return to Thunder Ridge Overlook, we meet Gloria and her husband. They are traveling and camping in a truck with a properly fitting camper shell. They spent an uneventful night at the overlook.

After a cold morning at the overlook, it warms up as we descend into Petites Gap, and we are in short sleeves by 10:40 a.m. We see pretty red flowers that look like flames, and beautiful streams of water running down the side of the mountain. We meet a group of three guy thru hikers, SGT Pepper, Leafguy, and SouthButt. Rocket and I are concerned about SouthButt's trail name, however his friends explain he likes SouthPark and he started at the Southern end of the trail, so he wants to be called SouthButt.

By 2:30 p.m. we can see James River winding below us through the mountains. We see more flora and fauna, and a small stream trickling down the mountain on its way to the James River. When we finally reach the James River footbridge there are people jumping off into the water.

Rocket says, "It looks fun, but logic says the water is still cold."

"I am tempted to try it anyway," I say "but I don't have anywhere for the dogs to go while I jump, and I don't want to be cold."

There are people everywhere; on the bridge, hanging on the side of the bridge about to jump into the river, and cluttering both ends of the bridge! The dogs are like kids, with a hundred dollars to spend, in a candy store. They are so excited, they don't know what to be excited about next. They are smelling everyone and everything we pass!

Sundance meets us at the bridge, and brings trail maps and books, along with his dog.

"Hey Girl with 4 Dogs, and Rocket. I wondered what time you would get here. I already saw your Dad at the parking area."

"That's cool," I say. "How long have you been here?"

"Not long," Sundance says as we walk across the bridge. Sundance continues, "When I hiked the AT, there were days when I couldn't find water, because the springs and streams had dried up. I went days without water. I was even hallucinating one time it was so bad. My lips were dry, cracked, and bleeding."

"Luckily, we haven't had a shortage of water," Rocket says.

We meet Dad at the other end of the bridge and continue talking about trail survival while Sundance waits on his wife to pick him up. It's been two hours and she hasn't shown up. After a while Dad offers to give him a ride home.

Rocket looks at me in disgust when we look in the cab and says, "Your Dad volunteered to give Sundance a ride, but he's not helping us clean up the cab! There is nowhere to sit and, look at this!" She gestures to a full container with urine.

Why Dad, why?

The full urinal is sitting proudly in the cab with a neon sign saying, "this is so disgusting."

"I think I'm going to puke," I exclaim irritably.

Rocket and I clean up the cab, discretely removing the urinal.

We wait in the parking lot with the dogs, while Dad takes Sundance home. The cab would have been crowded with all of us plus Dad's junk.

"We forgot to get the food out of the truck before Dad left," Rocket remarks.

"At least we remembered our jackets. My sweat is cooling and the sun is setting. I didn't realize Dad would be gone for so long."

The dogs enjoy barking at the trains flying by on the train tracks.

**Day 68** In the morning, we wake-up early with the trains zooming past on the tracks a few yards away from the parking area.

I see a proud Cardinal watching over us from the branches of a barren tree as I feed the dogs.

John's Hallow Shelter is two miles away. There are beautiful butterflies at the shelter eating gross, malodorous trash someone left in the fire pit. It smells like BM!

We meet Squash from Georgia. He hikes fast and leaves us quickly behind.

Rocket and I stop for lunch at Big Rocky Row and meet hIrSch.

We finish eating at the same time, but hIrSch also hikes fast and leaves us behind.

Next, at the top of Bluff Mountain, we see the monument for Ottie Cline Powell, a four year who wandered away from school November 9th and was found dead April 5th seven miles away on top of Bluff Mountain. When we see the monument, there are trinkets and toys on top of and around the monument.

Tears fill my eyes and threaten to spill down my cheeks as I think about a cold little boy lost and alone on top of the mountain.

Rocket says, "We should leave something here."

"What do we have to leave?" I ask. "We have food, but we aren't supposed to leave food on the trail. The wild animals will get it."

Rocket looks is her backpack and says, "I have change and this hiking pole stopper I found."

After looking in my backpack I find a "We can also leave wild flowers and pretty leaves."

"Okay," Rocket agrees.

We say a silent prayer before we continue hiking.

"I suspect foul play," I say to Rocket.

"Me too. We are huffing and puffing hiking up the mountain, and we are a lot older, and have been hiking for months. How could a child end up here?"

"I think someone kidnapped him."

"It is so sad," Rocket says.

Later we discover an apple tree at the Punchbowl shelter. There is no fruit on it yet.

"Why does the shelter stink like urine?" Rocket asks.

"I wonder if someone was too lazy to go to the woods in the night and peed under the shelter?"

"I'm glad we don't have to sleep here," Rocket says.

"I'm glad it doesn't stink at the picnic table," I say.

The dogs start barking and we look up to see two thru hikers joining us.

"Hello," Rocket says as the hikers approach. "I am Rocket and this is Girl w/ 4 Dogs. What are your trail names?"

"I am Johnny Appleseed and this is my friend Mango."

We talk about the trail how long they've been hiking, etc. Mango says, "We had a great time in the Smoky Mtns. We had beautiful, sunshine, and no snow."

"It was great, however, I got trench foot," Johnny Appleseed says.

"Really?" I say. "Can I see?"

"Sure," Appleseed says, "Although not many people ask to see my nasty feet."

"I'm a nurse," I answer. "I've never seen trench foot. I hate to miss a chance to see something new."

He lets me see his feet. He, he, ha, ha.

"Do you want to see too?" He asks Rocket.

She adamantly shakes her head "no."

"Your feet don't look bad," I say.

"Yeah, they are mostly healed except my toenails."

At Robinson Gap Road, we meet Carrot Top (wife), Follow Her (husband), and their dog Shadow. Then four miles later we meet Dad near USFS 39, Reservoir Rd. and drive to town for overnight parking.

**Day 69** Dad looks at the map then says, "If you girls start at Salt Log Gap and hike south back to Reservoir Road you will have more downhill hiking."

I look at Rocket. She says, "I'll hike today if we hike downhill."

"Okay," I say. I know Rocket is missing home more each day.

We meet the Red Team- "Red Riding Hood" and "Red Wagon." They are hiking 20 to 30 miles a day, steadily north.

Later, we meet Hard Charger and Johnny B. They are hiking the entire AT in sections. Once we make it to Reservoir Rd., Dad picks us up. There is a school bus passing on the road. The dogs investigate melted ice someone left as trail magic.

We sleep in the truck at Salt Log Gap on the forest road. There is a parked bulldozer.

I hope the PoPo's don't come tonight!

**Day 70** April 27, 2011 Another misty, drizzly day is upon us. We are hiking North to VA 56, Tyre River Suspension Bridge. Early in the morning, as we are eating breakfast, we meet, Hans Solo, from

Maryland and Coffee Break, from Seattle. Hans Solo uses an umbrella for his rain gear. They are headed South.

Halfway through the day, Rocket and I take a break at The Priest Shelter. It is rainy, and misty with creepy fog. The fog is so thick, we can't see the privy from the shelter. There are side trails everywhere, we pray we won't get lost.

Ahhh, relief.

After emptying our bladder Rocket and I sit in the shelter eating cheese and crackers. As we are sitting it feels like tiny fingers are penetrating our skin, stabbing needle thin icicles all over. The dogs are restless. The fog is extremely thick. We see it moving and swirling around. It feels as if we are in a strange horror movie. The suspense is heavy and any minute something bad is going to happen.

The 4 Dogs will protect us.

"I am getting cold sitting here," I say, "and the fog is creepy."

"I agree," Rocket says. "It wasn't cold before we came, but it is eerily chilly now. I'm ready to go."

We are relived when we leave. I can see the tension leave the dogs. It is warm as soon as we reach the main trail from the shelter.

We end the day at the Tyre River suspension bridge. It is peaceful with the water gurgling nearby and the green trees providing shade and fresh air.

**Day 71** It rains all night, and now it is chilly.

Rocket says, "Let's listen to the weather forecast. I don't want to hike if it's raining."

Dad turns on the radio in the truck and also starts driving.

Dad must be going to the gas station

There is music for a while then, the weather forecaster says, "We are under a tornado warning until 9 a.m. Eastern Time."

"So, if there is no longer a tornado warning at 9 a.m. do you want to hike today?" I ask Rocket.

"I don't know. Probably not. I'm not hiking when there are tornado warnings!"

Dad stops the truck and I look around. I can't believe this! It's only 7:30 a.m. and Dad has us at Dripping Rock on the BRP 9.6. Rocket isn't hiking, but I have to hike because we used gallons of gas to get here! I am pissed!

"I can't afford joy rides so I guess I'm hiking even if there are tornado's," I say glaring at Dad.

## Girl (Hiking) with 4 Dogs

I stomp out of the truck, grab food, my backpack, and rain gear. It's still pouring down rain. I ask Dad, "Well since you brought us here and I'm the only one hiking can you at least feed the dogs?"

"Yes," Dad answers. "You know you don't have to hike."

"Yeah right, like I can afford to waste gas returning to this spot tomorrow and the next day just so we can hike downhill, and it looks like I'm the only one hiking so it is a waste even coming here! I like hiking uphill better, it's easier on my knees than going downhill!"

Dad says, "I hate to mention it, but the truck is on empty."

I throw money at Dad and stomp off down the trail. The dogs start whining even though it is raining. They would be soaking wet in minutes, and I haven't figured out a way to change their wet fur.

The least Dad can do is take care of them today!

Fine! I'll hike in tornados! I guess if I hadn't heard the weather forecast, then I wouldn't know to worry about tornados. Since my hands are free I'll use an umbrella along with my rain gear.

I like the umbrella, but it doesn't keep all the rain off.

I see signs for Humpback Mountain.

Am I hiking in the right direction?

I am supposed to be hiking south back to the Tye River bridge, however more and more evidence indicates I am hiking north toward Waynesboro, VA and Humpback Mountain, instead of away from it.

I don't care! I'm not stopping in this torrential down pour to look at the map either!

It's not long before there is a rock boulder to climb. It's raining enough cats and dogs, I am glad I don't have the 4 dogs with me, so as to decrease my risk for injury. 4 Dogs slipping and sliding, along with my own struggling, seems quite dangerous. I have to use both hands on the slippery rocks. The umbrella is now in my backpack.

When it finally stops raining I dig out my map. I am headed to Waynesboro not Tye River. I consider letting Dad and Rocket worry when I don't show up at Tye River at the end of the day, but since I have enough phone signal, I send Dad a text message, letting him know I will finish in town.

God can always throw kinks in any plan. I want this, and I want that, but God has his own plans. I can work with God's way. "He will never leave me nor forsake me" Hebrews 13:5.

After the initial rain, I couldn't ask for a more beautiful and sunny day.

The trail near Paul C. Wolfe Shelter is flooded, and I get wet feet crossing. I hear rustling in the bushes and see a snake slithering away from the shelter.

Later there is a lone chimney scowling at all hikers passing by with his flat nose sticking out and his wide square mouth daring anyone to start a fire inside. Next I see a tiny waterfall trickling out of the mountain and farther down there is a large waterfall flooding the trail!

Toward the end of the hike, the trail is confusing. There is a washed-out bridge. I have to follow an alternate route from HE_ _! There are twists, turns and dead ends everywhere! I wish I had Kujo, or one of the other dogs to help me find my way.

I have to back track again!

What is that large mammal like thing in the distance? Maybe an overgrown ground hog, beaver, or little person in a fur body suit? It is roughly the size of one of the big dogs, but it stands on it's back feet and is fatter.

I hike toward the furry anomaly and somehow manage to navigate the trail maze to new scenery, which includes a white blaze.

I exit the trail at US 250. There are complicated spaghetti-like road crossings, and a visitor center. I send a GPS signal, and attempt to call Dad on the cell phone. I get the voicemail. Repeatedly.

Dad's phone battery only stays charged a couple of minutes at a time, and he doesn't have a normal battery charger. He either has to take the battery out and put it on a multiuse battery charger, or he can charge it by holding wires onto the battery connector part of the phone. Either way, he has to have the phone off in order to charge it.

I can't have a detailed phone conversation with Dad so I leave a message. He calls back to inform me there are multiple visitor centers. Rocket has signal on her T-Mobile phone and we are finally able to meet-up.

The dogs are rocking the truck they are so excited to see me!

Girl (Hiking) with 4 Dogs

     In town, we shop at Big Lots and buy $5 movies to watch on the laptop. We sleep in the truck at the Wal-Mart parking lot; 24/7 bathroom with flushing toilets, running water, and access to food!

     What luxury!

     I didn't see anyone else hiking all day!

     **Day 72** Today, I hike south from Dripping Rock. I have Kujo, Mtn. Goat, Digger and Instigator with me. Rocket takes another zero day. I cross paths with thru hiker, Moose, then I see thru hikers Just Renee and Slow Poke hiking a section with her mom from CA.

     Later, I meet a day hiker with her two dogs. Off leash! The dogs run up to us, barking, and trying to start a ruckus. My dogs start growling.

     As we pass, the woman snarls, "Dogs behave better when they are off leash!"

     I look at her grit my teeth, raise my eyebrow, and say, "I can tell your dogs are really listening. That's why they are still bothering me and not with you, right?"

     She huffs and puffs and finally gets her dogs. As we are passing I say, "Last time Kujo was off leash at a dog park, he bit and injured the dog who came running up behind him."

     After that, I meet more thru hikers, Duck, Fig, and their German Shepherd Willett. They carry their dog past. Huah. The final group for the day are four hospital hiker guys who are hiking to raise money to build a hospital.

     Then, I end the day at the majestic Tye River.

     "Dad," I say, "I'm taking tomorrow off."

     **Day 73** It's Saturday sleep in day. At least as much as the dogs will let me. Once I finally wake up I take the dogs across the street and down by the river. After a while Rocket joins us. I say, "It sure would be fun to swim in the Tye River if it wasn't so cold."

     "It is cold for the end of April." Rocket replies.

     The dogs finish drinking water, then Mtn. Goat and Instigator are straining at the leash to go up the hill to the truck while Kujo and Digger are pulling in the opposite direction to get in the water.

     "I'm going to take Mtn. Goat and Instigator back to Dad, then bring Kujo and Digger back to swim. Do you want me to bring back your flip flops?"

"No, I'll come with you," Rocket answers.

Dad is awake munching breakfast in the cab.

After I leave Mtn. Goat and Instigator with Dad, I return to the river. Kujo loves the water and swimming. Digger likes the water, but he's trepidatious about swimming.

Rocket and I throw sticks in the water and Kujo won't come back until he brings a stick with him. We have to throw a second or third stick if he can't find the original one, otherwise he swims in circles looking for the stick. I don't want him to get too tired and drown in the river.

We throw one stick for Kujo, and a second one to Digger, but Kujo thinks he has to have all the sticks. I predict dire results if the two dogs start fighting in water over their heads. Next, we throw only Digger the sticks while I hold Kujo's leash. Digger won't go past where his feet touch. Finally, Rocket uses Digger's fascination with splashing rocks to lure him to deeper water. She keeps throwing rocks in the water, just ahead of Digger. After a while, he ventures past where he can touch in order to get the rocks.

My baby is swimming! (Sniff, sniff). Of course, once he gets out, we have to throw him a stick to bring back. When the stick floats downstream, he swims after it. Rocket and I run down the river bank chasing him! Our cheap flip-flops are flip-flopping off our feet as we run through the brush!

"Gotcha!" Rocket shouts as she snatches up Digger's leash.

Shortly thereafter we return to the truck to check on Dad and relax in the sun.

It is a peaceful and relaxing day. We laugh a lot.

A little bit after noon, a van drops off a cackle of men with backpacks who hike toward 'The Priest," a really tall mountain. They spill out in an organized fashion.

"I wonder what they are doing?" I ask aloud.

A day hiker answers, "They are training in the military."

I watch another group of two guys remove a heavy backpack and a large round cylinder.

"What are you guys training for?" I ask.

"We are going winter hiking this year. We have to be able to carry at least 50 pounds of gear for winter mountain climbing and camping."

"Wow! Your gear looks pretty heavy."

Girl (Hiking) with 4 Dogs

Later, Dad helps day hikers with directions. Lastly, we see thru-hiker White Wolf, from the Smokey Mtns., and Goose, who is now hiking with White Wolf.

After a while, we drive back to Waynesboro, VA and take a shower at the YMCA. At the YMCA, the staff give hiker bags with shampoo, toothbrush, toothpaste, and chap stick. Rocket trades with me, so I can have the neon yellow toothbrush, and I luck out and get Burt's Bees Chap stick.

That night, we splurge to watch, "Water for Elephants," starring Reese Witherspoon, at the Zeus theater. My mouth waters as I eat movie theater popcorn!

Ahhh, the luxuries of town: Being clean, smelling good, and having soft, clean-feeling hair. Real food, popcorn, and entertainment. Why would anyone want to hike in the woods for days at a time smelling like sweat and stink?

# Chapter 9: Shenandoah National Park

**Day 74** May 1, 2011 "Rocket," I plead, "just because it looks like rain doesn't mean it's going to rain. Please, hike with me today."

Rocket answers, "I don't like being cold and wet. I'm not hiking 19 miles today!"

"Okay," I sigh. "Here's money for the park pass Dad, I'll see ya'll in a few hours."

Just after passing a little bunny hiding in the green sun warmed grass, I see Bears Den Mountain Communication Towers." There is a group of towers, with a sitting area. The seats look like former tractor seats and are in a semi-circle. Later, I tell Rocket it was her alien space station trying to find her to take her home, and she missed them.

Next, I meet a section hiker named Pringle. She shares a funny story about one time when she offered a thru hiker's dog jerky, and the hiker asked if he could have the jerky instead!

I see more lady slipper flowers and meet section hikers "Mack" and her "Dad."

I end the day at Black Rock Gap, Skyline 87.4. The Skyline is basically the same as the BRP, it just has a different name. Once I finish hiking, and meet up with Dad and Rocket we have to drive out of the park to find somewhere to sleep for the night. We consider the campgrounds within the park, but the ones close to us are closed for the season.

It takes about 30 minutes to find a remote location in which to park the truck overnight. I bid Dad and Rocket goodnight, then climb sleepily into the kennels with the dogs.

**Day 75** The following day is beautiful, sunny, and warm. Yeah! Rocket hikes with me, along with all four energetic dogs.

After hiking a few hours, Rocket says, "Let's eat lunch on the rock. It's in the sun and we won't have to sit on the ground."

"This does look like a great place for lunch," I say, taking off my backpack which has Mtn. Goat and Digger hooked on the right side and Kujo and Instigator on the left side.

Rocket and I pull out trail mix, jerky, cheese and crackers, then climb on the huge warm rock. It doesn't take Instigator long to find a hole under the rock. He digs furiously to make the hole bigger, then he turns around in circles about three times before finally laying down in the cool dirt.

After finishing lunch, we hike another couple of hours before taking another break in the middle of the trail. There are pretty yellow flowers and white butterflies on both sides of the trail. Rocket raises her face to absorb the warm sun rays.

BARK! BARK! BARK! Bark!

My heart leaps into action! Rocket and I both look franticly around!

Suddenly another thru hiker appears.

"Hey," I say to a male hiker with dark brown hair. My hand is holding the outside of my chest as if that would keep it from exploding. "You startled us."

He looks warily at the dogs and says "Really?"

"Yeah," Rocket adds. "We were very relaxed."

I pull the dogs to the side and he passes without difficulty.

"What's your trail name?" I call after him.

"Moose," he says.

"Cool, I was hoping to meet a moose on the trail. Now I have," I joke.

Moose laughs before saying, "You girls have a good day and be safe. I saw a bear a mile or so down the trail. I think you'll be okay since you have the dogs, but be careful."

"We will. Thanks." Rocket says.

The dogs bark their goodbye's as well.

We stop for an end of the day potty break at Pinefield Hut (aka shelter). It is 0.1 mile off the main trail. Many hikers are settling in for the evening; one is taking a nap in a blue and green Eno hammock, while another is fixing supper, a third group is washing dishes.

"Hey Squash," I sputter in surprise. "I didn't think we would ever see you again!"

"I slowed down some in order to hike a section with my friend, Prom Date," Squash replies.

"It's good to see you," Rocket says. "Good luck on finishing the trail."

"Thanks."

We also meet Windscreen and Hermes before retracing our steps back to the trail.

There is a stream on the way to, and on the way from, the shelter. There is a lot of water, and not many rocks. Mtn. Goat doesn't want to get his feet wet (well neither do I), and there isn't enough room for both of us on the same rock. When he maneuvers to share my rock, I am knocked off balance and land both feet in the water! I glare at Mtn. Goat and stomp the rest of the way across the stream. I hear faint snickers behind me.

After a half mile, we meet Dad at Skyline 75.2, for a total of 14 miles. We contemplate staying on the trail for a few days at a time, but Rocket is worried about where Dad will stay, so we continue to meet up daily.

There is a nice parking area off the main Skyline Road. It has a big field, and a place to picnic in the grass.

"Let's eat here," Rocket suggest. "Then we can drive somewhere to park for the night."

"I wish we could stay parked here, but it's not worth being fined or thrown in jail for overnight parking on government property," Dad comments.

"I agree," I sigh as I eat hot Roman noodles and canned beef.

The sun is setting and I yawn sleepily, "I'm going to get in the cages with the dogs to sleep for the night. Dad you and Rocket can find somewhere to park for the night and I will see ya'll in the morning. I don't want struggle getting in the cages with the dogs later."

"Okay, goodnight," Rocket and Dad both chime.

They are driving around in circles! It has been at least an hour! Life is much easier for the dogs. I'm glad I don't have to stress out with Dad and Rocket about why they are driving so long to find somewhere to park. Is Dad trying to bankrupt me? Does he hope I won't have money to put gas in the truck and I will have to quit and go home? I'm not going to let his passive aggressive maneuvers cause me to fail!

After a while, I fall asleep. Finally, around 11:00 p.m. the truck stops moving. I roll on my left side and idly pet Digger before falling asleep again. Peaceful, dreamless sleep.

About an hour later, I wake up to bright, flashing blue lights.

Girl (Hiking) with 4 Dogs

Oh well, another police check.

I peer outside the bars on my cage and blink sleepily. There are lots of blue flashing lights! More than I've ever seen at one time, even at a bad traffic accident! There must be at least 4 police cars!

I look around. Rocket isn't moving around in the cab. She's probably sound asleep with the sleeping bag over her head. Dad is snoring loudly laying across the tailgate of the truck in front of the cages. There isn't much I can do, since I am fastened in the dog cages.

Dad doesn't sleep in a sleeping bag. He bundles into layers of clothing, and occasionally, he wraps up in a dirty old comforter. He is unshaven and looks homeless and raggedy.

I wait quietly, and patiently until the policeman wakes Dad up. I'm not sure if he can see me. There is a lot of tension emanating from the policeman. I feel like I should keep a low-key profile right now. It might look strange if they see me sleeping in a cage with four dogs. I stay low, but I can still see what's happening. On the other hand, if they can see me, I want them to know I am ok.

I give a slight wave just in case.

After a bit, the policeman says loudly, and repeatedly, "Sir are you okay?" "Sir! Are you okay!?"

Dad finally wakes up, and sits up on the tailgate, shielding his eyes and mumbling, "I'm fine," in his cheerful, calm, polite voice.

The policeman asks again if he is ok, making sure Dad isn't hurt or injured in anyway. Then, the policeman explains, "We got a call indicating, 'man down.'"

I peek out the side window of the camper shell. There are more than four police cars, two ambulances, a fire truck, and a K-9 unit semi-surrounding the truck. The officers are on high alert, as are the K9 dogs. The 4 dogs are standing in the kennels giving low growls, and gruffs. I am trying to calmly, and quietly "shush" them.

I am usually a very quiet unobtrusive person.

The police officer asks Dad for his ID. In the meantime, there is another officer investigating the cab of the truck where Rocket is sleeping. They are flashing the flashlight in the truck, but she doesn't immediately wake up. As usual, her head is covered with the sleeping bag. In the morning, when it is time to get up, I crawl to the back kennel, reach through, and tap on the glass. She sleeps while I feed the dogs etc., then I wake her up a second time.

After multiple taps on the glass from the police officer, eventually, Rocket wakes up. The officer asks if she is okay, then he asks if she has any ID. She quickly wakes up the rest of the way. Her eyes widen in alarm, and she starts to get out of the truck. The officer has a flashlight shining on her and a gun close to his right hand.

Rocket starts to reach for her shoes, but decides it is safer to get out barefoot.

Once she is out of the truck, the blond-haired officer points to the floor board, "You can put your shoes on."

"I'm okay," Rocket responds gingerly walking on the gravel to the back of the truck. Her ID is in the back of the truck in the backpack on top of the kennel I am in. When she reaches on top of the dog cages to get her ID, I ask her to get mine out too.

The dark-haired officer who had been talking to Dad earlier, hadn't noticed me until I spoke. Then his jaw drops and he gets a baffled look on his face. After a minute, he asks shakily, "Is there someone in the cage?"

Rocket quickly explains that it is no different than when I sleep in the tent with the dogs. The officer is speechless.

Rocket hands the officer both our ID's. After taking them back to the police car for a few minutes, he returns our ID's, then tells us "You can't stay parked here."

I say "I thought it was okay to park on the side of the road at the edge of a field if you get tired while driving."

"Normally that is okay," the dark-haired officer explains, "however the person living on top of the hill isn't okay with you parking here and he won't leave us alone until you leave."

Dad explains, "My daughter and her friend are thru hiking, we are staying off the Skyline Parkway because we know that it is illegal to park overnight. We thought it was legal to pull off the side of the main roads to take a nap if you are sleepy. Where do you suggest we go?"

The officer begins giving verbal directions. He gets agitated when we seek clarify of his directions. The blond-haired officer finds paper and pen and writes the directions down for us.

"Stop, take Right, Next stop take Right, North Street veer Left…"

Girl (Hiking) with 4 Dogs

They also suggest in the future asking at the gas stations where parking is permitted.

I can imagine how bizarre and concerning it could be to see a strange, white truck, with out of state plates, and a too short camper shell parked on a rarely used road, in the middle of some fields, with an enigmatic person laid out on the back of the tailgate, covered in rags.

Thanks guys for your help. Sorry for all the drama. In conclusion, the place to sleep is George Washington Forest.

The forest sounds soon lull me back to a restless sleep.

**Day 76** Another beautiful day of hiking with Rocket and the dogs. There is a tree with new green leaves bursting forth and reddish maroon leaves unfolding underneath. There is also a plant resembling an umbrella. There is a large green leaf with seven extensions shielding a pure white flower from the harsh sun rays. We see yellow flowers, and wild strawberry flowers, along with white blossoms in the trees. The birds are singing. We see a robin and a bird's nest and new ferns unfurling.

We stop at Hightop Hut. While there we meet hikers; "Yeller" and "Cork Dork." A half a mile later near Hightop Mtn. we meet "Head Straight." He is hiking south from New York and started mid-March.

At the end of the day we meet Dad at the South River Picnic Area.

Dad says, "Do you girls want to watch one of the movies we bought at Big Lots?"

"Yes," Rocket and I answer.

"We have, Man of the Year."

"What was that about?" I ask.

"It's the one with Robin Williams," Dad says.

"That sounds good," Rocket says.

"Yeah," I agree. "He's pretty funny."

Just before we start the movie we see two hikers come off the trail.

Rocket and I introduce ourselves, then the new hikers introduce themselves, "I'm Pilot and this is Shera. We were hoping to meet "The Girl with 4 Dogs."

The dogs are tied up outside the truck so they can continue to get fresh air, so I introduce the dogs. Shera is excited and pets the dogs. Shera has a European accent.

Pilot says, "We were hoping to thru hike the AT, but Shera is here on a visa and has to return home in a couple of weeks. She won't be able to finish the whole trail in time.

It starts raining, so we say good bye. I load up the dogs and Dad, Rocket and I stay dry in the truck.

After the movie is over, Man of the Year with Robin Williams, I walk the dogs, then use the bathroom again, before driving out of the park into the forest again to sleep for the night.

My Gortex, water proof, hiking boots are worn out. After 902 miles on the AT and 50 miles on the PMT, they are letting water leak in, and rubbing blisters. It's time to wear my lighter weight, breathable ASICS.

**Day 77** Another zero day for Rocket.

I stomp off with Kujo and Digger into the cold sleet filled May day.

It's three miles to Pocosin Cabin. It is a log cabin. The door is locked, but there is an overhanging open shelter with a picnic table underneath and a rock outdoor chimney. There are three cans Coleman type propane on the shelf above the chimney. There is a little bench to the right of the chimney and a stack of cut firewood.

After passing Pocosin Cabin, I meet "Straight On," and "Forward," a retired couple from New Hampshire, Ranger Sue, and Jack and Jan, a couple from Connecticut. One of the couples tells a story of having to make a huge circle from the trail, in order to avoid a bear and her cub. Bears are extremely protective of their cubs.

After 18.4 miles of hiking, I finish the day at Hawksbill Gap. We all agree to pay to stay in the nearby campground.

As I'm coming back from the bathroom, I hear a baby wailing very loudly. When I get back to the truck, and ask Dad and Rocket if they heard the baby wailing, they say "no."

How did they not hear the wailing?

Rocket says, "That wasn't a baby that was your dog making that horrendous noise!"

"Wow!" I say. "I didn't know Mtn. Goat was that good at imitating humans!"

"Yeah," Dad adds, "He started whining as soon as you got out of sight and he didn't stop until you returned."

**Day 78** Rocket takes another zero.

In Shenandoah, the trail frequently crosses the road and meanders through various campgrounds and welcome centers.

I see a few deer, and the dogs see a lot more, based on the lunging they keep doing trying to get away from me. I also pass horse stables, and multiple solar panels.

I take a break to enjoy the view. Little Stony Man Cliffs have a natural pool of water in a rock crevice. The wind is strong enough to blow Mtn. Goat's ears. I'm inspired to sing, "I believe I can Fly…" (R. Kelly).

During the day I meet Lisa, Noah, DaFence, Bryon, and Grey Beard Beaver (section hiker who finished in 2008), and Guy from Michigan.

As I finish the day at the Panorama Parking area, there is a photographer, Eileen Brunner. She asks "Can you tell me how to get to a panoramic place to take pictures?"

"There are many beautiful places on the trail, but I don't have a clue how to get to them using the road," I answer.

Meanwhile the dogs are pulling me ever closer to Eileen so they can sniff her. She keeps cautiously backing away from us. Then she asks if she can take a picture of the dogs and I. I walk them in a circle and try unsuccessfully to get them to look at the camera.

After she finishes I ask, "Do you want to pet the dogs?"

"No," she answers. "I'm afraid of dogs. I don't want to get any closer."

Dad and Rocket finally arrive at our predetermined place, then we drive to Luray, VA and sleep in the truck, in a Wal-Mart parking lot.

**Day 79** Rocket takes another zero. Just before I leave the Panorama RR parking lot, she notices thirsty bikers headed to the water fountain.

"Wait!" Rocket exclaims. "There is a sign saying the water isn't potable!"

The bikers look disbelieving at first, but then Rocket shows them the sign.

Dad says, "We have fresh water in gallon jugs if you want some."

The female bikers, Sasha says, "Thanks for the water. I'm glad we didn't drink the hazardous water. We might have diarrhea later!"

The male biker, John says, "The sign is barely noticeable saying the water is bad."

"Yeah," Sasha agrees. "What would we do for water if you all weren't here?"

Rocket answers "I hope they fix the water soon before someone gets sick!"

Dad leaves a couple of gallons of drinking water at the water fountain for future thirsty hikers and bikers. I start hiking with the dogs.

In the silence of hiking without Rocket thoughts of AJ hover.

I pass a dandelion blooming on the trail.

I am a survivor. Storms come to drown me, the snow buries me in desolation, but I am strong. The sun will come and in solitude, I will bloom again.

Later I see a fern with four leaves extending like and evenly balanced star. In the center of the star-like shape a taller green leafy plant reaches for the sun.

I am hiking at least four to five miles an hour. I just passed Sgt. Pepper, Leaf guy, and South Butt. I don't want them to pass me again so soon. I pass a parking lot, but I don't see Dad and the white truck with the purple camper shell. I am at Skyline 14.2 and I need to meet Dad at Skyline 12.3, I think I have two more miles before I meet Dad anyway.

The next road crossing says, "Skyline 10.4."

It sit on the side of the road and try not to cry. Kujo puts his head under my hand. Instigator climbs in my lap. Mtn. Goat and Digger curl up beside me.

"I don't want to back track," I sniffle.

I pull out my phone to call Dad, but there isn't a signal.

I wipe my nose on my shirt, then rummage in my backpack for a snack. I didn't stop for lunch today. I eat cheese and trail mix, then peel an orange. I ran out of water an hour past.

Girl (Hiking) with 4 Dogs

While I'm still sniffling, a dark-haired guy in his late twenties approaches riding his bike. He sees me sitting beside the road and stops.

"Hi," he says. "My name is Andre. Do you need any help?" I notice he has an attractive accent.

"No," I answer "I'm taking a break before I hike back to meet my Dad and friend at Hogwallow Gap parking area two miles south. I'm doing a thru hike on the Appalachian Trail. The trail goes from Georgia to Maine. I notice you have an accent. Where are you from?"

"Sweden," he answers.

"How long are you going on your bike trip?"

"I started riding through the Mountains on the Blue Ridge Parkway, but I enjoy riding my bike so much I keep riding. I've been riding for months. Like you doing a thru hike. I am in the United States for two years, then I will ride my bike in South America."

"That's neat. I've never ridden my bike long distance. I notice you are going the same direction as me. If you see a white truck with a too short purple camper shell parked at the next parking area will you let my Dad and friend know I am on the way back to them?"

"Yes, I would love to," Andre` says. "Good luck on your hiking adventure."

"Thanks," I smile, "good luck on your riding adventure."

I resume hiking and see a family of deer crossing the road.

A few minutes later I see the white truck with the purple camper driving toward me.

"Yay!" I exclaim. Did Andre` tell you I was back here?"

"Yes," Rocket replies. "He said, 'your daughter is two clicks back' and pointed this direction."

"Thank you for coming for me." I say as I quickly load the dogs in the kennels, so we don't get run over being stopped on the highway.

I tell Dad and Rocket about my day as we drive to Front Royal, VA for the night.

Rocket says, "In the morning, I'm calling James to pick me up. I miss being home."

"Okay," I answer. "I understand. You always said you wanted to see how far you could go. Thanks for hiking this far with me."

Once in town, Rocket and I split the cost of a hotel room at the Blue Ridge Motel.

**Day 80** May 7, 2011 Saturday morning Rocket pays for a second night in the hotel room in Front Royal, VA. Rocket calls her husband, "Hey James, I'm ready to quit. Can you pick me up? We are in Front Royal, VA. I have a room at the Blue Ridge Hotel."

Afterward, we explore town. We visit with the employees at the visitor center, Ms. Wilson, Gail, and Don, then Rocket and I go thrift store shopping while Dad doggie sits. We find neat clothing styles and trinkets.

Once James arrives we have a last supper together. Then we load Rocket's stuff in his car. Dad and I sleep in the truck in the parking lot of the hotel. Dad sleeps in the cab and I sleep on the plastic food and storage bins beside the kennels. It's comfortable, but I miss snuggling with the dogs.

**Day 81** I wake up early and tap on the glass to wake Dad. I walk the dogs and feed them, then Dad drives me to the trail head.

Despite having the dogs, it is lonely hiking without Rocket.

There is a variety of plant life, chickadee plants, tall grass-like plants with white flowers, purple and yellow wild flowers, a purple iris, beautiful fields, a tree with a knot that looks like a rhinoceros's head sticking out, and a family of brown wild bunnies. I know Rocket would have enjoyed the flora and fauna.

I sing to myself, "F-i-i-ve wild bunnies, four walking dogs, three fence stiles (just kidding), two mild falls, and one lonely girl hiking!" (To the tune of Twelve Days of Christmas.)

The weather is nice and sunny. Also, the flowers are blooming and fuzzy. I don't feel like running and I'm not really funny.

I meet hiker "Goat" and another bunny at the Jim and Molly Denton Shelter. The dogs scare the bunny under the porch, it's late for a shower if I want to still meet Dad before dark. Also, I don't want to strip naked when there is only me and another male at the shelter.

After a brief visit with Goat, I rush off to finish the last three miles of the day and meet Dad at VA 55 Manassas Gap. It seems to be off the "White House Lawn."

"Dad I think we can stay parked here. I don't see any signs saying we can't."

"Okay," Dad says. "How was your day hiking?"

"It was quiet without Rocket. I'm sad to see her go, but I appreciate her staying with me as long as she did. I hiked 15.9 miles today!"

**Day 82** I'm out of SNP. I have a few miles before I am out of VA. It is pleasant and warm. There are tiring elevation changes. Ironically, now that Rocket is no longer here to see them, the trillium plants are finally blooming! I see a purple and white Lady Slipper starting to bloom, and a tree that looks like it is giving birth to a rock!

I stop at the Sky Meadows State Park Visitor Center. "Hey stranger," I say to Dad. He is filling up the water jugs at an outside spigot. He smiles and says, "Hey."

A few miles later I say aloud, "Kujo are you leading us in circles? This looks like the same brown tree we just saw. They must be re-routing the trail." I pat Kujo on the head. "I'm glad you are here." Mtn. Goat sticks his head under my head and I pet him too. Then Digger and Instigator look longingly at my hand. "It's time for a break." I put down the backpack, the dogs surround me, and I give them all attention and massaging. I wish they could return the favor for the massage.

I meet "Guy" from Colorado, and "Just Bob" at the Spring near Bolden Hollow.

I end the day at Morgan Mill Rd. It's a gravel road.

"Hey Dad, we made 19 miles today!" I say as I drop my backpack on the tailgate

"Good for you," Dad says.

As we are talking we hear breaks squeal and a loud thump from down the road. Dad says, "It sounds like someone ran off the road. This dirt road is full of twists and turns. I'm going to make sure they are okay."

"Sounds like a good idea. Since I don't have my shoes on, I'm going to stay here. I will keep the dogs from chewing thru their leashes and following us. I have my phone on. Call if you need me to come down." I stay contentedly sitting down on a plastic bin, on the back of the truck, resting my tired feet.

"Okay," Dad says and hobbles down the road. A little while later when Dad returns he says, "A young teenage guy ran off the road and got stuck in the ditch. He's shaken up, but not hurt. He was driving too fast on the gravel road. We tried to get the truck out, but he had to call a tow truck."

"I'm glad he wasn't hurt." As we are talking we meet the "Go-lyte" brothers. They are just starting on their thru hike. They are hiking the middle sections of the trail first. Also, we meet Stan, the trail maintainer for our particular section of the trail. He tells us about some of his hikes. Thanks for maintaining Stan!

**Day 83** 12:26 p.m. I see a glorious sign, "Welcome to West Virginia"

Wow! "I am finally out of VA! I am on the other side of the torturous, treacherous VA!" I jump up and down and spin in circles. "I made it! Yah-hoozie!"

I am at the top of one of many up and down rollercoaster mountains, but this time I am in another state!

Oh Joy, this one spot on the trail today has cell phone signal. I call mom at her work, and leave a message. Then I send Rocket a text.

I survived hiking 500+ miles in VA! It isn't the "real" halfway point, but it feels like!

# Chapter 10: West Virginia

**Day 83** May 10, 2011 Continued The adrenaline rush fades. I stand on Raven Rock and stare out over the endless expanse of mountains.

Why am I always alone?

My throat tightens and aches. I turn my back on the beauty and solitude and begin hiking at a brisk pace.

Five miles later, I detour to visit the Blackburn AT Center. I wish I hadn't wasted my time. It is off the trail. I can't visit inside with 4 Dogs. Worst of all, it is an uphill hike to get back on the trail!

"I would walk 500 miles and I would walk 500 more..." (By "The Proclaimers.")

I have walked 1000 miles!

After David Lesser Memorial Shelter, I meet Evie, hiking with her black Rotwielder, Viney. The dog is limping and she is carrying his food.

"What happened to your dog?" I ask as the 4 dogs and I pass.

Evie answers, "Viney is seven years old. He's not used to carrying a backpack. I think the weight of the food is hurting him."

"I'm impressed you can carry his food for him. I know it can be heavy!" I say glancing at my 4 dogs. "Good luck on your adventure!"

Only two more miles to Keys Gap, my rendezvous point with dad.

Yeah, he is waiting! It is a day park with picnic tables.

After a short break, I say, "Dad, it's only five miles to the next road crossing and the terrain has been easy so far, do you want to meet me at Chestnut Hill Road? I should make it in an hour and a half or less."

Dad answers, "It should be easy to get there. I drove on the road earlier."

"Thanks!"

I feed the dogs, and then get the pullers ready to hike some more. Shortly into the hike the terrain changes from dirt to rock! "Well boys," I say to the 4 Dogs, "I can't let these rocks slow me down."

Crap! Why did I leave my backpack with Dad in the truck?

I round a corner on the trail and stop short. Hey, I know these thru hikers.

"Hey guys. Ya'll have a warm looking fire going," I say to D'artagnon and the Three Bears.

"It is warm. You can join us if you want," D'artagnon says.

"I wish I could, but I'm supposed to meet my Dad at the next road crossing. How's the hiking going?"

We share trail talk for a bit. I tell them about some of the police drama I experienced in Shenandoah. They laugh so hard Kodiak falls off his rock perch! Then we all laugh harder.

"Well, I don't want to be hiking in the dark so I'm going to head on. Bye"

I depart with the dogs pulling the way.

My watch alarm beeps letting me know I'm running out of time before dark. I trail run. It is fun, but trepidatious. The wind is in my face, and the rocks twist my ankles. If I don't run, I won't make it to meet Dad before dark, and if I run, and twist my ankle, then I won't make it either.

Dear Jesus please help me make it to meet Dad without falling and hurting myself. Amen.

I rationalize that if I fall and hurt myself, at least my friends will find me tomorrow, and send for help. (Hopefully). Two dogs on each side does help keep me balance.

The first road crossing is hazardous. There is a sharp curve where the trail exits, so Dad asks if I can hike to the next crossing, a mile away. I say sure and take off running. It is getting dark, but it is only a mile. I am hyper alert when I trail run and somehow, I can see where I need to step. Also, having the dogs is a bit like having training wheels. If I start to fall one way, I can pull against the dog on the opposite side to counter balance.

I make it to the next road, US 340. Dad says, "This road is pretty busy. If you want to hike across the bridge the trail goes right to the parking lot."

"Okay Dad. I guess I can hike a little farther."

I finally make it across the Shenandoah River Bridge and meet Dad on the other side. There is a hiker walkway that is protected from the traffic by a concrete wall, a little more than waist high. Digger loves to bark at the traffic, but he is deterred by the wall.

I look over the edge of the bridge and see, ducks swimming in the water below the bridge. One of the ducks is on a small island, while another duck is trying to get to the island. It is swimming against the current, struggling to get to the island. It finally makes it.

I hiked 25.7 miles today! I dance a little jig.

"Dad! Look how much progress I made on the Appalachian Trail map today! I traveled a whole inch and I'm in another state!"

Dad smiles and agrees.

**Day 84** "Dad, since we are so close to Washington, DC, let's take a day to find the last church your dad built."

"Okay," Dad says.

Years ago, when Dad was a young boy in middle school, his dad, my grandfather, built churches for a living. My grandfather died in a car wreck not long after building the church in Washington, DC.

We drive around, and keep asking for directions, until we find the church. We park in the parking lot and look around outside.

I nearly jump out of my skin when someone behind us says, "Can I help you?"

We turn around and a friendly black man says, "I am Stephen Richardson, Administrative Pastor here at Dupont Park Seventh-Day Adventist Church. Are you lost or looking for something?"

"No," Dad says. "My daughter is doing a thru hike on the Appalachian Trail, and since we were so close we decided to look for the last church my Dad built before he died."

"What a coincidence that I am here. I forgot some paperwork on my desk and just drove back to retrieve it. It's Wednesday, but we don't have prayer meeting until 7:00 p.m. I have a few minutes if you would like to have a tour of the church."

"We would love to," Dad responds.

"Thank you so much for giving us a tour. I never knew my grandfather, but it's neat to see how the good works he did in his life live on. God is a miracle worker from working out the details so I can do this thru hike, to working out the details and timing so you can give us a tour."

**Day 85** It's two miles to High Street in Harpers Ferry, WV, the traditional halfway point and where the Appalachian Trail Conservancy is located. There is a lot of trail history in Harpers

Ferry, but not a lot of the trail. There have been many years when the trail didn't come to Harpers Ferry, due to various reasons, not the least of which, is the bridges' getting washed away.

The dogs and I have our picture take at Conservancy. We are number 73 for NOBO's.

Inside the conservancy, I meet "WaterBoy," "STRAWBERRY W/ FROSTiNG" '02 thru hiker, and "Tiger Bomb."

Hiking down the spiraling staircase with four dogs is a fun challenge.

Shortly thereafter we cross into Maryland.

# Chapter 11: Maryland

**Day 85** May 12, 2011 Continued Yeah! It's barely 11:00 a.m. and I'm already in Maryland. The terrain is easy and I fly past the turtle in the trail! I'm Super Woman!

"Ouch!" I twist my ankle.

In the afternoon, I meet Neil, a pleasant 79-year-old man taking pictures of Lady Slippers flowers. "You're doing great!" he says. "I'm surprised you can hike with all those dogs. You've got your hands full. I see hundreds of hikers each year, but I've never seen one with 4 dogs. Many hikers try to hike all of Maryland in a day, it's 40 miles. They miss so much beauty that way. I don't understand them."

"I'm amazed I can hike 20 miles a day!" I say.

I pass through Gathland State Park. I breeze through White Cliff. When it is HOT, the dogs finally get tired enough to stop pulling! Mtn. Goat, and Instigator, do a "lay down" protest. They decide they are taking a break with or without me. They literally lay down on the trail, and refuse to walk. If I want to keep hiking, then I have to drag them. I give up, and take a break too.

While the dogs are taking a break, I eat trail mix. Kujo and Mtn. Goat touch paws gently as they sleep.

I cross Monument Rd. then call Dad. When he answers, I say, "I am almost to our Rendezvous place."

Dad says, "I'm here. I bought ice cream. Andy just called and Kim is in labor!"

"Yahoozie!" I replace the phone in my backpack, and scramble over fallen limbs and debris. In no time, I've hiked the last mile to Washington Monument State Park to meet Dad.

My nephew, Caleb is born! He's happy and healthy and I haven't finished making his baby quilt!

Dad and I see a sign in the park indicating there is overnight parking for youth groups. We pay the parking fee and open up the Neapolitan ice cream.

Yummy!

I'm on my second bite when, one of the park rangers taps on the window.

He says, "The park is closing you will have to leave."

I respond, "The sign over there says youth groups are allowed to park overnight. We paid the parking fee and will leave in the morning. I am thru hiking and intend to start here early in the morning."

"I'm sorry, but you can't stay," he says again and looks discriminatingly at the dogs outside the truck.

I grit my teeth so I won't say something that will get me thrown in jail. The A_ _ HOLE saw me pay the parking fee and not five minutes later he came over. He doesn't even refund the parking fee and we haven't been here ten minutes!

Dad calmly says, "I'll help load up the dogs."

We backtrack to a B & B, and resume eating our now slightly melted ice cream.

My ice cream spoon is halfway to my mouth when there is another tapping on the glass. Seriously! What now!?

Grrr! There is another park ranger. I pray we won't have a drama fiasco, and that we can stay parked where we are. The second Ranger, Bill says, "I'm happy to see dogs hiking on the AT. My dog recently passed and I would like to give you trail magic to help with the dog's expenses, and to honor the memory of my dog."

"Thank you so much," I say "The dogs will love having a special treat." Bill leaves his card and tells us to call if we have any more problems with the other rangers.

Now the ice cream is all melted, but Dad and I finally celebrate Caleb's birth!

**Day 86** We arrive at the park entrance, but have to wait 30 minutes for it to open.

There is so much fog I can barely find the bathroom!

The 4 dogs and I crowd into the multiunit bathroom and I close the door so they can't escape. They sniff around the bathroom, drink from the toilet, and check out all the empty stalls while I take care of business.

Dad and I sleep in the truck at Raven Rock Road.

**Day 87** A few miles after getting started, there is a steep descending rock hill. Somehow, I fall. When I fall, the dogs are somewhat stopped, but when I am on the rock ground it causes tension on the leashes. Then the back two dogs, Digger and Mtn. Goat jump forward, thinking I'm pulling them forward. They have to jump, so as not to step on me. When they jump forward it pulls me forward and I fall down another rock level. Now, there is tension on Kujo and Instigator's leash. They jump forward, pulling me down another boulder. I can feel Mtn. Goat getting ready to jump again.

I have to stop this fall!

I can't use my hands to stop us because I am using both hands to hold onto the dog leashes. All the while we're falling down the hill like a slinky, one giggly flip at a time. Finally, I am able to stretch out one leg, and catch the toe of one shoe, under the edge of a rock. Using all my strength, I have just enough leveraged to keep the dogs from pulling me down the next level when they jump ahead again. I finally stop with my right leg stretched out as far as it can go with the toe caught under a rock. My left leg is bent at a 90-degree angle at the knee, and twisted back and to the side at an awkward angle. My arms are stretched in opposite directions, with each hand clenched in a fist to hold on to the dog leashes. All muscles are engaged. I can still feel my abs tightening to hold me steady.

I shakily get up and notice my left ankle is sore, but it doesn't feel broken. I have to make sure I step on it in proper alignment. I slow down.

Not long after recovering from, "the big fall," a four legged, happy, tail wagging, free reign friend shows up, while the 4 dogs and I are still gingerly descending the rock hill. I look warily ahead. The owners call their dog and put it back on a leash. I am able to drag my dogs past without falling. Again.

*Thank you God for keeping me safe and free from injury when I was falling like a slinky. Amen.*

At the Pen Mar County Park, I meet, Dan, at his cousin's Bar Mitzpa. He agrees to take a picture of me and the dogs.

The dogs refuse to look at the camera.

The mileage on the sign is totally inaccurate, but I am astounded at the magnitude of miles I've hiked, 1055.6.

The crossing at the MD/PN border shows the way I came from, but not the way I am going. I spend 45 minutes walking up and down the tracks on both sides looking for the trail. I finally find it, buried under overhanging spring tree growth. I mark the trail entrance with sticks and rocks pointing in the direction of the trail.

There are houses to the right of the trail. The people are having a party and laughing, but no one bothered to point me in the direction of the trail. After getting back on the trail, I see a wooden sign representing the Mason-Dixon line.

The dogs and I end the day at PA 16 parking area.

We see lots of hikers exiting the trail. It is Saturday. On May 14, 2011, we meet thru hikers Helmet and Whitney Houston. These guys are hiking an average of 30 miles a day! We also meet Ashley, Vikki, Moses, Hoochie, and Redbird.

# Chapter 12: Pennsylvania

**Day 88** May 15, 2011 "Ouch!" I exclaim as I stumble for the 15th time today! "People weren't lying when they said PA is rocky."

Kujo gives me a bored look in response to my outburst. Mtn. Goat, Digger, and Instigator pause from pulling long enough to give me a look that says, Hurry up will you?

The fog obscures many obstacles on the trail, including boulders and large rocks! My hands are tied up with leashes.

"Oomph!" The air is knocked out of me this time when I fall. I can feel a bruise forming on my knee.

I wish I had two more arms and hands so I can use hiking poles!

Kujo is my trail guide. All the rocks blend into an indiscriminate grey.

Two hours into the morning, I meet "Leaf" at Tumbling Run shelter, he says, "I'm glad to have water at the shelter because in the summer time the springs dry up!"

"Right now, there is more than enough water," I respond. "It either rains or there is already so much rain there are puddles on the trail every day!"

The fog finally clears, I pass a group of boulders laid out in a way that resembles Clifford the Big Red Dog.

Four more hours pass and I make it to Caledonia State Park. Where is Dad? He should be here by now! Maybe he can't find the park, or he doesn't know where the trail crosses in the park. I call his cell phone and leave a message, "Hey Dad. It's early and there is a five-way intersection less than four miles away. I'll meet you there. Love you. Bye."

So far today, I've hiked about 16 miles.

Less than two miles later I stop in awe as I gaze at the Quarry Gap Shelter. It has potted purple, white, and yellow pansy plants hanging from the porch. There is a flower garden with ferns and green stalks of what will be either daffodils or narcissus blooming in a few more weeks. The shelter has two sides with a picnic table in the middle. Above the middle is a yellow painted wood carving of a duck. The shelter is occupied.

One of the occupants, "Berky", says, "Be careful hiking. I saw a timber rattler earlier on the trail."

"I will. Thanks!"

A mile and a half later I reach the five-way intersection. It's a dirt road. I wait. And wait. And wait.

It starts to drizzle. I pull out my umbrella, but it doesn't keep the rain off the dogs.

After a while D'artagnon passes and invites me to hike with him, but I tell him I am waiting on my Dad. After waiting for over an hour in the rain, and getting colder despite rain gear and umbrella, I keep hiking. One umbrella isn't enough to keep myself, and four dogs dry. It is about 5:30. Darkness is coming. I try to call Dad, but he is tired of listening to me, and isn't answering his phone (he says the battery was dead, no signal…excuses). I already hiked about 20 miles, but after resting I have a little energy left.

There is a three-way gravel road coming up, then there is the PATC Milesburn Cabin, and another road after that. The cabin stays locked, but if I don't see Dad I can probably make it to Birch Run shelter. I don't want to be stuck in the dark in the rain! I force my tired legs to start running. I run as long as I can then I slow to a fast walk. I cover 3.5 miles in 1 hour. I have adrenaline in my veins. Slow breath in, "one-two-three" and out "one-two-three".

As I descend yet another hill I see a pretty stream, the PATC Milesburn Cabin, and oh glorious site, the white truck with the too short purple camper shell. I pick up the pace to catch Dad before leaves.

I hear the truck running. I sprint toward it yelling "Dad! DAD!" At the top of my lungs.

I finally reach the truck and tap on the window. "I sure am glad to see you." I tell Dad. "I thought it would be easy for you to find the five-way road, but I was wrong. I didn't know if you were getting my messages."

"Yeah," Dad says. "I saw your friend D'ar something earlier. I asked him if he had seen the girl with 4 dogs, and he said he had seen you. I was just about to leave to check my voicemail again. There isn't any signal here."

"I'm glad you didn't leave because if I hadn't seen you I was going to keep hiking."

I close my eyes and say a silent "Thank you Jesus for helping me connect with Dad.  Amen."

23 miles of hiking today.

Dad and I watch, "Mrs. Doubtfire" on the laptop.

Dad turns the key in the ignition on the truck.  It makes a pitiful "ngho, ngho nghugh" sound.  My heart stops beating, please don't tell me we are going to be stranded in the woods with a dead battery.

"Nghugh, Ughh, Vrooom!"

The truck finally starts.  Thank you again Jesus for your protection and mercy.  Amen.

**Day 89** I hike in the rain dog-less today.

It sure is quiet.

At Tom's Run Shelters I meet a family, Julianna, David, Dad, and Pole Broke.

"Hey," I say, "How are ya'll?"

"We're good.  We are trying to decide if it's going to stop raining long enough for us to hike into town without getting soaking wet."

"I know what you mean," I say.  "I usually hike with my 4 dogs, but I left them with my Dad this morning because of the rain.  Are ya'll thru hiking?"

"No.  We are hiking a section.  We are from Sarasota, FL."

"That's neat.  My cousin lives in Bradenton.  It's a long drive and she keeps moving farther and farther south!  It was nice meeting ya'll.  Good luck hiking and staying dry," I say as I resume hiking.  "I have 22.9 miles to hike today and I want to stop at the Pine Grove Store for the half gallon challenge!"

A half mile later I see the sign.

**1090.5 Springer Mountain South.  1090.5 Katahdin North.**

Halleluiah I make it halfway!

The sign is a well-made wooden trail marker complete with the official AT symbol, two small American flags, one on each corner, a mailbox, and a white blaze.

Thank you for making such a beautiful sign!

Three miles later I speed up as I approach town.  My mouth drools as I think bout the half gallon challenge at Pine Grove General

Store. They are supposed to be open from "mid-April to Memorial Day."

I speed pass a beautiful log home with white trim and a large screened side porch. The yard is green and manicured, with pretty white and yellow flowers blooming.

I race toward the store. Subconsciously thinking, there aren't many people here.

Grrrr! Pine Grove General Store is closed! They are only open on the weekend until after Memorial Day.

It's Monday!

The vending machine works. I splurge on a soda.

After 6:00 p.m., I make it to PA 94. Dad is waiting.

"I'm sorry you didn't get ice cream at the country store. We can go to town for ice cream. There is a Wal-Mart."

My mouth starts to salivate again. I hop in the truck, "Let's go."

On the way to the store we pass a Clydesdale Horse pulling a buggy on the country road. The driver has a long dark beard, a black suite, a black hat with a wide brim and a white shirt.

"I didn't know people still drove a horse and buggy," I tell Dad.

"I've seen a few interesting modes of transportation since we've been in Pennsylvania."

Once in the Wal-Mart we settle on buying a box of ice cream sandwiches. I can't resist buying a feather pillow. It's only $5!

As darkness descends, I snuggle into my sleeping bag. I have extra foam mats and sleeping bags on top of the plastic bins. I have a place at the top just big enough for my head, and I make sure my feet don't extend past the glass at the end of the camper shell, or they get wet when it rains. When we sleep in parking lots, I line the windows with extra foam mats, so no one can see me.

**Day 90** May 17, 2011 Ugh! Another lonely, rainy, and drizzly day. I navigate Rock Maze, then later meet Nature Bob near Butcher Hill Road.

He says "I am a high school teacher and part of the students' senior project is to hike from here to Harper's Ferry. We just got started from Boiling Springs."

"That sounds like a neat high school."

"It's a great way to have students appreciate nature and to increase their confidence, and survival skills," Nature Bob says.

"I have an older brother who took Home Economics in high school, but they did away with the program before I was old enough to go. I was so disappointed. I think it's good to know math and reading, but I also think survival skills are important. Good luck on your adventure," I say as we both continue on our way.

In Boiling Springs, PA, I stop at the ATC Mid-Atlantic Regional Office. They have a shower and a log book. Katmando and the 5 Guys are only a couple days ahead of me. John in the office asks how everything is on the trail. I assure him that everything has been calm and normal.

Towards the end of the day, near Bernheisel Road, I meet a local named Sarah. She works for an organic food dealer. She is trail running in the mud. She runs every day. She says she saw thru hikers earlier in the season and they looked miserable. One of them was Chainsaw who passed Rocket and I a while back in Tennessee.

My feet keep slipping in the mud when I walk fast. After talking to Sarah, I decide to trail run. My feet aren't slipping as much with running!

I finish the day with a clearly marked true "U-turn" which takes me under Conodoguinet Creek bridge and I meet Dad at Sherwood Drive. We talk about our day while we eat Ramen noodles.

The dogs greet me with tail wagging excitement and lots of tongue licking.

**Day 91**       Drizzly, dog-less day. I'm sick of sore, soggy feet day after day, slipping in slime, and sloshing through streams. I'm stuck with the silence of my melancholy thoughts.

If only I were prettier, if only I were slimmer, sexier, sweeter, smarter…richer.

If only, if only, if only…

If only I were loveable.

"Shut up!" I admonish myself. "Just SHUT UP!"

Tears roll freely down my cheeks to mix with the relentless drenching rain.

I run despite the hazardous terrain. Anything to stop the noise inside my head.

After Miller's Gap Road, I meet three male section hikers, they are Snobby, Rude and Brusque.

"Do ya'll know what the weather is going to be like over the next couple of days?" I ask.

"No. You should check the weather channel," Rude says.

"I thought since ya'll are just starting you might have an idea. Does it look like I'm carrying a T.V.? You obviously aren't thru hikers," I respond tersely.

"We're hiking from Duncannon to Harpers Ferry, maybe as far as Shenandoah," Snobby says, looking down his nose at me. (123-160 miles.)

I look back at him like, he's a piece of dog shit I just stepped in and say, "Well I started in Georgia and am hiking to Maine. Good luck on your adventure."

"Thanks," Brusque says in a nasally, high pitched voice as he brushes past.

A short time later, I pass a bench made from natural rock and take a quick break before moving on. After that, I hike through an endless green field with a narrow path worn into the grass from the steps of all the hikers before me. Other than a stick with the white AT blaze there is nothing man made to mar God's beauty. The view is so amazing, I feel like I'm walking in a piece of heaven.

Later I meet Croft at Hawk Rock View. The trail is treacherous. Visibility is hazy and the descent is steep and rocky, but the view is amazing. It is overlooking the lush green valley below.

Once we make it to a flat area, Croft and I stop for a break. "Where do you leave your dogs when you aren't hiking with them?" Croft asks.

"My Dad meets me at the trail crossings."

"I started a thru hike last year. I weighed 137 pounds when I stopped last year. I lost 77 pounds, but I gained some of it back. I didn't finish a couple of sections because it was too late in the season. I'm finishing up this year. I also want to lose the weight I gained back!"

"It's nice to be able to eat so much food while I'm hiking and not get fat," I say. "I fluctuate between 5-10 pounds of weight loss. I read it is impossible to carry enough food to prevent yourself from losing weight. The heavier your pack is the more calories you burn carrying it."

"I believe it. I'm going to Duncannon. Do you want to hike together? I might slow you down, since I'm not as young as you and I have to be careful I don't fall. Last year I twisted my ankle badly and it slowed me down."

"I would love to hike with you. I'm used to at least having my dogs to talk to, but the last few days I've been all alone. I'm getting tired of talking to myself."

At the convenient store, I get a burger, a piece of cake, and Dr. Pepper. I sit outside in the sun to eat. Then we hike to the Doyle Hotel. Croft says, "This is as far as my old bones will take me today. The Doyle is a great place to stay."

"It's tempting," I say, "but I'm meeting my Dad. It was nice to meet you. Good luck finishing the trail."

"Thanks, you too!"

Within minutes of passing up a warm dry place to stop for the day, a torrential downpour starts. I consider going back to the hostel, but I am soaked within seconds. I use the umbrella, but it is useless with so much rain swirling around. The sidewalk trail is a river, with enough water to submerge my shoes. Little orange flowers are beaten with rain until they fell apart, leaving orange petals floating helplessly down the sidewalk. I follow the petals to the bridge, then we part ways. They fall into the Susquehanna River and I begin to cross the bridge.

The vehicles drench me with a wall of water when they pass. The umbrella helps deflect the water sprayed from vehicles, but then I get wet from the rain pouring down on my head. It is stifling with my rain gear on, and I get wet and sweaty on the inside.

Lose, lose, lose wet situation!

Once I get onto the rural part of the trail, there are many trees down. One small tree, with bright, green leaves, is twisted in half and stabbed into the ground. I'm glad I wasn't standing there when the tree pierced the ground! Did all the damage and debris occurred while I was walking on the town section of the trail during the storm? Sometimes trail maintainers re-route the trail, and other times God does the re-route.

The rivers and streams are swollen with two to three feet of standing water in areas.

I finally make it to PA 225. Dad is waiting. He says, "I fed the dogs already."

"Thanks Dad." I change my wet clothes in the truck. I love to be warm, dry, snuggly, and cozy in my sleeping bag. After hiking 20 miles, any place to sleep feels like luxury.

**Day 92** This morning I caught Instigator with his nose wedged in the corner of the kennel and a piece of my foam sleeping mat in his little piranha mouth!

"Dad!" I call to the front of the truck. "I'm taking Instigator with me today."

"The weather forecast says it's going to rain again today."

"It's not raining now, and I don't think my sleeping mat can survive another day with Instigator's piranha mouth!"

I slosh through three inches of standing water. My feet are red with tender areas on the heels and a few toes. My right pinky toe escapes the confines of my now holey Asics.

About lunch time, I catch up with the hospital hikers, Boots and Danger while they are taking a break. Danger saw a live bobcat on the trail one day!

The AT continues on a gravel road. There is water roaring and rushing in to Rausch Creek. The bank is almost flooded! Stony Creek Foot bridge is made of two long wooden 2 X 8's fastened together. The bridge is only four inches above the water and the trail on the other side of the bridge has two inches of standing water. There is water everywhere! I can see the impact of the current on the small and medium size trees. If the rain doesn't stop soon the trees will be swept away!

Instigator looks like a drown rat.

In the field after Second Mountain, I see a man about my age hiking toward me. As he gets closer I say, "Hi, how far are you hiking?"

He says, "I'm just out for the day. What about you?"

"I'm doing a thru hike."

"I'm Doug and I'm a hydrologist." I look at him questioningly and he continues. "I currently work for the federal government and I check the sanitation of the water on the AT." He shows me his bag of supplies and continues. "So far, the water is good in this area, however farther south there have been reports of contamination. How do you manage hiking with four dogs?"

"It's not bad. I keep them on a leash otherwise they run away and don't come back!"

"Last year when I came I brought my dog. He ran off and when he came back he had porcupine quills all in his face. I had to take them out when we got home. He whimpered and whined the whole time."

We laugh together and talk a while longer before departing ways.

A mile later, after crossing two roads, I sigh, "I'm so tired, will I ever get to the Pa72 underpass?" I look at Instigator as if he has an answer. I keep hiking. I don't get far.

I look down at Instigator and ask, "Do you see where the trail goes?" He doesn't answer.

The trail has disappeared at a river crossing, at least as wide as a two-lane highway and a minimum of four ft. deep. I suspect in some places it is waist deep. I look up and down, and all around for white blazes on the opposite side of the river. It's after 7:00 p.m. Dusk is descending. I can't see anything except a well-worn trail with gravel on it, on the other side of the river.

I groan. I can't find a bridge anywhere! I consider my options. One, I can walk across and get wet, but I'm worried the current is too strong. I have no intention of drowning. Second option, is to cross on a wobbly, narrow log to the left about four ft. above the water. I start that route, but I can't figure out how to balance, and, carry Instigator across. He isn't a strong swimmer and would be swept away by the current, and he doesn't like water. Thirdly, I can backtrack to the last road crossing, about a half mile back. I don't like backtracking. Fourth option, is to go upstream, and cross on a narrow log, with water lapping over it. It isn't as wide here, but it appears deeper. There might be snakes!

I heft Instigator in my arms, hold on to low hanging branches, and wobble across the log with cold, rushing water. I make it to the other side. Then, I hike up hill to the road, and walk across the bridge to meet Dad.

I see Dad and say, "I'm glad you are here. It has been a long 25.6 miles!"

Dad says, "I had a little adventure today to." I raise my eyebrow in question. He continues. "One of the state roads is closed because of flooding. I detoured around, then I parked in the shade so the dogs wouldn't get too hot. The county road across from me had one to two feet of standing water so I watched the cars attempting to go through the water. The trucks had no problem. Some of the cars turned around, but one car was going too fast. He hit the water hard and his car stalled in the middle of the puddle. I went over and helped push his car out."

"Did the car start once it was out of the water?"

"He let it sit for a few minutes, then it started right up. Oh, about an hour before you got here I saw your friend StormSong. He was walking on the road and he stopped to pet Digger and ask how his foot is."

"That's pretty cool. The guys aren't that far ahead of me."

Whew, what a day! Water, water everywhere.

**Day 93** The dogs are dry with Dad. It's foggy with a chance of rain. What else is new? It rains for two weeks straight, with brief moments of something resembling sun. The trail, when it isn't rocky, is an excursion in river walking. I stop with wet feet at PA183.

**Day 94** A wonderful day of rest; I read, relax in the truck, then cut Instigator's hair with my tiny Swiss army knife scissors. It takes all day even though he's a little guy.

About 10:30 p.m. we have a "general" police check. i.e. supposedly it is routine. Probably one of the busy body hunters, concerned about us parking there all day.

**Day 95** It's foggy, but I bring the dogs with me.

Monotony is broken by an arrow shape made from rocks laid out on the ground telling me to turn right, then thirty minutes later I see a random, Boy Scout shelter in the woods. It has two long logs braced diagonally on trees. It has perpendicular logs across the top and two sides.

Near Phillips Canyon Spring I meet, Al. I ask "How do you keep from falling and hurting yourself when running on large rocks?"

Al smiles and says, "I don't know. I just see where I need to step."

He runs away.

Girl (Hiking) with 4 Dogs

I pause at a spring and let the tranquil sound of the water wash over and sooth me.

Next, I meet Dad at Broad St. and Penn. St. I feel rested, I only hiked 15 miles today. I sit in the back of the truck, and leisurely eat chicken Dad bought, and add bread and cheese.

Dad is in the cab of the truck for a long time. I glance to the cab once to see why Dad hasn't moved the truck, or come to the back to eat with me. His body is scrunched at an awkward angle and I see a massive, brown, semi-formed substance in a green bowl. I gag on the chicken in my mouth and quickly look away!

Twenty minutes later, we are ready to leave. Dad turns the key in the ignition. Nothing happens. The truck battery is dead. Dad wants us to push the truck out of the mud, and onto a main street. The mud is up to my ankles, squishy, and slippery. We use boards to keep the truck from sliding back into the hole it sunk into. After an hour of exhausting, useless, wasteful effort, we move the truck back 12 inches.

Finally, I can't take it anymore, I run up to a helpless woman who is bringing her blind family member home. She visibly jumps as I approach and she looks frantically side to side.

"I don't mean to scare you," I begin, "and I apologize if I smell sweaty. I'm thru hiking and my Dad met me here to re-supply." I gesture toward the truck. "The truck battery died and I can't push it out of the mud."

"I can't help you. I have to take care of my mom. She can't be left alone," the woman replies, "but I'll call my neighbor."

She calls the neighbor next door, Joel, and he comes out to give us a jump in his Toyota.

He is short and to the point. "Why didn't you ask for help sooner?" He has a northern accent. With my hands on my hips, I look at Dad and let him answer.

I won't plan any short days again for a while. I don't like being punished for it!

Once the truck is up and running, I take the dogs and hike a half mile to the next road crossing. I'd rather start from PA 61, Blue Mtn. Road. There is a beautiful piece of artwork, an old car painted in graffiti with all the colors of the rainbow at the parking area. Dad picks me up and we go to town. I gaze mournfully at my dirty, red, tender feet.

**Day 96** Rain and tornado warnings!

I wish I could find the courage to stop hiking.

Alone again. Always along.

I hike faster through the rain; Past Pocahontas Spring, past the broken blue egg shell on the ground. I pause to gaze at a split tree with a rock wedged between the limbs. The limbs will never touch again, but they are healthy and they are growing around and consuming the inflexible rock. Later I pass a small rock wall with a stream gurgling out of it.

I stop to catch my breath while hiking straight up a rock boulder. A local hiker, Frank and his dog, Aspen Grace, easily pass me.

I make it to the Pinnacle. Frank says, "The view is breathtaking when it's not raining. I see birds soar and once I watched an eagle. At night, the stars are amazing!"

"I bet," I say, still trying to catch my breath.

We (Frank) talks while I catch my breath.

At the end of the day, I meet Dad at PA 308. I am getting in the truck when the first torrential down pour starts. It stops long enough for me to feed the dogs, then, it stars raining again. Dad and I eat in the truck cab.

An hour and a half after stopping, a PoPo comes to check on us. He asks, "Are you waiting out the storm?"

"Yes," I answer. "We are waiting out the storm." I don't mention we will be "waiting out the storm" until in the morning.

We listen to the weather forecast in the truck. The broadcaster says, "We continue to be under a tornado warning. Seek shelter immediately."

I glance at Dad. He shrugs. It is what it is.

**Day 97** Finally, a sunny day.

I harness the 4 dogs to their leashes and set out.

Dew is still on the ground when I see Katmando at the New Tripoli Campsite. I say, "Hey, I never thought I would catch up to you. Are you still hiking with Niners, Stillwater, StormSong, and TreeBeard?"

"Yes. Niners daughter is hiking with us now, so we slowed down." Katmando idly pets the dogs. "Where is Rocket?"

Girl (Hiking) with 4 Dogs

"She quit just before West Virginia. She missed her husband too much. Where is everyone else?"

"They are still sleeping."

"Oh. Tell everyone I said hey. Maybe I'll see you on down the trail."

A mile later the dogs and I reach, The Knife Edge. As the name implies the trail resembles a blade (the rocks) protruding from the ground, and into the tree tops. Imagine the knife blade being tilted to a 120-degree angle. The trail runs along the top of the blade. There are no flat rocks to hike on and the trail continues this way for many yards.

The dogs are stoked and ready to lunge. I am trepidatious. It's a long way down. If I fall this time, it won't be a slow slinky fall. It will be more like, fall and break something. Hopefully, not my neck, or back. Instigator licks his lips in anticipation. Mtn. Goat and Kujo grin as if to say "we got this," and Digger looks like he would rather be somewhere else.

At least my friends are behind me.

I'd like to be able to crawl across on my hands and knees, but that won't work with the dogs. I glare at them and admonish, "No pulling," then with my heart racing in my chest, I slowly start across.

Katmando passes me while I inch my way across. So much for my friends being behind me.

I sigh in relief once My feet are on solid ground again.

I miss Rocket immensely. Crossing fallen trees and large rocks and boulders in the trail with dogs is a juggling act. I try to be the one in the front, but the dogs are impatient. Nor are they coordinated. Digger has mental delusions that he can't step over a waist high tree, he has to crawl under, and Instigator, the big dog that he is, can't crawl under, he has to go over. I often am stuck untangling leashes. Mtn. Goat doesn't wait for me to figure out the solution to the obstacles. He plows ahead. Then Kujo doesn't want to be in the back, so he is right on Mtn. Goat's heels. I laugh in exacerbation.

A couple of miles after the Knife Edge is Bake Oven. Probably named for all the rocks that are hot enough to bake me if I fall, and get lost in them. There are also huge oven sized boulders we have to maneuver through. Someone attempted to secure a tarp shelter over a boulder ravine, but it is blowing raggedly in the wind. As we exit Bake Oven, there is a golf ball graveyard, then a road hike.

After a road hike, there is a trail detour near Lehigh River. We start a steep accent. I feel like I'm climbing a never-ending ladder and soon I will evaporate as I reach the blazing sun. My water supply is low, but after feeling dizzy and lightheaded, I drink a few sips of water. Then I round a bend, and am faced with a steep, rock, boulder mountain.

I am speechless. How in the world am I going to navigate this obstacle with 4 dogs on a leash? Should I hike back down, call Dad, and ask him to take the dogs? No. I don't want to back track and I don't want to be defeated by a challenge. If Dad wasn't helping me then I would have to figure out a way to conquer the mountain. I could let the dogs off the leash, however then they might run off, or approach someone else, and make that person fall, possibly to their death. Or Third, I keep them on the leash and see if I can make it to the top without dying.

"Dear Jesus, please help us reach the top safely. Amen.

There are road construction workers waaaay below. If I fall, I hope they see and call 911 to pick up my body, and let my family know I'm not MIA I am just DOA.

Some places on the climb up are barely big enough for me, let alone me plus 4 dogs. I navigate one boulder at a time. I pick up Instigator and put him where I need him to be. Mtn. Goat is a great leader climbing boulders. If he didn't look so much like a dog, you might think he was a goat. Kujo follows. Unfortunately, Digger is a full-grown baby and doesn't believe in his abilities to jump and climb boulders. While the other dogs move forward and upward, Digger hesitates and falls back. I hook his leash to a loop on my backpack so I can climb and hold on better. I let Mtn. Goat and Kujo lead, with Instigator and myself in the middle.

The dogs are happy. Their tongue hangs out to the side and it looks like they are grinning. From time to time Mtn. Goat tries to crawl into the cooler rock crevices.

We come to a halt. How are we all going to get to the next level? It's seven foot higher than where we are standing on a three-foot ledge!

Girl (Hiking) with 4 Dogs

After five minutes of standing, Mtn. Goat gets tired of being crowded with us on the three-ft. ledge, and he jumps up the seven feet to the next level. Kujo quickly follows. I gently toss Instigator up then begin pulling myself up using my toe on a narrow ledge for leverage. Digger is hesitant. He puts his paws up on the boulder, and makes a puny attempt to jump up to the ledge, then he falls all the way back, jerking me backwards in the process. After the third time of being jerked backward, I finally have to let him off the leash.

It is sink or swim for him. He is too big for me to lift or carry, and too clumsy for me to keep him on his leash. Falling and dying is a real possibility even without Digger pulling me backward!

The rest of us keep going. Digger whines, and fusses, carrying on until we get about 30 ft. ahead and start around a corner where he can't see us, then he finally overcomes his fear and insecurities, jumps the ledge, and follows.

We make it to the top safely! I could have died.

"Thank you Jesus," I whisper.

I sit at the top to rest for a minute. My throat is dry, I'm hot, but I'm not sweating anymore. I reach for the spout on my CamelBak and realize I'm sitting on it. My butt is now wet. I shift my weight and grasp the spout. I get two drops of water before sucking only air.

Even though I am out of water, I pass a reservoir of water because I am hoping to make it to the post office in town before it closes. I've been hiking all day. I must be close to finishing.

After another hour of hiking I still haven't reached the road. My throat feels like a desert, my tongue is like sawdust, and my legs feel like lead. Mtn. Goat keeps doing his lay down protests. There are little streams of water crossing the trail. I hike upstream and pump water.

I dig out my cell phone and turn it on to call Dad. When he answers I say, "Dad can you pick up the "General Hiker" mail from the post office? I'm not going to make it to Little Gap Road before the post office closes. We have to have the new truck tags mom sent before June."

Dad says, "Yeah, I can pick-up the mail. We probably need to put more gas in the truck soon."

I sigh laying back on a warm rock. "Okay. Thanks."

After the SuperFUNd Detour, we hike through tall grass. The ticks are so thick I stop frequently to fling 10 to 20 at a time off my socks. It is so HOT! We take multiple breaks.

We finally make it to Little Gap. I meet Captain Max. He is planning to hike 500 miles of the trail doing about 10 miles a day. Mtn. Goat is covered in ticks! His fur is white with black polka dots. Normally, he's just white. I find 194 ticks on him, and crush them between rocks, while waiting on Dad. I look really hard for 6 more ticks, but I can't find any. There aren't as many on the other dogs, less than 20. I heard somewhere that ticks like white.

I only hiked 18.9 miles. It took all day!

Once Dad arrives, I thank him for getting the truck tag. I tell him about my near-death experience climbing the boulders and he agrees to keep two dogs at a time going forward.

**Day 98** Kujo, Instigator, and I meet "Whole Wheat" and "Too Tall." They are from North Carolina and are hiking the trail in sections. Too Tall is having problems with his knee.

The terrain is rocky, but flat most of the day.

I meet Dad at Fox Gap, 24 miles today. While we are eating, and relaxing outside the truck the dogs alert us to three guys approaching. I do my customary greeting and find out they are section hiking form New York and California. Shortly after they pass a group of locals drive up and unload seven boxes of pizza.

I ask, "Are ya'll having a party?"

One of the guys answers, "We are camping with friends at Kirkridge Shelter. They already have drinks at the shelter."

"Have fun," I say.

I was hoping they were giving out trail magic.

**Day 99** What in the Crazy World is going on?! It's 5:20 in the morning and the SUV that just pulled up beside ours in the parking area is rocking and moaning! Obviously, they are not really industrious, raring to go hikers! The dogs are excitedly barking and won't shut up!

It makes a lot of fucking sense now. When AJ said he had to go into work early and stay late. He was going to fuck around in Hoochie Momma's van!

I'm sick to my stomach and about to puke! I'm shaking and having heart palpitations. I grind my teeth to keep from screaming. I see a haze of red and struggle to keep myself from going to the vehicle next door to interrupt the rendezvous. I continue to shake in rage and disgust.

Get a fucking room people!

After my rude, early, awakening by infidels moaning, and rocking the SUV beside our truck, I can't go back to sleep. I hurriedly feed the dogs, discuss with Dad where to meet at the end of the day, then I snatch up Mtn. Goat and Digger and I start hiking.

Are women who have illicit trysts, in someone's vehicle, away from civilization, the same ones who end up as a "missing person" in the news headlines? He could easily fuck her, kill, her, and throw her in the woods.

By the time I reach Kirkridge Shelter a half mile away, I've calmed down.

Ahhh, relief. I love privies!

After seven miles, the trail exits the woods onto the road. It goes through Delaware Water Gap, PA, then crosses the Delaware River on interstate 80 and enters New Jersey!

# Chapter 13: New Jersey

**Day 99** May 26, 2011 Continued "Wow! I'm in New Jersey now."

It is 9:30 a.m. and the heat is sweltering! The dogs and I are at 314 feet, hiking on the steaming asphalt! I'm worried about the foot pads on Mtn. Goat and Digger. Once we are off the bridge, they walk in the grass.

I have to pee again, but there isn't any tree coverage! After another mile of hiking I see a welcome center up ahead. There is an outdoor bathroom. The BR is a plain concrete building. Inside there is what appears to be a metal trash can bolted to the floor over a deep hole (permanent port-a-john?), with a bed pan shaped seat (all one unit). It is blessedly cool inside. The dogs don't want to leave. I would stay longer, but the smell is too malodorous.

After the road hike, it is a relief to get back into the woods. The Delaware River area is refreshingly cool. The air is fresh and crisp. It is impossible not to breathe deeply. The Creek parallel to the trail is high with rushing, gurgling water racing around and over the rocks to get to Delaware River.

I see a black snake skitter across the trail, and then rattle its tail in the leaves. I'm sure it isn't a real rattle snake because the head isn't diamond shaped, and I don't see any rings on its tail to indicate a true rattle. Impressive survival techniques.

A short time later, there are waves of military school boys finishing a section of the trail as part of their education. Most are not scared of dogs, but one ran off the trail into the woods as we got closer. I called after him, "The dogs are on a leash." He stayed in the woods as we passed giving us a wide berth.

We pass grade school military guys all day. All the guys are incredibly polite and respectful. Some of them asked, "Can we pet your dogs?"

"Yes," I answer. "They like it and it keeps them sociable." Mtn. Goat and Digger sit and grin while they get petted. When the guys stop petting them, Mtn. Goat reaches out his paw toward the kids hand to try to get more petting while Digger shoves his head under the kids hand to let him know he wants more attention.

Girl (Hiking) with 4 Dogs

As they pass each kid asks, "How much farther to the parking area?"

At first I was able to answer, "Only a couple of miles." However, the stragglers have as much as six to ten miles to go.

They assured me, "Our ride is picking us up at the parking area." They look as tired as I feel. They started at High Point, and will end at Delaware Water Gap. It is a five-day trip for them. There are 100 in the group.

By noon I reach Sunfish Pond. It is a 41 acre, acidic, glacial pond. There are only a few types of fish able to survive in the pond. It has been a registered national landmark since August 21, 1935.

An hour later Mtn. Goat insists we take another break. I can feel myself melting and burning from the sun and heat. We stop for water and a snack break near the rock creations around the north end of the lake. One sculpture resembles a dragon, it has a long rock neck, a balanced rock on top for the head with smaller rocks to look like eyes, then surrounding rocks make the body and tail.

Life is wonderful and amazing! I am so thankful for the opportunity to experience a fraction of the fantastic world I live in!

It is still incredibly HOT!

Two hours later Mtn. Goat insists on another break. We have a long way to go, 20.8 miles total. Mtn. Goat and Digger lay in the streams to cool off. At one of our impromptu stops, we sit in the shade and look out at the lake below us. The scene is framed perfectly by a low hanging branch at the top and a small tree with spring green leaves on the bottom left. God is good all the time.

The other challenge for the day is Digger trying to catch frogs. There seems to be a record number of frogs on the trail. They like to wait until they are sure Digger is close, then they jump right in front of him, and into the bushes. Digger lunges immediately after them, and when he jumps in the bushes after them, he jerks my arm practically out of socket, pulls me off the trail, and into the bushes as well.

Ahh, do I scream or do I laugh!? Laugh, screaming makes my throat dry, and I'm out of water.

I pass another group of military school freshmen hiking. They are not finishing today.

I ask, "How much farther to the road?"

"It's less than five miles," one of the leaders answers.

"Good, I can wait to pump water. My Dad is meeting me at the road and I have water at the truck."

"You should see our supply leaders at the road too. They have plenty of water if you need some."

"Thanks," I say. "Good luck on your trip."

"Thanks, you too."

I pass the turn for Mohican Outdoor Center. I want a shower, but I don't have a way to keep up with the dogs while I'm in the shower, so I keep hiking.

I finally make it to Millbrook-Blairstown Rd. I stopped sweating about 30 minutes ago. Just a little longer until I can assuage my thirst.

I sit down on my backpack to rest for a minute. I don't see Dad so I send him another SPOT GPS, letting him know I am at the road. I also send him a text message, but there is very poor service. I'm not sure if he will get the message. While I am resting, one of the guys with the military kids at the road offers to fill up my water bottle. I feel like royalty sitting on my backpack, on the edge of the road, with my feet stretched out, and being served cold, delicious water. In return, I share hiking experiences and encouragement.

I hope some of the students hike the trail when they graduate.

Mtn. Goat and Digger are sprawled out beside me on the side of the road.

After a while everyone leaves, either to hike the next section, or to drive home to prepare to deliver supplies for the next day. I am still waiting for Dad. I am never sure if he isn't waiting because:

1. He doesn't know where I am.
2. He's at the wrong place.
3. I'm at the wrong place.
4. He doesn't think I could possibly be finished yet.
5. He wants me to keep hiking.
6. He's lost.
7. The truck is broken.
8. The GPS or text message didn't go through.
9. He's sleeping or in a diabetic coma.
10. He's still playing or exploring in town.

Girl (Hiking) with 4 Dogs

When Dad finally arrives, he says he knew where the trail crossed, but he didn't want to wait with all the people. He decided to come back after they left. Excuse # 11, "Thanks!"

There is new junk in the truck, a partially falling apart Fischer Price kids table and chair. I have to re-arrange everything in order to get the dog food out.

"Dad, why do you have a table in the truck?"

"I want it for Caleb when he comes to visit."

"Kim and Andy are probably not going to bring Caleb to your house. You have too much junk everywhere."

Dad doesn't say anything so I continue, "There is no room to sleep in the back with the table there. Do you want to keep it in the cab with you?"

"It won't fit," Dad answers.

We argue a while longer before compromising.

Dad says, "I can disassemble the unit, keep the chair, and trash the table."

"That sounds like a great idea. The table is scratched up and cracked anyway and we would hate it if Caleb hurt himself on the jagged plastic."

Finally, I can feed the dogs, then eat hot chicken roman noodles. While savoring every morsel of food, I see a lone hiker approach from the north.

I introduce myself, "Hi, I'm Girl with Four Dogs. How are you?" I ask. "Can we help you?"

"Maybe," she answers. "My trail name is "Bells" because I hike with bear bells. I started a thru hike at High Point three days ago, but I'm just too tired to go on. I always wanted to do a thru hike, but I'm exhausted."

"Maybe if you take a couple of days off you will feel like continuing," I say.

Dad says, "Thru hiking is very difficult. There is nothing wrong with quitting."

"I just can't keep going," Bell says. "I keep falling and I can barely move."

Dad wins. We drive all the way back 20+ miles to take her to Delaware Water Gap. We eventually drop Bells off at The Church of the Mountain Hostel. She is extremely thankful, and gifts me with her rain gear, she says she will never use it again.

As we head back to Blairstown Rd., we see "The 5 guys" walking in town.

I feel like I lived three days today!

Hours later, I am finally able to go to sleep, listening to a wonderful frog symphony, and hoping they will eat more of the mosquitoes biting me! I am a strong fan of deet. The more the merrier. I spray myself, my hair, sleeping bag, pillows, clothes, window screen, and camper shell. Dad, on the other hand, refuses pesticides, or bug repellent of any kind. I don't know how he can stand the mosquito's biting him, and buzzing in his ears!

**Day 100** May 27, 2011 Great, wonderful sunshine! It's time to get up and get ready to go. Kujo and Instigator are the lucky ones today.

After hiking a couple of miles, I traipse off trail and dig a hole for a BM. A short while later, I traipse off trail again. This time I have a purely water like stool. I don't feel sick, but when I drink water, if I don't sweat it out immediately, then it comes out from the wrong orifice. If I don't drink water, then I am fine. This happens four times. Eventually, I drink just enough water to sweat it out. I can eat food without any adverse effects. I wonder if my body is confused about how to function properly?

I hike my longest day of the trip 28.8 miles!

The dogs and I end the day at High Point State Park. The sun is setting with pink, blue and purple hues suspended over the tree tops.

**Day 101** I take a zero day in Port Jervis, NJ.

I say to Dad, "My hair is such a mess. It's oily and nasty. I can't stand it. I wish I could take a shower, but the hotel rooms are too expensive!"

Dad says, "If you want to wash your hair, I can help you rinse it with gallons of water from the truck."

"That's a great idea! Thanks."

After washing my hair, I shave my legs and arm pits using a bowl and soapy water. It has been three weeks since I last shaved, and I'm about to lose my mind!

I talk to "Berky" and meet thru hiker "Juice" at High Point Park State Headquarters. They have a flushing clean toilet inside!

Girl (Hiking) with 4 Dogs

Now it's time to go sightseeing and shopping! Dad and I find fantastic yard sales, and meet neat people. The dogs relax in the kennels. I buy a pink and white quilt, with girls wearing sun bonnets on it, for only $5! (Later, Piranha, aka Instigator, chews part of it!)

At Blakey's, I find a unique, handmade, teal green pottery bowl that looks like it has broken glass in the bottom.

**Day 102** I am hiking on the border of New Jersey and New York with Digger and Mtn. Goat.

We hike through the marshes on planks. The dragonflies zoom around, but Digger is too hot to chase them. I see a group of small red mushrooms beside the planks.

Next, we traverse through fields of cows looking hungrily at us. The calves are butting heads with each other, and the bulls scowl.

At County 519 I meet section hikers, Steve, David, and Daisy. Then, at County Rd. 615 I gag while passing two decaying deer carcasses. Next, at Oil City Road I pass Joan and her husband from Connecticut.

After another road hike, the dogs and I, enter the Wallikill Reserve. There is tall grass with white seeds at the top and purple wild flowers everywhere. Ann and Dan from New Jersey point out a baby deer hiding in the grass. It is so tiny and still has spots. His spots help him blend in with the white tops of the grass. He is curled up in a ball, but his head is raised and his ears are alert. Surprisingly, the dogs don't notice it. Joan says fawns don't have an odor. It helps protect them from predators.

Not long after the baby deer, I see a ground hog disappear into his hole, never to be seen again! The dogs smell it, pull at their leashes, and sniff the ground trying to hunt it down. Eventually, I convince (drag) them away. Mtn. Goat loves hide and seek.

Digger steps on the tail of a blacksnake, and doesn't even recognize he stepped on a living being.

At 6:40 p.m. we approach the Pochuck Creek suspension bridge and gaze in aww at a family with at least eight children wearing dresses!

I catch up to Dad in Vernon, NJ, highway 94 at the base of Wawayanda Mountain, pronounced "way-way-yon-da." There is a red and yellow gladiola blooming.

Dad says, "Today when I was parked in the parking lot of the Fresh Market a police man came up to the truck. The policeman said, 'You need to make sure the dogs in the back of the truck have water. It's too hot for them to be without water all day.'"

"Did he give you a ticket?" I asked.

"No. I gave the dogs water in their water containers, but most of it spilled out in the kennel when I was driving over here."

"Well, we can keep water in their kennels. I'll just have to clean it up when it spills. It was hot for us today too."

Dad continues, "There was also a woman in the parking lot who accidentally locked her child in the car! I kept pouring cold water on the outside to keep the car cool until the locksmith could get the door open."

"That's scary! If it took more than a couple of minutes, I would break out the window of the car to save my baby. I'm sure she was glad you were there to help."

As we are talking various people come and go to their vehicles. Some are nice, some are snobs, some are without, and some are with dogs. There is a family with a Basset Hound who gives us trail magic for the dogs, along with alcohol and paper towels to help get the ticks off. We also meet Kim and her family. Kim's brother owns a hostel in New Hampshire. She strongly encourages me to stay there.

The final memorable person of the day is a guy who runs up and down the mountain for exercise.

**Day 103** I only have Mtn. Goat today because the thru hiker book says there is a ladder somewhere, and Mtn. Goat is the only one who can discern how to use a ladder.

It's sweltering hot again and we are hiking on hot, wet, slippery rock boulders.

Mtn. Goat lays down on the trail frequently and refuses to budge! During our noon break, I sit in the shade and fix my lunch. I pull the crust off the bread for Mtn. Goat, I lay my sandwich on the zip lock bag. I turn to reach inside my backpack to get trail mix, and then I turn back and reach for my sandwich to take a bite. It is nowhere to be found! All I see is a lone zip lock bag and a smiling happy dog!

Girl (Hiking) with 4 Dogs

As we are eating a few hikers pass us. One of them slips on the rocks and busts her butt. We look at each other and I say, "Yeah, it's pretty slippery. I've fallen a few times today myself."

During another break, I share my map with a family from New Jersey and their friends from New York. Less than a mile later I see the NJ/NY border line painted on a rock. It's a 20 foot drop from the top of the rock to the ground.

# Chapter 14: New York

**Day 103** May 30, 2011 Continued There is no ladder, but there is a practically straight up, maybe 15 feet, climb. Mt. Goat can't jump to the top on his own. I find a quarter inch crack in the rock, 4 ft. up, and then I brace my leg so Mt. Goat can use it for leverage to jump to the top. After that, with a little bouncing, and a lot of straining, I am able to hoist myself up, and we continue on our way. Next there is a 30-foot climb. The rocks on either side are smooth and vertical. In the middle, there is a 3-foot crevice with navigateable stepping rocks. Another rock climb has a cascading waterfall parallel to the trail.

I laugh and say, "Hey," as I see the runner from Wawayanda Mtn., hiking the opposite direction from me. He is hiking with a friend today.

He says, "You should hike into Bellvale and have ice cream from Bellvale Farms. They have the best ice cream and they have an outdoor water spigot. You can get your dog some water."

"Sounds fun. Have you ever seen a ladder on the trail?" I ask.

"No. Why?"

"The thru hiker book says there is a ladder, but I didn't see it."

"Maybe it washed away last year."

Bellvale Farms shop is busy! I get Mtn. Goat some water then hook him to my backpack and loop the leash around a bench while I wait in line. The lady in front of me waits until it is her turn to order before she even looks at the menu. I bite my tongue so I don't cuss her out. Thankfully, there is more than one person helping customers. The lady is still looking at the menu when I leave!

I have a scoop of Pistachio and a scoop of Cookie Dough in a waffle cone. I give Mtn. Goat a bite of Cookie Dough. We both lick our lips as we eat the cold, refreshing, and yummy ice cream!

The ice cream shop is a half mile detour, round trip.

It's now 5:35 p.m. On the road hike back to the trail I run. Mtn. Goat barely has to walk fast to keep up. I see PoPo's on patrol near an abandoned building. I slow down until they pass. Once I get on the trail I have seven miles to hike before ending the day at Mombasha Rd.

Girl (Hiking) with 4 Dogs

**Day 104** I can hike 24 miles in about 8 hours. Today, it's up one boulder and down another. All day long. Kujo handles the rocky, boulder filled terrain in stride. I have carry Instigator a lot, and I can't get a fast, consistent pace going.

It is HOT! Again.

The elevation ranges from 163 feet at Bear Mountain Recreation Area to 1368 feet at Fingerboard Shelter.

After 30 minutes of hiking the trail becomes nebulous. The sign says to go straight, but there is no visible trail. The visible trail goes west, however the entire terrain is worn down and trampled. Kujo and I agree to go west following the clearer trail. After 8 minutes of hiking the trail suddenly ends. There are piles of debris and fallen trees blocking the trail. I detour around, but there is no trail on the other side. I backtrack to the sign and look more diligently for an indication of a trail. There is a faint line of fresh dirt headed in a straight-ish direction going up Buchanan Mountain. It eventually parallels the dead-end trail I previously hiked. I have Kujo sniff the trail and we start off north following fresh dirt.

At the top of the mountain we stop again to evaluate the trail. "Dear Jesus," I pray. "Please help us make the correct decision on which way to go. Amen." We follow the fresh dirt again.

Kujo, Instigator, and I hike another mile, cross East Mombasha Rd., then look at Little Dam Lake. Behind us is a well-made wooden footbridge, resting neatly on the ground. In front of us is a rock stepping path across the water. There is a horizontal 2 X 4 at the far end of the water with two vertical 2 X 4's fastened to it, extending in the air, and holding nothing. The rocky trail continues into the woods on the other side of the lake.

With Kujo in the lead and Instigator in the back I precariously proceed across the rocks in the water with one leash in each hand. Instigator baulks at getting his feet wet. I gently tug him while balancing on a rock. Meanwhile Kujo not so gently pulls me when he jumps to the next rock. I jump to the next rock and Instigator is forced to accompany me.

Once civilization is behind us the trail is much easier to follow.

I see five snakes; two of which Kujo steps on! Freaky! One of the five is a dark, black Timber Rattle snake. One of them is brown with black markings and has a triangular head, although initially he looks friendly, and nonpoisonous. Maybe an Eastern Hognose snake. Another one is light brown with dark brown/black ovals on each side of his face and light brown and dark brown diamonds on his back. The fourth one is black, but he doesn't rattle at me, and the fifth one is brown with a light brown stripe down it's back. I throw sticks at two of the snakes to make them evacuate the trail.

Most of the day Kujo drags Instigator and I around, trying to pull my arm off. Then he looks back as if to say, "Come on slow poke." Inevitably, with him pulling me along, I don't see the snakes until after he's disturbed them.

What should I do if one of the dogs gets bit by a rattle snake?

One option, is to use the SPOT GPS for emergency help, but I'm not sure rescuing an animal is an emergency. A second option, is to leave the injured dog behind and go for help. The draw backs are that my dog would hurt himself more trying to follow, and/or another animal would attack, or he wouldn't stay put and would get lost. The best option, using the cell phone to call for assistance can be hit or miss in regards to having a signal while in the woods, so plan B is essential. The fourth, and most likely option, is to bring the injured dog out with me for help. I could attempt to carry the injured dog out, in which case I would wish the injury on Instigator, since he is the smallest. Or maybe I could make a travois to drag out the injured dog. I don't think I can carry a 75-lb. dog any significant distance.

I've never seen a rattle snake, but it would be interesting to do so.

The dogs and I pass a tree possessively holding a rock into the ground. Next, we cross another stream. On the north end, there is a dilapidated rock retention wall. After that we squeeze through the lemon squeezer. Kujo looks back, and smiles with his tongue hanging to the side of his mouth, "This is fun. What's taking you so long?" his eyes and body language say.

I respond, "You're smaller than me. You don't have to squeeze as much to fit through the crack between the boulders in the trail!"

His eyes and face continue to laugh.

Girl (Hiking) with 4 Dogs

A couple miles before we reach the William Brien Memorial Shelter, there is a rustling in the blueberry bushes off to the side of the trail.

I look back, and see a big black snake bolt from laying stretched out, to a coiled, ready to strike, position. It's at least four feet long. I can hear the eerie rattling. It is not leaves. I stop 15 feet away, and take out my rinky, dinky camera phone, since my high tech, expensive camera, with zoom is broken. I turn on the camera phone, wait for it to start up, then I aim, and take a picture. I am sweating from the heat, but then I start sweating in fear, and having heart palpitations. I pray the dogs and I aren't going to die from a lethal snake bite while waiting on my exceptionally slow camera to take a picture! The rattling intensifies, penetrating my eardrums. I've heard snakes can strike quickly.

After taking the picture, I turn off my camera phone and bolt away. Five minutes later we cross a stream on stepping stones. Then 20 minutes after that I see William Brien Memorial Shelter. I look for the log book and make a note about the rattlesnakes in the area. It's 7:43 p.m. I have 9.4 miles to hike before reaching Bear Mountain Recreation Area.

The eerie rattling sound haunts me for hours afterward. I either keep hearing rattle snakes, or I am seriously paranoid. I am also hot and tired. Maybe I am paranoid, delusional, and suffering from heat exhaustion. The trail is narrow, barely wide enough for me. The dogs walk beside me disturbing bushes and inciting rattlesnakes!

As I approach Bear Mountain the trail is urbanized. It is wide, clearly marked, and large sections are wheelchair accessible. There are no roots or protruding rocks to trip me, and the two-thousand steps are evenly spaced.

Perkins Memorial Tower stands proudly overlooking the New York City skyline.

The sky is white with pink hues and the river is blue in the distance.

My feet drag as I continue. Will this day ever end?

Part of the Urban trail is blocked with green construction mesh. To the east there are five piles of perfectly cut rock, 6-foot-long, 3-foot-wide, and 1 foot tall with at least 10 rock "steps" in each pile.

I continue to scramble to Bear Mountain Recreation Area, hoping to arrive before it is too dark to see the trail. I finally make it as the moon and stars begin to shine.

I started my day early. It takes 13 hours to hike 24 miles, but it feels like an eternity.

Dad is waiting.

I sit in the parking lot and rest then Dad helps me feed the dogs.

A woman park visitor and her four children, want to pet the dogs. I warn them to leave Kujo alone. The family leaves shortly after Kujo growls at one of the boys.

There are at least three PoPos at the park for security. It isn't long before one of them approaches. "I'm thru hiking," explain. "It took longer than I expected to hike the 24 miles on my agenda. I was planning to stay at the Bear Mountain Inn. I didn't realize there was 'renovation in progress.' Is there any way we can stay parked in the parking lot tonight?"

The officer replies, "I get off at 11 o'clock p.m. I will check with the oncoming shift. Be careful," he says nodding his head in farewell before driving back to the station.

"I'm going to be Dad. Wake me if we need to move."

**Day 105** June 1, 2011 I yawn and glance at my watch. 7:30 a.m.

I tap on the glass to the cab, "Dad," I yell. "Do you want Instigator and Kujo in the kennel or hooked on the truck?"

"You can leave them on the truck."

"Okay. I've got Mtn. Goat and Digger. I'll see you this evening at Long Hill Road."

I walk through the recreation area to the bathroom. I bring Mtn. Goat and Digger in the stall with me.

As I walk through the park, there is garbage strewn sporadically about. Paper plates, napkins, and chicken bones. Memorial Day was two days ago. The vultures are picking at the trash. At least it's not thru hikers.

There are grills shaped like owls, other birds and animals. A lake is visible behind the picnic tables, rugged green mountains frame the lake. Digger tries to pull me in the trash can after the buzzards. I pull him back and continue walking toward the zoo.

Mtn. Goat and Digger aren't allowed to go into the zoo, so I look around for the blue blaze alternate trail. I walk to the side of the building, down the road, everywhere I can think of, but I can't find the trail!

The zoo closed.

How am I going to find the trail? Digger and Mtn. Goat aren't giving any indication which way to go. My respirations speed up, my throat is squeezing closed. I don't want to finish hiking late again! I force myself to take slow deep breaths. I look across the Hudson River, "Duh, I have to cross Hudson River at some point. I'll hike across on the bridge and look for the trail again on the other side. There is only one bridge across the river."

There is a concrete walkway for hikers on the side of the bridge portioned off with a two-foot-high barrier between us and the cars. Once I get to the other side, I look south and see the blue blaze for the SOBO's is clearly marked. After the bridge, the road splits into a "y."

"Which way do we go? Eney, miney, miney, mo..." I start to the right, but it feels weird. I look at the map, back-track, then I go left. It's been half a mile and I don't see any blazes. I'm wondering if I made the wrong choice when I finally see a faint opening in the trees off the side of the road. I duck under the low hanging branches and see the trail continuing in the woods.

I let out a sigh of relief. Once I'm in the woods I can easily follow the trail.

Seven miles later I cross through another town. I hook the dogs to the backpack, leave them outside, and look briefly inside the AT Market. It is too expensive.

I grab up the dogs and we continue hiking.

After another seven miles, I meet Marathon Mouse at the stream north of South Highland Rd.

He says, "I started the trail on February 14th. I started at Springer Mountain. I had to take time off for a wedding and other family events, so I flip flopped. When I returned to the trail I started in Maine and am hiking south. I was concerned it would be too late in the season to finish in Maine if I continued going north. I have heard some hikers were unable to summit Katahdin in September, due to snow and freezing rain last year."

"Sounds like a good idea to go north to south then. I started hiking February 17th. I have to finish by August. Good luck finishing the trail."

After another seven miles, I meet Silver, Poison Ivy and GOJO near Fahnestock Trail. They are hiking the trail in sections.

Three plus miles later on top of Shenandoah Mountain I see a 911 memorial flag painted on the rocks, along with the directions for North, South, East, and West. It's been almost 10 years since the tragedy of September 11, 2001.

Another half mile and I meet Dad at Long Hill gravel Rd. The parking area is flat, quit, and only big enough for about three vehicles.

**Day 106** It's two miles to the RPH Shelter. It is luxurious for hiker standards.

Next, at Hosner Mountain Rd. I meet "Elvis Trailsley," a 4,000 miler who helps maintain the trail.

We talk for a bit then he says, "Your trail name should be 'First Lady of the AT.' You are the first 'lady' I've seen on the trail."

I look at him questioningly and he continues.

"Many women on the trail don't act like ladies."

"I like the name," I say, "but I'm going to keep the name 'Girl with 4 Dogs.' My friends I started with won't know who is signing the trail log if I change my trail name."

"I understand," he says. "Remember to treat all your water. The water this low comes from a cow pasture higher up. If you have time, get a bite to eat at the 'Mtn. Top Market Deli.'"

"That sounds delicious. I'll call my Dad and see if he wants to eat there too. Thanks for the information and thanks for posting the sign reminding everyone to properly treat the water before drinking it."

As I exit onto NY 52 I meet "Major Miles," he is hiking while on leave from the military. I also meet "Reverend" who follows me to the Deli. I am desperately hoping Dad finds the Deli. "Reverend" talks a lot about when he used to drink heavily and use drugs. He also has tattoos all over his arms.

Girl (Hiking) with 4 Dogs

He says, "I'm a changed man since I got pancreatic cancer. I've hiked the AT before, but I want to do it again before I die. I take pain medicine for the cancer."

I look at him, raise my eyebrows, then ask, "How do you fill your prescription while you are hiking?"

"I call ahead to the pharmacy, then when I make it to the town they have it ready for me to pick up."

I respond, "Oh. Well, my Dad should be here any minute, but I'm going to go inside to get something to eat."

"I don't have any money. What with the cancer and all I barely make it day to day."

"I know how you feel. I'm not working and I may not even be able to finish the trail. My Dad doesn't have money either. He has a bad leg and can't work anymore. I only carry a few dollars for emergencies, if I were to run out of food or need to make a phone call."

Reverend looks at me again walks closer. Kujo growls and snarls his teeth. Reverend says, "He wouldn't really bite would he?"

"I'm not sure. He has bitten a few people, but only when he is provoked or protecting me."

"I guess since I don't have any money for food I'm going to keep hiking." He looks at me trying to give me a pitiful, poor me look.

I say, "Ok. Good luck on the trail."

Since he backed himself in a corner Reverend slowly proceeds to get is stuff and he finally leaves. I hook Kujo and Instigator to my backpack, then to the picnic table and go inside to buy food.

Dad finds us. I have a Philly steak sandwich, and Dad has an Italian dish. I eat all of mine, and Dad shares a couple bites of his.

I give all the dogs water from a doggie water bottle. When I squeeze the bottle, the water squirts up the straw, and into a bowl on the top. They sit and wait their turn, then lap up the water. Digger being is the sloppiest. I swap dogs with Dad.

After 10 more miles of hiking I approach a 3-foot-wide wood walkway going over a swamp. It has metal support spikes in the ground, then a framework of wooden 2 X 4's with a sheet of plywood on top. It's wide enough that Mtn. Goat, Digger and I can walk side by side. Suddenly, the plywood walk ends, there is only the wooden framework over the swamp. There is a sign pointing to the right, into the swamp, and a rinky dink path parallel to my luxurious plywood path. The rinky dink path is two 2 X 4's side by side supported by wooden braces barely off the ground.

Now I'm being pulled in half! Mtn. Goat is in front running forward and Digger is in the back hunched to the ground and shaking! I gently coax Digger forward.

Once we are off the planks I stretch my aching arms.

Two miles later I see the Dover Oak tree, just after crossing County Road 20. It is the largest Oak tree on the AT. It is huge and twisted at the base. There are many branches. Most of the branches are larger than 30-year-old oak trees. While taking pictures, I hear a car slowing down.

I hurriedly resume hiking.

A male voice calls, "Wait." It sounds like Reverend. I pretend like I can't hear him.

I can hear footsteps close behind me. They sound heavy and foreboding. I round a curve and run until I can't catch my breath, then I continue hiking as fast as my legs will move. I have chills running up and down my spine. I'm hoping serial killers won't be able to keep up.

I slow down to navigate the curved bridge going over the stream. There is only a rail on one side. I squish Digger against the rail and let Mtn. Goat lead across the stream.

A half mile later I meet Dad at the Appalachian Trail Railroad Station. I grab all the dogs and take them to potty away from the trail.

I sit on the tailgate on the back of the truck in the warm sunshine and converse with Dad about the day.

"Just before you arrived at the Deli there was a "thru" hiker named "Reverend." He kept talking about his past drinking and drug use."

"He doesn't sound like a reverend to me," Dad says.

"Me either. If you meet him, please don't' give him a ride."

**Day 107** My shoes are quickly saturated from dew on the ground. Kujo and Mtn. Goat bolt after a baby bunny. I have to reign them in.

In the trail log, I see I'm not far behind the Red Team. I keep seeing Squirrel's name but I've never met Squirrel. I smile; it is thrilling to hike fast, and far by foot in a day. It's an amazing feeling of wonderment, joy, and accomplishment.

I pass a wooden water tower and think about a book I read in high school, Don Quixote. It is full of knightly adventures.

I hike on the border of NY/CT for a while before officially entering CT. The trees make interesting creaking, groaning, moaning and rattling (at least I hope it is the trees) noises.

Are the trees about to fall on my head?

The trees appear to be a hundred feet tall. The tops disappear in the blinding light of the blazing sun. The branches are scarce, especially close to the ground. Probably the weight of the snow in the winter knocks off the branches.

# Chapter 15 Connecticut

**Day 107** June 3, 2011 Continued 'Tis the season for Poison Ivy. Fa la la la la, la la la la…

I stoop to rub more dirt on my ankles and legs.

If I put dirt on my skin, then the oil from the plant will bind with the dirt rather than my skin, decreasing the likelihood of me getting the itchy bumps.

Camouflaged by green leaves, Kujo, Mtn. Goat and I, pass a rotting log with moss growing on it in the shape of a hedgehog.

A few miles later, we meet two guys hiking a 500-mile section, SOBO to West Virginia.

During our brief conversation, I discover, the blonde hair blue-eyed one is considering going to Graduate School at Emory University in Atlanta and his brother plays bagpipes.

"I used to drive to Atlanta once a week for free bagpipe lessons from Atholl Highlanders Pipes and Drums. I got stuck on one of the songs on the practice chanter and haven't been back since."

Blondie's friend has dark brown/black hair. He doesn't talk much.

My thoughts turn bleak. Will I ever meet my prince charming?

Before I get too despondent, I happen upon a group of three ladies hiking.

As we are passing I say, "Hey, how are ya'll?"

"Good. How are you? Where are you from?"

"I'm good. I'm from Georgia. I guess my southern drawl is obvious up north. Are ya'll from here?"

"Yes, we are from Connecticut. Are you thru hiking?"

"Yes. I started in February. The trail is beautiful!"

We continue talking a while then I remember I have four miles to hike before dark. I pass "Caleb's Peak," and "St. John's Ledges."

After St. John's Ledges, there is an incredibly steep descent with little room to stand. I tell Mtn. Goat and Kujo to "sit" and "stay." We have to proceed slowly in order to keep me from flying head over heels downhill. I go down one level, then anchor myself on a rock or root with one hand, and let the dogs down, one at a time, to the next level. I position myself so if I fall, or get pulled down, I will land on my butt, one of the areas that no matter how much weight I lose, still has plenty of padding. The pain in my knees is excruciating. They begin to quiver with each downward bend. I have my own weight with the backpack, and then the dogs pulling on me. My knees burn and shake, and there is no relief.

Halfway down I see a family of four climbing up. I contain myself and the dogs to the side and let the family scramble past. As they pass the dad says, "You got your hands full. How do you do it?"

I give a half smile and say, "Very slowly. About how much farther is it to the road?"

"Not far once you get to the bottom. Good luck."

I laugh and say, "Thanks. I need it!"

I finally reach to the bottom. Wow! That was fun, but very tricky.

I see the dirt road where Dad is supposed to meet me, but I don't see Dad. I manage to get a call through to Dad. When he answers, I say, "Hey Dad, I'm at River Road. Where are you?"

"I'm at River Road," he answers.

"Okay. I'll walk up the road some. Let me know if you see us."

I hike up and down the road. but I still don't see Dad.

"Do you see us yet?" I ask.

"No, but I am looking at the road map. Where you are connects to where I am in four miles."

"Okay. I'll wait here until you get here."

"The problem is the road is only accessible with a four-wheel drive vehicle."

"What about Kent road? Will it bring you to where I am?"

"Some of the roads are closed still. I can try to make it on the dirt road, but the truck might get stuck."

"The truck would probably fall apart! Fine! I've already hiked 24 miles. What's another 4? It looks flat. If I don't make it before dark, then I'll sleep on the trail! Bye!" I say and hang up.

I turn the phone off and stuff it in the top of my backpack. Using a tree to brace against I put my backpack back on look at Kujo and Mtn. Goat and say, "Let's go."

They jump up from their break and look like they have been resting all day.

I run until my lungs are burning and I feel like I'm going to pass out, then I walk fast. I force myself to run at least two minutes, then I can have a one minute break. I focus on taking slow refreshing breaths. In 2-3-4 out 2-3-4.

It is dusk. I am fatigued, but I keep running. I pass Stewart Hollow Brook Shelter.

"Dang it!"

The shelter is not supposed to be directly on the trail. I look around in delirious confusion. Another hiker and his girlfriend see the baffled look on my face.

"You got off on the blue blaze trail for the shelter. The AT continues that way." He points to the right.

"Thanks," I gasp out.

The girlfriend says, "Hey! Are you The Girl with 4 Dogs? I've been hoping to meet you!"

"Yeah," I smile.

"I'm "Zippers" and this is my boyfriend, "Stretch.""

"Nice to meet ya'll." I'm panicking on the inside. I have 2.5 miles to go. It's almost dark!

Zippers says, "I know you have to go. Hopefully we'll see you down the trail. Good luck!"

"Thanks! Good luck to ya'll too."

I take off running down the hill.

Stretch says, "Not that way. See the blaze on the tree to the right?"

"Yeah. Thanks again." My face is hot and red. I'm glad it's fairly dark.

I take off at a fast walk, then run once I'm out of sight.

It's dark when I make it to the truck. It takes an hour and twenty minutes to travel 4.8 miles. On the treadmill, I can run one mile in seven minutes.

Today, I hiked from New York to Connecticut, a total of 28 + miles!

I don't say a word, I just feed the dogs, shove food in my mouth, then put the dogs in the kennel, and crawl into my sleeping bag in the back of the truck to go to sleep.

I can look out the window and see the forest, rather than feeling exposed in a parking lot. It's humbling to sleep in the truck. Being homeless is inexpensive, but mentally challenging. I want to be someone that God is proud of.

**Day 108** While Dad is still sleeping, I cook macaroni and cheese from the box, with the thick cheese sauce in the aluminum packaging, and add additional pasta. My mouth is watering as I add canned beef stew.

When Dad wakes up I ask, "Hey Dad, can you make some of your delicious pan popped popcorn?"

"Yes," he answers. He looks as happy as a kid in a candy store using his one burner propane stove while cooking popcorn. I remember Dad making stove top popcorn for us as kids. He taught me to put oil in the bottom and 2-3 kernels. Once the kernels pop, then it is okay to put enough popcorn in the bottom to just barely cover the bottom. Wait a few minutes until the popcorn starts popping, then shake, shake, SHAKE, until the popcorn slows to 1-3 seconds between pops. Turn off the heat and voila, Popcorn!

"Since our pan is so small, can you make a second batch?" I ask.

"Certainly," Dad says grinning.

"Thanks. I hiked so much yesterday, I'm taking today off. I just want to relax and read. I like resting on Saturday Sabbath."

"Okay. I'm going to make the trail entrance easier to see after the road hike. It's obscure by the spring growth. I picked up a large trash bag of trash from the area yesterday."

"Good job. It's neat that you can be a part of the trail maintenance team!"

"It makes the environment nicer without all the trash."

"I'm sorry I was grumpy yesterday."

"It's okay." Dad has a good sense of humor, and generally a positive attitude.

"I appreciate your help."

Around 10:00 a.m. we meet a couple out walking with their dogs. My dogs bark excitedly. Next there is a lady camping with a group of Girl Scouts. The lady says her daughter enjoys hiking on the AT. One of the Girl Scouts is terrified of dogs.

I say, "Instigator is little. He won't bite. He loves to be petted. Do you want to feel his soft fur?"

The girl, screams and runs past.

All four dogs want to chase her. They scream (bark) excitedly too!

Their eyes are bright and excited, tails up and wagging, teeth showing in a wide grin, and tongues hanging out slobbering all over the place. They keep looking at me for permission, but I have to shake my head "no." They remain hooked up to the truck, and the campers pass by.

"Dad. I think we should go to town or something. If we stay parked here all day, then we might get in trouble for parking the truck overnight two nights in a row."

"It's a long way to town from here. We can stay parked. No one will care."

"I want to go to town. Maybe they will have a Best Buy and I can get my camera fixed."

Dad reluctantly agrees and we load the dogs in the kennel.

There are no Best Buy's in town.

"I should have detoured to Best Buy when we were in New York. I've hiked myself away from civilization!" I complain to Dad.

"I did mention there was a Best Buy nearby a few days ago…" Dad trails off.

"I remember. Hopefully I'll learn from this to seize opportunities when they are closer!"

In town, there is a red antique air compressor with free air. We continue driving until we find McDonalds. I used to eat at Burger King, but they no longer have Mocha Joe's.

While at McDonalds, I watch in silent amazement! There is someone in the drive thru who doesn't speak English fluently. She can't hear on the headset. She keeps messing up everyone's order, and giving out the wrong food. Now, the main dining room is backed up with a huge line. The kitchen staff is having to make every order at least twice. The original order is handed to the wrong customer and then has to be made again when it gets returned.

I tap my feet and roll my eyes. The young lady at the front counter keeps getting interrupted from taking orders to deal with the irate drive thru customers who keep coming in the front door.

Girl (Hiking) with 4 Dogs

Dad and I have simple sandwiches from the dollar menu a cheeseburger and chicken sandwich for each of us. I see the sandwiches drop into the ready rack, however it is another ten minutes before it makes it from the ready rack to us.

I ask Dad, "Why do they have someone working in the drive thru who doesn't speak English? It's hard enough to hear what people say through the speaker when there isn't a language barrier."

"I don't know," Dad answers.

The front counter girl looks like she is about to cry. I used to work at Burger King, so I understand how she feels. I cry when I am overwhelmed, tired, or hungry!

We enjoy our food, once it finally arrives! Yummy! Wonderful food. I like to eat.

Before we leave, we take the gallon jugs to the bathroom to fill up with water. People look at us funny when we carry the water jugs into the bathroom.

I want to say, "Why are you looking at me with disgust? Just because I'm not normal doesn't mean I'm abnormal. I'm not homeless, I'm traveling, and I need water for myself and the dogs. We drink gallons of water. It's easier to use a faucet than to pump or treat it. If we are near a flowing water source, I don't treat or pump the dogs' water, I just give it to them," but I bite my tongue and continue to fill up water bottles.

The McDonalds water is HOT!

Kim sends us a picture of baby Caleb snuggled in his car seat. He is so adorable with his blue and white checkered onesie, and blue and white bib with a train, an airplane and the words, "Thank Heaven for Little Boys."

After a day in town, we return to River Road for overnight parking and sleeping.

**Day 109** Mtn. Goat and Instigator are with me today.

We cross CT 4. Cornwall Bridge is to the east. It is a red wooden covered bridge.

We are on Iron Mountain Bridge in Falls Village, CT. The trail markers say to continue straight, so I do. There aren't any more blazes so I backtrack. There are no blazes to the right. I finally go to the left.

I'm ready to scream.!

Instigator is dragging behind. I look back and he's gotten something green all over his face. He looks up at me and smiles, then stomps forward.

I bust out laughing!

Next, we travel over the water and through the woods; hiking on the AT we go... We pass an outdoor shower, but it looks cold, and I don't have time to take a shower because I wasted so much time trying to find the trail when it turned off the main road, onto Water Street.

I see a beautiful waterfall cascading over the rocks and forming and inviting pool. Later I encounter a porcupine having a bad day and missing quills on his butt. Throughout the day there are bright green fields with green trees and mountains in the distance. At 8:25 p.m. I pass a rock taller and four times larger than me, and shaped like a thumb.

Four miles after the thumb, I have a final road walk for the day, then I meet Dad at Under Mountain Rd. 24.3 miles.

**Day110**: June 6, 2011 Kujo, Digger, and I start off the day with a climb up a five-step wooden ladder. Kujo easily jumps. I have to give Digger a boost from behind.

Next, we have a road hike through town. We pass a rustic three story wooden house with a connected garage on the ground level. Green trees on a hill are behind the house.

Once we enter the woods again we summit Bear Mountain and see the Travis Owen Mason Monument established in 1885 which is the highest point of the trail in CT. Shortly after that, we cross in to Massachusetts!

# Chapter 16 Massachusetts

**Day 110**: June 6, 2011Continued Savages Ravine Campsite is the first campsite after crossing into MA. There is a large gurgling stream nearby and the trail follows the stream for a while. The sound of the rushing water is relaxing.

Digger destroys my serenity when he suddenly barks and lunges after a squirrel. Kujo is right behind him.

While hiking on Laurel Ridge, I meet "Cracker Jack," whose friends snuck all kinds of heavy gear into his backpack; including snow pants, binoculars and a pound of Cracker Jacks! He grew up in Georgia and is hiking home in sections.

He says, "In April tornado's destroyed Pecan trees on my parents' farm. They are devastated. This year will be tough for them financially."

"I'm sorry to hear that. I saw damage on the trail from the storms." We talk a little longer then continue on our respective paths.

Another SOBO section hiker wears Chaco shoes and thus has the trail name "Chaco."

The trail is rocky with small and large boulders. I have to run and pretend to jump up the boulder in order to get Digger to jump up. Once he is on the next level I climb while holding both his and Kujo's leash.

It's difficult to run when I feel like I am evaporating from the heat! While resting before my next running leap, I meet "Talks-a-Lot" from Sarasota FL. She talks a lot. After catching my breath, I bid "Talks-a-Lot" good luck on her NOBO hike, and race up the next boulder.

Later, as I struggle up yet another boulder, I wonder how "Talks-a-Lot" is faring. Kujo and Digger are in competition on who has the most endurance and can pull the most consistently on their leash!

On Mt. Everett I meet Deidre from Albany, NY. She is hiking a section of the trail. Next I pass Hemlocks and Glen Brook Shelter. They look like tiny rustic wooden cabins, with steep sloping tin roofs.

I continue to evaporate as I hike up Mt. Bushnell

There is evidence of storm damage on the trail and it is apparent the trail maintainers have been hard at work cutting fallen trees off the trail. I walk through a narrow passage where a tree fell across the trail. The tree was about 13 feet in diameter. The trail maintainers cut a section out of the tree so hikers can pass through. There are thick layers of fallen branches on both sides of the trail.

On rocky elevations, I see rock mounds marking the trail. Trees are nonexistent in places.

The sky is crystal clear. I can see for miles over the tops of the fully blooming trees to the never-ending mountains in the distance.

The heat saps my energy as I descend Mt. Bushnell headed for MA 41 near South Egremont. At 819 ft., thick swarms of evil swamp mosquitoes attack every non-covered piece of my skin. They viciously bite and chomp my skin, sinking their needle-sharp proboscis deep into my tender dehydrated flesh.

I take off running, wanting to scream, but my dry parched throat won't make a sound. Nor will my paranoid brain let my mouth open in case the mosquitoes try to get inside.

I leave one swarm behind and slow down to gasp in warm, stifling, humid air. I see another swarm approach. As they get closer I sprint through their black masses. My legs burn and are weak and shaky. I picture my lifeless body laying prostrate on the ground with swarms of mosquitoes devouring me. Then I see Kujo and Digger helpless beside me. I must go on!

I have to pee like a racehorse!

While running, I dig the toilet paper out of my pocket, make sure the dogs are hooked securely to my backpack. Then in between swarms, I drop my backpack, race into the woods, drop my pants and pee as quickly as possible. My bladder is extremely full. I wince as I feel mosquitoes bite my buttocks. I wipe, jerk up my pants, zoom back to the dogs, snatch up my backpack, and run wildly away from the mosquitoes of doom!

I make it to MA 41. The mosquitoes lurk eerily in the shadows of the woods. Only a few are brave enough to follow me onto the road.

Are the mosquito's biting the dogs? Kujo and Digger are happy to run with me.

Girl (Hiking) with 4 Dogs

I look warily around as the trail leaves the road to enter a swamp. There is a dilapidated section of boardwalk leading deeper into the swamp. It is four feet wide, and leaning crazily to the right side at a 45-degree angle. The planks quiver, shake, creak and groan under our weight. The right edge of the planks dip closer to the water. The left edge rises toward the sky. The planks are going to break soon and someone is going to plunge into the swamp water.

I inch my way forward. Who knows what lies in the black murky water under the footbridge. Suddenly Digger leaps off the plank into the mucky water. It is up to his chest. Simultaneously, I see a large dark animal slither into the water. It has a big long tail, beady slanted eyes, and sharp yellow teeth.

Is it a Baby Loch Ness Monster? Or maybe a boa sized water moccasins?

The trail finally exits onto South Egremont Road. I hike on the road past the Shay's rebellion Monument. The mosquitoes are blessedly absent. I hike another short stint thru the woods, then I see a tunnel of light at the end of the woods!

I finally make it to Boardman Street. I sit on my backpack and pet the dogs while I wait for Dad.

No mosquitoes! I can rest and recuperate!

Once Dad arrives, he tells me about his day in town and I tell him about the Mosquitoes of doom. As we are talking, I see "Tiger," ("Tigger").

"How are you?" I ask.

"I'm good now. I had to slow down to let my Achilles tendon heal. I'm bummed I forgot my hiking poles at the grocery store in town today."

"That sucks," I say. Before I can say more Dad say, "I can drive back to town and get them for you. Where exactly did you leave them?"

"That would be awesome if it's not too much trouble. They are right inside the door at the Big Y Foods, but how will I get them from you?"

Dad says, "Let's look at the map. We can see where the trail crosses the road again. I'll go first thing in the morning to get the poles. It looks like we can meet a MA 23."

"Okay, that will work," Tiger says. As they are talking I offer an orange.

Dad continues, "See the GPS coordinates for MA 23? They are written in a different format than the ones that come from the SPOT GPS. I created a formula to convert from one format to the other. I'll show you."

Dad continues to drone on and on about the conversion for the GPS. Tiger doesn't even have GPS. He listens patiently.

I interject, "Dad, Tiger still has five miles before he reaches the next shelter. It's getting dark."

Dad continues as if I haven't said anything.

I go to the other side of the truck and unhook the dogs. I take them for a walk and get ready to go to bed.

I miss my mom.

**Day 111** Instigator and Mtn. Goat enjoy slightly cooler weather.

There are fallen logs placed across the trail. There is white lettering that says, "STOP" and an arrow pointing to the right. "Ahh, yes. I see the trail continues this way," I say tugging the dogs to the right.

At the Ledges, just before Mt. Wilcox Shelter, I pass section hikers, "D.C. Cook," "Hailey Hardcore," and "Rocket" from DC.

Three miles later at East Brook, I catch up to "Magic Bags," who we drove to the Blueberry Patch Hostel weeks ago. He looks surprised to see me.

"Where is Rocket?" he asks.

"She quit."

"How are you managing the dogs without her?"

"It's not easy. I cut down to two dogs a day after the rock mountain in Pennsylvania.

At the end of the day, as I am crossing Goose Pond Rd., I say, "hey," to some kids riding their bicycle.

They ignore me!

They could at least wave! Maybe they are scared they smell bad, and didn't want to waft the malodorous smell from their arm pits by waving. And maybe it's good they didn't get too close, I wouldn't want their putrid attitude to rub off on me!

A few feet later, I see the white truck with the purple camper shell and head towards Dad.

Once I arrive he shows me the new GPS he bought.

"Yeah!"

"Now I know where you are and how to get to you. It's frustrating when the maps don't show the smaller roads, or they don't have them labeled very well."

I give Dad a hug. "Did you have any trouble finding Tiger today?"

"No. He was waiting when I arrived. He was happy to have his hiking poles and he took off. He wasn't running, but he can move fast."

I look around and notice a junk pile on the other side of the truck. I raise an eyebrow at Dad.

"There was a metal frame chair I couldn't pass up. It will make a great seat when we are eating supper outside the truck."

I sigh. "Did you find somewhere to put your dumpster diving treasure where it won't be in the way?"

"Yes. It fits nicely between the side of the truck and the kennel."

I sigh again and look for myself. It fits okay.

Dad asks, "Are you still considering staying at Upper Goose Pond Cabin?"

"It's sounds lovely, but I'm tired after hiking 23 miles. I don't want to hike another 3 miles, plus it's getting dark and I don't want to risk getting lost." I yawn. "I'll see you in the morning."

**Day 112** Digger and Mtn. Goat are my companions today. In the morning, the sun shines through the trees, knocking off the chill from the night air. I wistfully look at the trail for Upper Goose Pond Cabin. Maybe next time.

I have to keep going. One foot in front of the other. I can't slow down. The painful memories are too close behind.

How did I ever believe he loved me?

What is wrong with me?

"Come on boys," I call to the dogs. I start running.

My birthday is tomorrow.

I pass the monument explaining how the Mohhekennuck club donated land to the National Park service in order to preserve the wilderness in 1982. The monument is concrete and reminds me of a gravestone marker. To the left of the monument is a falling down, lonely, rock chimney. Everything else was destroyed a long time ago.

I bite my lip and hold my breath, but the tears still roll down my cheeks. Nothing lasts forever. Mtn. Goat and Digger stop sniffing around and stuff their head under my hands. I try to laugh. I wipe my nose on my shirt, take a deep breath and say, "I'm okay. Let's keep going."

At least my dogs care about me.

I see a big Turtle digging in the dirt. She is about a foot long and six inches wide. I wonder if she is laying eggs?

It's getting HOT! We still haven't entered deep woods hiking. We pass beautiful wooden two story homes nestled in the trees. My mind drifts to home and family.

Finally, we enter the woods, it's a little cooler, but still hot. I hike up Becket and Walling Mountain and gradually the painful memories are pushed back into the dark corner of my mind.

"Stay there!" I yell.

Mtn. Goat and Digger look at me in surprise.

"It's okay. I was talking to myself." I give them each a head and back massage.

I take a shaky breath and remind myself, "I can do this. 'I can do all things thru Christ who strengthens me.'"

I think about the story of Job and Joseph in the Bible. They were both worse off than me.

Up ahead is Finerty Pond. The water is calm as I look out from the trees on my side of the pond. On the other side the bank is peaceful. It is bordered with green brush, then trees, and green mountains in the background.

At West Brach Road, I think about going to see the "Cookie Lady," but the thought of slowing down has me cringing.

After Washington Mtn. Road, I meet Melissa Anne (Ironically my sister's name) and her mom Dianne from St Louis Missouri. They are hiking a section going south.

"Can I pet your dogs?" Melissa asks.

"Sure. They love the attention."

Dianne says, "How far are you going?"

"I'm meeting my Dad in Dalton today, but I'm hiking the entire trail from Georgia to Maine.

Girl (Hiking) with 4 Dogs

"When you get to Dalton there is a guy in town who is friendly to hikers. We stayed last night, showered and camped in the front yard. He has a water spigot on the outside of his house and he gave us ice cream when we stayed there."

"That sounds delicious! How will I know which house is his?"

"He has two hiker poles stuck in the ground in front of his house."

"Thanks. I'm looking forward to finding him. Good luck on your hike. I wish my mom could hike with me, but she was teaching when I started, and now I'm too far away."

Melissa says, "It is fun hiking with my mom."

Dianne adds, "It is very tiring! Good luck on your thru hike."

Ten more miles to Dalton! The terrain is mostly flat and easy.

Towards the end of the day, after Kay Woods Shelter I see a guy tent camping off the trail.

"Hey. You didn't want to camp in the shelter?" I ask

"No. It is more peaceful in the woods than being crowded in a shelter."

"It might not be too crowded on a Wednesday. I like staying in the shelters, but I can't do it much with the dogs."

"How far are you hiking with the dogs?"

"I started in Georgia in February. I'm going all the way to Maine. My trail name is 'Girl with 4 Dogs.'" I hold up the dog leashes. "Do you have a trail name?"

"No. I camp a few days at a time. I enjoy the peace. My name is Christopher. You should write a book about your thru hike with the dogs. You have a different perspective than anyone I have met."

I look at him with interest. "I haven't thought about writing a book. When I finish hiking, I have to get a job to continue to pay my mortgage. I'm a nurse."

"You have a remarkable experience to share," Christopher looks at me intently.

"It sounds like a neat idea." I chew my lip then add, "when I was in middle school I was in remedial English. I might not be any good at writing."

"You can do it and it will be a great book! Write from the perspective of having the dogs with you."

"I'll definitely consider it, but I'm not making any promises. Thanks for the advice."

Christopher smiles and says, "Write the book and good luck. Bye Girl with 4 Dogs."

"Bye Christopher."

A little while later I take a break by Barton Brook. The dogs rejuvenate by laying in the stream. I contemplate Christopher's advice. Having the dogs with me does make hiking immensely more challenging. They can't go inside buildings, so if I didn't have Dad helping, then re-supply and showering would be impossible. The dogs scare away the bear, and other wildlife, however, they are great companions and they make me laugh.

I use my water filter to pump fresh water to drink. I wash my face to cool down and soak and scrub my feet in the stream.

As I hike the rest of the way into town I pass a girl from Canada hiking, and Russ, a local guy who saw a bear on the trail last week.

The trail exit's the woods near a set of railroad tracks. Kujo and Instigator are hooked on trees. I feed the dogs, then say to Dad, "I'll take Kujo and Instigator and hike the 2.6 miles through town. One of the hikers I met today told me about a house where the guy gives ice cream! He also has a water spigot outside. We can fill up the water jugs."

"Okay. I followed the trail markers in town so I can help you find it if you need me too. It's marked clearly for the most part."

"Thanks"

Dad meets me at the house with the hiking poles in front. The owner isn't home, but we meet some of the other hikers staying at his home, "Forgetful," "Julius" (lord), "Knicker Bocker," "Speedy Gonzales," "Zeus," and "Itchy loaf." We exchange trail experiences as Dad and I fill up the water jugs.

When the host returns, he glares at Dad, Kujo, Instigator, and I.

I look at him and say, "The thru hiker book said you allow hikers to get water and the other campers didn't think you would mind."

The host, Tom, growls "I guess it's okay."

Girl (Hiking) with 4 Dogs

"I met a mom and her daughter today. They said you have a shower available. May I take a shower? It's been a while since I've had one."

"NO," he snaps. "the basement is full of water! No one else can take a shower today! You can leave when you finish. Dogs aren't allowed," he snarls and looks at Kujo and Instigator.

Kujo snarls back.

Instigator barks and looks defiantly at Tom.

I raise my eyebrows and look questioningly at the other hikers. Silently asking is he always like this? I glance at the truck, it's a good thing I don't have all 4 dogs out.

We finish getting water and I turn to leave. Tom doesn't offer any ice cream.

Within minutes of leaving inhospitable Tom's, it starts raining. A torrential downpour. I have my umbrella, but it is totally useless. I might as well be standing in the ocean!

Dad stops the truck. I shove Kujo in the kennel and Instigator in the cab.

I keep hiking, in the pouring rain, to the parking area, where we spend the night. I retrieve Instigator from Dad and load him properly into the far back kennel, then I crawl to my sleeping area and change into clean dry clothes.

I have a red rash the size of a dinner plate, on my inner thighs!

Whah, Whah, Whah! I wanted a shower for my birthday!

I got one from nature.

**Day 113** Yeah, my rash is gone this morning!

The day starts off with mild weather and ok terrain. Kujo and Instigator are bouncing around. When Mtn. Goat whines when we leave him behind. Instigator turns his head back, stomps his right paw, yaps "It's my turn," then turns back to me and stomps down the trail.

Around lunch, the clouds darken.

We are climbing higher and higher. The trail keeps spiraling upward. It's steep! We cross the road a hundred times! Each time has less visibility for oncoming traffic speeding around the curves!

Loud thunder blasts moments before rain burst forth hammering down in buckets, shovels, cats, dogs, pigs, and everything in-between. Kujo and Instigator are drenched. Kujo likes the rain, but not this downpour. He is trying to get under the umbrella, but it isn't big enough to keep us dry! I hide under the trees, but it's no use. The trees are bowed under from the weight of the horrendous downpour. Instigator gets in my lap, soaking me. It is like we are standing in a river.

I put up the umbrella and embrace hiking in the deluge!

I'm close to the top of the mountain. Closer to the lightning. Closer to the thunder. At least the air smells nice, like Christmas Trees.

"Oh Christmas Tree, oh Christmas Tree..." I sing shivering. I want to hide in the trees until the storm is over...I have 22 miles to hike.

"Keep going. Keep going." I chant.

I reach the summit of Mt. Greylock. I am just in time to see a beautiful pinkish purple bolt of lightning strike the tower. It is breath taking, and nerve racking

I spend the next hour, or more, looking for where the trail re-enters the mountainous woods. I-am-F-R-U-S-T-R-A-T-E-D! I want to keep hiking, and I can't, because I can't find the trail!

I find an emergency shelter made of concrete and rocks at the top of Mt. Greylock. It's open! At least we can stay dry while trapped on the mountain!

Sniffle, sniffle. "It's my birthday and I'll cry if I want to, I'll cry if I want to..."

"Dear Jesus," I pray, "Please help me find where the trail goes. Amen."

The rain slows to a mere drizzle. I explore every option like a detective in a mystery novel. One trail circles Veterans Memorial Tower. Other trails sprout off to various viewpoints. "There has to be a trail going down the mountain other than the one we hiked up. Can you find the trail Kujo?"

Kujo smiles and wags his tail. He leads us north and to the right of the emergency shelter. The trail is going in the correct direction, but I don't see any blazes. Kujo looks at me.

"We can try it for a while. Hopefully we'll see a blaze soon."

Please be the correct trail.

After a couple of miles, I finally see a blaze! It is mostly downhill from there, literally.

Girl (Hiking) with 4 Dogs

The dogs are excited and in a hurry to finish. Me too! I am soaking wet and cold. We pass Wilbur Clearing Shelter on the way to the road to meet Dad. There are a lot of switchbacks, going back and forth, back and forth. The dogs keep trying to pull me over the edge of the trail, straight down, instead of following the switchbacks.

The rain finally stops. I stand on the edge of a mountain overlook. It's clear enough to see the mountains in the distance. They are dark blue with white tops from the evaporating water. The sky is a faint pinkish purple, and there is one cloud that is a darker purple and is in the shape of a heart with wisps floating away at the top.

"Happy Birthday to me…"

I have enough phone signal to listen to birthday wishes from my family and friends, then I meet Dad at MA2. I feed the Dogs, and then I eat hot Roman noodles and cheese while sitting on a plastic bin in the back of the truck. It is not a gourmet birthday dinner, but it is all I want.    A local truck driver, Dalton, visits. He assures us overnight parking is allowed.

I just want to go to sleep and be warm.

**Day 114** The next morning "Zippers," "Stretch," and his dad pass our parking area while I am eating breakfast.

"Dad, I'm gonna feed the dogs then catch up to Zippers."

"I can take care of the dogs It's still cloudy. Do you want to leave the dogs with me?"

"I'll just leave Kujo and Instigator. It might not even rain today."

Less than an hour later I catch up to Zippers, Stretch, and His Dad.

Zippers introduces me to Stretch's dad.

"Do you mind if I hike with ya'll today? I get tired of hiking alone."

"That's fine," Zippers says.

"Where did ya'll start from this morning."

"About three miles away at Wilbur Clearing Shelter."

"I must have been right behind you. That explains why the dogs were so eager to lunge down the switch backs and they tried to take the side trail to the shelter."

Yay, someone to talk to!

The trail is rugged, but beautiful. Stretch and Zippers get ahead, but I am determined not to let Stretch's dad pass me. The terrain slows me down, but the challenging areas are intermittent. I have Mtn. Goat and Digger. It's hard climbing with a backpack and two dogs. There are steep climbs, and my cardio and respiratory system want me to slow down.

After I finally get to the top of the hill, I need to pee! I have been holding it since this morning. One major drawback to hiking with other people is that it's more challenging to find the "private" bathroom, especially when sandwiched in between the group.

The dogs have two tasks to accomplish while I take care of business. One is to bark when someone is within sight or smell distance, and the second is to scare them senseless so they don't pass while I'm indisposed. No more getting caught with my pants down!

I keep a zip lock bag with toilet paper in my pocket, I take it out while I'm running to the woods, in order to cut down on time. I have another zip lock bag for the trash. I wrap the trash in leaves to eliminate odor, and to make it easier to distinguish which bag has the clean TP.

Of course, just as I am finishing, the dogs start barking. I rush back, sling on my backpack, and look nonchalant, like I wasn't just coming back from the "bathroom."

After four miles of hiking I see the border sign for Massachusetts and Vermont.

# Chapter 17: Vermont

**Day 114** June 10, 2011 Continued Waiting at the top of the hill near the sign for MA/VT border sign are Stretch and Zippers. They are taking a lunch break. I join them. Stretch's dad isn't far behind.

We all eat lunch sitting on the boulder rocks. I have trail mix, cheese, crackers, and beef summer sausage. They have flour tortillas with sauce, chicken, and cheese. It looks better than anything I can cook, even when I'm at home with a full kitchen and refrigerator. My mouth is salivating.

I ask Zippers, "Did you dehydrate all your food?"

"Yes. I spent months planning and drying food. I have boxes prepared with dates and addresses for my family to send out. We only have a few items we have to buy in the store. I have the food in freezer bags. For supper, we are having beans and rice. We put the food in our Nalgene water bottle, add water and let it reconstitute while we are hiking. It will be ready to eat this evening."

"Wow! I dried a few items, mostly jerky, but I'm nowhere close to as organized as you are. I only had a month to get ready to hike. At home steaming broccoli in the microwave is my idea of cooking."

"What foods did you dry?" Zippers asks.

"I dried jerky, strawberries, peaches, kiwi, fruit rolls, and broccoli. Is it difficult planning where to pick-up your re-supply package?"

"At the beginning of the trip, we mapped out our mileage for each day. We stick to our plan. We don't take any zero days."

I give the dogs a few bites of sausage to snack on.

"I'm impressed. It was nice hiking with ya'll, but I've gotta get going. I'll see ya'll down the trail."

Three miles later, at Seth Warner Shelter I accidentally take the trail to the water instead of the trail to leave the shelter (those sneaky dogs made me do it; Mtn. Goat is laughing under his breath).

Near the stream, I see moose tracks. Later, there are wooden planks to hike on and the trail is lower than the pond. There is ten foot of brush and trees between the trail and the planks. Mtn. Goat hikes in the front and Digger is behind me.

I would hate to be hiking the trail in a rainstorm or flood. Not only would I get lost, I would probably be swept away. That's assuming there is even a trail to get lost on. Maybe, if the trail is marked well-enough, I can swim. Or if I have a blow-up air mat, then I can float across. That sounds like fun, but the dogs would still have to swim!

I pass through Congdon Shelter and briefly meet, "Bitchless." He is sad and stressed because his dog died in March. I also meet "Singing Dave," who is much more cheerful.

I end the day at VT 9 near Bennington VT. There is a Rec. Center in town and I am determined to have a shower today. I keep persisting with Dad until we finally find the Rec. Center.

I enter the Rec. Center and search frantically for the shower.

A kind voice says, "Hi, I'm Betty. Are you a thru hiker?"

I laugh and say, "Yes. I guess you can smell the hiker stink?"

"I've smelled worse. I hiked the trail last year. The shower is through those doors. We can talk more after you finish."

Ahh, this is heaven, a long HOT shower. I am human again.

After I finish my shower, Betty and I talk. On the way out to the truck I meet Jaw-Johnson, and Carrie Fabricius. I introduce Betty to Dad and the 4 Dogs. She encourages me that I can finish the trail, and I encourage her that she will survive going through a divorce.

Later, Dad and I park at the edge of a Wal-Mart parking lot near the trees. It closes at 10:00 p.m.! There are three Wal-Mart's in my town and all three are open 24/7.

**Day 115** I take a zero day in Bennington, VT.

Dad drives through the other side of the shopping center to explore The Price Chopper Grocery store. Dad and I split a box of Krunch Bars. I also buy stamps, then send post cards of the dogs and I from our visit at the Harper's Ferry, West Virginia. The dogs expressions are from stern to goofy.

In the evening, Dad and I drive to McDonalds to fill up the water containers, and eat. I fill my containers all up at one time, struggling a little as I carry them back to the truck.

However, Dad fills his containers up one at a time, and carries them back to the truck. Hobbling with each trip.

While inside McDonalds, I notice a group of "ladies" looking in Dad's direction, and making disparaging comments under their breath. And then, they start pointing at Dad. I am staring at them and clenching my jaw. My heart starts racing. I am more SOB (Short of Breath) than I ever was on the trail. I am having a huge internal battle. I am normally "calm, cool, and collected," as Dad would say. I don't like talking to strangers (although sometimes I do), and I definitely don't like confrontations. I ask myself, "Am I going to let these 'ladies' talk about my Dad?" They are sitting here thinking they are so high and mighty that they can put down my Dad. He's my Dad, I can be negative if I get frustrated, but these complete strangers have no idea how kind and helpful my Dad is, and I will NOT let them talk bad about Dad!

I take deep breaths, so I can speak when I approach the "ladies" (Marge, Helen, and JoAnn). Then, I get up from my seat and proceed to the table where they are sitting. With my hands on my hips, and my feet slightly apart for comfort and balance, in case I have to start punching, I boldly ask them, "Are you talking about my Dad?"

One of the women says, "I saw you looking over here and I wondered if you knew the man."

More likely I was glaring. I say, "That is my Dad. He is helping me with a thru hike on the Appalachian Trail. I have my four dogs with me and we frequently have to fill up our water jugs. He limps because he has a venous stasis ulcer on his leg!"

"We are so sorry," one of the ladies exclaims. "We were just concerned."

I give them one last glare and say, "Okay."

I'm sure we all talk about others when we are bored. Just be careful who is eavesdropping on your conversation. I, for one, am always listening!

After eating, we return to park the truck at the edge of the Wal-Mart shopping center. There is another truck parked nearby. It has a light on the top.

"Hi, I'm Dan," the guy says.

"I'm Girl with 4 Dogs. We've had police drama in the past. Do you think they will care if we park here overnight?"

"No. I park here all the time. Let me know if ya'll need anything."

There are beautiful fireflies all in the woods behind the truck. The rain on the roof of the camper shell lulls me to sleep.

**Day 116** The weather is cool and wet, but I grab Kujo and Instigator anyway. We hike quickly and don't take a break until Goddard Shelter ten miles away. The elevation at the shelter is 3573 ft. I meet Echobe, and MOM, which stands for Miracle on Miles. They are finished hiking for the day. MOM turned 75 this year.

MOM, who is a guy, says, "I'm hiking the AT in sections. I've always wanted to hike the whole trail. I have a phone my family insisted I bring with me. I have to keep in touch every day! If they don't hear from me for more than a 24-hour period, they get worried. They check my mail and send money from my retirement check when I need it. When I get to town I'll take a couple of days off and stay in a hotel"

"That sounds very luxurious. There are a few places on the trail where there isn't any signal, but I can usually get a signal at least once a day. Burr! It's cold. I wish I was finished for the day. I have another 12 miles. Do ya'll mind if I leave the dogs here for a minute while I run to the privy? They are hooked to my backpack."

"You can leave them," MOM says.

On the way back from the privy, I hear Kujo growling and Instigator barking. I sprint back to them and give them a, "what are you doing that for" look. Then I apologize to the thru hiker approaching from the south, "Bot," who wants to be a botanist.

"Sorry about that. He doesn't usually bite. I have him now if you want to pass." I say, hoisting on my backpack.

Bolt, bolts past and continues down the trail.

"I'm not staying at the shelter so don't leave on my account."

"Oh, umm, I have a couple of friends up ahead I'm trying to catch up to," Bot says.

"Really?" I ask. "I haven't seen anyone in a while."

Now Kujo is wagging his tail. Maybe his scruff is up because it's cold!

Instigator yaps and stomps hi feet.

"Yes," he says and continues down the trail.

I sigh, I don't understand people these days.

I struggle into my backpack. MOM calls out, "Good luck!"

I shiver again and Echobe says, "Keep movin"

"Good idea," I call back.

Girl (Hiking) with 4 Dogs

Staying at a Bed and Breakfast would be lovely. If only I had the time, and money.

I catch up to Bot and his friends at the Glastenbury Mountain Tower. They are drying their yellow and green tent. It flaps in the wind, like a kite stuck on the tower.

I end the day at Stratton-Arlington dirt Rd. While waiting on Dad to catch-up, I meet a family from Arkansas. One is a Physical Therapist, and one is an Occupational Therapist.

Rhonda says, "We both obtained travel positions for VT. When we are off work, we travel and explore the area. After this contract is up we will visit somewhere else and do the same thing."

"So, you get paid to see the world. One job contract at a time."

"Yes. It works great for us."

"Did ya'll forget your cooler?" I ask as they are getting in the car.

"No. It was here when we got here."

There is a plethora of mosquitoes. When Dad finally arrives, I spray on the. I don't even want to hear the "zzzz" of those evil creatures. The first words out of his mouth are, "I am glad I have GPS. The Stratton-Arlington Road was difficult to find even with navigation."

"I'm glad you have it too. I don't worry as much about you getting lost, or not being able to find me. Dad I guess the cooler is trail magic. I was talking to a couple and It's been here all day. Shall we see what's inside?"

"Yes."

I open the lid. "Here are some oranges and banana's. Oh, look! A lonely pair of Smart wool socks! If the socks are still here in the morning, I'm going to give them a home."

"The fruit is tasty.

Thanks for the trail magic!

**Day 117** I mentally wish my friend Pauline a Happy Birthday as I hook up Mtn. Goat and Digger. She's on a sailing trip around the world!

Almost as soon as I start hiking on this bright and sunny morning I have to cross a swampy field. The entire field is in 6-12 inches of standing water. At first I jump from one thick grassy clump to the next, but the clumps are deceptive.

Splash!

Whah, pouty lip, boo hoo, I don't want wet feet!

Once my feet are soaking wet I slosh through the field at a reasonable pace.

Next, we laboriously hike up Stratton Mountain. I quietly reflect on the amazing beginnings of the Appalachian Trail. This is the Mountain where Benton MacKay started dreaming about the AT. There are evergreen trees surrounding the small clearing and a couple of sitting areas made from large rocks along with a trail register book.

As I approach Stratton Pond Shelter, I hear a splash! I jump up and run around the corner, hoping to see a moose!

Nothing.

"Oh well," I say to Mtn. Goat and Digger, "let's keep walking. Maybe there is a moose around the corner."

Eventually, we make it to Manchester Center, VT my stopping place for the night. 17.6 miles.

**Day 118** About ten miles in on a 26-mile day, the monotony is broken up by meeting hikers doing the "Long Trail." However, "Tiger Lilly" and "Lilly Bell" are staying dry inside Peru Peak Shelter today.

There are three planks back to back, with a couple of inches of water on each plank. When I step down on the center plank, it submerges completely underwater. My feet are briefly submerged before I jump onto the last plank and make it safely to the muddy bank on the other side. When I look back, the middle plank is now perpendicular to the end planks.

I don't know how the next person is going to cross the stream without jumping in!

A few miles later where the Old Job trail branches off to the east, I stop to talk to a park ranger. While we are talking, I hear Zippers say, "Hi Girl with 4 Dogs!"

"Hey, how are ya'll. Where is your Dad?" I ask.

Stretch says, "My Dad will hike with us again when we get to Katahdin."

Zippers answers, "I almost lost my glove crossing the stream back there!"

Girl (Hiking) with 4 Dogs

"I almost fell in when the board I was standing on started slinking," I respond.

We haven't gone far after leaving the park ranger when Stretch, abruptly says, "I'm going to hike ahead." Then he looks at Zippers, "You can catch up."

After he is around the corner I say, "You don't have to hike with me."

"It's no problem, Zippers says. "Stretch really likes to hike by himself. Most days he hikes ahead and we stop for lunch together, then he hikes ahead again."

I say, "I enjoy having someone to talk to. When did ya'll start hiking?"

"We started in the middle of March. We hike 15 to 18 miles a day. We hike fewer miles when we re-supply."

"You don't take a day off when you re-supply?"

"No. We would have to pay for lodging if we take a day off."

"That makes sense. I hike 20 to 25 miles a day, then I take a day off, but I can sleep in the back of the truck."

The miles fly by. At the end of the day we pass a rock gathering. It reminds me of the rock sculptures at Sunfish Pond. Just after the rocks is the Greenwall Shelter.

Zippers says, "This is where we are staying tonight. Let's exchange numbers. If we don't see each other on the trail, we should get together after the trail."

We exchange numbers and I hike another mile and a half to meet Dad at VT 140, Wallingford, VT.

I tell Dad, "I wish I could stay in shelters more, for the camaraderie, but it's so difficult with the dogs."

"I can always keep the dogs."

"I know, but I don't feel right leaving them behind. It's hard enough only taking two dogs a day. Besides, I don't always know what to say when I'm around people, or I say the wrong things, or I say the right things, but people take it the wrong way."

"You won't' get any better at socializing if you aren't around people."

"True, but it's so hard. I want to fit in, but I don't know how."

"Just be yourself," Dad reminds me. "You are a unique and special person. Don't worry about what other people think. Just be yourself!"

"You're right, but being myself wasn't good enough for AJ."

"That's because AJ has his own issues and insecurities."

I cut Dad off, "I'm going to take the dogs for a walk."

Dad calls after me, "The trail goes up that hill and crosses the road. There is a larger parking area at the top and the AT passes right thru it."

"Thanks Dad."

It doesn't take long to get to the parking area. I'm feeling better. It really doesn't matter what other people think about me. The important thing is for me to like myself, and I do.

The parking area is large and enclosed by trees. It's cool and quiet.

Not too long after we arrive, someone else drives up in a pick-up truck. I look warily out from the back of the truck. Dad is already on his way to meet the newcomer. He looks harmless. He's about Dad's age, a little shorter, and thinner with bits of grey in his dark hair.

Dad says, "Hi, I'm Malcolm and this is my daughter, Girl with 4 Dogs. She is hiking the AT and I am helping with the dogs."

"I'm Mr. Morris. I come out here sometimes to relax. I have a home in Vermont, but I don't stay there often. I don't like being enclosed by four walls."

"Do you think it's all right for us to stay here overnight?" I ask.

"Sure. I've stayed a few times myself and I've never had any problems," Mr. Morris answers. "I know the area pretty well if you need to know where else to stay or how to find the trailheads."

Dad says, "If you know where the Appalachian Trail crosses the roads that would be helpful. It can be difficult to find the trail crossings."

"That it is," Mr. Morris says. "I can help you. Do you ever go caving?"

I answer, "I've been a few times, but I don't go often."

"I have a cave named after me, Morris Cave. I love to go caving. Wait here a minute I want to show you something I found."

Girl (Hiking) with 4 Dogs

A couple of minutes later Mr. Morris returns, "I found this crystal in a cave one time. I want you to have it for good luck!" Mr. Morris says and gives me a small clear crystal.

"Wow! Thanks," I say, "I've never had anyone give me a crystal."

"It's not worth any money."

"It's valuable to me. Thank you!"

While we are talking, we briefly meet Snorkel.

"Hi," I say as she approaches.

We introduce ourselves and she says, "I'm so glad to meet the Girl with 4 Dogs! I've been reading about you in the trail journals, and I passed some of your friends who were talking about you."

"Wow! I didn't know I was that popular. Do you want to meet the dogs?"

"Sure," Snorkel says.

I introduce her to Kujo, Mtn. Goat, Digger, and Instigator. They give their approval with tail wagging and licking.

"It's getting late," I say, "How many miles are you hiking today?"

"30 miles today."

"That's a lot of miles. How do you do it?"

"I've hiked the trail before. I'm in college and I take the summer break to hike the trail. This is my third time."

"You don't get tired?" I ask.

"Once I get to the White's in New Hampshire I will have to slow down. There is no way to hike 30 miles a day in those mountains!"

"Besides going to school what are your hobbies?"

"I like to rock climb."

I laugh and say, "That explains why you are in such great shape. How many pair of shoes do you go through?"

"I have a friend who ships me a new pair every few weeks. The last time I received them I didn't need them so I gave them to another hiker."

"How long will it take you to hike the entire trail?"

"Not more than three months. I better get going. I have four miles to go before dark!"

"It was great meeting you Snorkel."

Dad, the dogs, and I hang out with Mr. Morris a while longer before calling it a night.

**Day 119** I harness Kujo and Mt. Goat today. They are pulling ahead fiercely. It's wet and slippery. There's moss, pine straw, pine straw on top of the moss, on top of the rocks. More moss and more pine straw on top of more rocks. I fall. I get up. I fall again. I get up. I fall again.

"Stop pulling me!" I shout and jerk Kujo back. Then I glare at Mtn. Goat and say, "Stay back. You can't get in front of me or Kujo!"

Shortly after falling past Minerva Hinchey Shelter we pass "ST" (Sarah from Tennessee). She is hiking a section going south.

She says, "You look dirty. Is the terrain up ahead really rough?"

"No," I answer. "My dogs keep pulling me over and the rocks are slippery with pine straw."

ST looks at me as if I'm crazy. She says, "Maybe you should slow down."

"I agree. Good luck on your hike."

"Bye."

Just after lunch the dogs and I cross over Clarendon Gorge on the suspension bridge. It's just wide enough for Kujo and Mtn. Goat to walk side by side going across, and I trail behind. It's a long way down, with a solid rock wall on one side and large dangerous rocks below. The water is sparkling and effervescent as it rushes away. My heart races as we maneuver across the bridge. I say a silent prayer of thanks that there is a chain link fence to keep us from falling off the edge of the bridge. The bridge is 30 ft. long and at least 30 ft. above the gorge.

It's warm and sunny, with fresh air, and green trees. I breathe deeply of the crisp refreshing air. This is life. This is freedom!

Later I pass "JAWN," an Ohio section hiker. Then near Keiffer Road I pass "Bellie/Crazy Bell."

She says, "I'm hiking the long trail. I hike a section on the trail, then I hike back to my car. I move my car to the next section and repeat the process."

"It sounds like you will hike a lot of miles and not cover much distance. Good luck!" I say.

Next I pass "BushWack," who says, "I'm hiking the Long Trail with injuries." Then I pass "Cricket," "Willow," and their dad, "Shark," from New Jersey, New York, and Florida respectively. Lastly after Pico camp I pass "Zero." He is sleeping in the grass as I pass. He wakes up when Kujo and Mtn. Goat start sniffing him.

"I'm sorry," I say. "I was trying to pass without them getting close, but the trail is narrow."

He says, "Wait a minute and I'll hike with you. I started hiking north from Maryland in January." He quickly rolls up his sleeping bag and stuffs it in a bag.

"It sounds like you had some cold days of hiking," I say. "Good luck!"

"Are you staying at the Churchill Scott Shelter tonight? I can hike with you."

"No, I'm meeting my Dad further down the trail," I say as I resume hiking.

"Oh. I've been thru hiking for a while." He starts walking toward me and Kujo growls.

"Okay. Are you having fun?" I walk faster.

"Does your dog bite?"

"Sometimes," I answer.

Once I reach the parking area near US 4, Zero continues to the shelter. Dad is waiting for me.

Dad says, "I went with Mr. Morris today. He showed me different places where the trail crosses the road along with some of the historical sites nearby. Tomorrow we are going to tour Killington, VT"

"That's awesome!"

I hook my phone up to the truck charger.

"Dad, Andy and Kim sent a one month picture of Caleb in a bear outfit. Do you want to see it?"

"Yes," Dad says and I show him the picture. "He looks warm in his brown blanket." I hiked 23.8 miles today.

**Day 120** June 16, 2011 In the morning I meet a local man who is a Veteran, he says "You be careful hiking with your dogs. The terrain gets harder from here. When you get to Mt. Washington sign the visitor book on the top. Next time I go to Mt. Washington I'm going to look for 'Girl with 4 Dogs.' I want to know you've made it."

I smile and say, "I'll make it and I'll sign the book. Thanks for letting me know about the terrain. I'll be careful. I only take two dogs at a time. I'm taking Digger and Instigator today."

There is frost on the plants this morning. There is a green plant with blue tear drop shaped flowers.

Kent Pond is breathtaking. There is a small water fall, and a refreshing clear pool of water, surrounded by lush, green trees. Digger especially loves to hear the birds singing in the trees. He pulls me along trying to catch one. There are so many sounds. Some days when the birds sing it seems like they are cheering me on. One day the birds were singing "Shep-pherd" (which is Kujo's real name). He loved it! One sounds like a squeaky wheel, and another one sounds like breaking glass. Yet another trills, "high main-ten-ance," "dramatic fall," "hik-ing pole," and "Kelly's bird." The versatility is amazing. It's like kids saying, "I can make this sound, can you?"

At Thundering Brook Road, I narrowly avoid drama passing a woman and her "off leash" dogs. Had Kujo been with us bad things could have happened! However, Digger, is calm and forever loves everyone and everything and Instigator who is all bark, and only a tiny bite. I hold my dogs in check while she slowly rounds up her belligerent four legged companions.

She says, "I think they are only barking because they want to play with your dogs."

I grit my teeth and try to smile. I sarcastically say, "I appreciate the control you have over your dogs. I hope you have a wonderful day." I look pointedly up the hill where one of the two has run off again and continue hiking on the trail.

After hiking 10 miles, I am in dire need of a bathroom. I detour to Stony Brook Shelter and search frantically for the privy.

"Grrr, Grrrr" "Yap, Yap, Yap"

"Can I have five seconds of peace to use the bathroom?" I grumble.

The barking and growling intensifies. I quickly wipe and jerk up my drawers. I immediately see "Zero" a few feet away as I exit the bathroom.

"Hi," he says. "We meet again. I saw a snake at the privy last night. It was really big around and 5 feet long."

"Okay. I'm not scared of snakes."

"Snakes can be deadly. You should be careful. Do you want some coffee?"

"Sure," I answer.

"Okay. It'll take just a minute to heat water. Do you have a stove?"

"Sorry, I don't carry my stove anymore."

"I'll have to make a fire to heat the water. Do you have any protein bars?"

"No. I don't eat protein bars."

"What else do you have to eat?"

"I don't carry extra food. I have just enough for today. I don't have time for coffee after all. I have a long day ahead," I say and start toward the trail.

"Can I hike with you today? It's not safe for you to hike alone with snakes around."

"Sure," I answer. "I have a lot of miles to cover so I really need to get started."

"It'll only take a minute for me to get my stuff."

Zero grabs his stuff.

Not long after Stony Brook Shelter, the trail drops 20 feet from a rock boulder. There is a ladder for hiker use, but Digger and Instigator have to have another way down.

Zero goes down the ladder first then he says, "If your dogs won't bite I can help catch them when they jump."

"They probably won't bite unless I am in danger. It's a big jump from here, but if we go west the boulder isn't so high."

I lean down and gently toss Instigator to Zero. He catches him easily. Then I unhook Digger's leash so it won't snag and tell him to jump. He hesitates at first. I roll on my stomach, then inch over the edge and drop down. Digger is right behind me. Zero catches him and puts his leash on.

"Thanks for your help," I say. I share trail mix and cheese and crackers, then we continue hiking.

Zero is 22 years old, tall and skinny, with red hair and blue eyes.

Zero starts talking. He says, "My dad left us when I was two years old. I am the youngest of four biological siblings. I also have step siblings and half siblings on my mom's side. I don't ever see my dad. My oldest brother is 37. We used to all have to share a bed growing up. When I was in college I had a roommate, who was studying to be a neuro surgeon. I like to smoke pot. Do you smoke pot?"

"No. I don't smoke or drink. I never had the need. I don't drink either. Alcohol tastes disgusting and it's expensive."

"You acquire a taste for it."

"I have no need to acquire a taste for something so disgusting," I say.

"Well, I like to smoke pot and masturbate to relieve sexual aggression," Zero says.

He continues talking. What am I supposed to say to a comment like that? Was he sexually abused at some point in his life?

"Dear Jesus," I pray silently, "Please keep me safe." I focus on stretching my legs and lengthening my stride. I keep my breathing calm with slow deep breaths.

I know I can out hike Zero.

Soon Zero says, "Can we take a break? I need to catch my breath."

"I'm not tired, but you can take a break if you need to. I still have a lot of miles to cover."

"No, I'll keep up, but can you slow down some?"

"I can't slow down much or I won't be able to meet my Dad at the end of the day. He would be worried if I don't show up."

After a few minutes Zero says, "I have to stop to use the bathroom."

"Okay, I'll keep walking slowly to give you some privacy," I say.

Zero answers, "You can stay nearby. I don't mind."

"I insist you should have your privacy. You should be able to catch up."

"Well I have to pee. Don't go far it won't take a minute."

Zero stops on the trail and starts to take out his penis. I hike quickly ahead. As soon as I round the corner out of his site I take off running. My lungs are burning. My heart is racing out of my chest. I focus on my breathing.

I know Zero can't catch up.

Girl (Hiking) with 4 Dogs

"I am strong. I can keep running. I am strong." I repeat over and over again as I keep running.

After a few miles, I have to stop running, but I keep hiking as fast as I can.

The day drags on. Now, every few miles I see blue tie-on trail markers that say "Wtr Bar." I fantasize about ice cold water. A nice bar set-up at the shelter, with my choice of flavored Dasani Water; Lemon, Strawberry, or Grape. Frozen into an ice-cold slush. While I am sipping on my refreshing beverage, I have a dark haired, blue-eyed, hottie to massage my aching, sore, tired (dirty and smelly) feet. Then, he sincerely asks if there is "anything else" he can do for me.

About this time, I trip on a root, and fall face first into the ground. Just kidding, but I get distracted paying attention to the terrain and forget about my desire for cold water (and the rest of the fantasy), until the next time I see the blue flag saying, "Wtr Bar." Then the fantasy starts over again, with an innocent desire for ice cold water.

I never see any bottled water growing from the trees. Trail magic is scarce up north.

Those trail maintainers should be sued for false advertisement. They could at least have water of some kind! I would be happy with hot water. The scalding effect can be misconstrued as soothing. Although, I can't handle lukewarm water. Ewww!

I pass the turn off for Winturri Shelter. I know there isn't going to be cold water waiting for me there and I don't want to chance Zero catching up.

I continue trucking along, I'm thinking, I'm going fast. I did, after all leave Zero in my dust. Oh yeah! Then, along comes a trail runner. First, I have to make sure I'm not back in my "Wtr Bar" fantasy (the hottie part, 'cause this guy definitely meets my eye candy requirement). Then, I realize, I am moving at a snail's pace compared to this guy.

I blink, now, my eye candy is long gone! He moves too fast!

Ahh yes, but I do get to see him on his return trip when he passes me as if I am standing still. In fact, I am standing still on the side of the trail, in order to make it easier for him to pass, to keep Instigator and Digger out of the way, and to inconspicuously rest going uphill. Hottie, is running with his little black dog, with white on its chest.

I pick-up the pace, but I am still slow. I contemplate the likely hood of having to perform CPR if hottie has an accident, the mouth-to-mouth part has appeal, but dragging him to the road is not tempting. Actually, CPR never crosses my mind, I'm just trying to keep my mind occupied because I'm hot, thirsty, tired, and hungry. The dogs aren't answering any of my questions and I already know what my answers are. I'm running out of things to talk about.

Just before we arrive at the truck, the dogs and I have to walk through a field of cows, which Digger loves. I am not thrilled. I don't want Instigator to start something, and get us all mauled.

On the other side of the field on the outside of the fence, there are oranges for trail magic. Shortly after the oranges we finally make it to the truck!

Dad is waiting with Mr. Morris at Barnnard Gulf Road. They saw the runner, whose name is          (aaat    I'm    not    telling. Imagine how embarrassing it would be for me if the guy knew what I was thinking.) They talked with him, to see if he had seen me. He said, "yes," and told them I was hiking fast (he is probably just being nice), and not far behind.

Dad says to Mr. Morris, "We have canned kidney beans, potatoes, and peanut butter if you want to share a meal with us."

"Okay," Mr. Morris answers. "I have canned sardines, crackers, donuts, and candy to contribute."

"Sounds like a great meal!" I say as we say grace and eat together.

Delicious! There is indescribable joy in sharing a meal with a new friend.

"Thank you, Mr. Morris, for your kindness, friendship, and my special crystal," I say.

**Day 121** I yawn and stretch, forcing my sleepy eyes to open. My number one priority is to hike 22.7 miles to reach Hanover, NH before 5 p.m. I must make it to the rec. center for a shower!

As I leave the truck in the morning, the trail follows the road, in overgrown grass, before randomly crossing the road, and entering the woods. Kujo leads the way with his nose to the ground.

Girl (Hiking) with 4 Dogs

"Apples!" I exclaim excitedly reaching into a plastic bag hanging from a limb over the trail. My mouth waters as I take a bite. Juice trickles down my chin. I hastily wipe it on my shirt sleeve.

As the trail travels farther away from the road it becomes increasingly swampy.

Next, I enter a forest of maple trees. There are strings connecting the maple trees and buckets fastened onto hundreds of trees.

After three hours of hiking I summit one of many small mountains. I can see for miles! It looks like ski slopes on the sides of the mountains. Light green pathways surrounded by darker forest green.

It's amazing and breathtaking, literally. It's high altitude, the air is thinner. I stop to gasp for air.

Nine miles later, at Woods Road, I pass "Going Home," a section hiker.

Throughout the day, the terrain is a roller coaster up, then down hills and ski slopes, and so are my emotions. I am exhausted and tired. I want to take a break, but I can't because I have to make it to town in time to take a shower. I am desperate for a shower. I squeeze back tears. I don't have time, energy, or enough hydration to cry. My throat is tight, and I am having a difficult time breathing. I have to focus on deep healing breaths in, and let all the stress out, on the exhale.

I am near my limit of endurance.

Finally, a shaded, cool, downhill stretch. There are dead brown leaves on the trail, there is big green ferns alongside the trail, and a canopy of green trees over the trail to keep the sun out. Kujo and Mtn. Goat have excited grins on their face. They look around in awe and expectation at all the sounds of the forest.

After 20 miles of hiking in the mountains, the dogs and I exit the trail onto Elm Street. Not long after reaching the road, I meet "Short'N'Sweet."

She has a wooden fence outside her house with pink roses climbing on the fence and blooming. She also has orange and yellow flowers planted beside her mailbox. She has a cooler with food. On the outside is a sign that says "Thru Hiker Trail Magic." There is a Tupperware container for "Compost."

As I rummage inside the cooler I find water, desserts, fruit, and homemade goodies!

"Hi, I'm Short'N'Sweet," a middle age women says as she exits the house.

"I'm Girl with 4 Dogs. This is Kujo and Mtn. Goat. The other two are with my Dad."

"I brought water for them. Is it okay if I let them have a doggie treat too?"

"They would love it! Are those your boots with the pansies growing in them?" I ask.

"Yes. I hiked with my son some last year. My son 'The Brain' hiked the whole trail last year. He is an Engineer. I'm a nurse practitioner. When you hike thru the Whites in New Hampshire you must stay in the Huts."

"I've heard it can be expensive to stay in huts and I don't have extra money," I say.

"Most of the huts allow you to 'work for stay,' which means as a thru hiker, if you help in the kitchen with the dishes or with whatever they need, then you can stay without paying. It's part of the thru-hiking experience."

"Okay. Thank you so much Short'N'Sweet. I never would have considered staying in the huts if you hadn't told me about the work for stay option. It's neat that you are a nurse practitioner. I am a nurse. I have two miles to go before make it to the rec. center to take a shower. You don't want to know how long it's been since I've had a real shower!"

"If you don't get there in time, you can come back here and take a shower. By the way have you met anyone unusual on the trail?"

"I did meet a guy named Zero. He made me uncomfortable, but I out hiked him. He's probably a day or two behind. Thanks for the offer for a shower."

Kujo and Mtn. Goat rest quietly throughout our conversation, but as soon as I stand up, they jump up and are ready to go.

"Bye. Thanks again for the trail magic."

It's a short easy hike to the VT/NH border located on the bridge going over the Connecticut River.

# Chapter 18: New Hampshire

**Day 121** June 17, 2011 Continued Hanover, NH is extremely crowded. Kujo Mtn. Goat and I take up the entire sidewalk hiking thru town. There is a college reunion going on. The streets are incredibly busy, along with the businesses. Kujo is tense, breathing hard, and hoping to avoid people. Mtn. Goat, however, is happy, smiling, and begging people to pet him.

Kujo growls and gets his scruff up when other dogs pass, while Mtn. Goat wags his tail and whines to be friends. I look at Kujo and say "Are you serious? We have to hike all the way across town. Can you please calm down?"

Kujo smiles and wags his tail at me as if to say, "I'm just playing."

I finally make it through the crowded streets. I see the white truck ahead. Once I reach it I say, "Dad, can you take care of the dogs while I grab my stuff and head to the shower."

"Yes, I can keep the dogs. They have a washer inside too if you want to wash your clothes," Dad says. "Oh, I have a Stromboli and lasagna if you want some."

I look at Dad suspiciously. He never buys restaurant food unless he's eating at an all-you-can eat place. "How much was that?" I ask.

"I got it from the trash." I give him an 'are you serious?' look. He continues, "It was on the top, and hardly even touched. The woman took one bite and dropped in the garbage."

"No thanks, I'm not that hungry. I'm going to get my shower before they close." I grab my bag of dirty laundry and some money. It's $3 for a shower and $2 for laundry, soap included.

The Richard Black Rec. Center is refreshingly and freezingly cold. Jeanne shows me where the showers are. Both the washer and dryer are downstairs in a cozy little room with the shower to the right.

The shower water is amazingly hot. There is a bench in the shower. I sit my puny, weak, exhausted self-down and enjoy the hot shower. I hiked 22.7 miles with barely a break. I deserve this luxury!

After my shower, I am rejuvenated. "Dad," I say, "I need to find a store with hiking shoes. Mine have holes in the sides and they don't have good traction. I'm also looking for a light weight warm sleeping bag that is made in the U.S.A. I don't need my minus 5-degree bag in the summer months. If I'm going to spend a lot of money on a quality sleeping bag I want it to be made in the U.S.A."

"Hanover Outdoors is closest."

We load up the dogs and I get into the truck. On the dashboard is the yummy looking Stromboli. Umm, it smells so good. My mouth is watering and my stomach starts growling. I've had beef summer sausage, cheese, crackers, oranges, and trail mix for days on end.

Dad says, "I saved the Stromboli and I cut off the edge that was eaten."

I resist. I haven't had food since my stop at Short-N-Sweets. I'm not possibly going to eat from the trash can. I argue with myself, you didn't take it out of the trash can. True.

Dad says, "I've never had a Stromboli taste so good."

My stomach is kneading and yelling at me, "Please I want delicious food!"

"Okay Dad. I'll eat the Stromboli. If it doesn't kill me, it'll make me stronger."

"You don't have to eat it," Dad says smiling.

"It looks and smells too good to resist," I say as I bite into the Stromboli. "I can't believe I'm eating food from the trash, but it is very tasty!"

We make it to the shops and peruse the stores. After looking Hanover, we drive to the Mountain Goat store.

The first thing I notice inside the Mountain Goat Store is a human size, upright, white mountain goat manikin with grey shirt, black shorts, and an orange and grey shoulder bag. It has black hoofs for hands, a long, white, tapered goatee, and multicolored boots on its feet.

"I like this store," I say to Dad. I look around and find the shoes. I'm on my second pair of Asics, since Shenandoah. They are comfortable, light weight, and dry faster than boots. I rotate between two pair of shoes when I hike in the rain. I like Asics, but I need something more trail worthy, with better traction. I decide to get purple, Montreal Trail Runners. The red Solomon's are too tight.

Girl (Hiking) with 4 Dogs

As we drive through town Dad says, "Do you see the parking lot over there? That is where the parking coordinates are for overnight parking. It's not on the trail."

"I'm glad you realized I wouldn't look for you there," I say. "I would have been devastated if I couldn't take a shower because I didn't have anywhere to keep the dogs once I arrived at the Rec. Center."

"It was easy to find the Rec. Center."

"Hey, let's have pizza tonight. My treat. I read in the hiker guide that "Ramunto's" gives a free slice of yummy cheese pizza to hungry hikers!"

We have a total of four huge slices of pizza between Dad and myself. It was all so very delicious!

Dad drives us back to the parking lot with the parking coordinates. It's looks like a school parking lot. It's restful and surrounded by trees.

**Day 122** I hear a vehicle driving around in the parking lot. I cautiously glance outside the window and see a patrol car cruising by. An hour later, just before dawn, I hear another vehicle. It's the patrol car again. I try to go back to sleep, but the dogs are oblivious to my desire to sleep in. They begin licking themselves and scratching in their kennel.

"Fine," I grumble. "I'll take ya'll to the potty!"

I load the dogs back into the truck, then I knock on the glass to the cab to wake Dad up.

Groggily he says, "Huh?"

"We probably should move the truck. The PoPo has been by twice. I don't want him to tell us to move," I say.

"Okay," Dad says. "We can go after you feed the dogs."

"I already fed the dogs and took them to potty again."

"I can show you where the trail goes after the Rec. Center."

"Okay. I can even walk all four dogs from the Rec. Center to where the trail goes into the woods. I'm taking the rest of the day off from hiking today. I want to take you out to eat for an early Father's Day meal. I'm sorry you're stuck with me, instead of being with the rest of your kids and meeting your first grandson."

"I don't mind," Dad says. "Andy says, Caleb mostly sleeps right now."

I finish hiking through town, then Dad and I explore the town. We park the truck in the shade and fill the dogs bowls with water. There are book stores, specialty stores, and authentic places to eat.

For lunch, we narrow our choice to "Molly's Balloon," and have a delicious turkey burger and fries.

Dad points out, "The fries are the cheapest thing on the menu."

"Dad, you can have whatever you want. It's Father's Day and I want it to be special for you. I'll even buy desert if you want."

"I would rather get a gallon of ice cream at the grocery store later."

I laugh. "Okay."

After lunch, we drive to the edge of town to let the dogs out for exercise, fresh air, and to replenish their water. The only place we can find to park is at the CVS Pharmacy. There is a sign explicitly saying, if you aren't a customer, then they will tow your vehicle.

Dad says, "I don't think we should park here."

"I'll go inside and buy something, then we will be customers."

Dad grudgingly comes with me inside. We buy snacks and use the bathroom then return outside to the truck.

I'm sure they would love to tow the white truck with the purple camper. It's not stylish or classy, like those of the reunion people, nor did our attire fit in with their high dollar, sophisticated suits and dresses. Grunge, dog hair clothing vs. designer suits. At least I smell good and look clean.

The CVS has shade and is on the edge of the main shopping strip. The temperature is hot but, tolerable. I am very glad we are headed north. I'm not sure the dogs could take hiking in southern summer heat. Since we are hiking steadily north, the weather is mild most of the time, especially when we are on the trail and at elevation.

A lot of the stores are more geared for winter sports, than they are for hiking.

"Short-N-Sweet" had offered to let me stay with her if I needed to. I want to, but I get stuck and can't make myself call her. If I go, will she let Dad and the dogs stay too? I would be imposing…even though she offered…Long sigh. (I'm getting better at getting out of my comfort zone, but I'm still not there yet).

Girl (Hiking) with 4 Dogs

**Day 123** In the morning I hear the PoPo patrolling again. This time he stops beside the truck. I see him getting out and walking to the side of the truck. Since I sleep inconspicuously in the back of the truck with the dogs, when the PoPos' come by, they don't notice me. I lower myself slowly below the window, and cover my head with the sleeping bag and spare supplies.

The PoPo knocks on the glass of the cab. I hear Dad moving around and he eventually rolls down the manual truck window.

The PoPo asks, "Is everything all right?"

"Yes," Dad says.

"Okay," the officer says. "I patrol this area so let me know if you need anything."

"I'm good for now," Dad says. The officer leaves.

It makes me feel indigent when the PoPos' check on us even when they are friendly and respectful. However, it doesn't seem to bother Dad.

After the officer leaves I go to the cab. "I'm ready to start hiking," I tell Dad.

He agrees and we drive to the trailhead.

"Happy Father's Day Dad! I'll meet you at Lyme-Dorchester Road," I call as I head off down the trail. I bring Digger and Mtn. Goat with me. We've barely started and I have to use a rope to climb a rock boulder. Mtn. Goat bounds right up the boulder. I pretend to run and jump, but Digger only makes it halfway. Next I climb to the top, then help pull Digger up with the leash.

A girl running arrives. She says, "Can I help?"

"Yes, thanks." I answer in relief. She pushes Digger from behind while I'm pulling on the leash. He finally makes it. She is in Grad. School to be a marine biologist.

We finally make it to the top of the boulder and the marine biologist continues on her run.

Next I meet Renea, who is hiking with two friends.

Then, after Velvet Rocks shelter and at the pond I meet, 'Uncle Bert,' 'Auntie Em,' and their daughter, who are hiking a section of the trail. They are from Maine.

Five miles later while hiking up Moose Mountain, the dogs and I meet nurse Morene, her husband, two boys, and a girl with their dog Fin. The dogs sniff each other while we talk.

Morene says, "You should move to New Hampshire and get a job at Dartmouth Hospital."

"That sounds like a neat idea, but right now I'm trying to pay off my house, and my current yard, at least so far, is dog proof. I have a fence tall enough that Mtn. Goat can't jump out, and the bottom of the fence has poured concrete, so Digger can't dig out, Kujo keeps away intruders, and Instigator chases everyone around in circles inside the fence. Also, my sister helped me put the fence up, so it has sentimental value."

"Well if you change your mind, I'm sure you can get a job. Good luck on your thru-hike."

Later while hiking up Moose Mountain, we take a break near (in) the "brook," which appears to be the same thing as a stream, or we can just call it a body of water. Mtn. Goat is panting. He lays down it the brook and refuses to get up for 10 minutes. Occasionally he laps up water. It's shady. I finish drinking the water I brought and pump more water to drink for later. The water is ice cold. Digger followed Mtn. Goat's lead and is laying in the water. I douse myself in cold water and gasp as it takes my breath away.

While I am refilling water, I look up and see Digger is paralyzed. I jump up and run to check on him. I do a complete body scan, and find a tiny, harmless, inchworm on the fur on his left flank. Digger is completely, and utterly immobilized. Once the worm is gone, Digger wriggles and squirms in his usual out of control manner.

Maybe I should keep a few worms on hand, so when he is being too rambunctious, I can just throw a worm on him, to make him stop in his tracks.

The next section of the trail looks like a Christmas Tree Massacre! Was there an anger management session that got out of control, or maybe an anti-Christmas psychopath or the Grinch was let loose to destroy the trees. No, I think the Grinch has a good heart. The trees are down and cross-wise and upside down. It is a mess! Poor things, but it smells fantastic! Maybe they smell better than if they hadn't been through such a disaster. All the broken limbs surely release more of the sweet fir-like perfume.

Girl (Hiking) with 4 Dogs

At the top of Moose Mountain, after all the huffing and puffing to get there, I look at Mtn. Goat and Digger and say, "Hey look there is a box, probably with trail magic, maybe water or candy."

I open the box. Sigh. No food. It's some kind of geo-catch! Grrrr!

I'll forgive this cruelty, since the trail is marked so clearly. Not only is it easy to follow, but also the trail markers are very aesthetic, showing where the hikers are, water source, camping, and a picture of a moose. Thank you for your hard work and diligence to keep people like me from getting lost!

I reach Lyme -Dorchester Road and see Dad, but there isn't much of a parking area. I consult my thru hiker book and realize the trail crosses the same road again in two miles. The second crossing has the parking coordinates.

"Dad," I say. "The trail crosses this road again in a couple of miles. I'll trade the dogs then meet you there."

"No, I think this is the place. You know sometimes the roads don't connect."

"Yeah, but the other area has the parking coordinates. If we park here we might get a ticket, but if we park at the parking coordinates, then we should be safe from PoPo drama."

As Dad and I are arguing over whether or not the trail crosses the road again, a local guy drives near, and Dad flags him down.

The guy glares at us and glances at his watch, but as Dad limps closer his expression softens.

Dad says, "We are looking at our map and wondering how far this road continues."

The guy looks at the map with us and says, "Yes, this road goes on for at least five miles. It looks like the trail crosses the road again farther north. It looks shorter to hike on the road and I'm sure it's easier."

"No. I want to stick to the trail," I answer. "Thanks for your help sir. Dad I'll see you at the next road crossing."

The trail is quiet and enclosed by deciduous trees. There are large green ferns on both sides. Towards the end of the hike, there is a concrete trail marker stating the mileage thus far, 1730 traveled (really 1758 for this year) and 410 to go (really 423).

When I reach the second crossing for the Lyme-Dorchester Rd., it is peaceful and quiet. The dirt road isn't busy, and there is a convenient water supply for the dogs and myself. There is a large smooth rock on the edge of the stream that is shaped like a chase lounge. I would sit and relax, but it gets cold as soon as the sun starts going down. I shiver and put on my warm down jacket. Dad and I fix yummy Roman noodles, and talk while hanging out on the back of the truck. I apply bug spray. Dad refuses.

I look back on my phone to show Dad pictures, but I can't find them! What the blankety, blank, blank?! Where are the pictures, and why is this happening to me? I am about to start the most rugged, and probably the most beautiful section of the entire hike, and I don't have a working camera. My expensive camera doesn't even come on anymore.

The world is totally not fair!

Shortly after the realization that my camera is broken, we meet a couple finishing up a day hike, Josh and Annie. They are working in the area, but are originally from out west. They moved to NH for work.

Josh says, "I heard you say your camera isn't working. I have a disposable camera you can have. I don't remember what pictures are on it."

"I would hate to take something with your special memories on it," I say.

"There's only a few pictures. Mostly sceneries."

"If you're sure you don't mind, I would love to be able to take pictures while in New Hampshire."

"I don't mind," Josh says and hands me his camera.

"Thanks." I say as they drive off.

It brings tears to my eyes (not really at least not right now, but I was really touched).

About 30 minutes later, I meet the "tight-ass-family." Anorexic mom, weakling dad, and two snobby middle school age children.

As they exit the trail I say, "Hi."

The mom looks in our direction, then quickly looks away and whispers to her husband and kids, then herds everyone quickly toward their car. She glances back in our direction twice.

Girl (Hiking) with 4 Dogs

They are all wearing matching dorky, mosquito net, name-brand hats on. I think the mom must have instructed them (in a nasally voice of course, with her lips pursed) "Now go straight to the car kids, don't make eye contact. We don't know what these people are capable of. They might want your mosquito net hats, you know how special those are. We'll be sure to pray for them on Sunday when we go to church, but right now, don't acknowledge that they are human, and totally ignore them."

When I read the Bible, it says that God loves us all equally, whether I'm a smelly, stinky, backpacker, or a squeaky-clean professional. I'm sure neither of them is a nurse, but they might have been Doctors (JK).

I want to shout, "Do you think that God created you and not your neighbor? He created all of us. If you were born in different circumstances, you might be a different person," but I refrain.

So, for the "tight-ass-family," who wouldn't even wave, relax. Anal retentiveness leads to constipation. A painful experience, and if you don't get that taken care of, it can lead to major complications, ruptured colon, ostomy, hospitalization, and even death!

We are all human, and we all have our strengths and weaknesses.

**Day 124** Today is my sister Melissa's birthday. Unfortunately, I don't have any phone signal, but I called a few days ago, when I had phone signal, to wish her a Happy Birthday. There are more and more times when I don't have phone signal.

It's all up hill in the beginning, 1124 ft. to 3230 ft. I take a break at Smarts Mountain fire tower. Kujo and Instigator are hooked to my backpack and waiting at the bottom. I climb to the top and look down. It's a long way to the bottom. The evergreen trees border the clearing where the tower is. The evergreen branches are filled with green needles and it looks like I am surrounded by perfect flowering Christmas trees.

When I was a child we had the opportunity to climb up a fire tower in our area, I went up, not quite halfway, then I got scared and went back down. Once the other kids were at the top, spitting on everyone at the bottom, I wanted to go back up, but my mom wouldn't let me.

Don't let your fears hold you back, because you might not get a second chance...

After the fire tower, I meet "B.J" and "Ever Ready" section hiking with an RV. When they finish a section the RV is waiting for them.

The dogs and I pass Hexacube Shelter. "Puller" aka Kujo, is dragging me around, trying to catch up to people ahead of us. Kujo is as far ahead of me as he can be while contained by his leash. All of a sudden, he disappears! I look down and see he's stuck in mucky mud up to his armpits. He doesn't know if he should jump to get out, or swim, so he's trying to do both. He looks confused and his face says, "Help. Please?"

Of course, Instigator and I stop as soon as we realize the trail is no longer terra firma. There is four feet of sinking mud. I side track it by stepping on the bushes beside the trail, and carrying Instigator so he won't drown.

We continue. Kujo is no more cautious than before he fell in the mud.

We are slopping around on the mucky trail maze, then climbing down rocks, when another dog barrels down upon us. My heart stops. Kujo lunges, with a growl, and snarling teeth, almost unbalancing me. The other dog backs away. Once he is with his owner, I can breathe again and we are able to pass safely and continue on our way. Instigator continues barking and egging on the drama.

Next near Mt. Cube south peak, we meet "Tinsy" and "Winsy" who are from NH, and a few miles later near Bracket Brook, I meet Alyssa. As we pass she says, "You must be 'Girl with 4 Dogs.'"

"Yes. How did you know?" I ask.

"I've heard about you from other hikers and I'm friends with 'Short-N-Sweet.'"

"That's cool," I say.

"On the trail and in trail communities, everyone knows everyone," Alyssa says.

"Tell 'Short-N-Sweet' I said hey," I say as I continue hiking.

"I will and good luck," Alyssa answers.

Four miles later, as I pass the turn for Ore Hill shelter, I briefly note a sign posted saying something about the shelter being closed for maintenance. A couple of miles later I meet "Flash," a writer on dog-human relationships.

"How far are you going today?" I ask.

"Only a couple more miles to Ore Hill Shelter," Flash answers.

"I think it's closed," I say.

"The map doesn't say anything about it being closed."

"I guess you'll find out who's right when you get there." I say. "Good luck with your writing."

"Thanks." Flash answers.

Seven and a half miles later, the dogs and I end the day at NH 25. 23.9 miles.

**Day 125** I eventually realize that my phone is still taking pictures, however it saves them under the date January 5, 1980, when there is no phone service.

I tap on the glass to the truck to wake Dad up. "Dad, it looks like I will enter White Mountain National Forest today. The guy, Gary we met at Dickey Gap said it would be hard to hike in the White's with the dogs. I fed them and loaded them back in the truck. Do you mind keeping them with you?"

"That is fine. I can keep them," Dad answers.

"Okay. I am planning to make it to Franconia Notch. If it doesn't look like I'll make it that far in a day I will send you a text message, or a SPOT letting you know I am ok."

"If you want I can meet you at Kinsman Notch. You can pick up your tent and sleeping bag then, that way you only have to carry it 9 miles instead of all 25 miles," Dad suggest.

"That sounds like a good idea. I'll see you at Kinsman Notch then. Bye," I say and head off down the town trail.

I squint as I look ahead for trail markers. The thru hiker book says I hike on Long Pond Road, then High Street road.

Where are the trail markers?

Finally, a white blaze! It looks like I turn into the field. There is a trampled grass.

Where do I go now?

There are three possible directions to travel and no blazes in sight!

I wish I Kujo was here. I feel empty and lost hiking alone.

I go right, no blazes and it' s heading the way I came. Straight ahead is a dead end. Next, I go to the left. It looks promising, an old dirt road. Still no blazes. I hike a few minutes, but it doesn't feel right, so I turn around. I pray. Before I get back to the three-way trail split, I check out the perimeter of the field.

"Are you serious?" I exclaim. Low and behold, hidden by the grass, and overhanging trees, I discover a trail! I hike in a few feet then turn back to see if there are any white blazes. I don't see any blazes, but I do see a well written detailed sign for the SOBOs saying, 'stay to the right of the field' so you don't get lost. We love you SOBOs and will guide you clearly. We hate the NOBOs, so we'll let them waste hours trying to find the trail. Hugs and kisses my wanted ones.

I travel from 1130 ft. elevation to 4802 ft. elevation over a 5-mile distance. At the top of Mt. Moosilauke, I meet "Summit 48." He is challenging himself to summit 48 mountains in a month.

There are rock piles, but no trees. I'm shivering and the wind is stealing my breath. I don't want to chitchat. I try to send a text message to Dad, but it fails. The phone says I have signal, but maybe it is too windy. I keep going.

Going down the mountain, the trees are astonishing in their beauty. They are full of green leaves. There is a stream of white water going down the smooth rocks of the mountain. The downward descent from Mt. Moosilauke is almost straight down. There are wooden boards secured in the mountain to act as steps. I venture off the trail to look at the stream running parallel to the trail. It's a straight down vertical drop! I carefully ease back on to the trail.

How do trees grow in this environment?

I make it to meet Dad at NH 112, Kinsman Notch, to pick-up more food, and my sleeping bag, but he isn't there. I try calling and texting for 15 minutes. My goal is Franconia Notch, and I know if I wait on Dad, there is no way I can make it. Finally, I leave a message letting Dad know I can't wait any longer and I will either stay at Lonesome Lake Hut or meet at Franconia Notch parking area.

Today is AT hike naked day! I don't want to see any naked hikers, nor am I hiking naked!

Kinsman Notch is 1870 ft. The highest peak of Kinsman Mountain is 4358 ft. The next few miles of the trail are very rugged and tiring. Mile after mile of elevation changes, rock climbs and falls. I love it! After conquering Mt. Wolf, I pass "Blondie" at Eliza Brook Shelter. Next, I tackle North and South Kinsman Mountain. Every few feet I stop to gasp for air. I call Dad, and leave another message, telling him I probably won't make it to Franconia Notch, and not to worry.

I pass shrubs with pretty white spiky cotton bally shape flowers, and I glance at the thick soft looking moss alongside the trail. I pass a pond that reminds me of a water slide. The water rushes down the smooth rocks, twisting and turning, sloshing up the sides of the rocks, and exiting in a frothy burst into the large pond at the bottom.

When I get to Lonesome Lake Hut, there is an hour of daylight and only three miles, so I chicken out of asking to work-for-stay at the hut. I don't have my sleeping bag.

The hut is made from wood and is in an octagonal shape. There is a huge lake with mountains surrounding it and a wooden dock behind the hut. Two geese are exploring.

The trail is easier now. I run. There are planks, and a few extremely large rocks. It's getting dark. I have to stop running because I can't see. It gets dark earlier in the Mountains, and, there is a lot of tree coverage blocking the sun.

Well, now I can use my head lamp.

I don't have Kujo to help me stay on the trail. I don't want to get lost in the woods, or die from exposure. I don't want to change my goal, ask for help, or even do what normal people do, and work-for-stay at the hut.

What is wrong with me? The Hut is beautiful! Now, if I want to go back I have to pay an arm and a leg. I can't afford to lose those, because I have to work to make a living, and feed my numerous dogs and my cat.

I can't see the trail anymore. It's too dark. All I see is water with a tree in the middle, and what might be a white blaze on the tree in the middle of the water.

Why is there a white blaze on the tree in the middle of the water? Am I supposed to cross the water in the dark, on slippery rocks I can barely see?

Why yes, I am, and that's what I get for making bad choices, instead of enjoying the luxuries offered for work for stays.

I wish I had my sleeping bag.

I cross the river. My feet get wet! They always do, at the end of the day, and they're sore. I have a mile and a half left. The trail is wide and easy to follow. I hope there's no poison ivy.

Dad's not answering his phone.

After the trail exit's the woods, it goes under US-3/I-93. It's dark and scary. I can't see the trail good enough to follow it the small distance to Franconia Notch parking. I still can't reach Dad by phone. I turn the battery off. The phone is dying.

I feel homeless. No food, no shelter, no sleeping gear. I want to be close enough to the road so I can hear Dad if he comes to find me, but I don't want to be so close that everyone driving by can see me. I consider hitchhiking, but it is after 11:00 p.m.

I put on all the warm layers I have in my backpack. I am still chilly. Sweat is cooling and cold. I'm no longer hot, and I don't want to keep cooling.

Should I hang out at the bottom of the hill near the woods, or on the side of the hill in the tall grass? It might be warmer in the woods, and easier to get comfortable than on the hill, but then it would be harder to get back to the top of the hill, if Dad is near. Sometimes Dad honks when he is close…

After settling against tall weeds to semi-keep from rolling down the hill next to the highway, I try out my emergency blanket that I carry in my backpack. It is waterproof (I think) and I don't want to get dewed-ed on. Plus, then I can determine if it is worth its weight. I sit back up, and dig around in my backpack until I find the emergency blanket.

The blanket is made like a sleeping bag, where I can crawl into it. It's impossible to keep the blanket from snagging on the weeds. I usually sleep with my backpack under my knees, but this time I sleep halfway on top of it, on the hill, for warmth, and protection from the ground, as well as to keep me from rolling down the hill. I am horizontal, with my head slightly diagonal, to keep all the blood from rushing to my head. The Emergency blanket is warm, but it doesn't let moisture out.

Girl (Hiking) with 4 Dogs

I sit up again and wriggle out of the extra layers so they don't get wet from sweat. I check my phone to see if Dad responded, and maybe I am hallucinating, or wishful thinking, but I hear a horn.

Eventually, Dad finds me, and I don't have to sleep by the edge of the highway after all.

We spend what is left of the night in one of the parking areas. It's barely a block away. I crawl in my sleeping space beside the kennels and fall asleep almost immediately. I hiked 25.7 miles, not counting what I hiked when I couldn't find the trail early in the day.

**Day 126** "Good morning Dad," I greet him as he gets out of the truck. "Do you want me to leave the dogs out for you today or do you want me to load them in the kennels?"

"You can load them in the kennels. The truck is almost out of gas," Dad says.

"Are you serious? We just put gas in the truck two days ago!"

"I have to drive more to get to the road crossings in the mountains."

"Fine! I'll load the dogs up and we can drive somewhere to get gas. Yay! I busted my butt yesterday hiking, so I can waste time putting gas in the truck!"

I sit sullenly in the cab while we drive to the gas station. There is road construction and only one lane of traffic is open.

A half hour later, we finally make it to a store with a gas station. In the parking lot there is a four wheel old timey yellow car and a three wheel old timey green car, one wheel in the front and two in the back. Dad says "I remember seeing a car like that when I was a boy!"

"It looks like a neat car. Why did they stop making them?"

"They were dangerous to drive."

The gas is expensive.

Inside the store there is locally made jerky, and candy. The store has a friendly and cozy atmosphere, like a big happy family. The cashier lady smiles and talks as she rings up my snack purchases.

On the way back to the parking area, I have Dad drop me off on the highway where he picked me up the night before.

"Thanks for the ride Dad. It sure felt nice this morning when the air was crisp and cool. I can finally start hiking now that it sweltering hot!"

Dad wisely doesn't respond.

It is a short distance to the parking coordinates. Almost within sight.

It's after 10 a.m. when I get started.

As I slowly trudge up the mountain, Kya passes me. I look back and see Foster and Squash.

What!?

They passed me months ago, hiking 30 miles a day!

"Hey guys! How are ya'll? I figured you would be finished by now," I say excitedly.

Fosters says, "Kya lost her backpack on the trail and I had to order a new one and wait for it to come in. Another time I had equipment break and had to wait for it to be repaired. It set me back a few days."

"Have you seen anyone else I might know?" I ask.

"Youngin' is hiking with us, but he stayed at Lonesome Lake Hut last night. The friends he started with already finished so he and I started hiking together. I couldn't stay at Lonesome Lake Hut because they wouldn't let Kya inside."

"That seems unfair. Kya is so well-behaved it's easy to forget she's a dog."

"She is a certified therapy dog as well, so she should have been allowed to stay," Foster says.

"What about you Squash, why haven't you finished the trail already?" I ask.

"A friend flew down to hike with me. She couldn't hike 20 miles a day."

"It's great to see ya'll again," I say as they pass me.

How can they pass me so quickly, and easily, while we're hiking up a mountain?!

After a few minutes of relentless straight up hiking I have to stop to catch my breath.

Why do I get so winded climbing straight up the mountain?

I stay focused, deep breaths slowly in, then slowly out. One step at a time.

Girl (Hiking) with 4 Dogs

I pass Liberty Spring Campsite and catch up to and pass Foster and Squash. They are talking to "Newt," a female SOBO. She doesn't wear bug spray and she is covered in red, raw, oozing bug bites.

"Hey again," I say in passing.

Keep moving. No time to talk. Slow and steady wins the race.

Foster and Kya, Squash, and Youngin' pass me!

The 2800 + feet elevation increase, over a three mile stretch, is leaving me short of breath. The additional almost 1000 ft. increase over the next four miles doesn't help my lungs oxygenate my body any better. The elevation on top of Mt. Lafayette is 5260 ft. above sea level. The elevation at the beginning of the day was 1428 ft.

At the turning point for Greenleaf Hut I catch up to Youngin' and Foster while they are taking a lunch break.

"How far are ya'll going today?" I ask.

"We are going to Galehead Hut. Where are you going?" Youngin' asks.

"I planned to go to Greenleaf Hut tonight, it's a mile out of the way, but Galehead is another six miles. I don't know if I can hike that far before dark."

"I'm sure you can make it," Youngin' says.

"I don't hike as fast as you guys," I say.

"Let's flip a rock. If it lands with the chipped side up then go to Galehead and if it lands with the chipped side down then go to Greenleaf," Youngin' suggests.

"Okay, flip the rock."

Youngin' flips the rock and it lands chipped side up.

"Galehead it is," I say. "If I don't make it before morning, then send someone to look for me, okay?"

"You'll make it," Youngin' says and pats me on the back.

I grab some trail mix out of my backpack, take a few bites of cheese crackers, and beef summer sausage and continue toward Galehead Hut.

The guys bound past me like runners on an obstacle course. They use their hiking poles to pole vault down boulders and to stabilize themselves on the loose rocks.

I don't have hiking poles. I slowly and gingerly lower myself down the boulders and cautiously maneuver over the looser rocks.

I try to keep up with the guys, but they easily leave me behind. I'm a big girl. I can hike by myself. My throat is constricting. I don't want to be alone on the trail at night! I gasp in air. I purse my lips to breath in slow deep breaths.

I lengthen my stride, but it is difficult to hike fast. My knees are aching, even with both knee braces on. The heat makes the neoprene brace unbearably hot. The sweat and friction cause heat rashes on my knees, but the pain without the brace is almost unbearable.

I laugh ironically and tears roll down my cheeks.

I'm alone again.

I sip on water from my CamelBak, multiple small sips to wash away the tightness in my throat.

I focus on the beauty around me. The sky is clear and blue. I can see for miles in all directions. I'm healthy. I'm thru hiking the Appalachian Trail!

I don't need anyone!

In my lonesome musings, I realize guys hiking fast and taking long breaks is similar to other guy behavior. There is an expression comparing guys to girls; guys are like an express train, fast, and girls are like a freight train, slow, but once they start they keep on going!

I take a bite of trail mix, but I can't chew, breath, and hike. I stop hiking to chew and breath, then I put away the trail mix and focus on hiking and breathing. The sun is sinking below the horizon.

A few miles before I arrive at Galehead Hut I meet "P.J."

"It's almost dark. How far are you hiking today?" I ask.

"My total trip is 54 miles. I'm hiking and sometimes running from Hut-to-Hut through the White Mountains."

"54 miles is a long distance. Can you hike that far in a day?"

"I'll have to hike at night. Last year someone completed the challenge in 24 hours."

"Wow! Good luck and be careful. Some of the terrain is very treacherous!"

"Thanks. Good luck on your thru hike. You only have about two more miles to Galehead. I just left from there. They gave me food and I filled up my water."

Girl (Hiking) with 4 Dogs

After P.J. is gone I cross a stream coming down from the mountain. The water is clear and ice cold. I'm parched.

What doesn't kill me, makes me stronger, I say to myself and scoop fresh, unfiltered, untreated water from the stream to drink.

Delicious! It is the best, most pure water I can remember drinking. It is cold and soothing as it trickles down my parched throat.

The trail is treacherous. It goes straight down, like rock climbing, without a rope, and with a 'brook" of running water to keep me company as I climb. The entire climb is wet and slippery. I can see how someone could slip and fall 20 feet to their death!

I miss the Dogs, but I'm glad to be dog-less while hiking thru the White's. Having even one dog is dangerous, more work, and I wouldn't be able to stay in the Huts. Foster lets Kya find her own way, off leash, and that works for them.

It is dusk when I arrive at the hut, last as usual. I am relieved to be there before dark.

Youngin' says, "I knew you would make it."

"Barely," I reply.

The Hut personnel are putting away the soup and salad when I arrive, but they let me make a plate from the leftovers. I meet Michael, Christopher, Hilary, Adam, Philip, and Amie. They are energetic, talkative, and helpful. Most are in high school or college and they work in the huts during summer break. I'm envious.

I am glad there is food, and a warm dry place to sleep, and I am super glad I am able to do "work-for-stay." I help scrub and clean the kitchen stove after eating. I am all around "glad." I just wish I had stayed at Lonesome Lake Hut last night!

God worked it out so I could meet up with my hiking friends. It is motivating to hike with someone else. "My God is an awesome God…" I need to relax and trust God. He always knows what is best, but I don't always listen. Thank you God.

At Galehead Hut, thru-hikers get to sleep on the floor in the dining room after everyone goes to bed. Lights are out at 9 p.m. Most of the Huts have a natural energy source, such as solar or wind power, and they try to be self-sustaining.

Youngin' and I are the only thru hikers tonight. Foster stayed for supper, but he wasn't allowed to stay inside with Kya.

"I heard you stayed at Lonesome Lake Hut last night. How was it?" I ask Youngin'

"It was great! There weren't many guests staying so I got to sleep in a bunk. All I had to do for my work-for-stay was tell the guest about my thru hike."

"I almost stayed last night, but I chickened out."

"There was plenty of room."

"Thanks for encouraging me to hike to Galehead."

"I didn't think you would want to hike out of the way to make it to Greenleaf, then have to backtrack in the morning," Youngin' says.

"I'm glad I caught up to ya'll. I'll see you in the morning."

"Goodnight."

**Day 127** The staff at Galehead Hut fix a huge breakfast of eggs, bacon, fruit, and coffee. After eating Youngin' and I sweep the community area and bunk rooms, then begin our day hiking.

The Pemigewasset Wilderness is obscured by the thick heavy fog. I am ecstatic to start from Galehead Hut. There are places I hiked yesterday that I would definitely not want to hike when there is poor visibility. It was difficult enough hiking when it was dry and sunny!

I stumble frequently as I squint to see through my foggy, scratched lenses.

I make out the shape of a few green shrubs, but the rest of the scenery is hidden in fog.

After seven miles of hiking, I take a lunch break at the Zealand Falls Hut.

"Hi Youngin' we meet again," I say.

"Yes. I'm staying here tonight. I'm going to enjoy every minute of being in the White's. I'm going to stay in every Hut I can. They have great leftovers if you are hungry."

"Pizza and Soup. It looks delicious. Nothing beats hot soup on a cold, wet day!"

I give a donation for the food, then sit down and eat.

I meet JoeG and Jeff "Easy Dog" while at the Hut. "Enjoy the White's," JoeG says as I don my backpack.

"It would be a lot more enjoyable if it was a little e warmer," I respond.

I hike seven more miles to meet Dad at the Ethan Pond Parking area for re-supply.

I arrive at the parking area, but I don't see Dad.

Should I hitchhike to town or keep waiting?

It's raining. Rain = Cold.

I sent a text message, and a GPS for Dad at the top of the mountain.

Didn't Dad get the info? Is he lost or at a different place? Is he playing around in town?

I barely have enough signal to get another text out, then I settle myself to wait…

I'm shivering so I get up and pace up and down the road.

Finally, I see the truck.

When Dad stops, I ask, "What took you so long?"

"I didn't know which road you were going to stop at. Since it is only mid-afternoon I thought you would keep hiking," he replies sarcastically.

"Dad, it's 25 miles to the next set of parking coordinates! There is no way I can hike 40 miles in one day!"

Dad drives to the top of the parking area. I walk the dogs.

I don't mind waiting, I'm used to that. I have been at fault plenty of times, but not this time. I guess if Dad feels good about letting me wait in the freezing, rain, then that's his business. I only have 345.1 miles left! Dad's probably trying to piss me off, so I will quit. Then he can be right, since he only gave me 60% odds of completing the trail. Or, if I don't appreciate him properly, he'll leave me stranded with 4 dogs, and a truck I can't take on the trail!

**Day 128** It's cold this morning. I start at 1443 ft. elevation, dip down to 1265 ft. before making a steady climb to 5096 ft. elevation.

I stop briefly for a snack break, and potty time at Mizpah Spring Hut. It's warm inside, compared to outside. Julie, her husband and kids are playing card games at the tables inside. Becky is reading a book. Patch and Croo are laughing and talking.

Julie says, "You can join our game if you want."

"It looks fun. I remember as a kid we used to play games on the weekends. I'm thru hiking the AT so I only stopped to use the bathroom. I have six miles to hike before I make it to Lake of the Clouds Hut."

"What is your trail name?" Julie asks.

"Girl with Four Dogs." I explain how I got my trail name and that the dogs are with Dad while I hike through the White's. While I'm talking the other guests meander over to listen.

After a while we say our goodbye's and I continue toward Lake of the Clouds Hut.

My daily hiking mileage is half what it was, but it takes the same amount of time!

It is uphill all the way, and even that doesn't help me stay warm. It is foggy and wet. The trail is difficult to see, and challenging to follow. There aren't many trees. No blazes. There are piles of rocks everywhere, left, right and straight ahead!

Am I following the pile of rocks to go to the Lake of the Clouds Hut, or am I on another trail?

I see a few hikers headed south. I ask them which trail they are on.

"We are leaving from Lake of the Clouds Hut," one couple answers.

"Thanks," I say. "I'm going to the Lake of the Clouds Hut."

I can't stop shivering. I have my red ear warmers on, a t-shirt, fleece long sleeves, then my North Face Summit Series jacket. I have my sleeves pulled down to cover my hands, but I can still barely feel them.

"I can't believe it's J-June," I stutter passing another hiker. "It's f-f-freezing!"

"Mt. Washington Weather is unpredictable. It is reported they have the highest winds in the country."

"I believe it! My hands are turning blue!"

Next, I see a cluster of green bushes with purple flowers. As I walk through the bushes, it feels like someone turned on a space heater. I crouch down and contemplate snuggling into the foliage for the night. I can easily curl up and go to sleep.

"What are you doing!" my inner voice shouts at me, "this isn't the Lake of the Clouds Hut!"

"I know, but it's warm."

Girl (Hiking) with 4 Dogs

"Get-up and get to the HUT!"

My inner nuisance won't leave me alone so I get up and continue hiking. As soon as I leave the protection of my little bush friends, the wind ferociously torments me. It pushes me to the side of the trail. I push back by leaning into the wind. The wind suddenly stops blowing and I fall from the lack of resistance. I get up glaring. The wind starts blowing again and swirling in tiny circles. Laughing.

I stomp onward into the white haze going up the mountain!

I finally see the outline of the Lakes of the Cloud Hut. I notice a dog tied outside the hut as I go in. I take off my backpack, check with the staff to make sure I can stay for the night, then I rummage around in my backpack for my dry clothes and my down jacket, after that I head to the bathroom to change.

The bathroom is a deluxe porta-potty. The toilet seat sits over a large hole. Periodically the Hut staff have to shovel out the excess waste. There is an entry way on the outside of the hut that opens to the potty.

I meet the staff, Emma, Marie, Lacey, Gil, Margaret, Hannah, William, Nick, Anderson, and Madison, and ask what I can do to help. Margaret suggest I wash dishes. The water is heavenly warm. The staff talk as they work and it seems like everyone gets along.

I learn it is 49 degrees outside, the wind is blowing at 31 mph, with gusts of 49 mph wind.

Foster comes to help wash dishes.

"How did you manage to stay?" I ask.

"They have emergency accommodations in the basement where hikers can stay if they have dogs. They are more flexible about letting people stay when the weather is bad. Kya and I have been here since this morning."

"What have you been doing all day?"

"I had chocolate covered strawberries this morning. I talked with the other guests, took a nap, and ate some more."

"I noticed a dog tied up when I came in. She looks cold. I'm worried her."

"I saw Matt, the dogs owner, go outside a few minutes ago. He's probably taking his dog to the basement now."

"Good. I would expect him to take care of his dog first. I'm finally warming up. It was freezing out there today."

During clean-up after supper I meet Matt. He is 30 years old.

I listen as he and William talk.

Matt says, "My sleeping bag is extremely heavy. It got wet a few days ago and it has not dried out since. It is not very warm either. I have had if for a few years. I was sleeping at a church shelter and one of the church members gave it to me."

William says, "We don't have any sleeping bags here, but we can find you a blanket and a change of clothes if you need it."

"I need all the help I can get," Matt says.

"What kind of work do you do?" I ask.

"I used to help farm, but I hurt my back. I always wanted to hike the trail."

"Where did you start hiking and how long have you been on the trail?" I ask.

"I started in Gorham, New Hampshire a few weeks ago. It's harder than I thought. I don't have good equipment like some hikers."

"I noticed your dog was outside when I first got here. She looked really cold."

"She's used to cold weather," Matt answers defensively. "Does anyone have a phone charger or a phone I can use? My mom buys minutes for my phone, but I'm almost out of minutes and the battery does not stay charged long."

William says, "You can use my phone and I will charge your phone. Where do you stay when you are not hiking?"

"Me and a friend used to jump on trains. We would ride them all night and jump off in the morning before we got caught. One night we overslept. I heard the train conductor coming. I tried to wake her up, but she wouldn't wake up. I jumped off and hid under the train. The train conductor found my friend and beat her, then threw her off the train. He hurt her so bad she can no longer work. She gets a disability check and is always in pain."

William asks, "Did you sue the man? He should not be allowed to go unpunished!"

"Nobody would listen to us," Matt says. "I found an abandoned building to live in one time. I invited some friends to stay there with me. There was no one using the building. A few weeks later the owner somehow found out we were there and he kicked us all out and boarded up the place! He checks on the building all the time now. It's just not fair, we should be allowed to stay there if we want! He was not using the building. It's just falling apart."

I join the conversation, "I heard of a man who was staying in an abandoned building. He found out he had AIDS from an unfaithful girlfriend, then he got drunk and fell down the elevator shaft and broke his neck. Now he's paralyzed. Do you know what he did next? He sued the owner of the building! Just because something exists, doesn't mean you are entitled to it. It seems like people who get something for nothing are the least appreciative!"

"I should not have to pay to use something if no one else is using it," Matt raises his voice. He continues talking to William. "If I am hungry and I see a field of corn, I should be able to pick the corn and eat it. It does not matter if I planted it."

"What about the people who have to sell the corn to feed their family?" I ask

"They have enough for me too. I'm only one person," Matt retorts.

I look at him and raise my left eyebrow, "What if everyone thought the same as you?"

"Everyone should be allowed to eat!"

Blah Blah Blah, he goes on and on and on with his failure mentality. If everyone has his mentality, then there would be nothing for anyone to be entitled to!

I watch how Matt manipulates people, telling them his hard luck story. He finds his next victim to manipulate. Then, the good Samaritan, William, comes and caters to Matt (the entitled one). "Let me help you." Let me give you what you need, so you can continue to live in your delusional world where everything is free. You poor, poor soul, your life is so hard, blah, blah, blah. The Giver and the Taker.

I finish the dishes and walk away from all the Bull Shit coming out of Matt's mouth.

I talk to a few other guests. There are people from all over the world at the Hut. A few don't speak English.

I'm lost in my thought sitting on one of the benches in the dining hall looking out at the wall of white surrounding everything. Maybe, I am in the wrong, and I should just go around mooching off of everyone else, and not contributing anything. Of course, the Bible also says, if you don't use your talents then you will lose them, and it says the poor will always be with you. What if we are all takers? Then who will plant the fields, and tend the gardens for food? Who will build the rundown building for someone else to stay in for free? Who will drive and repair the train for people to ride on? There are so many liabilities now days. If someone gets hurt, they blame the owners. Then they sue, wanting money for their ailments. Biting the hand that feeds them. It's all your fault. Blah, Blah, Blah. Maybe only stupid people work. Why work when you can get stuff for free?

I notice the staff congregating in the front of the room. They are getting ready to put on a skit to relay the rules of the Hut. They have outrageous costumes, and mops on their heads.

Fosters sits beside me during the skit. Afterward we exchange foot rubs.

"I love a good foot rub," I say, "it's so relaxing, I could just fall asleep."

"You can join me in my bunk in the basement. I can continue your massage," Fosters suggests smiling.

"Is there a way to the basement without going outside?" I ask.

"Unfortunately, no, but I'll warm you up as soon as we get inside."

I'm leaning toward going to the basement, despite the cold path to get there, when Nuisance conscious steps in and adamantly tells me, "You are not going to the basement." "Why not?" I argue inside my head. "I'm 31 one years old. I've been married and divorced. I'm lonely." "You are worth more than a one night stand," Nuisance argues. "Are you serious?!" I argue back. "Foster has dark hair, he is handsome, and muscular, and he takes care of his dog!" "You're not going," Nuisance conscious puts her foot down.

"You've been quiet a long time," Foster says. "I'm going to bed. Are you coming with me or not?"

I sigh and answer, "No. My memories of nearly freezing to death today while hiking are still fresh in my mind. I don't want to be cold again."

"Goodnight," Foster says and leaves to go to the basement.

Girl (Hiking) with 4 Dogs

I curl up on the floor in my -5-degree sleeping bag and wonder what it is like in the basement.

**Day 129** I eat breakfast, then help clean up the kitchen for my work for stay. I see Foster leave before I finish packing up. He didn't even say good bye!

I check my thru hiker book, I stay on Crawford Path Trail at the four-way intersection. I'm going to Mt. Washington summit at 6288 ft., then toward Madison Spring Hut today. I put on my backpack and hike to the sign. According to the sign, Foster started in the wrong direction.

Oh well, he deserves to be lost for not waiting.

It's blindingly foggy this morning, but not as windy or cold.

It's only a mile and a half to the summit of Mt. Washington. When I get to the top of Mt. Washington, I get turned around and confused. I find the visitors center, and sign in. Then I wander around looking for the trail. It is so foggy, I can barely see my hand in front of my eyeball!

After a little while, I see Foster and Kya. I don't mention seeing him go the wrong way this morning. Instead I ask, "Do you know where the trail goes from here? I can't find it."

Foster says, "I just left the summit. I'll walk you to the sign."

"Thanks," I say. "Can you take a picture of me by the sign?"

"Sure."

After taking my picture, we start down Mt. Washington together.

"Is that a train I hear?" I ask Foster.

"It sounds like it."

A few yards later we see the light on the train as it goes down the mountain. It's only a few feet away from us.

As we descend Mt. Washington the fog thins. It's easier to keep up with Fosters today. It's mostly downhill.

"Where are you from?" I ask

"Michigan," Foster answers.

"Are you dating anyone back home?" I ask

"No. Are you?"

"No. I've been married and divorced already. I dated a guy, but he was too violent. He got into a fight with his boss! When you date, do you date more than one person at a time?"

"When I was in college I had a girlfriend at school and one at home."

"When you have a girlfriend and date, what all is involved?"

"What do you mean?" Foster asks.

"Well do you just go to the movies and hang out or are you intimate?"

"If the girl wants to have sex, we have sex."

"Even though you are seeing more than one person?" I ask incredulously.

"Sure, why not?"

"Aren't you worried about STD's? What if she is sleeping with someone else too?"

"I'm not going to get an STD. Besides she wouldn't have sex with anyone else."

"Since my divorce, I've learned guys think just like you. I've learned to make sure my guy agrees to an exclusive relationship. I won't share!"

My knees are aching and I slow down as we descend toward the hill. Foster increases the gap between us.

The weather is improving. The sun is out and chases away the chill of the morning. It is tranquil in the vast openness of the mountains.

Six miles after Mt. Washington, I see Madison Spring Hut in a valley between Mt. Adams and Mt. Madison. As I get closer I see Kya resting outside the hut. Once I get inside I see Foster talking to Stretch and Zippers.

"How are ya'll?" I ask coming inside.

"We are upset," Zippers says. "We got up early this morning to make sure we were the first two at the hut. We wanted to work for stay. The hut personnel won't let us stay. They say it is too early to stop hiking and the day is too beautiful for us to stay due to 'inclement weather.'"

"That sucks," I say. "Have you stayed in any of the huts?"

"No!" Zippers answers.

"Hmmm, it looks like the next hut is about 14 miles away."

Girl (Hiking) with 4 Dogs

"That is too far. We started at Nauman Campsite this morning. We've already hiked 12 miles," Zippers replies.

"Where will you stay?"

Stretch says, "We will spend the day here, then hike three miles to the Osgood Tent site."

"Where are you going?" Zippers asks.

"I am meeting my Dad at Pinkham Notch. I have some food I store in the truck for re-supply." I answer.

Fosters asks, "Can I ride with you to town? Matt did not have food for his dog and he stole mine. I have to replace Kya's food!"

"Sure," I answer. "It was good seeing ya'll. I'm a slow hiker and I have eight miles to hike before meeting Dad. I'll see ya'll next time. Too bad you couldn't spend the night in the hut. It's pretty nice."

"Bye," Stretch and Zippers say.

"I'll catch up." Fosters says.

I set off down the trail. The White Mountains are refreshingly pure. I'm surrounded by natural beauty and fresh air. There are no artificial signs or thick clouds of smog to mar God's creation.

The terrain is rugged and hiking is slow, but peaceful. Fosters easily catches up. Occasionally we talk about random things, but mostly we enjoy the solitude of nature. At Parapet Brook, we argue about which direction the trail is going. We take Fosters recommendation and end up at a park a few miles from where I was expecting to meet Dad. We eat a late afternoon snack while waiting on Dad to find us.

"Yay! I see the truck." I say. "Hey Dad, I'm glad you found us. Fosters needs to go to town to buy dog food. He feeds Kya raw meat and I don't have any, I only have dry dog food."

Kya, rides in the cab of the truck.

By the time we finish shopping and driving back to the parking coordinates it is late. Dad settles in the cab to sleep and Fosters and I head to the back of the truck.

"Fosters, if you want to sleep in the truck you can. You can have my sleeping area beside the kennels and I can sleep in the kennels with the dogs. I used to do it all the time," I say.

"Are you sure?" Fosters asks.

"It's fine. My dogs aren't barking so bad at Kya. You might not be able to stretch out all the way, but it's comfortable on the plastic bens."

"Okay." Fosters says.

We settle in for the night. It takes a while to settle my hormonal mind. She keeps telling me how much more enjoyable it would be to snuggle with a strong handsome man instead of four hairy dogs. I remind my hormonal self that I am not going to be involved with someone who thinks it's okay to sleep with multiple women at a time. If I was going to sink that low, I could have stayed with AJ. Eventually I fall into a dreamless sleep.

**Day 130** June 26, 2011 Burr, it's cold once I leave the warmth of the truck.

"Dad," I say. "It will be at least two days before I meet you at US 2. I'll send you a SPOT GPS when I am ready to be picked up. I love you and thanks for taking care of the dogs for me." I give Dad a hug, grab my backpack and start hiking with Fosters and Kya.

Wildcat Mountain is intense and beautiful. I have to use my hands when climbing. The terrain is rough and Foster and Kya leave me behind. After five miles of hiking I see signs for Carter Notch Hut, but it is challenging to find the trail to the Hut. I reach a dead end. There are guys fly fishing, and they tell me how to find the Hut. They are actually staff off duty.

When I look to my left I see a blaze on the other side of a flooded, marshy area. I climb halfway up a tree and jump over the marshy area to get back on the trail without getting my feet wet.

Why is everyone looking at me strangely? I just want dry feet!

At the Hut, I see Foster. He is talking to Beth, one of the Hut staff.

"Have you been here long?" I ask.

"Not too long. I had to get to the bathroom."

"Understandable."

"They have left over pizza and cookies from last night. Help yourself. They have to throw away leftovers to make room for tonight's meal." Fosters says.

"Okay. I'll eat a few bites. Are you staying here tonight?" I ask.

Girl (Hiking) with 4 Dogs

"I'm thinking about hiking to the Rattle River Shelter. It's another 13 miles. What about you?"

"It would be fun to stay, but I would feel better if I keep hiking. In fact, I need to get going."

Fosters starts off with me, but he gets tired of hiking slow and leaves me behind. Again. He says, "I will meet you at Imp Campsite, then we can hike to Rattle River Shelter together"

I finally make it to Imp Campsite, it's off the main trail. When I arrive, Fosters says, "I'm going to camp here tonight."

"You can stay, but I'm not paying $8 to camp on the Appalachian Trail. I am going to Rattle River Shelter. Have fun camping."

Tears roll down my cheeks as I hike back to the trail. I'm hungry, exhausted, and lonely. "Screw my agenda!" I sob, but I keep hiking north.

The trees and terrain absorb my sorrow. I have to concentrate to navigate the trail without falling and breaking my neck. I sit on my but, roll, and carefully jump down boulders. The sun is sinking lower and I have to hurry.

A couple of miles before the Rattle River Shelter, some SOBO's stop to talk.

"We just left from The White Mountains Hostel, in Gorham, NH. It is amazing. It's not much farther, you should stay there tonight." Nandu says.

I wearily ask, "How difficult is the terrain from here to there?"

"It is fairly even and there are no mountains to worry about."

"Really?" I ask excitedly. "I met the owner's sister when I was in New Jersey. I do want to stay there. Thanks so much for reminding me. Good luck on your thru hike. Yahoo! I'm almost finished!"

"Good luck!" the guys call after me as I take off running down the trail my backpack popping me in the back with each step.

Two more miles. I can make it two more miles. I chant over and over to myself.

My God is AWESOME!

Screw hunger, loneliness, fatigue, and exhaustion, there is a shower at the end of the day!

I pick up the pace, pass right on by Rattle River Shelter; it looks lonely anyway. I run over the hills and through the streams (Yes, Wet feet again!) to get to the White Mountains Lodge.

It is so worth it! I arrive late, between 8-9 ish. I hesitate about knocking, but my desire for the luxury of a shower, a bed, and real food push me into action.

A friendly woman, Geri, opens the door, smiles and invites me in.

"What do you want first?" She asks. "A shower or something to eat?"

"A shower!" I exclaim.

"I will show you your room. If you want to pass out your dirty laundry I can start it washing while you are in the shower."

"That would be wonderful. Thank you." I say.

I jump in the shower and enjoy the hot water washing away the dirt, grime, aches and sorrows of the day. I'm glad I pushed myself so hard. I hiked 20.8 miles and I can take a shower!

After my shower, I put on shorts and a t-shirt I normally sleep in. I search my entire backpack, but I can only find one flip flop. The other one must have fallen out of my backpack while I was climbing over boulders today. I head downstairs barefoot. I don't want to torture my feet with shoes anymore today.

I meet Geri's husband Greg when I get downstairs.

Geri says, "Where are your shoes dear?"

I explain that I must have lost one.

"Come with me while Greg sets the table. We have a hiker box with extra flip flops. Pick out a pair you want."

"Really!" I exclaim. "You are so kind. Thank you so much."

I pick out flip flops then return to the table to consume a feast. It is marvelous! Yummy! The food is fantastic and there is plenty of it! Italian Pasta, salad with strawberries, bread, juice, and desert. It is worth the 20 + miles I hiked to get here. I am so immensely thankful I made it.

After supper, I converse with the other SOBO hikers staying at the hostel. They are fresh and ready to continue their big adventure. It's rejuvenating to socialize with them.

After a short time, I return upstairs to my bunk to crash. The bed is heavenly and clean.

Girl (Hiking) with 4 Dogs

**Day 131** I wake up early, but snuggle back in my sleeping bag the next morning. I deserve extra rest. The bed is soft, warm and cozy.

A few minutes later, the smell of bacon and eggs is a strong enough lure to get me out of bed and I quickly pack before heading downstairs.

"Good morning Geri," I say. "Thank ya'll so much for letting me stay here. I've had a wonderful time."

"If you don't mind, we have a tradition of taking a picture of everyone who stays here. Can we get your picture?"

"I would be honored."

After breakfast, I grab my pack and head outside. Geri takes a picture of me by the sign to the hostel. We bid each other farewell and I continue my hiking adventure.

I call Dad. "Hi Dad. I hiked more than I thought I would yesterday. I'm in Gorham NH this morning. Can you meet me at Hogan Road? It's a gravel road. I can re-supply and get the dogs."

"Okay," Dad says. "It might take me 30 minutes or so to get there."

"That's okay. I'll find a shady spot to wait. I know I didn't let you know ahead of time where I would be."

I see a dam and crystal clear water as I hike through town. I find Hogan Road, then I sit on my backpack and eat snacks in the shade while I wait for Dad to find me.

Once Dad arrives we visit a few minutes and eat lunch together before I re-supply and pick up my doggie companions.

Dad says, "I can keep all the dogs if you want."

"No thanks. I get lonely when I don't have at least one or two of them hiking with me."

Hiking isn't bad compared to what I'm used to. I pass pretty pink flowers, then there is a plank walk through the marsh and into the woods.

I meet a few SOBO's, "Just Tom," a couple "Moose Mulch" and "Appalashire Man."

I'm melancholy after passing the couple near Dream Lake.

When will I find my soul mate?

Lost in thought, Kujo and I almost plow down Valkyre. She is finishing her last section of the entire AT. She started last year and was unable to finish due to bad weather. This year she started in Katahdin and is hiking south to finish.

The sun is sinking below the horizon as I reach Carlo Col Shelter and Campsite just after crossing into Maine. Full Goose shelter is another 4.5 miles. I dare not try to make it. I drop the pack and the dogs. With relief, I use the privy. Next, I secure the food in the bear box. Then I grab rocks, and make a pile by my head, in case I need to scare any bear away. It is a quiet night. I am alone except for the dogs. We hiked 17 miles today.

# Chapter 19: Maine

**Day 132** June 28, 2011 On the way toward Full Goose Shelter, I have to crawl down a six-foot hole, around rocks, jump boulder to boulder, and maneuver two dogs on leashes! Kujo looks at me as if to ask, "How am I supposed to get down there? My paws don't work like your hands."

I put Instigator down and make sure there is plenty of slack in his leash. Then I look up at Kujo, smile and cheerfully say, "Come on Kujo."

He looks back as if to say, "Are you insane?"

"Okay. Sit. Stay." I carefully reach up and unhook his leash. "Okay. Come on." I repeat as I start to walk away.

Kujo looks frantically towards me. "Good boy," I encourage. I hook him back up on the leash and walk a short distance farther. I look ahead at an expanse of rock podiums. I let Kujo and Instigator off the leash and jump from one podium to the next. I feel like Q*Bert in the Atari game.

Hours later we reach Full Goose shelter. I eat lunch and talk to "Bucko," and "Ann and Alex" who are all SOBO hikers. I find the trail log and read a few pages before signing in. Snorkel stayed in the shelter a few days ago. In her log she writes, "...the storm hit before I made it to the shelter. My clothes are wet and the temperate has dropped quickly. I'm shivering and I know I have to get warm quickly or I will suffer from hypothermia..."

In the south, hypothermia in June is impossible! However, I can imagine someone freezing in the cold northern mountains.

As I look out the front of the shelter I see a squirrel sitting on a fallen log eating a nut. I have a multimillion dollar picture right in front of my eyes and all it cost me was sweat!

Another hiker arrives and Kujo starts growling.

"Okay boys, it's time to go." I nod at the new comer as we pass.

A couple of miles after the shelter is Mahoosuc Notch, one of the most fun and challenging sections of the trail. It takes two hours to hike one mile!

There are patches of SNOW on the ground in crevices in the rocks! It's the end of June, even peanut butter melts in June in Georgia!

It is fun crawling over boulders and through holes, spying random patches of snow in crevices, and enjoying the natural air conditioning. Even though the terrain is very rugged, and is physically, and mentally challenging, it is also surprisingly relaxing. The air is crisp, and refreshing, and the views are aw-inspiring. One place I jump from one boulder to the next, keeping plenty of slack in the leash. Another place, I have to inch through the opening on my elbows and toes. I attach the dogs to the backpack, push it through, then send Kujo and Instigator through. I feel like we are going in circles, but I trust Kujo to get us out of the wilderness.

On the north end of Mahoosuc Notch, I meet "Mtn. Chi" hiking south, then at Mahoosuc Arm I meet "Boyes Day Out" hiking south. He hiked the Pacific Crest Trail (PCT) in 2010. The miles drag by, along with my feet.

As I drag myself past Speck Pond Shelter, I hear someone call "Hey Girl with Four Dogs, how are you?"

I turn and to see Hickory. He passed me in February!

"I'm wiped out after hiking Mahoosuc Notch. I've been hiking all day and I've barely hiked 9 miles. I feel defeated."

"Have a seat and rest for a minute. I'll pump you some fresh water from the pond. It takes everyone a long time to hike Mahoosuc Notch. It took me three hours. Besides you have the dogs to worry about too."

"I guess you're right. How have you been? Have you seen any wild life on the trail?"

"I saw a rattle snake at the Paul C. Wolfe shelter in Virginia. It was coiled and ready to strike. I have seen other small animals as well. Have you seen any animals?"

"The dogs scare most animals away. I did see a porcupine, and I hope to see a bear and a moose."

We talk a while, then Hickory introduces me to "Deal," "Steady," and "Fire Marshall," who are all staying at the shelter.

As we part ways Hickory says, "Make sure to look for "Soda Mike" when you get to the parking area. He is a Ranger and he always has soda for thru hikers."

Girl (Hiking) with 4 Dogs

It's 4 and a half miles to ME 26. Once I arrive, I look at the information booth, then I walk to a sunny spot in the middle of the parking lot at Grafton Notch and collapse on the warm asphalt. The wind is blowing across my sweaty skin and goose bumps appear on my arms. I start shivering.

I sit up and dig around in my backpack until I find my long sleeves. I glance at the dogs. They are panting.

I lay back down in the parking lot. The sun is warm on my face and it heats my black shirt. I doze.

Suddenly the dogs are barking. I jolt awake and look up. Someone is approaching. I sit up and grab the backpack with both hands so the dogs won't cart it away.

As I unhook Kujo and Instigator form the backpack so I can hold their leashes, a man in his late 40's says, "Hi, I am "SODAMIKE." are you okay?"

"I'm fine," I answer standing up so I can shake hands. "I'm waiting on my Dad to meet me. Do you have any sodas?"

"Not today. I'm the ranger for this area. Usually no one is here this late in the evening. I am making my last rounds before I retire for the night."

I see Dad driving in with the white truck and purple camper. "There's my Dad. Do you want to meet him and the other two dogs?"

"Okay," SODAMIKE says.

I introduce him to Dad, then he leaves.

I complete my usual routine then fall exhausted into bed.

**Day 133** My watch alarm wakes me up, but I don't want to get up and hike today!

An hour later Dad wakes up and comes to check on me.

"Are you hiking today?" he asks.

"I am taking a zero day today. I'm going back to sleep."

"Are you sure? It's a beautiful day for hiking."

"Yes," I grumble and turn over and go back to sleep.

45 minutes later the dogs are barking. I roll over to glare at them then I look out the side window. I see Hickory hiking from the trail.

Out of courtesy I crawl out of the truck and go talk.

Hickory says, "I am glad I caught up to you. I am surprised you are not already on the trail."

"I'm thinking about taking a zero day. I think hiking long miles and strenuous days are starting to wear me down."

"You don't have to hike so many miles in a day. You should hike the Balds today, while the weather is nice and the sun is shining. The weather can change in a heartbeat. It is only 10 miles from here to Andover."

"That sounds like good advice. I'll try to catch up to you."

I finish my a.m. chores, grab Mtn. Goat and Digger, and start hiking after Hickory.

The elevation changes from 1514 ft. to 3662 ft. in a 3-mile span. It is steep getting to the top of West Baldpate and once on top I am at the mercy of the wind. Thankfully it is sunny and pleasant. Then I scramble down, before climbing up East Baldpate at 3802 ft.

Around lunch I pass Hickory. "Thank you so much for encouraging me to hike today Hickory. It is beautiful weather and I enjoy not stressing bout hiking 20 miles in a day. I really appreciate your pep talk. I'll see you again at East B Hill Road."

"Anytime," Hickory says. "We are all here to encourage each other. I will see you later."

The dogs and I take a break on the East Peak of Baldpate at 3802 ft. Mt. Goat and Digger sit in front of the sign, which is held in place by a pile of rocks surrounding the post, while I get out our snacks. Next, we have a long descent to Dunn Notch Falls at 1285 ft. over 5 miles with occasional ups and downs.

Our next rest break is at the Falls. Mtn. Goat and Digger cool off and drink water while I re-fill my water bladder. I use the Aquimira drops to treat the water. It is ready to drink in 15 minutes. We all sit and enjoy the peace of the water and the coolness of the rocks.

While we are relaxing another group of hikers come for water at Dunn Notch and Falls. It's a youth group on a self-discovery campout in the woods. There are different tasks on their schedule to complete, such as personal and group reflection, and to demonstrate basic survival skills.

Now, it is less than a mile to East B Hill Road. When I arrive, there is a large parking area surrounded by woods and Dad is waiting.

## Girl (Hiking) with 4 Dogs

I leisurely take care of feeding and walking the dogs for the evening. As I am finishing I see Hickory exiting the trail.

Hickory asks, "Does your cell phone have signal? I tried to call Pine Ellis Hostel to pick me up, but I don't have any signal"

"We can give you a ride to town," I offer.

"I do not want to impose, but I would love a ride to town. I am staying at the Pine Ellis Lodging. They have rooms for $20 a night."

"That isn't a bad price for a room. I might stay myself. Dad do you want to stay at Pine Ellis? I can pay for our room."

"I don't want to stay in a room. I would rather sleep in the truck and baby-sit the dogs."

Hickory says, "I can pay for both rooms. I would love to give you both trail magic."

"Okay," I agree.

Dad says, "No thank you. I prefer to sleep in the cab of the truck."

We arrive in Andover and find Pine Ellis Lodging. It is a large wooden house. Inside there are rooms with bunks, and there is a private room on the outside of the building.

The lodging has a friendly family atmosphere. Everyone is sitting around conversing. The other residents are encouraging and optimistic.

Dad shares information about the GPS system. He says, "There are two ways to write the GPS coordinates. You can write them in Degrees, Minutes, and Seconds, or you can write them in decimal degrees. Make sure you, whoever is meeting you, and whatever equipment you are using are all the same format..." Dad explains how the system works then he gives out handouts explaining the whole procedure. (Appendix)

I sit in the chair and stress. It seems like it takes hours for the explanation, but thankfully everyone listens politely.

After a while I yawn, and say, "If I don't see ya'll in the morning, good luck on your journey." Amp "lexus" says, "Good luck," Seth says, "Good luck and safe travels," Irene says, "Blessings," Robin says, "Outward bound," and Hickory says, "Trek On."

**Day 134** I yawn and stretch feeling refreshed. I take care of the dogs, then return them to the kennel and go inside for fresh, hot, mouthwatering coffee.

"Good morning," Hickory says. "There is a great breakfast diner in town. Do you want to come with me for breakfast?"

"What's it called?" I ask.

"The Little Red Hen."

I laugh, "That was one of my favorite books when I was a kid. Let me ask Dad if he wants to come and I'll be right back."

"I can meet you outside."

"Okay."

Dad is still asleep in the cab. I tap on the glass and when he wakes up I say, "Dad I'm going to get breakfast in town do you want to come?"

"No thank you."

"Okay. I'll see you when I get back."

Hickory meets me outside and we walk to the diner.

"Look at that crazy looking horse running in the middle of the street." I say to Hickory.

A truck driving down the street honks the horn and the goofy looking horse, with it's gangly legs, detours to the right, off the road, runs behind a building (the truck passes), then it runs back on the road. About this time, I realize why it looks so funny.

"Oh!" I exclaim. "That's a moose not a horse I've never seen a moose before. It's pretty big."

Hickory says, "It is actually small for a moose."

"It looks big to me! I finally see a wild animal on my AT hike and the animal is in town instead of the woods!"

At the restaurant, I have a yummy egg omelet with veggies and cheese, and another cup of fresh hot coffee.

Hickory and I talk about politics with the locals. The teachers are concerned about their retirement due to union changes. Who can blame them? I'm concerned about our nation's future too, especially considering the rate of debt our president is accumulating, and his take from the rich and give to the poor philosophy.

We finish breakfast, then return to the Pine Ellis. Dad is ready to go. Hickory quickly packs his gear and we ride to the trail head.

I bring Kujo and Instigator to hike.

Girl (Hiking) with 4 Dogs

Not long after starting, there is a climb up a rock wall. There are metal bars fastened in the rock to help me climb, but the dogs don't have hands. Hickory is already out of site down the trail.

I unhook Kujo from my backpack. I snap my fingers and point to the top of the boulder. "Go" I say. Once he is at the top I say, "Stay."

I put Instigator up a few steps, then climb up behind him. I lift him up a few more steps and climb up behind him until we make it to the top.

Once at the top, I hook Kujo back to the backpack. There is a SOBO at the top and we talk a few minutes. At least he is talking, while I let my heart rate return to WNL (within normal limits) and catch my breath.

At Bemis Mountain on a flat rocky area, I meet more SOBO's, Columbus, Lion Lilly (she is wearing all pink), and a girl hiking barefoot. She says the shoes keep rubbing blisters on her feet, so she hikes without them. OK. She must have really tough feet to hike the entire AT barefoot!

The miles keep getting longer! Will this day ever end?

I remember seeing a dog and owner near one of the shelters up north. The dog was a small black lab, about 40-50 pounds. He had his tail between his legs. He looked mistreated. I wonder if there was verbal and physical abuse, which led to low-self-esteem? It's tail was so far between its legs, I could practically see it under his chin. My dogs never look that sad, not even when they are getting in trouble.

23 miles today, and it is long. As I draw closer to ME 17, there is construction. I can hear the construction blast for a while. All the detour signs say make sure to stay on the trail, so as not to be accidentally blasted. Well, that's a great idea, but very difficult to put into practice, when the trail isn't marked clearly! There are multiple intersections where I can go one of three-directions. Eney, meney, miney, moe works about as good as anything else. I have Kujo to help. I trust his instincts better than my own.

Kujo, Instigator, and I make it to the top of the trail. It's after 6:00 p.m. Thankfully it is late enough that the construction workers aren't blasting anymore, because we exit the trail in the middle of the blasting zone! (I guess Kujo was following the old trail instead of the new one, or the scent of the workers).

Crap!

Where is the parking area?

Where am I? I look right. I look left. I walk a little to the right (it's downhill). I walk a little to the left (it's mostly flat).

No visible parking area.

I shiver. Five minutes ago I was sweating.

It's starting to drizzle, and the sun is going down. Brr, I can feel the temperature dropping. I pull out my black North Face rain jacket with Dry Vent Technology and put it on.

Dad either can't find the trail crossing, or he's waiting at the parking area, and I don't know where that is.

If I hitchhike to town, I can call Dad and let him know specifically where I am, my feet and rain jacket will stay dry, and if necessary I can buy something to eat and rent a place to sleep. I can't just stand here getting wet!

I think the closest town is to the left, but I'm not 100% sure. It's 11 miles away.

I could hitchhike. Hmm, how will that work with Kujo and Instigator?

Should I stay to wait on Dad?

Well, there aren't many people on the road, but I can at least try hitchhiking.

Avoiding inclement conditions, such as being cold, wet, and possibly hypothermic, are extremely strong motivators to get out of my comfort zone. I head to the edge of the street with backpack on, and dogs in hand. Even if I can't get a ride, I can at least ask where the parking area is for the trail.

Desperate to stay as dry as possible, as the next car approaches, I step in the street, maybe a fourth of the way, and wave frantically for the car to stop.

It keeps going. Ok, so I'm not great at hitchhiking.

It's raining harder now. I don't want to start walking in the wrong direction.

I pray and start pacing.

I look at the construction signs and manipulate them to make a shelter, to keep the wind, and rain off me and the dogs. Just about the time I am getting my "shelter" set-up, a van comes along going the opposite way from the one I intend to go. They slow down, then stop.

"Do you need any help?" the man asks.

"Do you know where the parking area is for the Appalachian Trail? I'm supposed to meet my Dad, but the trail is re-routed due to construction. I don't know where the parking area is."

"We are not from the area. We are here on vacation." He looks to his wife and asks if she saw a parking area. "We did not see a parking area. Is there anything else we can do?"

"Can you give me a ride to town? I can call my Dad and let him know where I am."

He looks at his wife and she nods. "We would love to give you and your doggies a ride. You can put your dogs and backpack in the back."

I hurriedly put Kujo and Instigator in the back with my backpack, then I jump inside the van. It feels like a blast of heaven inside the warm cozy interior.

"Thank you so much for the ride. It gets cold quickly when the sun goes down."

"We are glad we can get you and your dogs out of the rain. I am Joe and this is my wife Rita and our dog Coco."

"Nice to meet ya'll," I say. I look warily between Coco and Kujo and Instigator. Thankfully Kujo is being nice. No growls or snarling. "Is your dog a Pekinese?"

"Yes. She is. We passed you a little bit ago and turned around to see if we can help," Joe says.

"We vacation near here every year, but we have never met anyone hiking the Appalachian Trail," Rita says.

"It is a trail that starts in Georgia and ends in Maine. It is 2181 miles and it changes a little from year to year due to trail re-routes. Normally my Dad meets me at the end of the day, but I'm not sure where he is today. I'm going to call him again and let him know ya'll are giving me a ride to town. I haven't been leaving the phone on because the battery is almost dead."

Kujo and Instigator snuggle in front of the warm air coming from the vents.

"Hey Dad. I'm calling to let you know I got a ride to town. My phone battery is almost dead, but I'll turn the phone on and check my messages again in about five minutes.

I continue talking to Joe and Rita. After five minutes, I phone Dad again. This time he answers. "Hey Dad. I'm on my way to town."

"I'm ten minutes behind you in the truck. You can have them stop and let you out and I will be there shortly."

"I'm not waiting in the cold and rain. Hold on a minute. Joe, do you mind stopping at the next pull-out? My Dad is just a few minutes behind. That would save you time having to take me all the way to town."

"We can drive you wherever you need," Joe answers.

"Thanks Joe. Dad, Joe and Rita said they don't mind pulling over and waiting for you to catch up. I'll see you in a minute. I'm turning my phone off to conserve battery"

It is so nice, warm, and dry in the van. I don't care about wasting time or Dad wasting gas.

Dad meets us just outside of town.

"Thank you so much Joe and Rita for the ride. It was so nice to meet you. Thank you for keeping us warm and dry. Enjoy your vacation."

"You are welcome. Good luck on your hike."

I throw my backpack in the back of the truck, then I jump in the cab of the truck and let Kujo and Instigator ride with me up front.

Once we are all settled in Dad say, "If you had waited a few minutes I was on the way to the parking coordinates."

"I'm sorry Dad. I didn't know how long I was going to have to wait."

"The parking area is only a couple of miles from where the trail crosses the road"

Dad turns off the road and drives down a dirt road before parking in a small wooded parking area.

"This looks like a nice place to spend the night. It is secluded," I say. "I hope no one thinks we are going to bother the construction equipment."

"I don't think anyone will be back until in the morning," Dad says.

Girl (Hiking) with 4 Dogs

"Thanks for finding me. I'm going to take care of the dogs then call it a night. I'll see you in the morning."

**Day 135** July 1 Today is mom's birthday. I had planned to do something special for her, but instead I'm a thousand miles away. I talked to her a few days ago, when I had phone signal. She said not to worry about missing her birthday, and that we can celebrate when I get home.

Mtn. Goat, Digger, and I pass Moxie Pond. The dogs get muddy feet.

Then we ford Bemis Stream. I get wet.

I pass Chellie and Jose at the Little Swift River Pond Campsite.

A lovely, short, 13-mile day. I end the day at the parking area near ME 4. I have a leisurely supper with Dad.

Dad says, "I see your friends hiking all the time. Yesterday we talked for a while before they had to keep hiking."

"Who all have you seen?" I ask.

"The couple, the guy from Atlanta, the red headed kid, and the guy with the dog."

"Oh, that is Zippers, Stretch, Squash, Youngin', Foster and Kya. I didn't realize they were so close. I'm going to wait on them this morning. I've run out of internal conversations and I'm tired of hiking alone every day."

"I've seen them off and on over the last few weeks," Dad says. "The girl said they are going to re-supply tomorrow in Rangeley, ME."

"Great! I will meet up with them in the morning."

**Day 136** I yawn and stretch. Normally I take Saturday's off to rest. I start to snuggle in my sleeping bag when I suddenly remember my friends are hiking by today. I jump out of the truck, then hurriedly take care of the dogs and wait by the trail.

After an hour, Dad wakes up and keeps me company.

"Do you think they already passed and I missed them?" I ask Dad.

"I'm sure the dogs would have been barking if anyone passed on the trail," Dad answers. "Normally I see them late morning."

"Okay."

A little while later the dogs ears perk up and Barking Commences.

I look up to see Kya bounding down the trail, then Fosters, Youngin' and Squash in the lead, followed by Stretch, then Zippers.

"Hi guys," I say excitedly. "I thought I'd join you for a couple of days. I didn't realize you were so close behind me all this time."

"We have to re-supply today," Stretch says harshly.

"Okay. We can give you a ride to town if you want," I say.

"That sounds great!" Zippers says, glancing at Stretch and glaring.

"If there is room, Kya and I can ride too," Fosters says.

"We can always make room," I say.

"I'm going to hitchhike!" Stretch says shortly.

"I can hitchhike too," Squash says. "There is no need for all of us to cram in the truck. I like the challenge of hitchhiking."

"I will hitchhike with Squash and Stretch," Youngin' says.

"Okay, we'll see ya'll at the store in a few minutes."

I hurriedly load the dogs in the kennels. We fasten Kya in the back with the other dogs, then Zippers, Fosters, and I pack into the cab like sardines. Dad drives.

It's only nine miles into town.

We find the IGA Supermarket on Main Street. There is a descent selection of food items. Zippers purchases a few packs of cookies along with peanut butter and a few other items.

"Let's have ice cream before we go," Zippers suggests.

"That sounds like a great idea," I answer.

We purchase the ice cream and sit-outside to eat with Youngin' while Fosters finishes shopping.

Stretch approaches Youngin' and says, "Squash and I are going back to the trail. Are you coming?"

"No. I will ride back with Zippers."

"Fine! We will see you when you make it to the campsite," Stretch snarls, scowling at both Youngin' and Zippers before stomping off.

"If it's an issue, I can continue to hike by myself," I say to Zippers.

"You can hike with us," Youngin' says.

"Stretch always acts as if he is in a bad mood," Zippers says.

Girl (Hiking) with 4 Dogs

We eventually make it back to the trailhead. I thank Dad for his help and hook up Kujo and Digger to hike. It takes a few minutes to load my new supplies into the backpack and to put the dogs backpacks on. By the time I am finished everyone else is gone.

It's nine miles to Reddington campsite.

Am I really better off hiking with people if I'm still hiking alone?

Oh well, at least I will have someone to talk to at the end of the day.

After hiking two miles I approach the Piazza Rock shelter aka "Lean-to." As I get closer I see the rest of the group.

Zippers says, "Girl with 4 Dogs, check out the privy! There are two seats and a game board in between!"

"Wow! This is neat," I say.

Zippers and I pose as if we are playing a game while using the privy and Youngin' takes our picture.

We start off again together. It isn't long before I fall behind while hiking up Saddleback Mountain despite Kujo and Digger pulling me ahead. I'm carrying my tent again and three days worth of food. I finally reach the top of the mountain. My friends are nowhere in sight.

Everyone is in a hurry to get to camp before dark.

It's hot. My mouth is parched and my throat feels like sandpaper. My CamelBak is empty.

"Come on boys," I say as I rush down Saddleback Mountain.

A gnat flies in my throat, blocking my airway.

Ahuak, huak Cough, Gag.

I can't Breathe!

I'm dying!

I don't want to eat a gnat, but it's better than dying.

I slow down to focus on producing saliva in my parched mouth. I suck as much saliva into my mouth as I can. There isn't much.

I forcefully swallow.

The gnat doesn't budge.

I stop in the middle of the trail and lower my head. Kujo and Digger are still pulling. I almost fall on my head. I cough as forcefully as possible.

Nothing.

I forcefully suck more spit into my mouth and milk my salivary gland. I swallow again as if my life depends upon it.

Finally, the gnat goes down.

I gasp in refreshing hot air!

My heart rate and breathing return to normal and I cautiously resume my descent down Saddleback Mountain.

Kujo, Digger and I finally arrive at the campsite. The surrounding foliage is green and the ground is brown and soft with decomposing leaves. The side trail is faint. I don't see my friends. I briefly wonder if they continued on without me.

Oh well...

The camping sites are also faint and there is a sign stating the campsite is undergoing re-construction.

Where is everyone?

I find the privy and drop my backpack to the ground.

Halfway through emptying my bladder I hear, "Grrrr" coming from Kujo.

"It's okay, Kujo," I say in a calming voice as I hurriedly finish.

When I step out of the privy I see Kya cautiously approaching. I tell Kujo, "Thanks for letting me know someone was coming, but you can stop growling now."

I look around and see the others setting up camp uphill, behind and to the right of the privy. I walk over. Stretch and Zippers are in the center of the clearing with Squash and Youngin' set up not far behind them. Fosters is set-up farther down the hill and to the right of everyone else. I glance quickly around the area and realize there is no room for my tent.

Stretch and Zippers are cooking their food, Squash is eating already cooked food, Youngin' is setting up his WhisperLite Stove, and Fosters is feeding Kya.

I sigh to myself and say aloud, "I just wanted to say hey before I set-up my tent. Thanks for letting me hike with ya'll."

Zippers says, "Come hang out with us once you finish setting up."

Girl (Hiking) with 4 Dogs

"Okay. Thanks," I say as I turn and walk away.

I find a fairly flat place uphill and to the left of everyone else. It set-down my backpack with the dogs hooked up and quietly set-up my tent. Once I finish, I grab my food and the dogs food and head back to the central campsite to eat.

"I'm back," I say as I get closer.

Zippers looks up, glances at me holding all the food and the leashes and asks, "Do you need any help?"

"No thanks," I say.

"Are you sure?" Youngin' asks.

"Yeah," I answer.

I cautiously set the food down so I can hook Kujo and Digger up to separate trees to eat. I stand up and proceed to take Digger's leash.

One minute everything is calm and the next there is growling and snarling teeth!

Kujo and Digger are rolling on the ground biting and snarling!

I snatch them apart. I look up and everyone is watching with disapproving frowns. Youngin' has a slight bit of sympathy on his face.

I swallow a few times, take a deep breath to relieve the tightness in my throat and say to Youngin,' "I guess I could use some help. Do you mind taking Digger?"

"Sure," Youngin' answers kindly.

I give him Digger's leash, then I take Kujo and hook him up on the opposite side of the camp. I take my time fastening him to a tree and giving him his food. He starts to eat when I set down his food. I say "NO" and make him sit and wait.

"Do you want me to fasten Digger to another tree?" Youngin' asks.

I swallow and take a deep breath before answering, "Yes. Thanks."

I slowly walk over to Digger and after he sits, I set his food down. Then I make sure both dogs are looking at me before I slap the side of my leg with my hand and say "Okay" giving them permission to eat.

There is a log at the central campsite. I sit-down by myself and eat my supper in silence. It's all I can do to keep the tears from trickling down my cheeks.

Conversation eventually resumes around me, but I don't join in.

I finish eating my cheese crackers and beef summer sausage.

It's getting dark.

I summon my courage and in as normal voice as possible I say, "Thanks for letting me eat with ya'll. I'm pretty tired. I'm going to call it an early night. Goodnight, I'll see ya'll in the morning."

Everyone says goodnight.

Youngin' offers to walk Digger back.

"No thanks," I say. "They have to learn to get along, besides, now that no food is involved they should be fine." I grit my teeth, but I can't stop a lone tear from escaping down my cheek.

Youngin' looks sympathetic and says, "Okay, I'll see you in the morning."

"Okay," I say and escape to my tent.

I'm happy it's dark.

"I'm glad to be alone," I tell myself over and over again as the tears roll freely down my cheeks.

The dogs are calm and contrite. Kujo is at my feet and Digger wiggles under my arm.

I left my sleeping bag with Dad to cut down on weight. I have my winter jacket, warm sleepwear, and the foot pad.

I miss my sleeping bag.

I stopped carrying my stove weeks ago. It was essential in the colder weather, but cold food taste fine in warmer weather. I usually add cold water to dry Roman, couscous, and instant mashed potatoes and it mixes fine. I also eat a variety of trail mix and candy bars in addition to Nutella and peanut butter.

With swollen red eyes, I eventually cry myself to sleep.

**Day 137** I wake up ready to face another day.

By the time I pack-up, and get the dogs ready, everyone else is gone.

Kujo and Digger are smiling and happy today. The drama of yesterday forgotten in their little doggie brains. They lunge ahead once we are loaded with our backpacks.

Girl (Hiking) with 4 Dogs

It's cool in the morning, but by the time I summit the intense steep Saddleback Junior mountain, I am hot and gasping for air. Youngin' and Zippers are just finishing a quick snack break. I forgo snacks in an attempt to keep up.

I fall behind again hiking up Lone Mountain and Spaulding Mountain, then I catch up again when everyone takes a lunch break. They are moving on as I crest the mountain. I grab trail mix from my backpack and eat as I descend the mountain.

As the day wears on it becomes cold and rainy.

At the bottom of Sugarloaf Mountain near Caribou Valley gravel Road, I again catch up to the rest of the group.

There is a group of hikers helping an older man hike out of the trail to the road. He hurt his leg. Squash, Stretch, Youngin' and Fosters help as well.

Zippers says to me, "The guys don't need our help. Let's hike to the campground and save tent spots for everyone."

"Great idea," I say and we continue to Crocker Cirque Campsite.

There is a clear spring a half mile before the campsite. Zipper rinses in the stream to get the hiking dirt off. Then dips her bandana she normally wears on her hair into the stream and uses it to cool off.

"If the water is dirty when we make camp, I use the bandana to filter the dirt and debris from the water before I put it in my water container. We treat all of our water, but it seems cleaner when there are no particles floating in it."

We are barely finished setting up our tents when the rest of the group arrives.

"How is the man?" I ask.

"I think he will be okay," Youngin' answers. "One of the group members has a four-wheel-drive truck. We helped the guy into the truck and his friend is driving him to the hospital."

"He is sturdy for being old," Fosters says.

The rain picks up and we all jump into the dryness of our tent.

Zippers announces, "Tonight is cookie night! All remaining cookies and assorted crumbs are consumed tonight. We re-supply tomorrow."

"Let's dig-in," Squash says. "I need to get started early tomorrow. I have about a week to finish the trail. I have a flight scheduled to take me home."

Zippers says, "You have to stay with us tomorrow to celebrate Independence Day!"

Squash thinks for a few minutes then says, "I guess I can hike a short day tomorrow, then do a Bonanza to finish the trail on time."

Conversation continues on mundane topics as we stay dry in our tents.

No more dog fights.

**Day 138** Monday July 4. Kujo and Digger are restless. It's morning already. I quickly pack my jacket and sleeping mat while inside the tent, then I hurriedly care for.

Everyone is packing up. I holler, "Good morning" and wave, then hastily return to my campsite to feed the dogs and finish packing my tent.

One-by-one everyone else heads down the trail waving as they pass. Zippers is last. She says, "We will see you in Stratton Girl with 4 Dogs."

"Happy Hiking. I'll see you later," I call back.

Finally, I'm ready to go. I eat a few handfuls of trail mix before hiking up Crocker Mountain. Eating, hiking up Crocker Mountain, and breathing is impossible.

I stop eating.

It's only seven miles to Stratton, ME.

Yay! Dad is here with the truck, and Mtn. Goat and Instigator. Stratton Motel and Hostel looks like a big white house with a green roof. There is a row of about five rooms extending behind the main house.

"Hey Dad. Did you have an okay time with the dogs the last few days?" I ask.

"Yeah, we were fine," Dad answers. "I let the dogs stay outside most of the day. Also we drove around Eustis. There are interesting historic homes in town."

"I'm glad you had a good time." We talk a while. I tell Dad about the man with the injury our group help off the trail. After a while I ask, "Do you want to stay in the hostel Dad? I can pay for another room. I'm planning to stay."

"No thank you. I prefer to stay in the truck and baby-sit the dogs. You go ahead and visit with your friends."

"Okay Dad. After a shower, I'm going across the street to the General Store to buy food. Do you want anything?"

"Nothing special. I can share whatever you buy."

"Okay. We are planning a cookout celebration for Independence Day. I'll buy enough to share with you. Thanks for keeping the dogs. I'm going inside to take a shower now!"

I enter through a side door. Zippers is scourging the refrigerator. There is a huge box of fresh strawberries inside. Zippers says, "Wow look at all these strawberries!"

I ask, "I wonder who is planning to eat all of these?"

"Sue and Knucklehead aka Endo and Miche said they are for everyone. They both did a thru hike in 2004. If they have shortcake at the store, then we can have Strawberry Shortcake for desert," Zippers says excitedly.

"That sounds delicious! I need to take a quick shower, then I can come with you to the store."

"Okay. Do you want to weigh yourself? The scale is by the refrigerator."

"Sure. Thanks." I walk to the scale and step on. "I think the scale is broken. It says I lost 10 lbs."

Zippers says, "I lost weight as well, but not 10 lbs. This kitchen is amazing. I would love to stay for a few days and cook every day! Hurry up with your shower so we can buy groceries. I'll think about what we can cook."

I find the shower and try not to spend too much time enjoying the hot water.

Once I finish showering, Zippers and I go grocery shopping. We see Youngin' and Fosters at the grocery store. We coordinate for everyone to buy a portion of the meal, hamburgers, hot dogs, buns, and pickles, onions and fixings, chips and cookies, and sodas.

"I don't want to participate in buying beer. I won't be drinking any of it," I say.

"That is fair," Zippers and Youngin' say.

We make our purchases and return to the hostel to cook. Once the food is ready I look around and ask, "Where are Squash and Stretch?"

"Stretch heard about a pizza eating contest. If he eats the whole pizza, he gets a T-shirt. Squash went with him. They should be back any minute, but we don't have to wait for them. Go get your Dad and let's eat while the food is hot," Zippers says.

We sit around the picnic table to eat. Squash arrives and joins us. Stretch won the contest, but he feels sick so he goes to his room to lay down.

"The food was great! Thank you," Dad says.

"You are welcome," Zippers says. "Not being able to cook is one of the things I miss most about hiking."

After lunch Squash and Fosters commence to drinking beer. Youngin' drinks a coke. Zippers and I clean up.

"I am Hot!" Zippers exclaims. "Does anyone want to go swimming?"

"I'll go swimming," I say.

"Me too," Youngin' says.

"What about ya'll?" I ask Squash and Fosters.

"Not right now," Squash says.

"Maybe later," Fosters answers.

"I'll bring my Neo air sleeping mat so we can have something to hold onto," Zippers says. "We just have to be careful not to get any holes in it."

"Okay," I say as I get in the water. I suck my breath in, "Burr, this water is cold!"

Zippers gets in next. "It's not bad," she says.

"Maybe it isn't cold to you because you live in Montana." I say.

Youngin' is still on the river bank. "Are you coming in?" Zippers calls.

"Not if it's cold," Youngin' calls back.

"It isn't bad once you get in. Just jump," I say.

"If you insist," Youngin' says and jumps in, splashing Zippers and I. We swim, play and splash until almost dark.

"My teeth are chattering. I'm ready to get out," I say.

"Okay. When we get out, let's see if the other guys want to play a game. Squash suggested beer pong earlier," Youngin' says.

Girl (Hiking) with 4 Dogs

We get out of the water and dry off.

"I've never played beer pong. How do we play?"

"We bounce a ping pong ball and try to get it in a cup. Whichever side misses has to drink a shot of beer, or water," Squash says glancing at me.

"Sounds fun," I say.

We play beer pong until it is too dark to see.

Squash says, "I'm going to bed early. I have a lot of miles to cover in the next few days in order to finish on time. Goodnight and bye everyone. It was fun hiking with you."

"Goodnight," I say.

"It was fun hiking with you too," Youngin' says.

"Good luck," Stretch says.

"Kill those miles!" Fosters says.

"Until next time," Zippers says.

I take the dogs for a short walk then load them into the truck.

"Goodnight Dad, I'll see you in the morning."

"Goodnight."

I go inside. Fosters, Stretch, Zippers, and Youngin' are watching the movie, Dirty Deeds, with some of the other hikers staying at the hostel.

Fosters starts flirting with me. Stretch and Zippers retire early, then Youngin.'

Fosters kisses me. My body starts to tingle. I kiss him back.

"It feels so good to be wanted," My Body says.

"Are you serious?!" My Conscious yells. "How far are you going to let him go?"

"As far as he wants," My Body answers.

"No, you're not!" My Conscious insists. "I have to live with you afterward."

"Are you serious!" My Body responds. "I haven't felt like this in a long time!"

"Does he have a condom?" My Conscious is ruthless. "Are you going to have unprotected sex when you know he has had sex with many women? Sometimes two or three sexual relationships at a time?

The kisses are more heated and my body is responding way too eagerly.

In between kisses, Fosters asks "Do you want to come up to my bed with me?"

The moment he stops kissing my conscious throws in another jab, "You do remember he's been drinking since this afternoon. He probably doesn't care who he sleeps with. You're not special to him. He's using you. JUST LIKE AJ."

"Do you have a condom?" I ask.

"No. It's too much weight and not enough opportunity to use it while I'm hiking. Squash says he never uses one."

"Not only could you get an STD, but he'll be talking about you to all his friends. Is it worth it?" My Conscious asks.

I have more self-respect than to allow this to continue.

I finally answer Fosters, "I can sleep beside you, but I'm not going to have sex with you."

"Okay, but you might change your mind," Fosters says grinning.

Long after Fosters falls asleep, I turn on my side and cry myself to sleep.

**Day 139** Squash is gone. He has 187 miles to cover in less than a week.

The rest of us have a leisurely morning. I say goodbye to the other hikers; "Carnivore" and "Purple," "Still" Ryan and Beka, "Frosty," "Laughing Star," and "Sits in Car."

"Dad, I'm taking Mtn. Goat and Instigator this time. See you in Monson," I hurriedly rush down the trail after the other hikers.

The trail is rocky with multiple large steps, and four ft. jumps. Mtn. Goat jumps up without difficulty. However, Instigator puts his paws up and attempts to jump, only to fall over from the weight of his pink camo backpack. He is carrying food for four days. On the rare occasions he makes a jump on his own, the corner on his backpack gets stuck. I have to stop, squat, and pick him up. After ten of these maneuvers my legs feel like jelly.

"It's only five miles to Horns-Pond-Lean-To," I remind myself out loud.

The trail continues to wear Instigator and I down. Mtn. Goat steadily leads. Our trek starts at 1414 ft., drops to 1257ft., then steadily climbs to 3376 ft. before settling at 3183 ft. at Horns Pond Leant-To aka Shelter.

There are trails branching in all directions. I keep following the biggest trail until I see the Shelters. A group of SOBO hikers are staying in one. I talk for a few minutes before checking for my fellow hikers in the second shelter. I see Zippers and Youngin' reading and relaxing. Stretch and Fosters are finishing up canned beer they hiked in.

Beer taste disgusting on a good day, I don't understand why it's so essential someone would carry a 12 pack for 5 miles to drink it. Then they have to carry the cans out for 3 and a half more days.

"Does anyone know where the privy is?" I ask the group at large.

"No. I went in the woods," Zippers says.

I glance around the group. Everyone shakes their head in the negative.

"Okay. I'll be back in a little bit. Do ya'll mind if I leave my backpack and dogs here?" I ask.

"Sure, you can leave your backpack." Zippers says.

"The dogs aren't going to start fighting, are they?" Youngin' asks.

"No, they won't be fighting. I'll fasten them to a tree so they won't run off. Thanks."

I retrace my steps and follow the medium size trail until I eventually find the privy. There are two privies side by side, and they are supposed to be composting.

Ahh, the luxuries of a toilet with a seat and a door.

I meander back to the shelter on wobbly weak legs. An adolescent almost runs me over on his way to the privy.

"What is wrong with your dog?" Youngin' asks as soon as I return.

My heart instantly stops beating.

"I didn't notice anything was wrong with him," I say. "Where is he? I'll check on him."

"He's okay now, but as soon as you got out of sight he started whining and bucking around. He sounded like a baby wailing!"

I start laughing, "He thinks he's human. He just sounds like that sometimes. He doesn't like being left behind."

"Why don't you let him run around some?" Fosters asks.

"I'm worried he won't come back."

"Kya has her freedom, but she always comes back."

"I'll let him off for a little, but I'm hooking him up for overnight."

As soon as I let Mtn. Goat off the leash, he bolts away out of sight and won't come back when I call him. Instigator is too tired to move.

"I hope he doesn't run anyone over," I say.

"He will be fine," Fosters says.

"I'm going to find somewhere to set up my tent. I'll see ya'll later.

"Why don't you sleep in the shelter?" Zippers asks. There is plenty of room."

"What if someone else comes later and needs to sleep in the shelter?"

"It's late enough I doubt anyone else is coming to the shelter," Youngin, says.

"I didn't think I was supposed to let the dogs sleep in the shelter."

"Kya sleeps in the shelter with me all the time," Fosters says.

"Okay. Thanks. If no one minds then, I'll sleep in the shelter. If I take the side by the wall I can keep Mtn. Goat and Instigator by the wall so they won't bother anyone."

Once sleeping arrangements are solidified I commence to eat supper and feed the dogs. As soon as Mtn. Goat hears the food, he comes running gleefully back. I hook him back to his leash while he eats. By now it is dark. I take Mtn. Goat and Instigator with me this time when I go to the bathroom, then I head back to the shelter for some much-needed sleep.

In the middle of the night I jolt awake when I hear a loud crash from the neighboring shelter. Mtn. Goat and Instigator growl. I cautiously grab the leashes and stealthily make my way to the neighboring shelter. I see the shadow of a large animal, a moose? running off into the woods. I ease back to bed and toss and turn listening to the dogs growl softly, until I fall asleep again.

Girl (Hiking) with 4 Dogs

**Day 140** July 6, 2011 It's morning already! I listen to the conversation about a moose attacking the neighboring shelter during the night. No injuries are reported. I shove a spoonful of peanut butter in my mouth, grab a granola bar, lug on my backpack, then race after everyone.

In half a mile, the incline increases by over 600 ft. I fall behind. I pant my way up the relentless rocky Bigelow mountain. I reach the top of South Horn before plummeting down the valley, then scrambling to even higher elevations on Bigelow Mountain, 4145 ft., a short steep drop down again then up to summit Avery Peak. I glimpse my friends packing up after a snack break.

"Hey ya'll," I say.

"We were just leaving," Stretch says.

"Do you need to take a break? I can wait for a minute," Zippers says.

'I'll eat a little trail mix. I'm not tired now that I'm at the top of the mountain. Thanks for waiting."

We pass Sweatpea, and Beardoh.

"Did Fosters tell you he is stopping at Little Bigelow Lean-To?" Zippers asks.

"He mentioned he had to slow down. He said his ride won't be here for a few weeks. His friends have to keep Kya when he summits Katahdin."

Zippers and I catch up to Fosters just before Little Bigelow.

"I'm going ahead," Zippers says. "I'll meet you at the next shelter."

"Bye. It was fun hiking with you," Fosters says.

I give Fosters a tight hug. "If you want to finish hiking with us, my Dad can keep Kya."

"No. I would still have to wait for my friends to pick me up. They are my ride home to Michigan. Why don't you slow down and finish hiking with me?"

"I have to keep going. If I slow down, life might catch up to me and I won't be able to finish. Do you have e-mail or something?" I ask. I write down his e-mail.

We hug again, then I depart to hike the last seven miles to West Carry Pond Lean-To. I look around as I leave. The thru hiker book says there are "tubs" for swimming, but I don't see any "tubs."

My throat aches and I feel like someone is squeezing the life out of my chest. I breath through my mouth and lean forward slowly trying to draw oxygen through my constricted throat and into my lungs. I exhale through pursed lips and gritted teeth. My jaw quivers and my teeth chatter. Each breath is shaky.

I keep walking one foot in front of the next. The trail blurs before me.

My Conscious says softly, "It's for the best."

I grit my teeth harder.

With each step, I chant over and over, "I don't care. I don't care. I don't care. Nothing matters, I don't care. Nothing matters. I don't care, I DON'T CARE, I DON'T CARE!"

There are dark foreboding clouds rolling in.

I swallow the lump in my throat.

Rain, rain come today, wash me away to a better day.

Wash me away.

Wash me away.

I look down at Mtn. Goat, Instigator.

So Loyal. So Loving. So Trusting. Unconditional.

Smiling. Happy.

They need me.

I take a deep cleansing breath, on the exhale I hug my four-legged companions, attempt a wobbly smile, and exclaim aloud, "I'm done. 'I can do all things through Christ Who strengthens me.'"

I look up at the darkening clouds, "I'm not ready to be washed away. Come on boys, lets out run the storm!" I say to Mtn. Goat and Instigator.

We reach West Pond Shelter.

"Hey everyone," I say as I put my backpack down in the shelter and remove the dogs' backpacks as well. I look at my water bladder, but it is empty. I sigh, I'll have to treat some before I drink some.

"I'm glad you made it before the rain," Zippers says.

"Me too," I answer.

"Do you want me to pump you some water?" Hickory asks.

"That would be fantastic!" I exclaim. "Do you need any help?"

"No. It will only take a minute. Go ahead and get settled in."

"Thank you so much. It's great to see you again by the way. How has your hiking been?"

"I am making it. I have a few aches, but I am hoping to finish this time."

"At this point, I think I would crawl if I had to in order to finish the trail. We are so close. Only 165 miles to go!"

Just as Hickory returns with water there is a torrential down pour. I close my eyes and say a silent prayer, "Thank you Jesus for holding back the rain until we are safe in the shelter."

Everyone insists I camp in the shelter with the dogs rather than set-up a tent in the rain.

I am reaching for my food bag when the leader of a group of girl hikers from Montréal, Canada says, "Please help us eat this food. We packed way too much. We have lots of leftover beans and rice. We do not want to have to carry this extra food."

"I'm not picky about food. If you have plenty I don't mind helping you eat it. Thanks!"

Shortly after the sun goes down, I squeeze myself, Mtn. Goat and Instigator near the wall and commence to fall into an exhausted slumber.

**Day 141** I see the foggy shape of Hickory hiking down the trail as I crawl out of the shelter in the morning. I quickly complete my a.m. routine and am ready to start with the rest of my group. Stretch hikes ahead, however, Zippers, Youngin', Mtn. Goat, Instigator and I all hike together. After four miles of hiking we take a break at East Carry Pond.

"Youngin', Girl with 4 Dogs, lets cool off in the Pond," Zippers says.

"I don't have a swimming suit."

"Come on. It will be fun." Youngin' says stripping down to his underwear.

"I am swimming in my sports bra and underwear. It's like a swim suit," Zippers says.

"Okay." I relent, self-consciously, stripping down to my underwear and sports bra.

There is a flat sandy bank leading into the water. I drag Mtn. Goat and Instigator in the water. They begin lapping at the water. Once they tire of it, I take them back to the bank and tie them up while I splash and swim with my friends.

After a while, Youngin' says, "I guess we better hike some more. We still have six miles to the shelter."

A short time later, we reach Pierce Pond Shelter. Stretch is fishing when we arrive. I hook the dog leashes to trees while I set up the tent and hang the food bag on a hook in the shelter. Instigator immediately digs a hole in the soft rich dirt. Then both Instigator and Mtn. Goat stretch and lay down. Mtn. Goat watches me intently.

"Hey Zippers and Youngin' look what I caught," Stretch says excitedly bringing a trout to the shelter.

"It looks small," Zippers says.

"All I had was a hook and a string to catch it."

"What are you going to do with it?" Youngin' asks.

"I'm going to cook it and eat it. Do you want some?"

"No thanks, I am walking to Harrison's Pierce Pond Camps, to put in a reservation for breakfast," Youngin' says.

"Do you mind if I tag along?" I ask.

"You can come with me. Let me know when you are ready."

"Let me grab some money and I'll be ready."

"I need to make reservations as well," Zippers says.

"Zippers, I will meet you at Harrison's once I finish cooking my fish."

We walk the short distance to Harrison's and I tie the dogs up outside because they aren't allowed in the building. There is an outdoor bathroom separate from the main lodge. In between the lodge and the bathroom, there are two tire swings hanging from a post secured between two trees.

The outside bathroom for hikers has a sign reading: "If it's yellow, let it mellow. If it's brown, flush it down." Northeasterners are more frugal with their resources and too much flushing might flood the septic system.

I see Hickory inside. "Hey Hickory. I am surprised to see you here."

"I left out early this morning to make sure I made it to the cabin in time to claim my reservation for tonight. Are you staying here also?"

"No. We are camped at the shelter, but I wanted to have breakfast here in the morning. It is good seeing you. I'm going to look around the cabin while I'm here.

One of the other guests is a lady who is weaving. "That looks fun," I say. "How long have you been a weaver?"

"For years," she answers. "Do you want to try? It's easy," she says moving over so I can reach the loom. "Make sure you go over, then under, then over and so on. Once you finish a line, push everything tight."

When it is time to leave, I say, "Thank you."

"You are welcome. Here is my card. My friend and I hand craft dolls. We sell the dolls and donate a portion of the profits to help women and children in need."

I glance at the card, www.thedolly-mamas.com.

"I'm so glad I met you. Thanks for the card and thanks again for letting me weave. I have to get back to the shelter before it gets too dark to see."

Stretch made it to the cabin and he and Zippers walk back together.

"I'll see ya'll back at camp. I'm going to try out the other trail to get back to the shelter," I say.

"I will come with you," Youngin' says.

"Wow! This trail goes across the dam," I exclaim.

It's a wooden dam at the level of the water. Some trees are involved in the construction. It shifts as we walk across. Mt. Goat is first, I'm second, and Instigator is last. My toe catches on a branch and I barely keep myself from falling face first in the pond.

Is it a beaver dam?

Once we are on the other side, Youngin' says, "I wondered if you were going to fall in."

"I wondered too."

We arrive back at the shelter and later that evening I meet, Rumblestrip, Optimist and Stopwatch.

Rumblestrip is an extremely fast hiker, he doesn't take breaks. He just keeps hiking, 30+ miles a day. I heard he is a Puritan on a journey, before settling in to his community.

Optimist and Stopwatch are married. They have hiked many trails and have published a book! They hike 20-30 miles a day!

By 9:00 p.m. The dogs and I are asleep.

**Day 142** "Good morning everyone!" Zippers yells as she wakes up smiling. "Who is ready for breakfast?"

"I already ate my breakfast. Bye." Rumblestrip says and sets off at a brisk pace.

"We are eating breakfast here." Stopwatch says

"You can eat with us at the cabin."

"No. We did not make reservations," Optimist says.

"I am ready for breakfast when you are." I say.

We hike the short distance to the Harrison's Cabin. Mtn. Goat has a sulky look on his face as he watches the door going inside.

"Yeah! A NOBO's delight 12 pancakes, juice, coffee, and milk," I say.

"This is the best breakfast on the trail!" Youngin' says.

"You didn't get sausage?" Zippers asks.

"I can barely finish what I have. Do you want my juice Youngin'? I know I can't finish it. I'm about to pop!"

"Sure. Thanks."

"How far are you hiking today Hickory?"

"I have not decided. Probably Bald Mountain. How far are you hiking?"

"Moxie Bald Mountain Shelter. Almost 23 miles."

"Good luck," Hickory says.

"You too."

I thank our host for a delicious breakfast and don my backpack and collect my dogs for the next leg of our adventure.

A short three miles later, we amble down the bank to wait at the rivers edge. Kennebec River is deep, wide, and has a strong current. It is highly recommended not to ford the river, and the ferry service has scheduled hours of operation. There is a short line for the "ferry" which is a red canoe, manned by a local man with a thick country accent, big burly muscles, lots of facial hair, a forest green shirt and a wide brimmed brown hat. He takes two hikers at a time across the river and brings back two hikers from the other side on his return trip.

Stretch and Zippers cross first. The ferry driver, "Hick" returns and asks, "Who's next?"

Youngin' moves forward.

"Is anyone else hiking solo?" Hick asks.

"I am, sort of. I have my two dogs with me," I say.

"Go ahead and get in, if that is okay with you?" he looks at Youngin'.

"The dogs aren't going to dump us over are they?" Youngin' asks.

"I will hold on to their leashes," I answer.

"Get in. The line isn't getting any shorter standing here," Hick says.

Youngin is already in the canoe. He gets out so I can sit in the middle with the dogs. Hick is in the back. He gives Youngin' one of the oars and says, "You can help paddle across."

I hold my breath and pray Mtn. Goat won't jump out of the canoe. He has tried to jump out of a moving car when the window was down.

Halfway across the river Mtn. Goat stands up and leans over the right side of the canoe. The entire canoe rocks wildly back and forth. I counter lean to the left, tug on Mtn. Goat's leash, and say, "Sit" while snapping my fingers. Mtn. Goat looks back as if to say, "I only want to see what we are doing." I raise my eyebrow and snap my fingers again. Reluctantly Mtn. Goat sits again, which rocks the canoe, but not as wildly as before.

Stretch and Zippers wait on the far bank. Once we exit the canoe they take off with Youngin' right behind them.

"Thanks for the ride Hick. I had fun, next time I come I should bring all four dogs."

Hick nods and loads up the next group of hikers.

I hike for miles and miles surrounded by mountains and trees. At Pleasant Pond Mountain, I catch up to Youngin' and Zippers.

"Look at the view," Zippers says. "The sky is clear and you can see for miles in all directions."

"We are on top of the world!" Youngin' exclaims.

I take a deep breath and absorb everything in. The trees on top of the mountain are not more then 10-20 feet tall. They look like spruce, or some kind of evergreen tree. Some are barren skeletons with dry, brittle, dead limbs, while others are thriving and green.

Mtn. Goat and Instigator find a small shady spot near group of short evergreen trees that block the setting western sun. Mtn. Goat wiggles his way under the low branches of the tree looking for a cool place.

"It is amazing up here," I finally say.

"We finished eating lunch. Are you going to eat anything?" Zippers asks.

"I'm not hungry yet. Breakfast was so big, I'm just starting to feel normal instead of stuffed. I know I hike slower than ya'll so I'm going to keep hiking. I'll see you later."

I descend Pleasant Pond Mountain and cross the road at the south end of Moxie Pond.

Where is the trail?

Great I have to ford the pond to keep on the trail!

The water is knee high, at the shallowest point. I can barely see the white blaze on the other side of the pond. Nothing else remotely resembles a trail.

I sigh, my flip-flops are not going to stay on crossing the stream. I don't want to puncture my feet with a protruding stick so I guess I'll leave my shoes on.

I try to keep my feet dry by stepping on trees and foliage. Mtn. Goat tries to jump on the same foliage and we both end up getting soaking wet. Instigator stays dry because I'm carrying him.

Zippers and Youngin' catch up just as I slosh out to the other side. I wait for them to cross, they have Crocs, and we hike together up Moxie Bald Mountain. At the top, we drop our backpacks and explore while we catch our breathe.

We finally make it to Moxie Bald Mountain Lean-to. The shelter is full. I set up my tent a few yards away. I briefly meet Pokemon and Logwalker, who are both SOBO's.

Pokemon asks, "Can I take your picture? I want to take a picture of everyone I meet on the trail."

"Sure," I answer. "Do you want to sign my thru-hiker book? I started having everyone sign it who I passed, but I haven't kept up with it."

"I would love to sign your book," Pokemon says. He takes our picture then says, "You are almost at the end. I'm excited to see people who have almost accomplished what I hope to accomplish."

"You can do it. Just take one step at a time. Good luck."

Optimist and Stopwatch are camping at Moxie Bald as well. They are using a Poncho/Lean-to for their shelter. It requires hiking poles for set-up, but ultimately uses less wt. because they don't have to carry separate gear for rain gear and shelter.

**Day 143** As I pack up my tent and take care of my four-legged friends, I hear snatches of conversation from the rest of my hiking friends and the shelter group.

Zippers says to Stopwatch and Optimist, "You should hike with us for at least part of the day. We are all going to town and it is only 18 miles."

Stopwatch says, "We have to make it to the store before they close."

"I'm sure we can make it to the store and still hike with Stretch and Zippers," Optimist interjects.

"We are ready when you are," Stretch says.

Two miles later I cross Bald Mountain Stream. It is a foot deep with slippery rocks all the way across. I carry Instigator and keep a tight grip on Mtn. Goat's leash as Mtn. Goat and I wade to the other side. There is a short steep climb up the embankment, then the trail levels out. There are adult trees with branches full of green leaves to provide shade and there are rocks and smaller saplings near the ground

Stretch and Zippers are sitting on a log having a snack break and Youngin' is sitting on another. They both have an excellent view of Bald Mountain Stream.

Zippers smiles and says, "We wondered how you were going to cross the stream with the dogs."

Youngin, laughs, "We almost fell in, but you crossed without any problems."

Stretch sits and scowls, "We have had a long enough break. Let's keep going. I want to catch up to Optimist and Stopwatch."

They change out of their crocs and back into their tennis shoes.

"Did you cross the stream in your tennis shoes?" Youngin' ask.

"Yes. I didn't bring any crocs. My shoes will dry quickly," I answer while idly petting the dogs.

We catch up to Stopwatch and Optimist at Piscataquis River. I can see them taking a break on the north side of the river.

The river is about 30 feet across and 3 feet deep. The water is clear, the rocks are big and slippery. I heft up Instigator again and hold on to Mtn. Goat's leash. I wade and he swims across to the other side. I gasp as the water reaches my thighs.

"The water is f-f-freezing," I say.

"It feels wonderful," Zippers says crossing to the north bank.

Once everyone crosses the river we continue on toward Monsen.

Optimist says, "We hiked on the Pacific Crest Trail (PCT) in some ways it is easier than the AT. There are less elevation changes."

Stopwatch adds, "The PCT is less populated so we had to have more items drop shipped. If we were late to pick-up our package other hikers thought it was trail magic and scavenged it."

Conversation continues on other topics. Zippers brings up the topic of unions, "Unions are important to make sure everyone is treated fair and are paid a fair wage. Without unions business owners can fire someone for no reason, or pay them less than they deserve!"

"If someone doesn't like what they are being paid they can always work somewhere else," I say.

"Unions provide a united voice," Stopwatch says.

"They also have union fees," Youngin' adds.

We continue to debate the pros and cons of unions. After a few miles, Optimist and Stopwatch pull ahead so they can make it to the store before 5 p.m.

We hike through green mountain forest and eventually make it to Monson, Maine.

Once in town, we see Optimist and Stopwatch at Lakeshore House Lodging and Pub.

Zippers says, "Let's get something to eat at the pub."

Stopwatch points out, "We are not staying in town. We have three miles to hike before we are finished for the day."

Optimist decides, "It is only three miles. We have finished re-supplying. We can eat, then leave right after we eat."

Girl (Hiking) with 4 Dogs

"I'm going to get settled. I'll see ya'll later." I say.

"You have to come eat with us," Zippers insists. "This is the last time we will all be together. I am sure your Dad will not mind watching the dogs. Please let us all eat together."

"Okay," I give in.

"Youngin,' you are eating with us as well?" Zippers asks.

Eventually we all agree to eat together.

Dad keeps the dogs for me while I relax in town. Kujo and Instigator lick all the sweat from my skin before I head back to the Lakeshore House Lodging and Pub.

The Pub is a beautiful two-story wooden historic home. It is painted white with dark trim. There is a tranquil lake behind the building. Kayaks and paddle boats are available to rent. Inside the pub there are hardwood floors and traditional restaurant style tables.

I order a cheese burger with lettuce, tomato, and onion and a side of fries.

"It would be amazing if the Appalachian Trail crossed into Canada!" Optimist exclaims.

"I think the trail should start as far South as Florida. Then it would encompass the entire East coast," I say.

"We are going to hike the Continental Divide Trail," Optimist says.

"I want to hike the Long Trail or the Wonderland Trail around Mt. Rainier," Zippers interjects.

We continue talking about various trails until Stopwatch checks the time and says, "It was nice eating with you, but we have to go. Good luck finishing the trail,"

"Thanks. It was nice meeting ya'll. Good luck on your future hiking adventures," I say.

I return to Shaw's where Dad is parked.

"I'm going to get a shower, then I'm headed to Monson's General store. Do you need anything?" I ask.

"You can get whatever you need. I can eat whatever is left over," Dad says.

As I exit the shower I can hear yelling form Stretch and Zippers private room. I quickly return to the general hiker bunks and grab $3 to start my laundry in the washing machine. Then I grab money so I can go to the store. Youngin' is on his way out the door also.

"Do you want company to walk to the store or would you rather be alone?" I ask.

"We can walk together," Youngin' says. "I get enough alone time on the trail."

Monson's General Store is small, but it carries the necessary trail food and protein bars. I talk to the owner, TA while Youngin' is still looking around.

"Where are you hiking from?" TA asks.

"I'm from Georgia, South of Atlanta," I answer.

"Oh, is that so? I used to live in Ft. Benning. Being military I've been everywhere. Do you know where Ft. Benning is?"

"Yes!" I answer excitedly. "Ft. Benning is close to my home town. How did you end up all the way in Maine?"

"Just traveling here and there. I've been running this store for a couple of years, but it is hard work. It's remote up here in Maine."

"All of Maine feels like country compared to Georgia. The trails are amazing. I wouldn't trade it for the world."

"It is breathtaking," TA concludes. "Are you ready to pay young man?" TA asks Youngin'

"It was nice meeting you TA. Good luck on running the store," I say as we leave.

"I'm going to check out Robinson's store, to see what they have. Do you want to come?" I ask Youngin'.

"No, they are more expensive and less friendly," Youngin' says.

I enjoy the short walk to Robinson's. No dogs. No backpack. No rocks or roots to trip over.

Youngin' is right, Robinson's is more expensive.

I return to Shaw's in time for leftover spaghetti from a SOBO cooking party. I offer money to pay for the food, but Val and Steptruth decline saying, "We were about to throw the food away. Help yourself to as much as you want."

"Thank you so much," I answer and dig in to delicious spaghetti and salad.

After supper, I explore Shaw's Lodging it is also a two-story white house, but it appears to be larger than the Lakeshore Lodging. They also have a large parking area and they don't mind Dad parking the truck overnight. The back of Shaw's has rooms with a balcony upstairs. The balcony overhangs to provide a shaded, sheltered sitting area on the ground floor. I meet Seskimo and Bash, Zach, CRMM, Val, Stephanie, and Rob Chillaxin at Shaw's. RWE T-coZee, signs my thru hiker book with a quote, "Nature does not like to be observed and likes that we should be her fools and playmates."

I wind down as the sun goes down. I have a last visit with Dad and the dogs before returning to Shaw's to snuggle in my twin-size bed with the yellow headboard, multicolored striped sheets and pink and orange comforter.

"Hey Hickory!" I exclaim upon entering the hiker sleeping quarters. "How long have you been here?"

"I just arrived. It has been a long day. I did not know if I would make it before dark. How long have you been here?"

"We arrived this afternoon. We have re-supplied and are ready to start the 100-mile wilderness tomorrow. Are you starting tomorrow too?"

"Possibly after I re-supply."

"I am so excited! We are almost at the end!"

"I have been this close before and did not finish. I hope I finish this year."

"Good luck! I know you can do it this year. Good night."

**Day 144** July 10, 2011 100 Mile Wilderness

"Yes Dad, I insist on taking all four dogs!" I repeat for the umpteenth time.

"You might get hurt. Maybe you should leave all the dogs with me, then you can keep up with your friends easier," Dad argues.

"Most of the time they aren't going to hike with me anyway. I started with four dogs and I'm going to finish with four dogs!"

"They have to carry a lot of food for a six-day hike."

"They will be fine Dad. I have the food in Ziploc bags to keep it dry. I will rotate the backpacks so it won't rub their skin. I checked their feet. They all look good. Each day their backpacks will get lighter. I will see you on Friday at Abol Bridge."

"If you don't get hurt," Dad mumbles under his breath.

"I won't get hurt. Love you bye Dad. Everyone else is ready to go."

I stop for a minute at the trail sign for the "100 Mile Wilderness."

This is it. I take a deep breath, then shift the weight of my enormous backpack, complete with sleeping bag, tent, and a six-day food supply. I untangle the leashes before setting off on the trail. There are green overgrown trees making a tunnel as I delve deeper into the wilderness. Each step takes me farther from civilization and closers to my ending destination.

I've hiked less than two miles when all of a sudden I find myself face first on the ground. The air whooshes out of my lungs as my chest hit's the hard, unforgiving ground.

The dogs are jerked to a standstill. They look back questioningly, "What just happened?" they seem to ask.

I plant my hands on each side of my body and slowly and shakily push up from the ground. I see a huge rock centimeters from my head. I pull my knees underneath me and my toe catches on the root that tripped me.

I breathe a sigh of relief. Nothing feels broken. "Thank you Jesus for keeping me from harm. Amen."

Once I'm on my feet again, I reassure the dogs by petting them and explaining, "I'm not used to hiking with all this weight in my backpack. I've got our tent, sleeping bag, and enough food for six days. You guys aren't helping with all your pulling. Let's slow down. We aren't going to catch up to everyone else, so let me not die trying."

There are a lot of water crossings: James Brooke, Thompson Brook, Big Wilson Stream, Wilbur Brook, Vaughn Stream, and many more.

"I give up. I'm not going to have dry feet tonight." I exclaim to the dogs.

They give me a happy, "This is fun walking in the water" look.

At one water crossing, I see Hickory sitting on one of many large rocks near the water's edge pumping water and taking a snack break.

"I'm glad to see you on the trail," I say. "You must have gotten up early to re-supply."

"I am used to hiking hours, so I could not sleep in this morning. I decided to get started early."

"Good idea. I'll see you next time," I say as I pass.

After hours of Mtn. Goat's backpack repeatedly slamming into my right calf muscle, I let him off his leash to give my leg a rest.

"Mtn. Goat, Come BACK!" I call as he runs away down the trail.

"Are you serious I grumble" Kujo, Digger, and Instigator look at me expectantly.

"No," I say sarcastically, "I'm not letting ya'll run away too."

I grimace as Mtn. Goat bolts past a south bound day hiker and brushers against her leg.

"I didn't think anyone else would be on this trail." I say contritely as we hike past the day hikers.

"Do you need any help catching him?"

"No. He will come back after he runs for a minute. I'm sorry he bumped into you."

"No problem. We have a dog at home. Your dog could get hurt running off on his own."

"I will put him back on his leash as soon as I catch him!"

I continue to whistle and call for Mtn. Goat. He finally comes back with a wide toothy grin and his tongue lolling to the side.

I give him a "so there" look as I hear the click of the leash on the collar.

I wave to my friends inside Long Pond Shelter, set-up camp and collapse.

It was a long15 miles today!

**Day 145** Barren Mountain, Fourth Mountain, Third Mountain, Columbus Mountain and Chairback Mountain, will the Mountains ever end? The dogs drag me up and down, up and down, over the rocks and thru the woods. Mile after relentless mile of terrain. I have 20.8 miles to hike and I feel like I'm moving as fast as a turtle!

After the numerous mountains, we descend to the West Branch of Pleasant River crossing. I look across the 3-ft. deep, 40 ft. across expanse of River and wonder, "How am I going to get across and keep my feet dry?"

As I look around I see Stretch, Zippers, and Youngin' changing into their Crocs. I wave and hike upstream. There is a small dam with large rocks protruding from the water. I unhook the leashes from my backpack and place them in my hands, then I gingerly proceed across the rocks keeping my feet dry.

I start to smile to myself, "Ha! I can cross this river and keep my feet dry."

Kujo is leading us across the dam.

Suddenly, the current pushes Kujo's foot off the rocks. He bobs under the water! I tug on the leash, but the current is too strong, and the bulk and weight of his backpack is keeping him trapped in the undertow!

My heart stops beating.

In an instant I jump into the waist high water next to the dam. I keep my left hand up to keep from pulling the other three dogs in, then with my right hand I grab the handle on Kujo's backpack and pull up and forward with all my strength.

Kujo's head clears the water.

I can breathe again.

Kujo frantically doggie paddles

Mtn. Goat and Instigator are struggling backward, Digger jumps in thinking we are playing a game.

"Come on," I say trying to sound cheerful and keep the panic out of my voice. We struggle across and down the river. I pull on the leashes to make Mtn. Goat and Instigator follow. Mtn. Goat takes a flying leap and lands on another rock sticking out of the water. I grasp onto Instigator just before he takes an unplanned dive underwater.

My heart is racing like a freight train. I can feel the blood circulating to my arms and legs with each erratic beat. I can feel blood pounding in my head.

We finally make it to the calm shallow side of the not so pleasant, Pleasant River. My legs are shaky as I exit the river on the gently sloping bank.

I take deep calming breaths.

"Why did you cross all the way up there?" Zippers asks while sitting on a log and putting her Salomon hiking shoes back on.

"I thought we might cool off in the water," I respond nonchalantly.

"That sounds like a great idea," Youngin' says.

"Where is Stretch?" I ask Zippers.

"He went ahead. He wants to make sure we have room at the shelter tonight."

"Thanks for waiting on me."

"No problem," Youngin' says.

"I'll catch up after I ring out my socks," I say.

A couple miles later, I catch up to Zippers and Youngin again.

"What are ya'll stopped for?" I ask

"There is a gorge and we do not see a bridge to cross on," Zippers answers.

I get closer and see a gaping hole in the middle of the trail.

"I can look up hill for a bridge and ya'll can check downhill. We can meet back in five minutes." I suggest.

"We have already looked," Youngin' says. "We are going to have to jump across."

My heart starts pounding again.

I bite my nails.

"Can one of ya'll help with the dogs?" I ask.

"Sure," Youngin' says.

"Absolutely," Zippers adds. "What do you need us to do?"

"Honestly, I want to see Youngin' jump first so I can visualize myself landing on the other side instead of in the ravine. Zippers if you hold the dogs until I jump across, then when I call let them go and Youngin' and I can catch them when they jump across."

"Let's throw the backpacks across first," Youngin' suggests.

"Good idea," Zippers and I agree.

"Is Instigator going to be able to jump that far?" Zippers asks.

"Youngin', would you mind jumping across with Instigator?"

"I can take Instigator with me," Youngin' says.

Youngin' jumps and makes it look easy. I take a few steps back, then I run and jump!

I sail through the air and land on the other side.

I laugh, "That was fun. You can let the dogs loose, one at a time now."

Zippers lets Mtn. Goat, then Kujo, and lastly Digger loose. They are like wild dogs jumping across.

"Thanks for your help ya'll. I couldn't have done it without you."

"You are welcome," Youngin' says.

"We will meet you at the shelter," Zippers says.

It takes another 10 minutes to load the backpacks on the dogs.

It's less than a mile to Carl A. Newhall Shelter. My shoes are finally dry.

Suddenly the clouds open up and there is a five-minute torrential downpour.

"Are you serious?" I moan aloud.

Ten minutes later I cross the stream before the shelter.

"Let's take a break and get our water for tonight and in the morning," I tell the dogs stopping at the stream for water.

I'm still soaking wet when I arrive at the shelter five minutes later. My hands are white and shriveled. I'm shivering, and my teeth are chattering.

I look longingly at the warm, dry shelter. It is crammed full. Another hiker has a German Shepherd snuggled inside. Stretch, Zippers, and Youngin' are dry and settled in the shelter.

I wave, too exhausted and miserable to speak, then find a flat spot for the tent. I quickly feed the dogs, then set-up the tent on the cold wet ground, before it gets dark. I have the poles color coded with zebra stripe duct tape so I can set the tent up without getting confused on where the poles go.

As soon as I finish setting up the tent the dogs rush inside with me right behind them.

I eat inside the tent, then snuggle and shiver with the dogs until we fall asleep.

**Day 146** Kujo and Digger are restless. I quickly change into my cold wet hiking clothes, find my flip flops, and take all the dogs out to potty before they start fighting.

It's barely dawn.

The shelter residents are starting to stir.

I dole out dog food, then add water to powdered milk and cereal I have in a Ziploc bag. I quickly guzzle down breakfast, then I stuff the Ziploc bag in my pocket to use for toilet paper trash later.

I remove snacks for the day from my food bag and store them in the top pouch of my backpack before cramming my food bag into the center of my backpack. My sleeping bag is stored in a water proof bag, then stuffed in the bottom zipper of my backpack. My camp clothes are in a Ziploc bag and stuffed wherever they will fit. I have a liter and a half of water remaining in my water bladder which I store in a slide pouch in the center of my backpack. Lastly, I cringe as I take down and stuff my soppy wet tent into the large center compartment of my backpack.

By the time I finish packing, the shelter is empty.

Our starting elevation is 1938 ft. and we hike as high as 3530 ft. on top of White Cap Mountain.

I shiver. Today's rugged Maine mountains are; Gulf Hagas, West Peak, Hay Mountain, then White Cap Mountain, and finishing the day with Little Boardman Mountain.

I hike alone most of the day except for the dogs. They are eager with relentless energy. Mile after mile of rough, uneven terrain, yet they have a toothy smile.

Huge evergreen trees surround and shield out civilization. Heaven must truly be at least this beautiful and serene.

Even when crossings streams, there are no bridges to scream of man's interference in God's creation.

After hiking almost 11 miles in silence and solitude, I catch up to Zippers, and Youngin' at East Branch Lean-to. They are talking to two guys from Tennessee, who are camping at the shelter.

I glance warily ahead.

"Did you guys come south?" I ask, hoping they can tell me there is a bridge somewhere for crossing Pleasant River.

"No, we are north bound," one of the men answers.

"We are hiking shelter to shelter until we get our trail legs," the other guy adds.

"Are you enjoying yourselves?" I ask.

"Absolutely."

After a few minutes of talking it is obvious Zippers and Youngin' are not going to cross the river first.

"It was nice meeting ya'll," I say to the Tennessee guys. "I have seven miles to hike before I run out of daylight. Wish me luck crossing the log over Pleasant River with these four dogs."

"I'm curious to see if you make it without falling in," one guy says as I slowly walk toward the river.

I laugh, "Me too."

I put the leashes in my hands and cautiously step onto the log. I precariously move forward. The log is about 3 ft. in diameter, at least 6 ft. above the water and 30 ft. across. Mtn. Goat is in the lead with his leash taught. Kujo is behind him, then myself, followed by Instigator, then Digger. My arms are stretched wide.

Inch by inch we make it across.

Once on the other side I grin and wave before continuing toward Cooper Brook Falls Lean-to.

The shelter is up on a hill resting on large rocks. There are multiple flat areas for tents. I find a cozy place toward the end of the line of tent sites where I can hook up the dogs on trees while I set up the tent.

Zippers arrives as I am laying out my tent.

"Once you finish let's go swim." Zippers suggests.

Zippers and Youngin' jump in the water while Stretch reads in the shelter. As soon as I finish setting up camp I join them bringing Kujo and Digger with me.

I suck in my breath as I step into the icy water.

I sigh, "This is lovely."

"I love swimming," Zippers says.

Youngin' is upstream swimming with long clean strokes in the water.

I tear my eyes away as Kujo bites at the water and Digger swims in circles trying to catch his tail.

Mtn. Goat and Instigator are whining for their turn so I return Kujo and Digger to the camp site and retrieve Mtn. Goat and Instigator. After a quick swim and an abundance of water lapping Mtn. Goat and Instigator are ready to return to the tent area.

All four dogs are now laying down near the tent watching as I return to swim with Zippers and Youngin.'

"I'm back." I announce as I slowly walk into the water.

Youngin' and Zippers are at the far end of the swimming area talking to Stretch, who is up the hill in the shelter. I unbraid my hair and swim under the refreshing water. I take time to swish my sweaty underwear and sports bra in the water to remove the sweat.

I frolic like a Mermaid until I'm too cold to swim anymore.

"It was so hot today, I think I got a heat rash on my inner thighs. I got one another time when I was hiking in hot humid rain," I comment to Zippers as we dry off.

"I found some body glide in the shelter. You can use it," Zippers offers.

"If the rash on my legs isn't better in the morning, I'll take you up on that offer. Goodnight," I answer.

**Day 147** Groggily I wake up to Mtn. Goat panting in my face.

He could really use a breath mint!

"Okay, I'm getting up," I say pushing his head to the side so I can breathe.

It is mostly flat compared to yesterday. I keep up easily with the rest of the group. We pass SOBO, "The Rock" and one family out section hiking.

After hiking 12 miles, we take the well-worn side trail through the wilderness to Pemadumcook Lake. The lake is huge! The water is calm.

"Girl with 4 Dogs, look behind Youngin', that is K-Tahd (Katahdin)," Zippers says.

"Wow!" I'm speechless. The trees snuggle right up to the edge of the lake. There are a few rocks in the edge of the water, and in the background, K-Tahd stands majestic. The clear blue sky is dotted with white fluffy clouds. The clouds make a halo around K-Tahd.

"I guess Squash has already summited by now. I wonder what it is like," I say once I can speak again.

"I am sure he finished easily," Stretch says. "I'm headed on to Wadleigh Stream Lean-to." He looks at Zippers, "You can catch up."

We all leave the lake and K-Tahd behind.

"Come on boys," I say to Mtn. Goat, Kujo, Digger and Instigator. "Did you have a nice rest? Me too. We have ten miles to go."

We plod along until we reach Wadleigh Stream Shelter. Instigator collapses on the ground, laying on his backpack on his left side, and his little head is gently resting on Mtn. Goat's back feet.

Digger lays down, but looks up as if to say, "Just give me a minute and I'll be ready to hike ten more miles!"

Mtn. Goat is laying down checking for ways to ditch the leash and run loose around the campsite.

Kujo is sitting up intently watching me to make sure I don't go anywhere without him.

While I dish out the dog food I notice a SOBO group with two teenage girls, "Cat" and "Trimble." They just graduated from high school. They are hiking with their guy friend, "Dude." The girls set-up the tent the three share and fix supper while the guy lounges by the campfire that "Fixed Scrotum," a local hiker, started.

I listen to the conversation drifting to me from the campfire, while I set-up camp.

"I have a Huntsman Survival Knife, nothing is going to get me," Dude says. "It has a stainless-steel razor sharp blade on one side and serrated edges on the other."

"I doubt you will need a knife that big on the trail," Youngin' says. "I had a knife the first 30 miles of hiking, but I never used it. Once I got to Neels Gap I sent it home."

"I do not have a problem with too much weight. Cat and Trimble carry the tent and cooking supplies," Dude says arrogantly.

Disgusted, I tune in to a different conversation.

Fixed Scrotum says, "I'm 39 years old. I have two girls and a third on the way. I lost my job three months ago and I haven't been able to find a new one. I hate Maine! I'm surrounded by sticks and there are not jobs unless you can get into the lumber business."

He throws a stick into the fire. Sparks burst into the air.

Stretch says, "Are you hiking the whole Trail?"

"No," Fixed Scrotum answers, "I have got to find work. I have to support my family!" He takes a guzzle of the beer he carried in and starts crying.

Hmm, I wonder what Zippers is doing. Oh, there she is talking to a hiker who just arrived.

"Girl with 4 Dogs, come meet "Grimm." We hiked a few days with him in Pennsylvania," Zippers says.

"Okay. Did ya'll already eat?"

"Yes. We are about to go to a swimming hole Fixed Scrotum mentioned. You are welcome to join us."

"The dogs won't tolerate me being out of sight. They would chew through their leashes. Besides it's almost dark. Aren't you worried about getting cold?" I ask.

"I will not be cold," Zippers says looking coyly at Stretch.

Girl (Hiking) with 4 Dogs

"Have fun. I'll see ya'll in the morning. It was nice meeting you Grimm."

"It's nice meeting you too. I have been trying to catch up to you since I heard about you in Pennsylvania. I didn't think anyone could hike with four dogs," Grimm says.

**Day 148** "Grimm is going to finish out the trail with us," Zippers announces in the morning.

"Okay," I answer as I finish loading up the dogs and start down the trail. We have 23.1 miles on the agenda today.

There are glimpses of K-Thad throughout the day!

The terrain is mostly flat, Grimm hikes ahead, however Stretch, Zippers, Youngin' the 4 dogs and I hike together.

After 17 miles of hiking, we climb to the top of the Rainbow ledges. The elevation is 1512 ft. and is the highest elevation for the day.

"Wow! We can see K-Thad from here," Youngin' exclaims.

"It is clear today, but I wish it was not so hot!" Zippers says.

"Seeing a rainbow on top of Rainbow Ledges with K-Thad in the background would be crème-a-la-crème," I say.

"Let's have lunch here," Zippers says.

I sit on my backpack to eat. Stretch, Zippers, and Youngin' sit on the ground in a semi-circle.

Mtn. Goat rustles through the bushes looking for a cool spot. When he finds the perfect place to rest, he closes his eyes in contentment. Kujo also crawls under the bushes trying to get out of the blazing sun. He squints his eyes against the penetrating rays of light. Digger wedges himself between me and a rock, then he looks at his feet in contemplation. I lean over and give him a short foot rub while inspecting his feet. They look healthy. Instigator plops down beside me and snuggles up to Digger. His bells jingle as he wiggles into a cool spot. The top of his head brushes against Digger's left foreleg and his chin is nuzzled on a rock. He's snoring in seconds.

As we are finishing lunch Stretch snorts, "All the trail books have the 'leave-no-trace' principle. Your dogs are breaking all the guidelines by laying in the bushes and digging holes under the trees!" He snatches up his backpack from the ground, winces as he pulls a muscle, and storms off down the trail.

I pet the dogs reassuringly and quietly pack up my lunch.

Youngin' waves as he passes and says, "Don't worry about him."

"Stretch is just sore and uncomfortable," Zippers says.

I nod in acknowledgement, but my throat is too tight to speak. My eyes are tingling.

"Do you want me to hike with you?" Zippers asks.

I force a smile, swallow, shake my head no, and manage to speak normally enough to say, "No thank you."

Zippers looks at me questioningly, then says, "Are you sure?"

I give my best actress face trying to give the impression that everything is great and wonderful, "I'm sure. I'll see ya'll in six more miles."

I have my emotions under control by the time I pass Hurd Brook Lean-to a couple of miles later. As I am about to pass the shelter a man and his son stop me.

"Are you a thru hiker?" the dad asks.

"Yes. I started in Georgia in February and I'm almost finished hiking over 2000 miles," I answer.

"Wow!" the son says. "Did you hike with your dogs the whole way? Can I pet your dogs?"

"Yes, you may pet the dogs, just if Kujo backs away then don't follow him. Yes, I hiked with at least two of them at a time for most of the trip." I explain some of the challenges with hiking with dogs and how my Dad is helping me complete my thru hike.

"We left a lot of Mountain House Meals in the hiker box in Abol. Please take some for the last stretch of your journey. We packed more than we need for our section hike. We want the excess to help thru hikers," the dad says.

I smile, "Thanks in advance for the Trail Magic!"

"What is 'Trail Magic'?" the son asks.

"It's when someone does something nice for a hiker."

"I like that," the dad says. He laughs heartily, "Help yourself to some Trail Magic when you get to town, if you can even call it a town since it is so small. You better get going before it gets too dark. Good luck."

"Thanks," I say gathering the dogs and placing them where they need to be for hiking. Once out of sight of the shelter I run. The sun is going down.

Girl (Hiking) with 4 Dogs

I see a sign up ahead and the back of Zippers green shirt.

"Zippers!" I call. "Wait a minute. Can you take a picture of me and the dogs at the end of the "100 Mile Wilderness?"

"Yes, but hurry."

"Thanks!"

I drop my backpack onto the ground and dig out my camera phone. Mtn. Goat, Digger, and Instigator lay down in exhaustion. I collapse onto my backpack to rest. Kujo sits up proudly and looks at the camera.

"CHEESE!"

Zippers tosses me the camera and rushes off to Abol Campsite.

I quickly stash my camera phone and hike to Abol Bridge and Campground to find Dad. He is waiting at the store. I rush over and give him a hug. We have supper together and I tell Dad about my adventures in the 100 Mile Wilderness. I pet, massage, and snuggle with the dogs.

"You can sleep in the truck if you want," Dad says.

"I know, but I'm trying to be more sociable. Are you okay taking care of the dogs and keeping them while I summit K-Thad?"

"I don't mind keeping the dogs. So tomorrow you will hike ten miles to Birches Lean-to and the next day you will hike the last five miles of the trail to summit Katahdin? Do you want me to meet you in Baxter Park to pick you up?"

"No. I think it is ridiculous that you would have to pay $15 to drive in the park just to pick me up. I will hitchhike out of the park to Millinocket. I'll call and send a SPOT signal from there."

We continue to converse as I pack my backpack for tonight and tomorrow. I pack my three liters of water, food, tent, and sleeping bag.

"Bye Dad, I love you. I'll probably see you in the morning."

I stagger as I put my backpack on and walk the short distance to the campground.

When I arrive at the Campground Grimm is already set-up. Stretch, Zippers and Youngin' are almost finished setting up their tent. I quickly lay out my tent and set it up.

"We are going to take pictures from Abol's Bridge," Zippers says. "Grim said the view is amazing. Do you want to come with us Girl with 4 Dogs?"

"Sure," I answer. "I'll just throw everything in my tent and I can finish setting up later."

We make it to Abol bridge shortly before sunset. K-Thad is so close! There is a calm lake with a few ripples where the water flows around a large rock, and a few more ripples from a smaller rock. The lake is bordered by rocks on the right edge, then tall green trees. There is a sandy section of the bank that jets into the water and there are a couple of teal green boats tied on the edge. The lake continues to curve around. On the opposite side of the lake from where we are standing there is a short span of green trees with Katahdin rising in the background.

I deeply breathe in the fresh, crisp air blowing across the lake. Its purity fills and cleanses me. I feel serene.

When it is too dark to see the mountain, we head back toward the campsite on the gravel road. Stretch, Grimm, and Youngin' are a few feet ahead.

Crash! Snap!

Everyone stops.

Youngin' slowly backtracks to Zippers and I. He whispers, "There is a moose up ahead. It ran into the woods a short distance, but then it stopped. We are going to try to get a picture."

We slowly and quietly move closer to the moose. I can see the dark brown body and lighter brown gangly feet. Every time Stretch and Youngin' get close the moose ambles further into the woods.

Grimm says, "I saw moose tracks by a small pond earlier today. Maybe that is where it is headed."

We hike off the main road on a narrow moose trail.

"Are you sure this is a good idea?" Zippers asks. "It is almost dark and we didn't bring a headlamp. What if we can't find our way back? There are no city lights visible."

"It's not much farther," Grimm whispers back.

A minute later we can see the lake. At the far side of the lake are two moose drinking water. The moonlight reflects off the water. The guys look for a way around the lake.

"I'm headed back to the campsite," I whisper.

"I am going back as well," Zippers says softly.

"There is a trail that goes around the lake," Grimm says.

Stretch looks at Youngin', Youngin' nods, "We'll come back in a few minutes," Stretch says.

Zippers and I make it back to camp. The guys aren't far behind.

"As soon as we got close, the moose bolted again!" Stretch exclaims.

I finish setting out my sleeping mat and sleeping bag then rejoin everyone at the campsite table. I take the far-right edge. Zippers is beside me, Youngin' is beside her and Stretch and Grimm are on the opposite side of the table.

Stretch, Zippers, and Grimm are laughing, but there is nothing funny that I am aware of. Youngin' looks uncomfortable.

I miss having soft fur to pet and four tiresome dogs to take care of. I shiver.

"Is anyone else cold?" I ask.

"No," Zippers says and busts out laughing. "I am hungry though. Let's have cookie night! We can buy more at the store in the morning."

"I'm going to get my down jacket, gloves and hat before I become hypothermic! It's July 14th! How can it be so cold!" I say as I head to my tent.

"I had to put my hat on earlier when I was cold," Youngin' says.

"I thought my long sleeve Under Armour shirt would be warm enough, but I was wrong." I admit.

Youngin' asks, "Does anyone have any cards?"

Grimm starts laughing, "I used to but I sent them back home. I have to take a piss!"

"I'm going to water a tree as well," Stretch says between chuckles.

Zippers is giggling too.

I scrunch my eyebrows, then look at Youngin' questioningly. Youngin' shakes his head slightly.

When Grimm and Stretch return, I smell a burning grass-like odor.

Holey shit!

I instantly hold my breath and lean away from Stretch and Grimm.

I have to get a job when I finish hiking, and I know I have to pass a drug test.

"It was nice visiting with ya'll, but I'm going to call it a night. I'll see you in the morning," I say while trying not to breath any contaminated air.

"Don't you want cookies?" Zippers asks laughing uncontrollably.

"I'm good. Thanks."

**Day 149** "Good morning ya'll" I call once I finish packing. "I'm headed to the store for breakfast. I'll see you later."

"I will be there soon," Grimm says. "I am expecting a package."

I check the store hiker box and select a couple of Mountain House Meals to take, then I order two cheese burgers with the works and take one to Dad in the truck. The store sells cheese burgers from 7 a.m. to 7 p.m.

While Dad eats his burger, I take care of the dogs before heading back to find the rest of my hiking group.

Zippers is making final food selections. I meet SOBO's "Earrings" and "Dog" before we are ready to leave.

I go outside to wait for Zippers. I pace restlessly.

I wave bye to Dad as he drives down the road. I can hear Mtn. Goat wailing like a baby.

I wish I could take them with me. Dogs are domesticated wild life. Are Coyotes or Red Foxes banned from Baxter Park?

Finally, Zippers is ready to go. Stretch, Grimm, and Youngin' are also anxious to depart.

"Let's go to K-Tahd campground!" Zippers exclaims.

After hiking a mile, I stop to register to stay in the Birches Lean-to. I'm number 26. Stretch, Zippers, Grimm, and Youngin' are out of site. Stretch and Zippers are staying with Stretch's dad and stepmom in the campground tonight.

Earlier I heard Youngin' say, "Sure, if there is room."

Is everyone staying with Stretches parents except me?

I am only hiking 10 miles today. So far everything is flat and boring.

Girl (Hiking) with 4 Dogs

I drag my feet. There is no reason to hurry. I will be sleeping in the shelter alone.

Hiking alone.

Sleeping alone.

Alone, alone, alone.

My cheeks are wet.

My throat is squeezing shut.

Alone.

I swallow down the lump in my throat and switch my thoughts to what Dad and the dogs are doing. I smile picturing Mtn. Goat, Kujo, Digger, and Instigator giving Dad a hard time.

I started this trail knowing once Rocket quit, then I would be hiking alone.

Alone.

It seems to be my lot in life.

The trail starts to blur again.

I'm changing the subject, remember? Focus on HAPPY thoughts.

I'm completing a lifelong dream! Many people dream, but few people fulfill that dream.

I can breathe normal again, although I still have an occasional sniffle.

Six miles after starting I see the side trail for Big Niagara Falls. I might as well sit down for lunch and enjoy the falls. I walk across the granite rock closer to the sound of rushing water and look for a place to sit in the shade. I see Grimm, Stretch, Zippers, and Youngin' sitting under a big leafy green deciduous tree, maybe a Hickory Tree, having lunch. It seems rude to ignore them so I walk over.

"Hey ya'll. Do you mind if I sit down?" I ask

"There is plenty of room, you don't have to ask." Zippers says.

"Thanks." I answer, taking out my usual trail food.

"Can you believe we are almost finished!" Zippers exclaims. "Has everyone arranged for transportation home? Stretch's Dad is driving us home."

` "My dad is driving me home." I say.

"I have a plane ticket home. I will hitchhike to the airport."
Youngin' says.

"I'm also flying home." Grimm says. "It has been an
amazing journey. I am so blessed to finish with friends."

I stay quiet and finish my lunch. We all leave together.
Grimm is in the lead followed by Stretch, Youngin', Zippers and
myself. Zippers and Youngin' talk about music from the Patsy Cline
era. I've heard of I Fall to Pieces, but most of the songs I don't know.
They also know songs from Bob Dylan, and Carole King. Whenever
they both know a song, they sing or discuss the lyrics.

We stop near the Daicey Pond Nature Trail parking area. The
guys rush off to find the privy.

"Are Grimm and Youngin' staying with ya'll at the
campsite?" I nonchalantly ask Zippers.

"Yes. I wanted to invite you as well, but six people is the
maximum allowed at the campsite."

"Okay, I was just curious," I say.

The guys return and I try my best to draaag behind as we set
off down the trail. We have less than three miles to hike. There is
nothing to aid me in hiking slow. No rocks, or mountains, or uneven
ground to slow me down. No dogs to distract me.

I want to ask, "Why are ya'll hiking with me today of all
days?!" but I remain silent.

I can't stop the tears from trickling down my cheeks. My
throat is tight and I can barely breath again. I don't want to be
gasping and wheezing for air.

It doesn't matter. Nothing matters, I remind myself over and
over.

"Are you okay back there Girl with 4 Dogs?" Zippers asks.

I swallow a few times before answering, "Yes, I'm fine."

"You seem quiet today." Zippers says.

Stop asking questions!

It's harder and harder to answer. I swallow a few more times,
"I'm tired and I miss my dogs."

I just want to be left alone in my misery.

I ignore my negative thoughts and focus on the song lyrics
Zippers is recalling.

After a few minutes, I say, "One of my favorite trail songs is If you're going through hell keep on going, don't slow down…, I think about it when I am hiking up the never-ending mountains."

We reach the fork in the trail. The left leads to the campground, and the right to the Birches Shelter.

"Bye. Thanks for letting me hike with ya'll. Good luck tomorrow summiting K-Tahd." I call rushing off on the trail to the shelter.

"You can come to our campsite if you want." Zippers says.

"Maybe later. I have to get settled in at the shelter, and I might take a nap."

"Come over later," Zippers says before rushing off after everyone else.

I wonder around on the gravel road before locating Birches Lean-to. No one else is around. There are two shelters side-by-side. I look at both then choose the one to the left of the approach trail. Is seems a tiny bit more private.

I get out my sleeping bag and sleeping mat, then I curl up in a ball, hold my down jacket in my arms, and sob. Deep racking sobs of rejection and loneliness. My breath comes in jagged gasps.

"I'm always going to be alone," I whisper. The tears are still rolling down my cheeks. My throat is tight, but I'm not shaking anymore.

So what if you are alone. Lots of people are alone. Happiness is a choice. A person doesn't make you happy!

I take a slow deep breath in.

"…Keep on going…If you're scared don't show it…"

I confront the pain of AJ's betrayal and rejection. My beautiful trusting heart is scarred with mistrust and doubt, but my heart beats on. Steady and strong.

I face down the loneliness. I will survive.

I will never leave you nor forsake you. God's still small voice penetrates my sorrow.

Confusion and questions screaming for answers.

Why?! WHY?! WHY!?

Both Job and Joseph in the Bible had it worse than you, and they trusted God. God knows the big picture. Trust in Him.

I take another deep breath. I can feel my heart healing. The pain is almost unbearable, but with each shaky breath the pain lessons.

I can do all things through Christ who strengthens me.

I search my soul for any lingering pain, negative thoughts, or feelings. I confront each bleeding wound that I've been running from. I clench my teeth. My body shakes uncontrollably. I want to run, but there is nowhere to go. No one to save me. No dogs to protect me. I make myself feel the pain. It washes over me in in wave after wave of impossible sorrow. H hold my breath, then gasp fin air.

I face it.

Unworthiness. Rejection.

I'm still breathing and my heart is still beating. The storm passes. The waves recede.

I am stronger now. I feel cleansed and refreshed. I recall William Shakespeare's Hamlet "To be or not to be." I will have peace in my sleep of death. I will fight the evil that threatens to consume me. I will stay true to myself. I am a daughter of my father in heaven. He loves me and will help me.

I blow my nose one last time and dry my eyes.

I take a deep breath. It is time to find the ranger station so I can pay my $10 camping fee.

I backtrack to find the Ranger Station and go inside to pay. There is a log book inside for NOBO's to sign. There are not many names listed.

"I'm here to pay the camping fee for staying at the Birches lean-to," I say when the Ranger looks up.

"Are you hiking North or South?" he asks. "We do not allow South bounders to stay at the Birches."

"I am finishing up a North bound thru hike," I answer trying to keep the irritation out of my voice.

"What is your name and do you have cash?"

"I have cash," I answer giving him my money. "My last name is MacKenzie."

He writes out the receipt and hands it over. "What is your trail name?" the Ranger asks.

"Girl with 4 Dogs." I answer pocketing my receipt and turning toward the door.

# Girl (Hiking) with 4 Dogs

The Ranger's head jerks up. "Where are the dogs now!" he snaps.

"That's a good question," I answer politely and continue out the door.

I return to the campsite, and grab a Mountain House meal to eat for supper. I add cold water and let it sit for a while to soften up. As I am waiting on my food, "Sol" shows up. He is dressed in worn Khakis and an old T-shirt. He's in his late forties or early fifties with medium length brown wild hair and no facial hair. His backpack looks heavier than most thru hiker packs.

"Hi," I greet him, trying to keep the wariness out of my voice. I'm undecided if I feel safer all alone or with a male hiker I don't know. "Are you thru hiking?"

"I am thru hiking in sections. I took a break to pick blueberries on a farm for money. It is hard hot work. I worked all day and barely got paid. I'm out of money already!"

"The rangers charge hikers a fee to stay in these shelters," I say.

"Well, I don't have any money. I guess they will have to make an exception. Do you have any money I can borrow?"

"I don't have any extra money. Sorry. I brought only enough to pay for staying in the shelter. I left the rest with my Dad. I'm meeting him tomorrow after I finish the trail."

"Are you thru hiking all alone?" Sol asks.

"I have some friends staying at the camping area, and some other friends who are not far behind. I normally hike with my 4 dogs, but they aren't allowed in the park. The ranger almost had a heart attack when I told him my trail name." I explain laughingly. I share some of my trail adventures as we both eat supper.

Just before dusk, I see a white truck pull up on the gravel road a few yards from the shelter. The word, "RANGER," is written in green lettering on the side.

I look at Sol and raise my left eyebrow.

The Ranger strolls over. He is younger than the one who works in the office. He has short black hair, a lean body and a friendly smile.

"Hi," he says as he approaches us.

"Hi." We answer back

"Are you thru hikers?"

"Yes," I answer.

"I thru hiked a few years ago. My trail name was "Puff" because I hiked so fast. What is yours?"

"My trail name is Girl with 4 Dogs."

"Where are the dogs now?"

"They are with my Dad."

"How are you getting out of the park tomorrow?"

"I am hitchhiking. It didn't make sense for my Dad to pay $15 just to drive in the park to pick me up."

"If he has the dogs in his vehicle, then he isn't allowed in the park."

"Are you serious?" I ask incredulously. "Even if all he does is drive in the park, pick me up, turn around, and leave? The dogs would never leave the vehicle. What is the big deal about not having dogs in the park? Do you keep the wildlife out too?"

"He would not be allowed in the park. The founder of Baxter park did not want domesticated animals scaring the wild life or polluting the pristine beauty of the park with feces."

"Can you elaborate? Are wild animals, such as fox and coyote trained somehow not to defecate in the park? And are they also trained not to scare the other wildlife? I suppose the wildlife have been trained not to be scared of the sound of noisy vehicles as well? If we didn't tell you there were dogs in the truck, how would you know?"

"Dogs are not allowed in the park!" Puff exclaims. "If you ever see dogs on Katahdin, it is because the locals use the old lumber roads to hike with their dogs. It is extremely dangerous to have dogs on the trail!"

My thoughts turn evil. Well, if I ever want to hike with the dogs on K-Tahd, I just need to find an old lumber road. Besides, there are ways to "pollute" the park without the dogs even being present.

"It's a good thing I decided to hitchhike because if I did need my Dad to pick me up, he would pick me up, with my dogs in the truck, and no one would even know they were in the truck!" I say defiantly.

Puff glares at me, "Be careful. Hitchhiking can be dangerous."

"As if I would have a choice!"

"Are you both staying here tonight?" Puff asks changing the subject.

"I am. I paid at the Ranger Station earlier. Do you need to see my receipt?" I ask sarcastically.

"Yes, I do. Are you staying as well?" He asks Sol.

I leave to get my receipt out of my backpack. I can hear Sol explaining his financial situation to the Ranger. His voice is escalating.

"Can't I do a work for stay?" Sol is nearly yelling now. "I'm down on my luck. I've been hiking and I don't have any money! It is my dream to finish the trail and hike Katahdin!"

"The rules say if you don't pay, you don't stay. I can drive you to Millinocket, it is about 20 miles away. You can look for lodging there."

"Can you come back in 30 minutes so I can pack?" Sol asks.

"No. I will wait here while you pack," Puff answers.

I return with my receipt. I can hear Sol cussing as he packs his belongings. I hand the receipt to Puff and ask with barely restrained impatience, "Is there anything else you need?"

"No. You are clear to stay," Puff says. He folds his arms across his chest, his brown uniform shirt is tight across his shoulders and his green pants fit perfectly on his muscular buttocks.

My thoughts wander. Too bad Puff is such an inbred asshole. He will probably spend more money in gas driving to and from Millinocket, than if he had just let Sol stay. It's not as if the shelter is in jeopardy of getting full tonight with a grand total of one occupant per shelter. Talking to Puff is like talking to someone who has severe brain damage! Does everyone in Baxter Park try to piss people off and make their last day on the trail miserable, or is it something they do without trying?

It's dark by the time Sol and Puff leave.

Finally, peace and quiet. I snuggle in my sleeping bag and fall asleep.

**Day 150** I wake up excited. I only have five miles to hike before I am at "the end!"

I hurriedly dress in my black Mountain Gear pants, and purple REI short sleeve shirt, then eat breakfast, don my red backpack, and head to the trail. There is a cool nip in the air.

I haven't even gone a mile when I see Stretch, his dad and step-mom, Zippers, Grimm, and Youngin' up ahead. They are removing an outer layer of clothing. Stretch's dad is carrying a day pack, and Youngin' is carrying his backpack. Stretch, Zippers, and Grimm have only their hiking poles.

I summon up what I hope is an authentic smile and forge ahead. Stretch's dad seemed friendly enough last time I met him.

"How are ya'll?" I ask cheerfully.

"We had a great time last night," Grimm says.

"It was fun, but cramped," Youngin' responds.

"Were there thru hikers with you last night?" Zippers asks.

"I was the only one to stay all night." I then explain about Sol. "Good luck today! I'm sure you will pass me again soon," I say as I shift my backpack weight and continue up K-Tahd.

Less than 10 minutes later, Youngin,' then Grimm, then Stretch and Zippers pass me. By now I am panting and gasping for air. I know my face is beet red. I am determined to keep a steady pace so Stretch's parents won't pass me.

The weather is perfect. Cool and sunny. I stop my relentless climb to look back on where I have been. The view is amazing, there is mile upon mile of thick forest, there is a river snaking lazily through the valley behind me. The sky is clear blue without a single cloud in sight. I continue hiking.

I come to a dead end. I am on a rock boulder with thick green trees on both sides of the trail. The trail runs smack into another rock boulder that is higher than my head. Even stretching I can't reach the top of the next rock. I look around until I see a tree on the edge of the trail with its roots exposed. I stretch my fingernails and use the roots to pull myself up. The root shifts down as I pull. I find a toe hold for my shoe, then I continue to climb until I can grasp the top of the boulder and pull myself up. I lay gasping for air. When I can breathe without feeling like I'm about to faint, I crawl to my hands and knees, balance the weight of my backpack, then I grasp a wobbly sapling, and gingerly stand. My knee braces provide some protection from the abrasive granite and give support.

My legs are shaky. I drink a few sips of water and eat a handful of trial mix, then continue up K-Tahd. Soon, I reach another dead end. There are no trees around to help me this time.

I try to climb the boulders, but I can't find a good foothold.

After five minutes of searching I see another hiker approach. He is about 5 foot 9 inches moderately muscular and hiking fast. I step to the side.

"You don't have to move. I can wait," he says.

"That's okay. I'm trying to figure out how to get up the boulder. I'll watch how you do it first."

"It does look challenging. I didn't know we would be rock climbing!" he says.

"My trail name is Girl with 4 Dogs. Do you have a trail name?"

"My name is William. I don't have a trail name. I'm in school to be a nurse and I'm only hiking a section of the trail," he says extending his hand. He has strong manly hands.

"Nice to meet you. Good luck in school. I'm a nurse, it's a versatile career."

He hoists himself easily up the boulder using a few cracks to gain leverage!

It's a stretch for me, but I dig my fingers in the groove in the rock and jump to get a toe hold in another crevice.

Whew!

"Thanks for showing me the way," I say as William disappears ahead of me.

I hike slowly to catch my breath. Fantastic fun!

I summit Katahdin. At the top, the weather is clear. I can see for miles. It is breathtaking, amazing, and perfect. I am on top of the world! There is only God's beautiful creation around me. God gave me the most marvelous day to finish the trail!

I wave to William and stop to read the Katahdin plaque.

Wow 2181 Miles! I accomplish a lifelong dream!

"Come take pictures with us!" Zippers calls. I look up to see her waving. Stretch, Grimm, and Youngin' have already taken off their backpacks and are eating a snack. I amble over for pictures.

There is an "A" frame brown sign marking the official end of the trail. I stand behind the sign with my arms raised in triumph! I conquered the Appalachian Trail! I conquered Katahdin!

I am FREE!

I didn't find my soul mate, but I found my soul.

# Epilogue

I have lunch with my hiking friends, then descend Katahdin via the Knife edge, a trepidatious line of rocks which give Knife's Edge its name. It feels safest to straddle the "blade" and slowly creep across its length. My heart beats wildly as I glance to the side of the trail. It is a sheer drop off.

I carefully watch my footholds, but I also have to glance up in case there is someone hiking toward me. There are no ideal places to step to the side of the trail, but some drop offs look less intimidating than others.

Youngin' got a ride to town with Betsy. Becca and Ryan gave me a ride to Millinocket and bought me a bottled water on the way.

Once in Millinocket, I go to the Appalachian Trail Café to eat, and wait on Dad. While I am looking at the menu, a group of guys invite me to join their table and tell them about my hiking trip. They are on their annual guys weekend/week out, and are curious about thru-hiking. I share the more interesting stories, and they are impressed. They are planning to hike the Knife Edge section tomorrow. I tell them it is easy peasy (JK). I tell them it is challenging, but worth it, and that if I can do it with a backpack on, then surely they can do it with just a day pack. Besides, they are guys and I'm a girl. They have longer legs and can take bigger steps. One guy is afraid of heights. I hope he does ok. It's a long way down.

The majority of the time these guys are talking and being impressed by my hiking trip, I'm thinking they really are the ones to deserve praise and admiration. They are all happily married. I want to tell them that hiking the AT is a lot easier than making a marriage work. Hiking is all about my choices. I either get up and hike, or I don't. A marriage is about making a relationship work.

At the Café, there is a sign-in board for thru hikers; Chain Saw, Whitney Houston, White Fang, Sali, Coach, Professor, Snorkel, Water Bear, Boy Howdy, Ice Axe, Rambler, Ryan Captain USA, Jacob, Lunch Box, Madeline, Natale, Space Cowboy, Victus, Squash, Renaissance, 2 Cor 5:17, Sam Pola, Solitaire, Tonic, Crue Design, Maxiclub, Girl w/4Dogs(Me), Red Dane, Missing Link, Solo.

Dad and I see thru hiker, D'art, at a grocery store before we leave Millinocket. He finished the trail today as well.

Then, unbelievably, we see one of The Brothers, Two Medicine, at a rest stop on the way home. His facial hair is grown out and I didn't recognize him at first, but he sees us with the 4 dogs and the white truck with the purple camper. It is really, cool and I'm glad he stopped to say hi! (His brother, Train Wreck, was diagnosed with Multiple Sclerosis, or something. Check out Bill and Bob's Excellent Adventures).

2017

Life continues to be full of challenges, but the strength I gained on the AT has stayed with me.

Dad died in August of 2015 after having a heart attack and stroke. A few months later, March 2016, Mtn. Goat tied of lymphatic cancer. I imagine them hanging out together in heaven.

Kujo died recently, April 2017, two months after being diagnosed with heart failure. His last two months were a miracle and a blessing from my Heavenly Father and his Son Jesus

Digger, and Instigator are still with me, although age is catching up to them.

My fiver year old daughter, Olivia, bosses them around.

Rocket is still happily married. Maybe one day she will start back in VA and finish the AT in sections.

Live your dreams Happily Ever After!

Contact me at:
 P.O. Box 8266
Columbus, GA 31908

# Appendix

I'm adding the GPS Coordinate Conversion Information my Dad used to find me while I was hiking on the Appalachian Trail. I scanned and edited his work into this book. I know he was working out some kinks and I have a few copies so I hope this is the most current. I always thought I would get his latest work when I was finally publishing this book. Unfortunately, life doesn't wait. My Dad had a heart attack and a stroke in 2015 and died after 3 days in the hospital.

Appendix: * Technical GPS Tips for Hikers And Drivers

A hiker, with a Spot Satellite@ GPS, can send his GPS location to a satellite by pressing a button. The satellite "texts" it to several friends' phones and e-mails. If the pick-up driver's cellphone has no signal, a "land" phone might help him get the GPS # from a "friend." A "Wi-Fi" hot spot (at some libraries, "fast foods", supermarkets, city halls and P.O.'s) may give her e-mail access.

Enter a GPS # into http://maps.google.com

For 36.12 $^0$N 86.67 $^0$W, type in "36.12,-86.67" (no quotes). Then, click map, satellite, center the "pin A", zoom in, rotate "N", see the airport. (For "East", change the "-" to "+"; or, omit the minus.

For better searches, have five numbers after the decimal.)

In areas without internet, enter the GPS # into a GPS device, smartphone or laptop with "built in" maps. Microsoft® Streets and Trips, with its optional USB GPS sensor, shows your present location on a bigger, laptop screen.

Maps, guide books and GPS devices show degrees minutes and seconds in three different forms. "Speak" the same language! Choose a matching degree form on your GPS. If the GPS batteries die, these "hints" can help you translate those forms.

| | | | |
|---|---|---|---|
| D | M | S | $36° \; 7' \; 12"$ |
| To | | | $36° \; +(7'/60)° \; +(12"/3600)°$ |
| D.D | | | $36.12°$ |

---

| | | |
|---|---|---|
| D | M.M | $36° \; 7.2'$ |
| To | $36°+ (7.2'/ 60)°$ | |
| D.D | | $36.12°$ |

---

| | | |
|---|---|---|
| D.D | | $36.12°$ |
| To | | $36° \; +(.12° \times 60)'$ |
| D | M.M | $36° \; 7.2'$ |
| To | | $36° \; +7' \; +(.2' \times 60)"$ |
| D | M | S | $36° \quad 7' \quad 12"$ |
| To | | $36° \; +7' \; +(12"/60)'$ |
| D | M.M | $36° \; 7.2'$ |

\* From "Hiking the AT with Four Dogs," ©Sandy MacKenzie.

**GPS Tips**

"Google" the GPS number. For $36.12015^0$ N $65.12^0$W, enter 36.12015,-65.12 into a Google search box, click map, satellite, zoom in, see "friend's location". For East, change that "-" to a "+" . (For better "finds", have five numbers after the decimal.) In areas without internet access, enter the number into a

Microsot@ Streets and Trips, or similar, computer program. To see the correct search input for 36 deg. 7 min. 12 sec., solve this: 36 + (7/60) + (12/3600). Answer: 36.12 Likewise for 36 deg. 7.2 min. solve: 36 + (7.2/60). Answer:

36.12

Maps and GPS devices describe degrees in several ways, which can be translated," as shown above and below. So, "speak" the <u>same</u> language!

**DD.DD to DD MM.MM**

$47.26250^0$ - $47^0$ + $(.26250^0$ x 60)' Answer: $47^0$ 15.75'

**DD MM SS to DD MM.MM** $47^0$ 15' 45" $47^0$ + 15' + (45"/60)' Answer: $47^0$ 15.75'

**DD MM.MM to DD MM SS**

$470$ 15.75' = $47^0$ + 15' + (.75' x 60)" Answer: $47^0$ $15^1$ 45"

**DD.DD to DD MM SS**

$47.26250^0$ = $47^0$ +$(.26250^0$ x 60)' = $47^0$ +15.75' = $47^0$ +15' +(.75' x 60)" Answer: $47^0$ 15' 45"

A hiker, with a <u>Spot Satellite@</u> GPS, can send his location to a satellite by pressing a button. The satellite "texts" it to several friends' phones and e-mails. If the pick-up driver's phone has no signal, a "land" phone might help him get that number from a "friend."

# References

Miller, D. "A." (2011). The A.T. Guide 2011 Northbound. A Handbook for Hiking the Appalachian Trail. Titusville, FL: Jerelyn Press. The References section (or Bibliography) generally follows the Notes section if there is one. The references text can be set in the same font and size as the Notes.

www.ingramcontent.com/pod-product-compliance
Lightning Source LLC
Chambersburg PA
CBHW020601270326
41927CB00005B/124